The Petty Demon

The Petty Demon

Fyodor Sologub

Translated and Introduced by S. D. Cioran
with an Appendix of Critical Articles
Edited by Murl Barker

ARDIS PUBLISHERS
WOODSTOCK & NEW YORK

This edition first published in the United States in 2006 by
Ardis Publishers
Woodstock & New York

WOODSTOCK:
One Overlook Drive
Woodstock, NY 12498
[for individual orders, bulk and special sales, contact our Woodstock office]

NEW YORK:
141 Wooster Street
New York, NY 10012

Ardis Publishers is an imprint of Peter Mayer Publishers, Inc.
www.ardisbooks.com

Cataloging-in-Publication Data is available from the Library of Congress

Book design and type formatting by Bernard Schleifer
Printed in Canada
ISBN 0-88233-808-0
1 2 3 4 5 6 7 8 9 10

CONTENTS

TRANSLATOR'S FOREWORD

IN GENERAL I feel that there is not much to be gained by trying to explain in great detail the literary and linguistic subtleties of the original Russian text to an English-speaking audience. Obviously those who know Russian can compare the original with the translation and come to their own conclusions. For better or worse the English-speaking reader finds himself at the mercy of the translator and can only hope that he is reading a "faithful" translation. Unfortunately, no two translators, or critics, are apt to agree fully on what "faithful" should mean. Faithful to what? The content? The style? The sensibilities of a reader who desires a smooth and readable text? Or perhaps a wonderful compromise among all these factors which is achieved through some magical formula in the sole possession of the translator? In any event, the reader does have the right at least to know what the translator thought he was trying to accomplish and how he set about it.

In the case of Sologub's *The Petty Demon* I have attempted to abide as closely as possible by the "content" of the original. Except in isolated circumstances I have directly translated what Sologub wrote without trying to "interpret" the content or to take undue license by striving above all for a musical or poetic effect in English. Nor have I attempted to adorn the original text, or worse, to delete words and phrases which did not "fit" well into English. I made a special effort to preserve the *lexical integrity* of the text by utilizing vocabulary items in English which I felt were of the same semantic value and level in Russian. My intention was neither to aggrandize nor to mitigate the effect of Sologub's language in order to achieve some desired effect. I took particular care in preserving the *frequency* or *repetition* of Sologub's vocabulary, for this is one of the hallmarks of Sologubian prose. While the author does not draw on a particularly rich and varied lexical store, nevertheless, he is extremely fastidious in what he does use and he consciously *repeats* his favorite words and phrases. The repetition of this selective vocabulary in Sologub's works was often meant to induce an incantational and hypnotic effect that is frequently reminiscent of music, poetry or even religious rites. The reader will also recognize, of course, that such repetition performs the role of creating convenient verbal leitmotifs for the various characters and situations.

I did, however, deviate from the above principles in two circumstances. The first was in rendering the counter-spells uttered by Peredonov. The second concerned the many puns and word plays that abound throughout the novel. In both cases it was my intention to avoid laborious footnotes which explain the actual content or meaning of the counter-spells or puns. In the case of the counter-spells I produced what I felt would be a reasonable English equivalent. As far as the word plays were concerned, I believed that it was more important to reproduce the spirit or intent of the Russian original while still creating a word play in English. In a few cases where I thought that the spirit of the original would be unduly violated, I reluctantly resorted to a footnote.

A final point concerns the translation of the Russian words *oboroten'* and *baran* because the attentive reader may notice a discrepancy between the text of the translation and various references made in the articles contained in the critical appendix. Some critics (and former translators) have rendered *oboroten'* as "werewolf" in English. The actual root of *oboroten'* is based on the word meaning "to change". I have chosen to translate the word as "changeling" rather than as "werewolf." Obviously a "werewolf" belongs to the category of "changelings" but both in English and in Russian the words *oboroten'*/"changeling" can indicate a human being that assumes the identity of *any* animal or bird, or even of another human being. This is obviously a very important theme in the novel when one realizes the great number of "transformations" or "changelings" that Sologub interpolates into the text. Peredonov's diseased imagination manufactures all manner of such phenomena: Volodin alternates between his human identity and that of a sheep; the playing cards become real kings, queens and knaves; Peredonov believes that Volodin is trying to kill him and assume his identity. Costumes are used throughout to depict changes in identity: Sasha dresses as a geisha girl; both Lyudmila and Sasha don various costumes in order to alter their personalities; Peredonov displays his own "changeling" aspirations by ordering a new uniform, throwing away his old hat and wearing his official cap. Finally, a great scandal is caused by Peredonov accusing Sasha of being a girl in disguise.

In the novel, Volodin is regularly described in terms of a *baran*. In Russian this means a "male sheep" or "ram." Some translators and critics have chosen to translate this quality in Volodin as being "ram-like." My feeling is that the word "sheep" is more neutral and evocative of Volodin's antics and behavior and at the same time it does not deny the fact that he is a male. Moreover, the word "ram" might suggest the appearance and qualities of the mountain variety to the English reader. This particular problem is a veritable Pandora's Box that I do not care to open any further since it touches upon a host of difficulties in translating the differences between male and female counterparts of the same animal and whether the masculine or feminine determination is used to create adjectival forms. For example, in Russian one says *baran'i kotlety* for "lamb" or "mutton chops," yet surely this does not mean that only the unfortunate male of the species ends up on the dinner table. I add this merely as food for thought to the readers of the text.

—S.D.C.

INTRODUCTION

As THE NINETEENTH CENTURY drew to a close, a diverse number of Russian thinkers and writers declared a metaphysical and aesthetic war against insipid materialism and vulgar utilitarianism in art and thought. The salvation of mankind lay in the search for a new spiritual idealism. The salvation of art lay in the creation of new forms of artistic expression. The inspiration for this new idealistic impetus came from at least two discernible directions. The first was a reaction against a predominant mood of pessimism in Russian literature and thought, which was perceived to be a legacy of the lugubrious and depressing themes of Russian civic art. The second was an acceptance of the "new art" of literary sensitivity that was being imported from France, England and other European countries.[1]

One of the earliest exponents of a renewed philosophy of idealism in art and thought was the Russian philosopher-poet, Vladimir Solovyov (1853–1900), who directed man's vision to the divine realm for inspiration:

> And man, as one who belongs to both worlds, can and must by an act of rational contemplation concern himself with the divine world, and finding himself yet in a world of contention and vague apprehension, he must enter into communication with vivid images from the kingdom of glory and eternal beauty.[2]

Solovyov's theories were to have a profound effect on a later generation of symbolist writers that would include both Alexander Blok (1880–1921) and Andrei Bely (1880–1934).

However, the first genuine "manifesto" of the new artistic and philosophical sensibilities is usually accredited to Dmitri Merezhkovsky (1865–1941) who wrote his famous treatise "On the Reasons for the Decline and on the New Tendencies in Contemporary Russian Literature" in 1892. Merezhkovsky was among the first in Russia to outline in great detail what he envisaged as the genuine requirements of the new artistic idealism that would do battle with the "suffocatingly dead positivism of the 19th Century." Referring to the works of Baudelaire, Edgar Allan Poe, Flaubert, Turgenev and Ibsen, Merezhkovsky distilled the essential ingredients:

... the three major elements of the new art [are] a *mystical content, symbols*, and the *expansion of artistic impressionability* ... only a *creative faith in something infinite and immortal* can ignite the soul of man, create heroes, martyrs and prophets ... People have need of faith, they need inspiration, they crave a holy madness in their heroes and martyrs.[3]

As we will see later, these words were to arouse a creative response in the heart of Fyodor Sologub.

While some writers of this "first generation" of Symbolists that included Merezhkovsky, his wife Zinaida Hippius (1867–1945), and Nikolai Minsky (1855–1937), devoted themselves to the creation of idealistic and inspirational content in the new art, other poets, such as Konstantin Balmont (1867–1943) and Valeri Bryusov (1873–1924) preferred to explore and promote new aesthetic forms and sensibilities:

> Rare and powerful harmonies exist,
> Shaping both scent and contour in a flower.
> Thus brilliance lies unseen by us until,
> Beneath the chisel, it blazes in the diamond.
>
> And I desire that all my dreaming visions
> That reach the light embodied in the word,
> Find for themselves their long-sought forms.
> (V. Bryusov, *A Sonnet to Form*, 1895)

In the works of Bryusov and Balmont there were, at times, simply the undeniable attempts to *épater le bourgeois*, to shock, amaze and anger. Hence Bryusov's notorious one-liner:

> O, cover your pale legs!

Virtuosity in form, musicality in tone and exotic dreamlike sensuality in content were the trademarks of Konstantin Balmont:

> Beneath this youthful, sickle-Moon
> That glows above the emerald Sea,
> You walk beside the waves with me.
> I whisper words, we silently dispute.
>
> This came to me in dreams one night,
> As combers roared in you and me.
> I saw with moonlight-flooded sight
> That you and I were sinking in the Sea.
>
> We were, in crespuscule and brine,
> Two ocean flowers, entwining blooms
> Of salt and sea—dreaming Moons
> And stars of novel lands and strange designs.
> (*Beneath a Lunar Sign*)[4]

In both treatise and poem these new prophets of exotic sensations attracted converts as well as enemies who labelled them "decadent" because of the unabashed eroticism and frequent escapism into realms of artificial experience. The designations of "Symbolist" and "Decadent" became confused and interchangeable in the minds of the conservative reading public who preferred less spicey fare than was being dished up. Scant distinction was made between those writers who seemed genuinely dedicated to seeking the creative synthesis of heaven and earth and those who were more inclined to an exotic aestheticism. The confusion was compounded by the fact that both Symbolists and Decadents shared a common interest in renewing artistic forms and were frequently attracted to identical themes and motifs. This initial movement which became known as Symbolism or Decadence, depending upon the aesthetic bias of the reader or critic, began to proliferate and diversify in the early part of the twentieth century as more and more writers and poets were attracted. A second generation of younger, or belated, writers, hastened to join the ranks of the new aesthetic modernism that held out such promise for a genuine renaissance in Russian letters. The second wave of Symbolism included such hopefuls as Andrei Bely, Alexander Blok and Vyacheslav Ivanov (1866–1949), to name only the most prominent. Bely and Blok apprenticed themselves in their early years to the established Symbolist masters like Solovyov, Merezhkovsky, Bryusov and Balmont, but rapidly developed their own aesthetic forms and philosophies.

The faint rustlings of Russian Symbolism in the early 1890's echoed across the frontier of the twentieth century and grew to resounding proportions in the literary world of pre-World War I Russia. Particularly after the aborted revolution of 1905, this literary tendency began to diversify and fractionalize as one literary-artistic journal after another was created as a rallying-point for a fresh alignment of Symbolist writers, thinkers and artists. Vehement *professions de foi* and militant "manifestoes" were hurled at friend and foe alike in a furious verbal barrage over literary matters pertaining to Symbolism. One might well characterize this period between roughly 1905 and 1910 as a period of "War Symbolism" in which long-time friends became foes overnight while implacable enemies were embraced as committed Symbolists moved from one literary camp or publishing house to the other.

It is fair to say that Russian Symbolism was never a lukewarm experience. The passionate alliances, the vicious rivalries, the fiery, often absurd, debates, the ridiculous antics and aesthetic poses of many of its adherents proved to be the rule rather than the exception. The hopes, dreams and aspirations of Symbolism were just as exaggerated, perhaps as futile, as the works they created.

Considering the many divergent theories of Symbolism proposed by its adherents over the course of almost a quarter century (from the early 1890s up until the Revolution) it is not an easy task to select a single salient or unifying theme, a single central tenet that would fairly represent the thrust of Russian Symbolism. However, a great deal of the spirit of Russian Symbolism might be summed up in the predominant concern for *transformation* or *transfiguration*. A priori this concept presupposes the existence, or even opposition, of two realms, be it the earthly and the heavenly, the human and the divine, the ugly and the beautiful. The desire of the Symbolist was to annul this opposition, to resolve it. The ugly, the earthly and the human were to be transformed or transfigured into their loftier counterparts. The method or magic formula for achieving this common design was as diverse as the membership and personality of Russian Symbolism. The philosopher-poet, Vladimir Solovyov, proposed a vision for the transformation of mankind that was essentially Christian, if unorthodox. In his theory of Godmanhood, he sought the union between earth and heaven in which man would ascend to the divine level and be transfigured. Both Bely and Blok, particularly in their younger years, were deeply influenced by Solovyov and espoused many of the principal tenets of his teachings on the divine purpose of art and the desire to achieve Godmanhood. Bely was the more active of the two in pursuing and developing new theories of Symbolist art that were usually eclectic and idiosyncratic. But over the years Bely invariably returned to the same Symbolist concerns: the resolution of opposites, the transformation of earth into heaven, man into the godman. Like Solovyov, Merezhkovsky was also fascinated by opposites. In his scheme for mankind's transfiguration, he sought a synthesis of the pagan and the Christian spirits to create a new being that would be beauteous in body and spirit. Merezhkovsky's own attempt to put theory into practice resulted in a series of grandiose novels wherein various historical figures were selected as symbolic incarnations of the mighty struggle between contrasting forces in mankind and the universe. His first trilogy was given the expressive title of *Christ and Antichrist* (1896–1905).

One of the most important and seminal ideas proposed by Merezhkovsky in his original manifesto of 1892, and which echoed the thoughts of Vladimir Solovyov, concerned the utilization of symbols to portray both metaphysical and artistic truths:

> Characters can . . . serve as symbols. Sancho Panza and Faust, Don Quixote and Hamlet, Don Juan and Falstaff, in the words of Goethe, are "schwankende Gestalten" . . . apparitions which haunt mankind . . . from generation to generation. It is impossible to communicate in any words whatsoever the idea of such symbolic characters, whereas symbols express the unrestricted aspect of truth.[5]

Indeed, every Symbolist worthy of the title felt obliged to create his own system of Symbols, his own symbolic mythology, and to personify the inexpressible truths of his particular vision. The cornerstone symbol of Solovyov's scheme was the Divine Sophia (the Divine Wisdom of God) who would inspire mankind to actively seek and participate in his own transfiguration through the process of Godmanhood. This archetype of the Eternal Feminine resonated through the works of other Symbolists such as Blok and Bely. They both created their own personal variants of Solovyov's Divine Sophia. Blok espoused the "Beautiful Lady" and Bely the "Woman Clothed in the Sun." Particularly during their younger years, these Symbols apotheosized their vague, at times inarticulate, at times verbose, longing for earthly transformation.

The role of the poet was viewed in a similar way by many of the Symbolists. Theirs was not a passive function. They stood as intermediaries between two realms, as heralds of transformed existence, the travellers between worlds who beckoned to others to follow. Vyacheslav Ivanov, a classical scholar and Symbolist poet who drew many of his archetypes and inspiration from antiquity, stated this Symbolist role as inspired messenger:

> And thus I am not a Symbolist if in the heart of the listener I do not arouse with intangible nuance or influence those incommunicable sensations which resemble at times some primeval remembrance . . .

> I am not a Symbolist if my words do not summon forth in the listener sensations of the connection between that which is his "ego" and that which he calls his "non-ego" . . . if my words do not convince him immediately of the existence of a hidden life where his mind had not suspected life; if my words do not move in him the energy of love towards that which he was previously unable to love because his love did not know of the many abodes it possessed.

> (*Thoughts on Symbolism*, 1912)[6]

Symbolism, as a vibrant, often chaotic force in Russian letters, lost ground with the approach of World War I and the Russian Revolution. Other -ism's (Acmeism, Futurism, etc.), while less ambitious in their designs, eventually proved to be more vigorous and attractive. Even the most stalwart and hopeful grew weary of maintaining their vigil of faith atop deserted mountains in expectation of the dawning of the new age so often heralded by the Symbolists. Succeeding times and generations do not readily accept the proposals of their immediate predecessors.

This, in brief and simplified terms, is the aesthetic landscape wherein the literary work and artistic sensibility of Fyodor Sologub blossomed and grew to prominence. While profoundly a part of that same Symbolist world, nevertheless he was at the same time a foreigner within it.

Fyodor Kuzmich Sologub (pseud. of F.K. Teternikov, 1863–1927) was one of the most striking curiosities produced by Russian Symbolism. His background, his profession, his age, even his appearance, made him a very unlikely, even ridiculous figure among the Russian Symbolists and frequently deprived him of the respect which was his due. Especially for the younger poets, Symbolism was as much a lifestyle, an aesthetic pose, as it was a genuine literary pursuit. Flamboyant dress, exaggerated manners, verbal pyrotechnics and suspect behavior were liberally flaunted as proof of membership in what must have seemed a somewhat exclusive literary club. Moreover, most Symbolists came from the middle or upper classes with strong intellectual traditions. Yet, hovering on the fringes of this pride of lions was Sologub, the son of a former serf, a provincial teacher for most of his life, balding, rather insignificant and hapless in appearance, awkward, taciturn and touchy, and looking much older than his years. And who had conceived the somewhat absurd-sounding pseudonym of "Sologub" for him? While Sologub was almost a solitary figure, almost an outcast within the very Symbolist circles he moved in, nevertheless, his works were undeniably a reflection of and a resonant echo of that same world.

Sologub was not an obliging person when pestered for biographical material. Perhaps his reticence was provoked as much by modesty or shyness as by embarrassment over his less-than-auspicious origins. Perhaps he sensed as well that people were more "curious" than "interested" in him. Critics frequently complained that he was a "Mister Incognito" or that he had no "genealogical table". In fact, it was only when he had passed the age of fifty and his wife, Anastasia Nikolaevna Chebotarevskaya, published a brief biographical outline of her spouse in 1915 that the wider world became more familiar with the unremarkable origins of a very remarkable writer. Most of our information about the writer Sologub comes from eyewitness accounts of contemporaries, whereas the first thirty years or so of his life is still mainly locked up in Soviet archives. Some of that material has found its way into print and has been incorporated into M. Dikman's introduction to the anthology of Sologub's verse published in the Soviet Union in 1975.[7]

Sologub's father was a former serf who died of tuberculosis in 1867, four years after the birth of Fyodor. The family had moved to St. Petersburg after the Emancipation where the father tried to eke out a living as a tailor. Fyodor's mother was a peasant. The mother, completely without means, bundled up Fyodor and a younger sister, Olga, and went off to work as a servant in the home of a cultured, yet sympathetic family that also provided for the young Fyodor's education. Fyodor's family ties were very close but very oppressive at the same time. Although there was a good deal of affection between mother and son, she beat and punished him for every possible misdemeanor. Sologub frequently recalled those vicious whippings and said that his youth was composed of the "hell of thrashings and the paradise of dreams." These beatings were administered by the mother well into Sologub's manhood, according to material quoted by Dikman in the introduction cited above. Psychologists may find some interesting connection between this particular fact and the additional fact that Sologub never married until after the death of his mother and his sister—when he was already forty-five. These whippings—which occupy such a salient role in most of Sologub's works, particularly in *The Petty Demon* and *The Created Legend*, permeated most of his earlier life, at home, in the parish school, even at the pedagogical school where he was regularly whipped at the request of his mother and his landlady even after the age of sixteen. School was not an entirely happy experience for the youthful Sologub. Although he was a diligent and excellent student, he felt awkward and isolated among his classmates who frequently made him the butt of their jokes. His readings during those years included the democratic critics like Belinsky, Dobrolyubov and Pisarev. His favorite Russian poet was Nekrasov; his favorite Russian novelist was Dostoevsky. In later years, he was to recall that the three works which had the most enduring impact on him had been Shakespeare's *King Lear*, Defoe's *Robinson Crusoe* and Cervantes' *Don Quixote*.

He completed his teacher training in 1882 and at the age of nineteen he took his family with him to his first post in the small provincial town of Krestsy (Novgorod Province). His mother died two years later. Sologub was convinced at a very early age that his genuine calling was literature. His first verses were written in 1875 and he even began a novel in 1879 which he never completed. He worked zealously at perfecting his literary skills and the sources for his inspiration were close at hand: the petty vulgarity of life in a small provincial town and the meddlesome incompetence and tyranny of school officialdom. Much of this material he was able to incorporate into a series of novels. His first novel, *Bad Dreams* (1894), depicts the life of a young provincial schoolteacher who experiences the same disparity between visions of a lyrical idealism and the nightmare of soul-destroying provincial life as did the youthful Sologub. During the three years he spent in Krestsy, Sologub began to submit the first specimens of his poetry to various publishers and he made a modest debut in print in 1884.

During the years of vulgar existence in Krestsy and his subsequent provincial postings, Sologub nurtured an almost escapist hope that literature would somehow deliver him from such a miserable existence which threatened to endure for the rest of his life. After three years in Krestsy he moved with his sister to Velikie Luki where he taught for four years. This represented little improvement over the coarse philistinism of his previous post. But Chebotarevskaya later claimed that the years in Velikie Luki provided the principal inspiration for the novel *The Petty Demon*. From all accounts, Sologub was a dedicated teacher and he had many altercations with the authorities on matters of curricula, pedagogical methodology and ethics. But tiring of the ceaseless conflicts there, he moved on to the Pedagogical Seminary in Vyterga. It was here that he became deeply interested in the French Symbolists and began to translate Verlaine.

Bearing in mind his literary ambitions, Sologub always tried to keep abreast of the literary and artistic scene in the capital by subscribing to newspapers and journals. He was among those who were sensitive to the first echoes of the "new art" that was poised to invade Russia from France and which had already begun to inspire the early prophets of Russian modernism, Merezhkovsky and Minsky. He made a special trip to St. Petersburg in 1889 to meet both Merezhkovsky and Minsky. On that occasion he did have a long conversation with Minsky on literary matters and Minsky invited Sologub to submit some verses for publication in *The Northern Herald*, the leading journal for modernism in those days.

Sologub's fondest dream now centered on moving to the capital in order to further his literary ambitions. In 1892 he received a teaching post in a St. Petersburg school and settled permanently in the city. Here he met frequently with Dmitri Merezhkovsky, Zinaida Hippius and Nikolai Minsky. Thanks to this connection he became a regular contributor to *The Northern Herald*. Both his first novel, *Bad Dreams*, and his first major story, "Shadows," were printed in this journal. He also contributed poetry, articles and reviews. His literary pseudonym was conceived in the editorial offices of this same journal.

Almost from the very beginning, Sologub seemed to be a curious phenomena in Russian Symbolism, for reasons other than his background, profession or appearance. While other modernists like Bely, Blok, Bryusov and Balmont were to trace meteoric trajectories across the heavens in their pursuit of everything from Aestheticism to Zoroastrianism, Fyodor Sologub seemed to remain the fixed star, introverted, isolated and immutable.

His verse was not experimental in form, but tended to be almost "classical" in its technical clarity, restraint and immaculateness. The content of those same verses did not vary greatly over the succeeding years. Rather they were seemingly subjected to endless variations on the same themes: rejection of this vulgar world of time and space, escapism into artificial realms fashioned in the poet's own fantasy and the desire to transform earthly existence. Such were the abiding leitmotifs of Sologub's verse:

From the worlds' decrepit misery
Where women wept and children babbled,
Into the clouded distances I flew
In the embrace of joyful fantasy.
And from the wondrous height of soaring flight
The earthly realm I did transform,
And thus it gleamed as bright before me
As darkly golden fabric spread.
And when aroused from dreaming vision
By life's befouling touch,
Back to the torments of my native land
I bore the unfathomed mystery

(1896)

A heavy pall of gloom and the inescapable odor of death clung to most of Sologub's verse. Death seemed the one noble consolation in a life often portrayed by Sologub as a vulgar and hideous, yet seductive wench, who lured man to the false charms of this world:

Cherishing my somber thoughts
Deep in waking, melancholy dream,
I have no remorse for this dark life
And I rent the transparent fabric,

The fabric of youthful expectations
And misty childlike reveries;
Far removed from vain desires.
Long prepared for death am I.

Deep in melancholy dream, cherishing pain,
I rent life's web assunder,
And know not how to conclude
For what purpose and by what means I live.

(1895)

So overpowering was the scent of death and decay in Sologub's verse, so complete the depressing aura of pessimism, that many years later, Maxim Gorky wrote what many critics took to be a most biting parody of Fyodor Sologub's preoccupation with death. The hero of Gorky's "Fairy Tale" was a certain Mister "Smertyashkin" (Mister Death) who makes his living at first by writing gloomy verses for obituaries and *in memoria*. However, his talent for somber verse is exploited by his wife and her enterprising paramour to make a sensation and a financial fortune on the literary scene. Subsequently, the term "Smertyashkiny" became synonymous in Russian literature with the "dealers-in-death," namely those writers and poets who during the pre-revolutionary era seemed to trade on the general pessimism and gloom of society to make a living.[8]

Sologub did not give up his teaching responsibilities as he began to move in the glittering circles of young aspiring poets, writers and artists in St. Petersburg through the later 1890's. Particularly with the publication of his first book of verse in 1896, there seemed little doubt that Sologub had become heir to the French decadent tradition in Russia.

In 1899 Sologub received a promotion as school-inspector for the Andreyevsky Civic School in the capital. Despite his acquaintanceship with the leading representatives of literary and aesthetic modernism in Russia, Sologub, withdrawn, and somehow ridiculous (after all, he was not only a decadent poet, but a teacher and a school-inspector as well!) never seemed to be entirely accepted by his literary colleagues who often made fun of him behind his back. His regular Sunday receptions, hosted by himself and his chronically-ill sister, Olga, were something of a contrast with those of other patron-practitioners of the arts:

> At the Merezhkovskys' everyone spoke loudly, at Sologub's in a hushed voice; at the Merezhkovskys' people argued excitedly and even passionately about the church, at Sologub's they deliberated over verses with the impartiality of masters and connoisseurs of the poetic craft. In the host's study, where stood somber, somewhat cold, leather furniture, the poets sat decorously, obediently read their verses at the behest of the host and then humbly listened to the master's judgments which were precise and stern, but almost always benevolent, yet at times cutting and merciless if the versifier had dared to come forth with frivolous and imperfect verses. This was the Areopagus of the Petersburg poets.[9]

If the person of Sologub was ignored or belittled by many, then the name was certainly to be reckoned with increasingly after the turn of the century. His poems, in particular, appeared in all of the leading Symbolist journals of the era, including *The Scales, The New Path, Questions of Life, World of Art* and *The Golden Fleece*. Despite the pejorative epithets leveled at him by Gorky and others, Sologub was also a frequent contributor of works to the popular political and satirical feuilletons of the day (*The Spectator, The Hammer, The Devil's Post*, etc.). In addition, he was always prepared to contribute appropriate works to miscellanies and anthologies in benefit of various charitable and humanitarian cause, in particular the struggle against anti-semitism and the campaign for women's rights. This meddling of a decadent poet and "pornographer" in political and social questions no doubt contributed to the general confusion surrounding Sologub.

The year 1907 witnessed a turning-point in Sologub's life for several reasons. He suffered a personal tragedy in the death of his sister to whom he had been very devoted. The same year, however, Sologub's reputation reached its zenith with the complete publication of his novel, *The Petty Demon*, which met with almost universal acclaim in Russia. Like his earlier novel, *Bad Dreams, The Petty Demon* drew on Sologub's pedagogical experiences in the provincial backwoods of Russia. In the "hero" of the novel, Peredonov, a rural teacher, Sologub incorporated all the vicious and petty vulgarity imaginable. Few characters in Russian fiction can even pretend to the ignoble and spiritual void represented by Peredonov who endowed Russian literature and social criticism with the term of "Peredonovshchina" (i.e., "Peredonovism"). In 1907, Sologub also completed twenty-five years of pedagogical service and retired, now able to devote himself entirely to literary activity thanks to a state pension and the critical acclaim accorded *The Petty Demon*. Rumors circulated to the effect, however, that his resignation was forced on him because of the apparent erotic motifs in the novel which included hints of the seduction of a young schoolboy by the beautiful and sensuous Lyudmila.

About the same time, Sologub added to his laurels in prose and poetry by developing an interest in theater and drama, writing half-a-dozen or so popular plays during the inter-revolutionary period for the leading theaters and directors (including Meyerhold). In 1908, Sologub's personal fortunes rose as well, for at the not-so-tender age of forty-five he became acquainted with and married the writer-critic, Anastasia Nikolaevna Chebotarevskaya. Young, vivacious, extremely eccentric, Chebotarevskaya took Sologub's career in hand, actively aiding him with his literary work and doing her utmost to promote his literary fortunes. In fact, in 1911, she gathered together and edited a number of critical reviews and articles on Sologub's work (mostly favorable!) and published it under her own name.

With his marriage to Chebotarevskaya, Sologub's formerly restrained and almost austere life-style altered, at least externally. At her insistence a larger apartment was rented, visitors now included not merely poets, but politicians, artists and entrepreneurs. Noisy parties and masquerades, at which Sologub, sad and perplexed, wandered about like a lost sheep, appeared to be his wife's inspiration. Chebotarevskaya suffered from some psychological malady early on in their marriage and her condition deteriorated over the years. Thus, Sologub had to care for her, just as he earlier had cared for his invalid mother and his sick sister.

In 1907, after the enormous success of his novel *The Petty Demon*, Sologub began the serialization of his greatest and most bizarre work, *The Created Legend* (1907–1913).[10] During its serialization *The Created Legend* provoked the critics' ire as few other novels ever did in the history of Russian literature. Initial perplexity gave way to general dismay and eventually ended in universal outrage. Many readers attacked Sologub for turning his back on the earlier brilliant portrayal of Peredonovism to indulge himself in his own willful fantasies: "[Russian social thought] . . . has lost a great master who, after Gogol, represents the most remarkable portrayer of that entire astounding slime of triviality of which Russian life is composed."[11] Gorky was in a perfect frenzy over Sologub's novel. Struggling for social conscience in literature, Gorky felt that writers like Sologub were anathema to the moral dignity and political future of society in Russia. He promptly cut off his affiliations with the journal that began the serialization of the novel, calling it "indecent". His letters were filled with expressions of disgust over the content of Sologub's work and he was particularly horrified at what he was later to call, in his address at the 1934 Congress of Writers, the presence of "eros in politics". This deviation was best exemplified in Sologub. Several letters to Lunacharsky in December of 1907 highlight his reactions and explain some of the origins for the animosity between Sologub and Gorky:

> You know, that rotten, bald-headed bastard by the name of Sologub is having his novel *The Created Legend* printed in the almanac *Shipovnik*. In the novel you find his hero, an indubitable sadist, and a certain woman who is a social democrat and a propagandist. She comes to him, strips naked, and after suggesting first that he photograph her, she then gives herself to the beast, gives herself like a chunk of cold meat. Anatoly Vasilievich, he ought to have his face smashed in for that! Get the book and read it. By God, you must![12]
>
> . . . You can say the filthiest things possible about Sologub and it would still not be enough for his vile, slimy, froglike soul![13]

If there were socially committed critics like Gorky who felt that fantasy and eroticism were incompatible with politics, others found the novel more or less symptomatic of their times: "This derangement of the imagination, this capricious mixture of the real with pure fantasy, the involuntary manifestations here and there of an erotic sensibility which is not entirely healthy, finally this disjointed and nervous, translucent style which reminds one of a careless first draft or comments for a notebook—all this represents the incontestable symptoms of a sick age."[14]

Indeed, how was the reader supposed to react to Sologub's hero, Grigory Sergeyevich Trirodov? He could not only communicate with spirits from the beyond, raise dead children from freshly dug graves back to a zombie-like existence, reduce his enemies to glass prisms, and concoct powerful potions in his secret laboratory, but he was also involved in politics, actively aiding various democratic and revolutionary organizations, as well as operating a very avantgarde school where both children and instructresses ran about in the altogether. Moreover, what did the reign of Queen Ortruda in the distant kingdom of the United Isles have to do with the plan of this modern-day poet-alchemist? And what could be more absurd than he, a Russian commoner, applying officially for the position of King of the tiny island kingdom in the Mediterranean after the demise of Ortruda? Finally, Sologub must have left readers shaking their heads in disbelief when Trirodov, in order to escape the brutal attack of the militant Black Hundred organization on his estate, takes refuge in his garden green house—which is actually a cleverly concealed spaceship—and blasts off into space. The fact that an old adversary, Peredonov, from *The Petty Demon*, is resurrected in *The Created Legend* as the vice-governor, certainly added to the general muddle. As one reader aptly mused: "It is difficult to find a parallel to this novel in the past of our literature . . . The reader, bewildered and wracking his brains, is given the task of trying to decide whether this is not some kind of joke."[15]

With his typical perverseness, Sologub himself was not forthcoming with any explanations. As reticent about the import of his fiction and poetry as he was about his own person, he seemed to feel that each reader was free to interpret it however he wished. As far as he was concerned, the introductory paragraph to *The Created Legend* explained all that required explaining:

> I take a piece of life, coarse and barren, and from it I create an exquisite legend, for I am a poet. Whether life, dull and common, stagnates in the gloom, or bursts forth in a raging fire, I, the poet, will erect above you, life, my legend which is being created, my legend of the enchanting and the beautiful.

Sologub, then, was exerting his will, his creative fantasy over the coarse material of this world and transfiguring it into something beautiful and divine.

Sologub's final major prose works, *Sweeter Than Poison* (1912) and *The Snake Charmer* (1921), display little of the willful and exquisite fantasy of either *The Petty Demon* or *The Created Legend*. Both of the later novels deal with the tragic fates of two women, the first a petite bourgeoise and the second a factory worker. Perhaps as a result of the criticism of his trilogy, Sologub appeared to return to more solid ground in these works. In *Sweeter Than Poison* we find ourselves once more in a provincial setting where greed, vulgarity and philistinism are rampant among the gentry and townsfolk. However, Sologub's last novel, *The Snake Charmer*, is more remarkable in that the heroine of the novel and the "charmer of snakes" is an attractive young girl from the working classes, Vera Karpunina. She is convinced that she has a holy mission to destroy a "nest of snakes" at her factory—namely, the factory owners and their toadies. The factory owner becomes hopelessly enchanted with Vera. In return for her favors, she extracts a promise from him that he will deed the factory to her so that she can then pass it on to the workers. No sooner does Vera receive the deed than she is murdered by her jealous fiancé who knew nothing of her self-sacrificing designs. Perhaps this novel represented Sologub's half-hearted and clumsy attempt to accommodate himself to the Revolution. At the same time, one must not forget that "democratic themes" were always very much in evidence throughout all of Sologub's novels.

Throughout his entire literary career, Sologub was prepared to write parodies and satires directed at the Tsarist regime. But with the outbreak of World War I, he joined the ranks of other writers who put aside their animosities and wrote very nationalistic and patriotic pieces. He might have been encouraged by the hope that eventually the War would change things and lead to a more democratic society. In fact, Sologub greeted the February Revolution with very positive feelings and threw his support behind the Constitutional Democrats and Social Revolutionaries. His stated ideal was that of a "European Humanitarian Civilization". However, he was not in sympathy with the October Revolution. Nevertheless he did involve himself in literary affairs after this Revolution and he became a leading member of a literary faction that called for independence and freedom in artistic expression. But that faction was short-lived. Together with his wife he joined a professional union of translators. In March of 1918 he helped to found and then became the first president of a writers' organization that was supposed to help writers live and work during those difficult years of War Communism. Because of disagreements within the organization itself, Sologub and his wife resigned and practically disappeared from the literary scene. Suffering material and artistic privations they applied to leave the Soviet Union in 1920. There is disagreement on whether permission was actually granted to Sologub and his wife to emigrate. In his correspondence Gorky claimed that it was not granted. In September of 1921, after several previous unsuccessful attempts, Sologub's wife committed suicide by flinging herself off a Petrograd bridge. Sologub was utterly crushed and he plunged into even deeper isolation. Nevertheless, he managed somehow to integrate himself partially into the new world of the Soviet Union. He served in various administrative capacities on literary bodies until his death in 1927. He was even the recipient of a number of more or less ritual honors. After the Revolution, for reasons that are apparent, Sologub confined himself mainly to translation and administrative duties. While his "Impossible Dream" might have fallen on deaf or coarsened ears before the Revolution, it would now have been drowned by the cacophany of revolutionary thematics and aesthetics. Those who desire a simplistic metaphor, but perhaps an apt one, might be tempted to say that Aldonsa, that vulgar wench of reality, now reigned over the ephemeral and exquisite Dulcinea. And, Sologub, who had emerged out of obscurity bespectacled, balding, slightly ridiculous and improbable, departed from whence he came.

Although Soviet critics willingly concede Sologub a place in the hierarchy of Russian literature for *The Petty Demon*, they have not hastened to publish his work. Too talented to ignore, too problematic to accept unequivocably, Sologub's works have made but fleeting appearances on the Soviet literary scene since the Revolution. With the exception of Sologub's inclusion in various anthologies, the only works to be reprinted since his death in 1927 are *The Petty Demon* (1933; 1958) and two anthologies of his verse (1939; 1975, reprinted 1978). Yet his literary legacy consists of seven novels, almost eighty stories, several novellas, half-a-dozen plays and more than a dozen books of poetry.

From the accounts of Sologub's wife, we know that *The Petty Demon* was begun in the early 1890's and was completed in 1902. Only after an effort of several years was Sologub then able to get it published (in incomplete form) in the journal *Questions of Life* (1905, Nos. 6–11). In 1907 the first complete and separate version appeared and this was rapidly followed by *five* reprintings. The novel was prepared for the stage and travelled about Russia, playing to enthusiastic audiences. Almost overnight Sologub became the toast of Russian letters and joined the popular troyka of Gorky, Kuprin and Andreyev. To this very day *The Petty Demon* is considered to be one of the great classics of Russian literature. The novel appealed to pre-revolutionary and Soviet critics alike and for very similar reasons: it was a masterful sociological exposé of provincial manners in Tsarist Russia, unmasking the hypocrisy, the bigotry and the philistinism that was symptomatic of Russian provincial society and officialdom. Most critics immediately seized upon what they perceived as the obvious affinities between *The Petty Demon* and Gogol's nineteenth-century masterpiece, *Dead Souls*. In his foreword(s) to the novel, Sologub himself seemed to insist that his depictions of provincial society were drawn with fidelity, that they had been based on first-hand experience. Most critics were prepared, for the moment at least, to overlook the other suspect themes in Sologub that touched on eroticism and sado-masochism. Furthermore, most readers were unaware of any deeper meanings in the novel because their appetites were satisfied by what they believed to be "naturalistic detail". Sologub did try to indicate in at least one interview that the novel could be read as a generalization and that Peredonov's madness was a reflection of something else: "Peredonov's madness is not a chance occurrence, but rather a general malady and it represents the daily life of present-day Russia."[16] But, unlike the ponderously significant novels of Merezhkovsky with their complex religious and pagan themes, with grandiose archetypes drawn from across the centuries, Sologub's novel was read at face-value by most. The deeply buried mythological and symbolic strata of the novel eluded the general readership. Symbolic personification and archetypes were just as important to the literary creativity of Sologub as they were to Merezhkovsky, Bely and Blok. His aesthetic mythologization was perhaps more obscure and idiosyncratic, but, as several of the critical essays contained in the appendix at the end of this volume indicate, Sologub had a conscious sense of the symbolic patternings which he was weaving into the sociological fabric of the text.

The bizarre, gray little creature of indeterminate shape and form, the *nedotykomka*, that seems to be a figment of Peredonov's incipient madness, has long intrigued readers and critics—and bedevilled translators. Theories on the identity and the significance of this enigmatic creation abound with the same vigor as the little beastie displays in scurrying across the pages of the novel and through the deranged mind of Peredonov. Readers will find several explanations of the *nedotykomka* in the critical appendix of this edition. Some of the debate focuses on whether the *nedotykomka* is an autonomous being or the sum total of Peredonov's neuroses and vulgarity rolled up into a single musty gray bundle which dissolves into dust or dissipates into thin air at every attempt of Peredonov's to touch, trap or destroy it. It has already been pointed out that, like other Symbolist writers of his generation, Sologub was also attracted to the idea of the symbolic incarnation, embodiment or personification of the artistic idea. The creation of his *nedotykomka* would seem to offer ample proof of this. English readers in particular, however, have been troubled by the exact meaning of the word in Russian. The actual form *nedotykomka* cannot be found in the usual reference texts and dictionaries and the closest variant one is apt to discover is *nedotyka* which signifies a touchy, prickly, sullen or even clumsy person. One source does provide the actual word used by Sologub.[17] *Nedotykomka* appears to be a regional variation on *nedotyka* and carries the same basic meaning. Two things may be of interest here. First of all, the variation used by Sologub is, in fact, accredited to the Novgorod region where he held his first teaching posts. Secondly, Sologub's variant is also a synonym for *nedotroga* which is a flower bearing the Latin name of *Impatiens non me tangere*—or, in simple English: "touch-me-not." Readers of the text will immediately discern the two-fold applicability of Sologub's choice of *nedotykomka*. Peredonov is constantly described as being sullen, touchy and even awkward. At the same time, the elusive *nedotykomka* is a genuine "touch-me-not" who defies all Peredonov's attempts to lay his hands on it. Linguistically, at least, this may shed some light on the identity of the *bête grise* in Peredonov's diseased world.

Readers may wonder about the surname of our hero, Peredonov. That, too, has given critics pause. The most likely suggestions have indicated that the root may well have come from Don Quixote, one of Sologub's beloved characters and an archetype with which he felt he had a great deal in common. In the case of Peredonov, we have, of course, the reverse image of the idealistic and chivalrous Spanish knight. A number of critics have already indicated the parallels that may well exist between Cervantes' novel and Sologub's where the sheeplike Volodin performs the role of Sancho Panza and Varvara appears as Aldonsa.[18]

Extensive discussions of educational organization and educational philosophy are omnipresent in most of Sologub's novels, not to mention many of his stories. One must recall that Sologub devoted twenty-five years of his life to this profession and had always been a deeply involved member of that profession. That experience provides a considerable amount of the content of *The Petty Demon*. In order to understand many of the circumstances and allusions in the novel it is necessary to have some knowledge of the educational system in Russia before the Revolution.

A Ministry of Public Education was established in 1802 under Alexander I, and this was the first genuinely well-conceived and organized attempt at creating an educational system in Russia. The country was divided into six educational circuits, each possessing a university at its center. These "circuits" were further subdivided into districts. Each university would have a pedagogical institute to train teachers. Furthermore, the new Regulations called for the establishment of one or more four-year gymnasia in every main town or city, some type of two-year secondary or elementary school in each district, and a one-year elementary school in every parish. These same Regulations allowed teachers to rise through the various levels of schooling by increasing their qualifications. This reasonably "democratic" and "secular" beginning, was, however, ruined when in 1815 Alexander virtually gave a large measure of control over the school system to the Holy Synod. That meant, among other things, that religious writings and the catechism would occupy a very important part in secular education for the rest of the century.

Under the reign of Nicholas I (1825-1855) this reactionary attitude to public education continued, indeed, deepened, because Nicholas felt that Alexander I's earlier reforms were too liberal. He did not care for the idea that peasant children might be able to ascend upwards through the school system or be allowed to mix with other social classes. He also preferred more emphasis to be placed on the formation of attitudes and character (namely, loyalty, piety and morality) rather than the acquisition of knowledge. New rules were issued in 1828 which stated that the village school as intended exclusively for the peasants; the country or district school was reserved for the merchant class; the *gymnasia* and universities should be the exclusive domain of the gentry or nobility. Specific social status was also attached to the teachers at the various levels. Those in the parish or village schools had little or no status and could only strive for the very lowest rank in the Table of Ranks (the fourteenth). Posts in the district schools and *gymnasia*, particularly the latter, obviously commanded greater respect and could only be held by persons of "free estate." The latter teachers could rise quite high in the Table of Ranks. Corporal punishment was reintroduced (after having been banned during the reign of Peter I). One of the most important—and insidious—new developments concerned the creation of the special office of the Class Monitor or Prefect. Essentially, this represented an official whose primary duties were not only to enforce the numerous regulations pertaining to the educational work of the students, but to maintain a watchful eye over the entire life of the student inside and outside of the classroom. Less euphemistically, the Prefect might well have been called an "academic policeman" or "spy." The chief disciplinary office in each district, however, was held by the Inspector who enjoyed a great deal of power. In actual fact, the Prefects were all answerable to him rather than the director or headmaster in each *gymnasium*. As a result, the Inspector ruled over a kind of Fifth Column within the school system. Another perquisite of an Inspectorship was the administration of corporal punishment. In the district schools the Inspector's power was even greater. Here the teachers were required to acknowledge him as their ultimate superior in all matters pertaining to their behavior and duties.

During the reign of Alexander II (1855–1881), there were many reforms within the educational system. But the reactionary conservatism fostered by Nicholas I often undermined those reforms. One of the most important changes concerned the development of the rural school system. In the mid-1860's, after the Emancipation of the serfs, elected county or rural councils (*zemstvos*) were created. These rural councils included members from both the wealthier nobles and the smaller landowners. Although the desire for liberal reform varied from region to region, nevertheless, these councils managed to improve the rural school system for the peasants. Naturally, the more conservative elements in the Russian educational system resented the work of the councils and did their utmost to undermine both the influence of the councils and the results of their pedagogical activities. Teachers in the *zemstvo* schools were regularly subjected to harassment and repression.

With the assassination of Alexander II in 1881, the reactionaries received fresh impetus to suppress liberal reform in the public school system. Under K. P. Pobedonostsev, the Chief Procurator of the Holy Synod, as well as other reactionary officials chosen by Alexander III (1881–94) and Nicholas II (1894–1917), there was a concerted attempt to exert the authoritarian influence of the Church over public schools. Curiously enough, the *zemstvos* were largely successful in resisting this move to sectarianize the schools, largely because they contributed the lion's share of financial support to the rural school system and the Government did not have the funds to wrest control from the councils. To counter this influence of the *zemstvos*, the Government created a plan to strengthen the parish schools so that they could compete with the secular or rural schools. The revised curriculum proposed for the parish school concentrated particularly on religious subjects (including prayers, the catechism and even singing Church music). Because of large amounts of funding from the Government, the parish schools actually burgeoned for a while through the later 1890s. But that growth quickly declined after 1905 and the *zemstvo* schools were clearly in the ascendancy. In the early part of the 20th Century the rural councils began to design a scheme whereby education would be accessible to the peasantry not only in theory, but in practice as well. This plan called for the organization and construction of schools that would be strategically located so that no pupils would have to go farther than two miles to attend school. Beginning with various reforms introduced after the aborted revolution of 1905, there was a see-sawing battle between conservatives and liberals to further "deform" or "reform" the educational system. In general, great progress was made towards expanding the educational system and liberalizing the regulations governing education in Russia by the time of the Revolution.[19]

Against this schematic background of educational progress and regression throughout the nineteenth and early twentieth centuries, the reader might better comprehend the social significance of Sologub's extensive preoccupation with and description of the educational milieu described in the novel. Peredonov, the tireless and tyrannical reactionary, obviously sees the teacher's role as being that of the moral policeman rather than the purveyor of knowledge. The supreme way of dispensing disciplinary punishment (and simultaneously gratifying his own sadistic lasciviousness) is to become an Inspector who controls the police force of school Prefects. The tension between the champions of the ultra-reactionary educational system of parish schools and rural council schools is portrayed in Peredonov's confrontations with the Marshal of the Nobility, Veriga, and the local *zemstvo* chairman, Kirillov. The question of varying social status within the system is reflected at many points throughout the narrative: Peredonov orders a new uniform in anticipation of his future Inspectorship and dons his official cap with the cockade while mocking those teachers in the lower school system who are not allowed to wear such a cap.

This was the kind of sociological detail that appealed to readers such as Gorky who could appreciate the accuracy of Sologub's portrayal of the educational milieu in Russia at the turn of the century.[20]

It is not by chance that Sologub gave Trirodov, the hero of *The Created Legend*, his own physical features and aesthetic views. Nor is it any less an accident that Trirodov is both poet and chemist, for who would be better endowed to transform the creative dreams of the poet into reality than such a poet-alchemist? Sologub's own dreams of transformation were as fervent as those of the other Symbolists. At the same time, however, he saw the impossibility of fulfillment. But not to dream, not to aspire—that would mean denial of the creative fantasy of the poet: "It is impossible to live without faith in a miracle . . . the miracle of transformation is impossible but it is essential . . . Only the ecstasy of creativity offers man a solution to this fateful contradiction."[21] Futile, yet beautiful dreams are the most alluring, the most exquisite, just as the love of Sasha and Lyudmila in *The Petty Demon* is exquisitely sweet, yet impossible. As a number of his poems reveal, Sologub must have readily identified with the hopelessly romantic, the eternally old, but eternally young hero of Cervantes' novel. Bedevilled by Aldonsa, beguiled by Dulcinea, that ridiculous epigone, Don Quixote, seeks the fulfillment of the impossible dream. Sologub must have caught in himself the wry reflection of that superannuated knight trapped in a time warp when he held the Symbolist's beloved mirror up to his own unprepossessing visage. Ridiculous as he might have seemed, he was nevertheless unwilling to abandon his beloved, his chaste vision:

> By him alone is love not quit
> Whose love is love immortal,
> Whose passion leaves that love unspoilt,
> Whose heart is proffered to the stars,
> Whose love by death alone is quenched.
> The earth knows none who love like this.
> Except that madman, Don Quixote.
>
> Before his eyes, Aldonsa stands.
> That beastly sweat concerns him not
> Which all its earthbound toil
> Doth offer to the blissful sun!
> Aflame with ardor unexpired
> He loves alone with heart so true,
> That wretched madman, Don Quixote.

That maid of low and common toil
To Dulcinea he transformed.
And bowing down before her feet
He sings to her the sweetest hymns.
Before that constant love of yours
What means the heat of youthful love,
Of fleeting love, O, Don Quixote!

(*Don Quixote*, 1920)

—S.D. CIORAN

NOTES

1. See Georgette Donchin, *The Influence of French Symbolism on Russian Poetry.* 'S-Gravenhage, 1958.

2. Vladimir Solovyov, "Chteniya o Bogochelovechestve," in *Sobranie sochineniy V.S. Solovyova*, III, 118.

3. Carl Proffer and Ellendea Proffer (editors), *The Silver Age of Russian Culture.* Ann Arbor: Ardis, 1971, p. 5.

4. *Ibid.*, p. 123.

5. *Ibid.*, p. 4.

6. *Ibid.*, p. 35.

7. See M.I. Dikman, "Poeticheskoe tvorchestvo Fyodora Sologuba," in *Fyodor Sologub. Stikhotvoreniya* (Biblioteka Poeta, Bolshaya seriya, Izd. 2-oe). Leningrad, 1978.

8. See the Introduction to the second set of textual variants by S. Rabinowitz.

9. G. Chulkov, *Gody stranstviy.* Moscow, 1930, pp. 146-7.

10. F. Sologub, *The Created Legend* (Parts I-III). Translated by S.D. Cioran. Ann Arbor: Ardis, 1979.

11. P. Kogan, *Ocherki po istorii noveishey russkoy literatury.* Moscow, 1910, III (vypusk I), p. 103.

12. Maksim Gorky, *Sobranie sochineniy v 30 tomakh.* Moscow, 1949–55, XXX, p. 44.

13. *Ibid.*, p. 46.

14. A.A. Izmailov, *Literaturnyi Olimp.* Moscow, 1911, p. 316.

15. *Ibid.*, pp. 309–10.

16. Quoted by M.I. Dikman, p. 33.

17. See *Opyt oblastnago velikago russkago slovarya* (izd. vtorym otdeleniem Imperatorskoy Akademii nauk). Sanktpeterburg, 1852, p. 126.

18. See the Preface by Andrew Field to Fyodor Sologub, *The Petty Demon*, Bloomington: Indiana University Press, 1970.

19. See W.H.E. Johnson, *Russia's Educational Heritage.* Pittsburgh, 1950.

20. For a more complete discussion of the works of Fyodor Sologub please see: Murl Barker, *The Novels of Fyodor Sologub.* Knoxville, 1977; Stanley Rabinowitz, *Sologub's Literary Children.* Columbus, Ohio. 1980.

21. Quoted by M.I. Dikman, p. 42.

AUTHOR'S FOREWORD TO
THE SECOND EDITION

THE NOVEL *The Petty Demon* was begun in 1892 and completed in 1902. It was printed for the first time in the journal *Questions of Life* in 1905 (Nos. 6–11), but without the concluding chapters. The novel appeared for the first time in a complete version in an edition by *Shipovnik* in March of 1907.

In the printed reviews, as well as the oral ones which I was obliged to listen to, I noticed two contrary opinions.

Some think that the author, being a very bad fellow, wished to present his own portrait and depicted himself in the model of the teacher Peredonov. Due to his sincerity, the author didn't wish to justify and embellish himself in any way, and for that reason smeared his visage with the blackest of colors. He embarked upon this amazing enterprise in order to deliver himself up to a kind of Calvary and to suffer for something or other. The result was an interesting and harmless novel.

Interesting because the novel makes apparent what manner of bad people there are in the world. Harmless because the reader can say: "I'm not the one he's writing about."

Others, who have a less harsh opinion of the author, think that the Peredonovism described in the novel is a rather widespread phenomenon.

Several people even think that by peering closely into ourselves, each of us will find the unmistakable characteristics of Peredonov inside.

Of these two opinions I give preference to the one which pleases me more, namely the second. I was not obliged to contrive and invent on my own. Everything that relates to the narrative incidents, the everyday life and the psychology in my novel is based on very precise observations, and I had sufficient "models" for my novel in my proximity. And if the work on the novel was so drawn out, then it was simply so that stern Ananke could be enthroned where once reigned Aisa, the disseminator of anecdotes.

True, people love to be loved. They like to have the lofty and noble aspects of their souls depicted. Even in malefactors they like to see glimmerings of goodness, of the "divine spark," as it was expressed in olden times. Therefore they cannot believe it when they are faced with a depiction that is faithful, precise, gloomy and wicked. They want to say:

"He's writing about himself."

No, my dear contemporaries, it is about you that I have written my novel about the Petty Demon and its sinister *Nedotykomka*, about Ardalyon and Varvara Peredonov, Pavel Volodin, Darya, Lyudmila and Valeriya Rutilova, Aleksandr Pylnikov and the others. About you.

This novel is a mirror, skillfully fashioned. I polished it for a long while and worked zealously over it.

Smooth is the surface of my mirror and pure its composition. Measured repeatedly and tested painstakingly, it possesses no distortion.

The deformed and the beautiful are reflected in it with equal precision.

January 1908

Author's Foreword to the Fifth Edition

A T ONE TIME it seemed to me that Peredonov's career was finished and that he would no longer emerge from the psychiatric hospital where he was placed after he cut Volodin's throat. But lately rumors have started to reach me concerning the fact that Peredonov's mental derangement had proved to be temporary and had not prevented him from finding himself at liberty after a certain time. Rumors, of course, that have little likelihood. I only make mention of them because in our times the unlikely does happen. I even read in one newspaper that I was getting ready to write the second part of *The Petty Demon*.

I heard that supposedly Varvara succeeded in convincing someone that Peredonov had cause for acting as he had, that more than once Volodin had uttered shocking words and had revealed shocking intentions and that before his death he had said something incredibly impertinent that had prompted the fateful denouement. I have been told that Varvara interested Princess Volchanskaya with this story, and the Princess, who earlier had kept forgetting to put in a word on Peredonov's behalf, apparently now was actively involved in his fate.

My information is unclear and contradictory on the subject of what happened to Peredonov after he came out of the hospital. Some people have told me that Peredonov joined the police service, as Skuchaev had indeed advised him, and was a councillor in a provincial administration. He somehow distinguished himself in this post and was making a good career.

From others I have heard that it was not Ardalyon Borisych who was serving with the police, but a different Peredonov, a relative of our Peredonov. Ardalyon Borisych himself had not succeeded in joining the police service, or had not wished to. He took up literary criticism. Those very characteristics that had distinguished him earlier were now evident in his articles.

This latter rumor seems even less like the truth than the first.

In any event, if I manage to receive specific information about the subsequent activities of Peredonov I shall pass it on in ample detail.

AUTHOR'S FOREWORD TO THE SEVENTH EDITION

THE ATTENTIVE READERS of my novel *Smoke and Ashes* (the fourth part of *The Created Legend*) already know, of course, the path Ardalyon Borisych is now following.

May 1913

DIALOGUE

(To the seventh edition)

"My soul, why are you so dismayed?"

"Because of the hatred that surrounds the name of the author of *The Petty Demon*. Many people who disagree in all else are agreed in this."

"Accept their spite and abuse in peace."

"But could it be that our work is not deserving of gratitude? Where does the hatred come from?"

"This hatred can be likened to fear. You are too outspoken in arousing conscience, you are too frank."

"But is there really no benefit from my fidelity?"

"You expect compliments. But this isn't Paris here."

"Oh, indeed, it's not Paris."

"You, my soul, are a true Parisienne, a child of European civilization. You've come in a fine dress and delicate sandals to a place where coarse peasant blouses and greased boots are worn. Don't be surprised when at times a greased boot stamps rudely on your delicate foot. Its owner is a decent fellow."

"But so sullen. And so clumsy."

May 1913

The Petty Demon

"I wanted to burn her, the wicked witch."

I

FTER THE HOLIDAY MASS the parishioners headed home. Some lingered in the churchyard behind the white stone walls under the old lindens and maples and chatted. Everyone was attired in holiday dress, exchanging amiable looks, and it seemed as though people were living peacefully and harmoniously in this town. Even happily. But it only seemed that way.

Peredonov, a teacher at the gymnasium, stood in a circle of his friends, gazing sullenly at them with small swollen eyes from behind gold-framed spectacles, and said to them:

"Princess Volchanskaya herself promised Varya, so it must be for certain. She said that as soon as Varya marries me then she will immediately take it upon herself to find me a position as an inspector."

"But how can you marry Varvara Dmitrievna?" asked the red-faced Falastov. "After all, she's your first cousin! Has a new law been issued that allows marriage to first cousins?"

Everyone burst into laughter. Peredonov's ruddy and customarily indifferent, sleepy face grew furious.

"Second cousin . . ." he growled, peering angrily past his companions.

"But did the Princess promise you yourself?" asked the pale, tall and foppishly dressed Rutilov.

"Not me but Varya," Peredonov replied.

"Well, there you go, and you believed it," Rutilov said with animation. "It's possible to say anything. Why didn't you go and see the Princess yourself?"

"Look, Varya and I did go but missed the Princess, we were all of five minutes late," Peredonov said. "She had gone off to the country and was to return in three weeks, and I couldn't possibly wait, I had to come back here for the examinations."

"There's something suspicious," said Rutilov and laughed, showing his rotten-looking teeth.

Peredonov grew thoughtful. His companions dispersed. Only Rutilov stayed behind with him.

"Of course," Peredonov said, "I can marry anyone that I care to. Varvara isn't the only one."

"It goes without saying, Ardalyon Borisych, that anyone would marry you," confirmed Rutilov.

They left the churchyard and slowly crossed the unpaved and dusty square. Peredonov said:

"But what about the Princess? She would get angry if I threw Varya over."

"Who cares about the Princess!" Rutilov said. "You don't have to pussyfoot around with her. Let her give you a position first, then you'll have plenty of time to get hitched. Otherwise you'll be doing it for nothing, blindly."

"That's true . . ." Peredonov agreed thoughtfully.

"You tell Varvara that," Rutilov pressed him. "First the position, you say to her, otherwise you don't really believe it. When you do get the position, then you can go ahead and marry whomever you take a fancy to. Best of all, take one of my sisters, there are three, choose any one of them. They're educated young ladies, clever, and it's not flattery to say that Varvara is no match for them. She can't hold a candle to them."

"Hm-hm . . ." Peredonov made a lowing sound.

"It's true. What's your Varvara? Here, take a whiff."

Rutilov bent over, broke off a shaggy stalk of henbane, crumpled it together with the leaves and dirty white flowers, and grinding it between his fingers, raised it to Peredonov's nose. The latter screwed up his face from the unpleasant heavy smell. Rutilov said:

"Grind her up and throw her away, and that's your Varvara. She and my sisters, now brother, there's a real difference for you. My young ladies are perky and full of life, just take any one of them and you won't be dozing off. And they're young too, the eldest is three times younger than your Varvara."

As was his custom, Rutilov uttered all of this quickly and cheerfully, with a smile, yet he was tall, narrow-chested and seemed consumptive and brittle. Sparse, closely cropped light hair stuck out rather miserably from beneath his new and stylish hat.

"Come now, three times," Peredonov objected listlessly, removing his gold spectacles and wiping them.

"It's really true!" exclaimed Rutilov. "Mind you don't dawdle, because as I live, those sisters of mine have their pride—when you feel like it later, then it'll be too late. But any single one of them would be more than pleased to marry you."

"Yes, everyone is in love with me here," Peredonov boasted sullenly.

"Now look, you just seize the opportunity," Rutilov urged him.

"The main thing for me is that I don't want her to be scrawny," Peredonov said with melancholy in his voice. "I prefer one that's a little plump."

"Don't go worrying yourself on that account," Rutilov said heatedly. "They're chubby little ladies right now and if they haven't quite filled out yet, then it's just a matter of time. Soon as they get married they'll put on some flesh like the eldest one. Our Larisa, as you know yourself, has become a proper dumpling."

"I would get married," Peredonov said, "but I'm afraid that Varya would cause a big scandal."

"If you're afraid of a scandal, then this is what you should do," Rutilov said with a cunning smile. "Get married right away today, or even tomorrow. You show up at home with your young wife and, quick as a wink, it'll be over. Really, if you want I'll go and throw it together quick—for tomorrow evening? Which one do you want?"

Peredonov suddenly burst into loud and fitful laughter.

"What about it? Is it a deal?" Rutilov asked.

Peredonov stopped laughing just as suddenly and said sullenly, quietly, almost in a whisper:

"She'll inform on me, the shrew."

"She won't inform about anything, there's nothing to inform about," Rutilov tried to convince him.

"Or she'll poison me," Peredonov whispered fearfully.

"You just leave everything to me," Rutilov pressed him heatedly. "I'll fix everything up for you just right . . ."

"I'm not getting married without a dowry," Peredonov cried angrily.

Rutilov was not amazed in the least by the new jump in the thoughts of his sullen companion. He protested with the same animation:

"You queer fellow, do you really think they have no dowry! Well, are you satisfied then? I'll run along and get everything organized. Only mind you, not so much as a whisper to anyone, you hear!"

He shook Peredonov's hand and ran off. Peredonov stared silently after him. He recollected the young Rutilov ladies, cheerful and derisive. An immodest thought produced the foul likeness of a smile on his lips. It appeared only for an instant and disappeared. A vague anxiety arose inside him.

"What am I supposed to do about the Princess?" he thought. "There's not a kopeck or any patronage backing them up, but with Varvara I'll get to be an inspector and later I'll be made a headmaster."

He glanced after Rutilov who was busily dashing off and thought maliciously:

"Let him run around."

That thought brought a listless and dull pleasure. But he grew bored of being alone. He pushed his hat down over his forehead, knit his light-colored brows and hastily made off in the direction of home through the unpaved deserted streets that were overgrown with grass that had been trampled into the dirt, wild radish and pearlwort with its white flowers.

Someone called him in a quiet and quick voice:

"Ardalyon Borisych, come in and visit us."

Peredonov raised his gloomy eyes and glanced angrily over the hedge. Standing in the garden behind the gate was Natalya Afanasyevna Vershina, a small, thin, dark-skinned woman, dressed all in black, black-browed and black-eyed. She was smoking a cigarette in a dark cherry-wood holder and smiling slightly as though she knew something that couldn't be said but that was worth smiling over. She was urging Peredonov into her garden not so much with words as with light, quick movements: she opened the gate, stood to the side, smiled entreatingly and at the same time confidently indicated with her hands as though to say: "Come in, why stand there?"

And Peredonov did enter, submitting to her soundless almost spell-binding movements. But he immediately stopped on the sandy path where he caught sight of the broken pieces of dry twigs and glanced at his watch.

"It's time for lunch," he grumbled.

Although the watch had served him for a long while, he gazed with pleasure at its large gold case just as he always did in the presence of people. It was twenty minutes to twelve. Peredonov decided that he could spend a little time. He sullenly followed Vershina along the paths, past the barren bushes of black and red currant, raspberry and gooseberry.

The garden had turned yellow and was a colorful profusion of fruit and late flowers. Here were many fruit and ordinary trees as well as bushes: low spreading apple, round-leaved pear, lindens, cherry with smooth shiny leaves, plum, honeysuckle. Red berries glistened on the elder bushes. Siberian geraniums with their delicate purple-veined pale pink buds blossomed thickly along the fence.

Milk thistle thrust its purple heads out from beneath the bushes. Off to the side stood a small, grayish, single-story dwelling with a wide summer kitchen leading into the garden. It seemed nice and comfortable. A portion of the vegetable garden was visible behind it. Dry poppy pods swayed back and forth together with the enormous white and yellow caps of camomile. Wilting, the yellow heads of sunflower bowed low. Among the herbs towered the white umbrellas of fool's parsley and the pale purple umbrellas of storksbill, while pale yellow buttercups and low flowering spurge blossomed.

"Were you at mass?" Vershina asked.

"I was," Peredonov replied sullenly.

"Marta has only just returned," Vershina said. "She goes to our church regularly. I laugh about it. I say to her: Marta, on whose account are you going to our church? She blushes and says nothing. Come, let's sit a while in the summer house," she said quickly without making any transition from what she had been saying earlier.

Standing in the midst of the garden in the shade of spreading maples was an old, grayish summer house: three steps up, a moss-covered dais, low walls, six pot-bellied, turned columns and a six-cornered roof.

Marta was sitting in the summer house, still attired for mass. She was wearing a light-colored dress with small bows but it didn't suit her. The short sleeves revealed her angular red elbows and her large strong hands. Incidentally, Marta wasn't really bad looking. The freckles didn't spoil her looks. Particularly among her own people, the Poles, of whom there were a fair number here, she even had the reputation of being good looking.

Marta was rolling cigarettes for Vershina. She was eager to have Peredonov look at her and be entranced. That desire betrayed itself on her simple-hearted face in an expression of nervous amiability. Incidentally, whether or not Marta was in love with Peredonov had nothing to do with it. Vershina wished to fix her up with someone (Marta came from a large family) and Marta herself wanted to please Vershina with whom she had been living for several months, since the day Vershina's old husband had been buried. She wanted to please Vershina on behalf of herself as well as of her brother, a student at the gymnasium, who was also a guest there.

Vershina and Peredonov went into the summer house. Gloomily, Peredonov exchanged greetings with Marta and sat down. He chose a spot where a column would protect his back from the wind and a draught wouldn't blow in his ears. He glanced at Marta's yellow shoes with pink pompons and had the thought that he was the target of their husband hunting. He always thought that when he saw young ladies who were being amiable with him. In Marta he noted only shortcomings: a lot of freckles, large hands and coarse skin. He knew that her father, a Polish gentleman, was leasing a small estate about six versts from the town. The income was small, the number of children large. Marta had completed the pro-gymnasium, one son was studying at the gymnasium and the other children were even younger.

"May I pour you some beer?" Vershina asked quickly.

On the table stood glasses, two bottles of beer, fine-grained sugar in a tin box, a silver-plated spoon wet with beer.

"I'll have a drink," Peredonov said abruptly.

Vershina glanced at Marta. Marta poured a glass, and moved it towards Peredonov all the while a strange smile, more fearful than actually happy, played over her face. Vershina said quickly, just as though she were spilling the words:

"Put some sugar in the beer."

Marta moved the tin of sugar towards Peredonov. But Peredonov said with annoyance:

"No, it's vile with sugar."

"Come now, it tastes good," Vershina said in a quick, casual monotone.

"Very tasty," Marta said.

"Vile," Peredonov repeated and cast an angry glance at the sugar.

"As you wish," Vershina said and in the same voice began to talk about something else without pausing or making any transition. "Cherepnin is getting to be a bore," she said and laughed.

Marta laughed as well. Peredonov looked on with indifference. He never took part in the affairs of others. He didn't like people, he never thought about them other than in connection with what benefits or pleasures he might derive from them. Vershina smiled complacently and said:

"He thinks that I'm going to marry him."

"Terribly insolent of him," Marta said, not because she herself thought so but because she wanted to please and flatter Vershina.

"He was spying at the window yesterday," Vershina related. "He sneaked into the garden when we were having dinner. There's a barrel under the window, we put it there to catch the rain and it was completely full. It was covered with a board and you couldn't see the water. He crawled up on the barrel and was looking through the window. The lamp was burning where we were, so he could see us but we couldn't see him. Suddenly we heard a noise. At first we were frightened, we ran outside. And there he had tumbled into the water. But he crawled out and ran off completely wet. There was a wet trail along the path. But we recognized him from the back."

Marta gave a delicate, cheerful laugh, the way well-mannered children laugh. Vershina related everything quickly and casually as though she were simply pouring it out (she always talked that way) and all at once she stopped, sat there and smiled with the corner of her mouth, which made her whole swarthy and dry face fall into wrinkles and slightly revealed teeth that were blackened from smoking. Peredonov thought for a while and suddenly burst into laughter. He never reacted immediately to what seemed amusing to him. His faculties were dull and slow.

Vershina was smoking one cigarette after the other. She couldn't live without tobacco smoke before her nose.

"We'll soon be neighbors," Peredonov announced.

Vershina threw a quick glance at Marta. The latter blushed slightly, looked at Peredonov in timid expectation and immediately averted her eyes once more into the garden.

"Are you moving?" Vershina asked. "What for?"

"It's a long way to the gymnasium," Peredonov explained.

Vershina smiled mistrustfully. She thought that it was more likely that he wanted to be closer to Marta.

"But you've been living there for a long while, several years now," she said.

"And the landlady is a bitch," Peredonov said angrily.

"Really?" Vershina asked mistrustfully and smiled crookedly.

Peredonov grew somewhat animated.

"She put up new wallpaper and it's disgusting," he explained. "The pieces don't match. Suddenly in the dining room there's a completely different pattern above the door, the entire room is done in a free pattern and small flowers and then over the door are stripes and polka dots. And the color is all wrong. We might not have noticed but Falastov came and laughed. And everyone is laughing."

"Imagine, what a disgrace," Vershina agreed.

"Only we're not telling her that we're moving out," Peredonov said, lowering his voice. "We'll find an apartment and just go, but we're not telling her."

"Naturally," Vershina said.

"Otherwise, to be sure, she'll cause a scandal," Peredonov said and a fearful anxiety was mirrored in his eyes. "And on top of it, why pay her for a month, for that kind of vileness?"

Peredonov burst into laughter over the happy thought that he would move out of the apartment and not pay for it.

"She'll demand the money," Vershina noted.

"Let her, I won't pay," Peredonov said angrily. "We made a trip to St. Petersburg, so we weren't using the apartment at the time."

"Still, the apartment was reserved for you," Vershina said.

"Makes no difference! She's supposed to do the repairs, so why are we obliged to pay for the time when we're not living there? And the main thing is that she's terribly insolent."

"Well, the landlady is insolent because your, um . . . cousin is a hot-tempered person," Vershina said, with a slight hesitation over the word "cousin."

Peredonov frowned and stared dully in front of himself with half-asleep eyes. Vershina started to talk about something different. Peredonov pulled a caramel out of his pocket, cleaned the paper away and started to chew. By chance he glanced at Marta and had the thought that she was jealous and would also like a caramel.

"Should I give her one or not?" Peredonov thought. "She's not worth it. Or maybe I should anyway, I don't want them to think that I begrudge it. I have lots of them, pocketfuls of caramels."

And he pulled out a fistful of caramels.

"Go ahead," he said and offered the candy first to Vershina, then to Marta. "They're good bonbons, expensive, cost thirty kopecks a pound."

Each took one. He said:

"Take more. I have lots, and they're good bonbons, I'm not about to eat bad stuff."

"Thank you, I don't want any more," Vershina said quickly and tonelessly.

Marta repeated the same words after her, but somehow uncertainly. Peredonov looked mistrustfully at Marta and said:

"What do you mean you don't want any! Go ahead."

From a fistful he took one caramel for himself and laid the rest in front of Marta. Marta smiled in silence and bowed her head.

"The boor," Peredonov thought. "Doesn't know how to thank you nicely."

He didn't know what to talk to Marta about. He didn't find her interesting—she was like all the objects with which someone else hadn't established good or bad relations for him.

The rest of the beer was poured into Peredonov's glass. Vershina glanced at Marta.

"I'll bring more," Marta said.

She always guessed without any words what Vershina wanted.

"Send Vladya, he's in the garden," Vershina said.

"Vladislav!" Marta shouted.

"Here," the boy responded quickly and close by, just as though he were eavesdropping.

"Bring some beer, two bottles," Marta said. "Inside the chest in the passage."

Vladislav soon came running noiselessly back to the summer house, handed the beer to Marta through a window and bowed to Peredonov.

"Greetings," Peredonov said with a frown. "How many bottles have you polished off today?"

Vladislav gave a strained smile and said:

"I don't drink beer."

He was a boy of about fourteen, resembling his sister, with freckles like Marta's, awkward and sluggish in his movements. He was dressed in a long loose shirt of coarse linen.

Marta spoke with her brother in a whisper. They were both laughing. Peredonov kept giving them suspicious looks. When people were laughing in his presence and he didn't know about what, he always supposed that they were laughing about him. Vershina grew uneasy. She was about to call Marta. But Peredonov himself asked in a spiteful voice:

"What are you laughing at?"

Marta gave a start, turned to him and didn't know what to say. Vladislav smiled, stared at Peredonov and blushed slightly.

"It's not polite in front of guests," Peredonov reprimanded them. "Are you laughing at me?" he asked.

Marta blushed, Vladislav was frightened.

"Forgive us," Marta said. "We weren't talking about you. It was about something that concerned us."

"A secret," Peredonov said angrily. "It's not polite to chat about secrets in front of guests."

"It's not really a secret at all," Marta said. "We were talking about the fact that Vladya is barefoot and can't come in here, he's bashful."

Peredonov relaxed, began to make up jokes at Vladya's expense and then he treated him to a caramel as well.

"Marta, bring my black shawl," Vershina said. "And while you're at it, take a look in the kitchen and see how the pie is doing."

Marta left obediently. She understood that Vershina wanted to talk to Peredonov and she was happy, in her indolence, that there was no hurry.

"And off you go," said Vershina to Vladya. "There's no reason for you to hang around here."

Vladya ran off and the murmuring sound of sand was audible beneath his feet. Vershina carefully and quickly glanced sideways at Peredonov through the smoke which she was emitting incessantly. Peredonov sat in silence, staring straight ahead with a vague look and chewing on a caramel. He was pleased that the others had left, otherwise, to be sure, they might have started laughing again. Although he knew probably that they weren't laughing at him, nevertheless, a feeling of annoyance lingered on inside him, just the way the pain lingers on and grows after touching a stinging nettle even though the nettle is long removed.

"Why aren't you getting married?" Vershina suddenly said briskly, quickly. "Why are you still waiting, Ardalyon Borisych? Varvara is no match for you, forgive me for being forthright."

Peredonov ran his hand through his slightly tousled chestnut-colored hair and said with sullen pomposity:

"No one's a match for me here."

"Don't say that," Vershina objected and smiled crookedly. "There's a great deal better here than her and anyone would marry you."

She flicked the ash from her cigarette with a decisive movement as though she were putting an exclamation mark to something.

"I don't need just anyone," Peredonov replied.

"We're not talking about just anyone," Vershina said quickly. "And since you don't have to go chasing after a dowry there would be a fine girl. Thank goodness you earn enough."

"No," objected Peredonov, "there's more for me to gain by marrying Varvara. The Princess has promised patronage to her. She'll give me a good position," Peredonov said with sullen enthusiasm.

Vershina smiled slightly. Her entire face, wrinkled, dark and seemingly tobacco cured, expressed a condescending mistrustfulness. She asked:

"And did the Princess herself tell you that?"

With the stress on the word "you."

"Not me but Varvara," Peredonov admitted. "But it makes no difference."

"You're relying rather a lot on the words of your cousin," Vershina said maliciously. "Tell me now, is she much older than you? About fifteen years or so? Or more? She must be close to fifty?"

"Come now," Peredonov said with annoyance. "She's not thirty yet."

Vershina laughed.

"Interesting," she said with unconcealed derision in her voice. "Yet to look at she's much older than you. Of course, it's none of my affair, but it does seem a pity from the point of view that such a fine young person can't live the way he might have deserved, given his attractiveness and spiritual qualities."

Peredonov looked himself over with self-satisfaction. But there was no smile on his ruddy face and it seemed as though he were insulted by the fact that not everyone understood him as well as Vershina did. Vershina continued:

"You'll go far even without patronage. How can the authorities not help but value you! Why should you hang on to Varvara! And it's not worth your while marrying one of the Rutilov ladies. They're all frivolous and you need a solid wife. You ought to take my Marta here."

Peredonov glanced at his watch.

"Time to go home," he said and began to take leave.

Vershina was certain that Peredonov was leaving because she had touched a raw spot and it was only because of his indecisiveness that he didn't want to talk about Marta right then.

II

VARVARA DMITRIEVNA MALOSHINA, Peredonov's mistress, was waiting for him, slovenly dressed but painstakingly powdered and rouged.

Jam pastries had been baked for lunch. Peredonov loved them. Varvara was waddling quickly around the kitchen on her high heels, hurrying all the while to have everything ready for his arrival. Varvara was afraid that the maid, the pock-marked, fat wench, Natalya, would steal a pastry or even more. For that reason Varvara wouldn't leave the kitchen and as was her habit she was scolding the maid. On a face that preserved some traces of a former attractiveness, she wore an invariable expression of querulous greed.[1]

As always, on his return home, Peredonov would be gripped by displeasure and melancholy. He made a noisy entrance into the dining room, flung his hat on the window sill, sat down at the table and shouted:

"Varya, serve lunch!"

Varvara carried in the food from the kitchen, hobbling adroitly in the narrow shoes she wore for vanity's sake and served Peredonov herself. When she brought the coffee, Peredonov bent down over the steaming glass and sniffed. Varvara grew alarmed and asked him with fright:

"What's the matter, Ardalyon Borisych? Does the coffee smell of something?"

Peredonov glanced sullenly at her and said angrily:

"I'm sniffing it to see whether poison has been put in it."

"Really, Ardalyon Borisych!" Varvara said fearfully. "God help you, why ever would you think up such a thing?"

"You laced it with poison hemlock!" he growled.

"What have I got to gain by poisoning you?" Varvara tried to convince him. "Enough of your tomfoolery!"

Peredonov went on sniffing for a long while and finally relaxed and said:

"If there really is any poison then you can invariably detect it as a heavy odor, just sniff a little closer, right in the steam."

He was silent for a while and then suddenly spoke out spitefully and derisively:

"The Princess!"

Varvara grew agitated.

"What about the Princess? What do you mean, the Princess?"

"The Princess, I'm saying," Peredonov went on, "let her give me the position first and then I'll get married afterwards. You write her that."

"But, Ardalyon Borisych," Varvara began in a voice that attempted to be convincing, "you know yourself that the Princess has promised only after I get married. Otherwise it's awkward for her to ask on your behalf."

"Write her that we're already married," Peredonov said quickly, rejoicing at his invention. Varvara was almost taken aback but soon regained her wits and said:

"What's the use of lying, the Princess will make inquiries. No, better you name the wedding day. And it's time to have a dress sewn."

"What dress?" Peredonov asked sullenly.

"Do you really expect me to get married in this work dress?" Varvara cried. "Give me some money, Ardalyon Borisych, for the dress."

"Are you getting ready to die?" Peredonov asked spitefully.

"You're a beast, Ardalyon Borisych!" Varvara exclaimed reproachfully.

Suddenly Peredonov felt like teasing Varvara. He asked:

"Varvara, do you know where I was?"

"Well, where?" Varvara asked anxiously.

"At Vershina's," he said and burst into laughter.

"You found yourself fine company," Varvara cried spitefully. "No use saying anything!"

"I saw Marta," Peredonov went on.

"She's all covered in freckles," Varvara said with growing spite. "And a mouth that's ear to ear, you could pin it on a frog."

"But she's prettier than you," Peredonov said. "Maybe I'll go ahead and marry her."

"Go right ahead," Varvara shrieked, all red and trembling with malice. "I'll burn her eyes out with acid!"

"I want to spit on you," Peredonov said calmly.

"No you won't!" Varvara screamed.

"I'm going to spit on you right now," Peredonov said.

He stood up and with a dull and indifferent expression he spat in her face.

"Swine!" Varvara said rather calmly as though the spit had refreshed her.

She started to wipe herself off with a napkin. Peredonov was silent. Lately he had become even cruder than usual with Varvara. Even before he had always treated her poorly. Reassured by his silence she said more loudly:

"It's true, you're a swine. It landed right in my mug."

A bleating, almost sheep-like voice was heard in the front hall.

"Stop yelling," Peredonov said. "Guests."

"It's Pavlushka," she replied with a smirk.

Entering the room with a cheerful loud laugh was Pavel Vasilyevich Volodin, a young man who totally in face and manners bore an amazing resemblance to a sheep. The curly hair was sheep-like, the eyes were dull and protruding—everything was just like a cheerful sheep. In short, a stupid young man. He was a cabinet maker and had studied earlier at a vocational school and now was working as a vocational teacher in the town school.

"Ardalyon Borisych, my good friend!" he cried out joyfully. "You're at home, having a nice old coffee and now here I am, sure as can be."

"Natashka, bring a third spoon!" Varvara shouted.

From the kitchen Natalya could be heard clinking the one remaining teaspoon: the rest had been hidden away.

"Eat, Pavlushka," Peredonov said and it was apparent that he wanted to feed Volodin. "It won't be long now, brother, I'll be stepping into an inspectorship. The Princess has promised Varya."

Volodin rejoiced and burst into laughter.

"Hey, the future inspector is having a nice old coffee!" he cried, clapping Peredonov on the shoulder.

"Do you think it's easy to step into an inspectorship? All they have to do is denounce me—and down comes the lid."

"And what's there to denounce?" Varvara asked with a smirk.

"Lots. They'll say that I was reading Pisarev*—and oi-yoi-yoi!"

"But Ardalyon Borisych, you just put that Pisarev on the back shelf," Volodin advised with a giggle.

Peredonov glanced cautiously at Volodin and said:

"Maybe I never had any Pisarev. Do you want a drink, Pavlushka?"

Volodin stuck out his lower lip, assumed the important face of a person who knew his own worth and then he said as he nodded his head like a sheep:

"If it's for the sake of company, then I'm always ready to have a drink, otherwise, uh-uh."

Peredonov, too, was always ready to have a drink. They drank vodka and ate the sweet pastries.

Suddenly Peredonov splattered the rest of the coffee out of his glass on the wallpaper. Volodin's eyes goggled and he looked around in amazement. The wallpaper was smeared and shredded. Volodin asked:

"What's wrong with the wallpaper here?"

Peredonov and Varvara burst into laughter.

"It's to spite the landlady," Varvara said. "We're moving out soon. But no blabbing now!"

"Excellent!" Volodin cried and burst into cheerful laughter.

Peredonov went up to the wall and started to kick at it with the soles of his shoes. Following his example, Volodin, too, pounded away at the wall. Peredonov said:

"Whenever we leave any place we always mess up the walls to let them have something to remember us by."

"You planted some dandies there!" Volodin exclaimed in ecstasy.

"Irishka will go out of her mind," Varvara said with a dry and mean laugh.

*Pisarev, Dmitry Ivanovich (1840–1868). A radical intellectual and critic of the 1860s. Prominent figure among the Russian nihilists. He was arrested in 1862 for being involved in the underground press and spent four years in prison. Died of drowning in 1868. Famous for making the statement that a good pair of boots was worth more than a Shakespearean tragedy. Very critical of Pushkin as a poet lacking in sufficient social consciousness. Pisarev held very utilitarian views about the purpose of art.

Standing in front of the wall all three of them were spitting on it, tearing the wallpaper and pounding at it with their shoes. Tired and satisfied after a while they turned away.

Peredonov bent over and picked up the cat. The cat was fat, white and ugly. Peredonov pestered it—he tugged at the ears and the tail and shook it by the neck. Volodin was roaring cheerfully and suggesting other things Peredonov could do.

"Ardalyon Borisych, blow in its eyes! Rub its fur the wrong way!"

The cat snorted and tried to tear free but it didn't dare show its claws—for that it would have been beaten cruelly. Finally Peredonov grew bored with this diversion and he dropped the cat.

"Listen, Ardalyon Borisych, this is what I wanted to tell you," Volodin began. "I kept thinking not to forget on the way here and I almost did."

"Well?" Peredonov asked sullenly.

"Now you like sweet things," Volodin said happily, "and I know a dish that will make you lick your fingers."

"I know all the tasty dishes myself," Peredonov said.

Volodin gave an offended look.

"Ardalyon Borisych," he said, "maybe you know all the tasty dishes that people make where you come from, but how could you possibly know all the tasty dishes that are made where I come from if you've never been there?"

Satisfied with the persuasiveness of his argument, Volodin laughed and bleated.

"They feed on dead cats where you come from," Peredonov said angrily.

"Excuse me, Ardalyon Borisych," Volodin said in a shrill laughing voice, "it may well be that people eat dead cats where you come from, but we won't go into that, only you have never eaten *erly*."

"No, I haven't," Peredonov admitted.

"What kind of dish is that?" Varvara asked.

"This is what it is," Volodin began to explain. "Do you know the *kutiya** they serve at funerals?"

"Who doesn't know *kutiya*," Varvara replied with a smirk.

"So you take a *kutiya* made from millet and add raisins, some sugar and almonds—and there's your *erly*."

Volodin began to relate in detail how *erly* was prepared where he came from. Peredonov listened somberly. Imagine, a funeral *kutiya*. Was Pavlushka trying to pack him off to the grave or something?

Volodin made an offer:

"If you want everything to be just right, give me ingredients and I'll prepare one for you."

"You might as well let a goat into the garden," Peredonov said sullenly.

"And he'll probably slip something else in as well," he thought.

Volodin was offended once more.

Kutiya is a pressed cereal pudding made variously from barley, millet or rice together with watered-down honey and raisins. It is usually brought to church at funeral services and then served afterwards at the wake.

"If you're thinking, Ardalyon Borisych, that I'm about to pinch some sugar from you, then you are mistaken. I have no need of your sugar."

"Stop all the tomfoolery," Varvara interrupted. "You know how touchy he is. Come and prepare it here."

"And you'll eat it all yourself," Peredonov said.

"Why is that?" Volodin asked in a voice that reverberated with insult.

"Because it's vile."

"As you like, Ardalyon Borisych," Volodin said, shrugging his shoulders. "I merely wanted to please you, but if you don't want it then have it your way."

"Why did the general bawl you out?" Peredonov asked.

"What general?" Volodin countered with a question, blushed and puffed out his lower lip offendedly.

"We heard, we did," Peredonov said.

Varvara was smirking.

"If you please, Ardalyon Borisych," Volodin began heatedly, "you heard, but perhaps you didn't hear everything. I'll tell you about the whole affair."

"Well, we're waiting," Peredonov said.

"This affair took place the day before yesterday," Volodin related, "about this very time. As you are aware, repairs are underway in the workshop. And, lo and behold, Veriga arrived with our inspector to look things over while we were working in the back room. Fine. I didn't concern myself with the reason for Veriga's appearance or what he wanted there, that was none of my affair. We will assume that I know that he is marshal of the nobility and has no connection to our school—but I won't go into that. He came, and fine, we weren't in the way, we were working away by ourselves. Suddenly they came into our room and Veriga, if you please, is wearing his hat."

"He was showing disrespect for you," Peredonov said sullenly.

"And, if you please," Volodin took up this line joyfully, "there was even an icon hanging in that room and there we all were without hats when suddenly he puts in an appearance like some kind of mameluke. I gave myself leave to say to him, quietly and nobly: Your Excellency, I said, please take the trouble to remove your hat because, I said to him, there is an icon here. Was I right in what I said?" Volodin asked and his eyes goggled questioningly.

"Smart fellow, Pavlushka," Peredonov cried, "that's telling him."

"Of course, why should they get away with it," Varvara threw in her support as well. "Good work, Pavel Vasilyevich."

With the look of a person who had been wrongly offended, Volodin continued:

"And suddenly, by his leave, he said to me: the cobbler should stick to his last. He turned and left. And that is what the whole affair was about and there's nothing more to it."

Volodin felt like a hero nevertheless. Peredonov gave him a caramel by way of consolation.

Another guest arrived, Sofiya Efimovna Prepolovenskaya, wife of the forest warden, a plump woman with a goodnaturedly devious face and smooth movements. They sat her down to lunch. She questioned Volodin slyly:

"Really, Pavel Vasilyevich, have you become a regular visitor to Varvara Dmitrievna?"

"It's not Varvara Dmitrievna that I've come to see, if you please," Volodin answered modestly, "it's Ardalyon Borisych."

"Haven't you fallen in love with anyone by now?" Prepolovenskaya asked laughingly.

Everyone was aware of the fact that Volodin was looking for a bride with a dowry, he had proposed to many and had always been refused. Prepolovenskaya's joke seemed out of place to him. With his entire manner reminiscent of a deeply offended sheep, he said in a trembling voice:

"If I have fallen in love, Sofiya Efimovna, then it would be no one's concern but my own and the other person's. And you are just doing this to make fun."

But Prepolovenskaya was irrepressible:

"Look," she said, "if you get Varvara Dmitrievna to fall in love with you, who then is going to bake sweet pastries for Ardalyon Borisych?"

Volodin puffed out his lips, raised his brows and no longer knew what to say.

"And don't be modest, Pavel Vasilyevich," Prepolovenskaya continued. "You'd make a good husband! You're young and handsome."

"Perhaps Varvara Dmitrievna doesn't care to," Volodin said, giggling.

"What do you mean, doesn't care to." Prepolovenskaya replied, "You're being painfully modest for nothing."

"And maybe I don't care to," Volodin said, clowning around. "Perhaps I don't want to marry other people's cousins. Perhaps where I come from I have a niece of my own who's growing up."

By now he had begun to believe that Varvara wouldn't be adverse to marrying him. Varvara grew angry. She considered Volodin a fool. He earned only a quarter of Peredonov's salary. But Prepolovenskaya wanted to marry Peredonov off to her own cousin, the buxom daughter of a priest. For that reason she was trying to embroil Peredonov and Varvara.

"Why are you proposing me for marriage," Varvara asked in annoyance. "Better you offer your little cousin to Pavel Vasilyevich in marriage."

"Why should I be about to take him away from you!" Prepolovenskaya protested jokingly.

Prepolovenskaya's jokes added a new turn to Peredonov's slow thoughts. And the *erly* had become firmly seated in his mind. Why had Volodin invented that particular dish? Peredonov didn't like to spend time reflecting. He always believed straightaway what people told him. So he had believed that Volodin was in love with Varvara. He thought that no sooner would he be hitched to Varvara than he would be poisoned with the *erly* on the road to his new inspector's position, Volodin would take his place, he would be buried under Volodin's name and Volodin would be the inspector. A clever plan they had hatched!

Suddenly there was a noise in the front hall. Peredonov and Varvara took fright. His eyes were riveted on the door. Varvara crept stealthily up to the door in the living room and opened it a crack, peeked through and then just as quietly, on tip-toe, balancing herself with her arms and smiling distractedly, returned to the table. Shrill cries and a racket were coming from the entry way as though a struggle was underway there. Varvara whispered:

"It's that bag, Ershova, drunk as drunk can be. Natashka isn't letting her in but she's still trying to barge her way into the living room."

"What are we supposed to do?" Peredonov asked fearfully.

"We have to move into the living room," Varvara decided, "so that she doesn't sneak in here."

They went into the living room and shut the doors firmly behind them. Varvara went out into the front hall with the faint hope of detaining the landlady there or seating her in the kitchen. But the insolent woman forced her way into the living room anyway. With hands on hips she stopped at the doorway and spouted words of abuse by way of a general greeting. Peredonov and Varvara fussed around her and tried to sit her down on a chair closer to the front hall and as far as possible from the dining room. Varvara brought her out a tray of vodka, beer and pastries from the kitchen. But the landlady wouldn't sit down, ate nothing and strained to get into the dining room but just couldn't identify where the door was. She was flushed, bedraggled and filthy, and she smelled of vodka from a long way off. She was screaming:

"No, you seat me at your table. What do you mean by serving me on a tray! I want it on a table cloth. I'm the landlady, so you give me some respect. Don't look at me like I'm drunk. I'm still a decent woman, I'm still my husband's wife."

Varvara, with a cowardly and impudent smirk, said:

"Don't we know it."

Ershova winked at Varvara, burst into a hoarse laughter and snapped her fingers jauntily. She was becoming increasingly impudent.

"Cousin!" she shouted, "we know what kind of cousin you are. And why doesn't the headmaster's wife come to visit you? Eh? Well?"

"Stop shouting," Varvara said.

But Ershova started to shout even more loudly:

"How dare you give me orders! I'm in my own house and I'll do what I want. If I feel like it I'll kick you out of here right this minute so there won't be hide nor hair of you. Only I'm being very gracious towards you. Live as you will, I don't mind, just don't go causing a nuisance."

Meanwhile, Volodin and Prepolovenskaya were huddling meekly by the window and keeping as quiet as can be. Prepolovenskaya had the trace of a grin as she kept glancing sideways at the rowdy woman, pretending to look outside. Volodin sat with an expression of offended importance on his face.

For the moment Ershova had become good-humored and said to Varvara in an amicable fashion while smiling drunkenly and cheerfully and clapping her on the back:

"No, you just listen to what I'm going to say to you. You sit me down at your table and serve me something grand to drink. And serve me some real spice cakes. Have some respect for your landlady, really, you dear girl of mine."

"Here are some pastries for you," Varvara said.

"I don't want pastries, I want some really grand spice cakes," Ershova started to shout, waving her arms about and smiling blissfully. "The ladies and gents are stuffing themselves with nice tasty spice cakes, real tasty ones!"

"I don't have any cakes for you," Varvara replied, growing bolder from the fact that the landlady was getting more cheerful. "Here, you're getting pastries, so stuff yourself."

Suddenly, Ershova figured out where the door into the dining room was. They were too late to stop her. Bowing her head, her fists clenched, she burst into the dining room after flinging the door open with a crash. There she stopped at the threshold, caught sight of the spattered wallpaper and gave a shrill whistle. She put her hands on her hips, planted one foot ostentatiously and screamed furiously:

"So, in actual fact, you want to leave town!"

"Come now, Irina Stepanovna," Varvara said in a trembling voice. "We weren't even thinking of it, enough of this tomfoolery."

"We aren't going anywhere," Peredonov confirmed. "We like it here just fine."

The landlady wasn't listening, she stepped up to a dumbfounded Varvara and shook her fists in her face. Peredonov was standing behind Varvara. He would have run away but he was curious to see how the landlady and Varvara would lay into each other.

"I'll stand you on one foot, yank on the other and tear you in half!" Ershova screamed fiercely.

"Come now, Irina Stepanovna," Varvara tried to convince her. "Stop, we have guests."

"Let's have your guests here too!" Ershova shouted. "What do I care about your guests anyway!"

Stumbling, Ershova plunged into the living room and suddenly changing both her speech and her entire behavior completely, mildly addressed Prepolovenskaya as she gave her a deep bow and almost collapsed onto the floor:

"My dear madam, Sofiya Efimovna, forgive me, drunken woman that I am. Only listen to what I'm going to tell you. Here you are coming to visit them and do you know what she says about your cousin? And to whom? To me, the drunken wife of a shoemaker! Why? So I'll tell everyone, that's why?"

Varvara turned a deep crimson and said:

"I never said anything to you."

"You didn't? You, a foul libertine?" Ershova started to shout, stepping up to Varvara with clenched fists.

"Quiet down," Varvara muttered with embarrassment.

"No I won't," Ershova screamed maliciously and turned to Prepolovenskaya once more. "She told me, the vile woman did, that your cousin is apparently carrying on with your husband."

Sofiya flashed an angry and cunning glance at Varvara, stood up and said with feigned laughter:

"I thank you most humbly. I never expected that."

"You're lying!" Varvara shrieked spitefully at Ershova.

Ershova gave an angry hoot, stomped her feet and shook her hand at Varvara and immediately turned to Prepolovenskaya once more:

"And the things, dear lady, that the gentleman says about you! That apparently earlier you used to gad about and only got married afterwards! That's the kind they are, the vilest of people! Spit in their mugs, my good madam, don't have anything to do with these kind of utterly disgusting people."

Prepolovenskaya blushed and silently went out into the front hall. Peredonov ran after her trying to make excuses.

"She's lying, don't you believe her. Only once in her presence did I say that you were a fool and that was only out of anger and, by God, I never said anything more. She's making it up herself."

Prepolovenskaya replied calmly:

"Come now, Ardalyon Borisych! I can see that she's drunk and she herself doesn't know what she's spouting on about. Only why do you allow all this to go on in your home?"

"Just try to imagine," replied Peredonov, "what can you do with her!"

Angry and embarrassed, Prepolovenskaya put on her jacket. Peredonov didn't think to help her. He muttered a few things more but she was no longer listening to him. Then Peredonov returned to the living room. Ershova started to reproach him noisily. Varvara ran out on the porch and tried to console Prepolovenskaya:

"You know what a fool he is, he doesn't know himself what to say."

"Enough of your worrying," Prepolovenskaya replied to her. "A drunken old woman will say all sorts of things."

Outside, around the house where the porch fronted, stinging nettles grew thick and high. Prepolovenskaya smiled slightly and the final shadow of displeasure disappeared from her white and plump face. Once more she grew friendly and amiable with Varvara. The insult would be avenged without any quarrel. They walked together into the garden to wait out the landlady's onslaught.

Prepolovenskaya kept looking at the nettles that grew along the fences in abundance. She finally said:

"You have a lot of nettles. Do you need them all?"

Varvara laughed and replied:

"Now what would I need them for!"

"If you don't mind I should like to gather some from you, we don't have any," Prepolovenskaya said.

"What do you need them for?" Varvara asked in amazement.

"I've got a use for them," Prepolovenskaya said laughingly.

"Honey, tell me what for?" Varvara asked with curiosity.

Leaning over to Varvara's ear Prepolovenskaya whispered:

"Rub yourself with nettles and you won't lose any weight. My Genichka became such a fatty from using nettles."

She was aware that Peredonov gave preference to fat women and disapproved of skinny ones. Varvara was crushed by the fact that she was slender and getting thinner. How could she put some more weight on? That was one of her most important concerns. She had asked everyone whether they knew of any means. Now Prepolovenskaya was certain that Varvara, following her suggestion, would zealously rub herself all over with nettles and in this way punish herself.

III

PEREDONOV AND ERSHOVA came outside. He muttered:
"Well, who would have thought it possible."
She was shouting at the top of her voice and was happy. They were going to dance. Prepolovenskaya and Varvara crept back into the rooms through the kitchen and sat down by the window to watch what would happen outside.

Peredonov and Ershova took hold of each other and started up a dance around the pear tree. Peredonov's face retained its customary dull expression and displayed nothing. The gold spectacles and the short hair on his head were bobbing up and down mechanically as though on some inanimate thing. Ershova was squealing, shouting and waving her hands while her whole body reeled.

She shouted to Varvara through the window:
"Hey, you prig, come on out and dance! You ashamed of our company?"
Varvara turned away.
"To hell with you! I'm dead on my feet!" Ershova shouted, collapsed on the grass and pulled Peredonov down with her.

They sat a while in each other's arms and then they started dancing again. And so it continued a number of times: first they would dance a while, then rest under the pear tree, on a bench or right on the grass.

Volodin was genuinely enjoying himself looking out the window at the dancers. He was roaring with laughter, making killingly funny faces, clowning, bending his knees up and screeching:
"They're really going at it now! Great fun!"
"Damned bitch!" Varvara said angrily.
"Bitch," Volodin agreed, laughing. "Just you wait, my dear old landlady, I'm going to do you a nice favor. Let's make a mess in the living room too. It doesn't matter now, she won't be back today, she'll fag herself out there on the grass and then go home to sleep."

He dissolved in a bleating laugh and started to prance like a sheep. Prepolovenskaya played the instigator:
"Of course, go ahead and make a mess, Pavel Vasilyevich, no need to play up to her. If she does come then you can tell her that she did it herself in a drunken state."

Jumping up and down and guffawing, Volodin ran off into the living room and started to scrape the wallpaper with the soles of his shoes.

"Varvara Dmitrievna, give me some rope," he cried.

Waddling like a duck, Varvara crossed the living room into the bedroom and brought back the end of a rope that was shredded and knotted. Volodin made a noose, stood a chair in the middle of the room and hung the noose on the lamp hook.

"That's for the landlady!" he shouted. "So she'll have something to hang herself with out of anger when you move out."

Both women squealed with laughter.

"Give me a bit of paper," Volodin shouted, "and a pencil."

Varvara rummaged around in the bedroom again and brought out a scrap of paper and a pencil. Volodin wrote "for the landlady" and fastened the paper to the noose. He accompanied all of this with amusing faces. Then once more he began to jump up and down furiously along the walls, pounding away at them with the soles of his shoes and shaking with laughter the whole time. The entire house was filled with his squealing and bleating laughter. The white cat, its ears laid back in fright, kept peering out of the bedroom and obviously didn't know where it should flee to.

Peredonov finally extricated himself from Ershova and returned home alone. Ershova had in fact exhausted herself and had gone home to sleep. Volodin greeted Peredonov with a joyful guffaw and cry:

"We've made a mess in the living room too! Hurray!"

"Hurray!" Peredonov cried and abruptly burst into a loud laugh just as though he were firing off a salvo of his laughter.

The women shouted "hurray" as well. A general revelry commenced. Peredonov cried:

"Pavlushka, let's dance!"

"Let's, Ardalyon, old boy," Volodin replied with a stupid giggle.

They danced away beneath the noose, kicking out their feet in a clumsy fashion. The floor was trembling under Peredonov's heavy stomping.

"Ardalyon Borisych is dancing his heart out," Prepolovenskaya noted with a slight smile.

"You're telling me, he's full of quirks," Varvara replied peevishly, nevertheless admiring Peredonov.

She sincerely thought that he was a handsome and fine fellow. His most stupid actions seemed only proper to her. He was neither ridiculous nor despicable to her.

"Let's hold a funeral service for the landlady!" Volodin cried.

"Give me a pillow!"

"What won't they think up!" Varvara said with a laugh.

She tossed a pillow in a filthy cover out of the bedroom. The pillow was placed on the floor as the landlady and they started to perform her funeral in wild and squealing voices. Afterwards they called in Natalya and made her turn the handle on the music-box while they themselves, all four of them, danced a quadrille, making absurd faces and kicking their feet up high.

After the dancing Peredonov was overcome with generosity. A gloomy and sullen animation gleamed on his swollen face. An almost mechanical decisiveness took possession of him—perhaps a consequence of the intensified physical activity. He pulled out his wallet, counted off several bank notes and with an arrogant and conceited expression tossed them in Varvara's direction.

"Take it, Varvara!" he shouted. "Make yourself a wedding dress."

The bank notes scattered over the floor. Varvara gathered them up smartly. She was not in the least offended by this manner of presentation. Prepolovenskaya thought spitefully: "We'll still see which one gets him." And she gave a venomous smile. Volodin, of course, never thought to help Varvara pick up the money.

Prepolovenskaya soon left. In the passage she ran into a new guest, Grushina.

Marya Osipovna Grushina, a young widow, had a prematurely wasted appearance. She was slender and her dry skin was completely covered in delicate little wrinkles seemingly filled with dust. Her face was not lacking in pleasantness, but her teeth were dirty and black. The hands were slender, the fingers long and prehensile with dirt under the fingernails. Superficially it wasn't that she seemed very dirty. Rather she produced the impression that she never washed and merely shook herself out together with her clothes. One had the feeling that if she were struck several times with a carpet beater, a column of dust would rise to the very heavens. The clothing on her hung in rumpled folds as though it had only just been pulled out of a tightly trussed up bundle where it had lain all crushed together for a long while. Grushina lived on a pension, the income from petty trading in secondhand goods and the interest on property secured loans. For the most part she carried on immodest conversations and attached herself to men with the desire of finding a husband. Unmarried officials were constantly renting a room in her house.

Varvara gave Grushina a joyful welcome: she had business that concerned her. Grushina and Varvara immediately started to talk about the maid in a whisper. A curious Volodin sat down with them and listened. Peredonov sat sullenly at the table by himself and kneaded the edge of the table cloth in his hands.

Varvara was complaining to Grushina about her Natalya. Grushina told her about a new servant, Klavdiya, and praised her highly. They decided to go for her right away to Samorodina River where she was living in the meanwhile at the home of an excise duty official who had received a transfer to another town a few days before. The only thing that stopped Varvara was the name. She asked in bewilderment:

"Klavdiya? But what will I call her? Klashka or something?"

Grushina advised her:

"You'll call her Klavdyushka."

Varvara liked that. She repeated:

"Klavdyushka, dyushka."

And she gave a screeching laugh. It should be noted that in our town pigs are called dyushkas. Volodin started to make an oinking sound. Everyone burst into laughter.

"Dyushka, dyushenka," Volodin prattled between fits of laughter as he screwed up his stupid face and puffed out his lips.

And he went on oinking and playing the fool until he was told that he was a bore. Then he went off with an offended expression and sat beside Peredonov and lowering his abrupt forehead like a sheep he stared at the stained tablecloth.

Varvara decided that she would buy the material for her wedding dress at the same time that she went to Samorodina River. She always made the rounds of the stores together with Grushina. The latter would help her to choose and to bargain.

Behind Peredonov's back Varvara stuffed Grushina's deep pockets with various victuals, sweet pastries and candies for her children. Grushina guessed that Varvara was going to be greatly in need of her services that day.

Varvara could not walk a great deal because of her narrow shoes and high heels. She would quickly tire. For that reason she rode in cabs although the distances were not great in our town. Lately she had become a frequent visitor at Grushina's. The cabbies had already taken note of that. All in all there were about two dozen of them. After seating her they no longer asked where to take her.

They got into a drozhky and went to the people where Klavdiya was living in order to make inquiries about her. There was mud almost everywhere in the streets even though the rain had ended by the evening before. At rare intervals the drozhky would reverberate along the stone pavement only to sink in the sticky mud once more in the unpaved streets.

On the other hand, Varvara's voice reverberated incessantly, frequently accompanied by the sympathetic chatter of Grushina.

"My goose was at Marfushka's again," Varvara said.

Grushina replied with sympathetic spitefulness:

"They're trying to catch him. And I should think so. A first-rate husband, particularly for that one, Marfushka. She never dreamed of one like that."

"Truly, I don't know what to do," Varvara complained. "He's become so prickly, it's really frightening. Believe me, my head is just spinning. If he marries someone else then I'm out on the street."

"Come now, my dear Varvara Dmitrievna," Grushina tried to console her. "None of those thoughts. He would never marry anyone but you. He's used to you."

"Sometimes he'd go off late at night and I wouldn't be able to sleep," Varvara said. "Who knows, maybe he's off getting married somewhere. Sometimes I toss and turn the whole night. They all have their eyes on him, those three Rutilov mares—they latch on to everyone. And that fat-faced Zhenka as well."

Varvara complained for a long while and from the entire conversation Grushina saw that she had something else in mind, some kind of request, and she began to anticipate with delight the money she would earn.

Klavdiya was to their liking. The wife of the excise duty official praised her. She was hired and ordered to come that same evening because the official was leaving that very day.

Finally, they arrived at Grushina's. Grushina lived in her own little house in a rather slovenly fashion with her three little children, who were shabby, dirty, stupid and mean as scalded whelps. Only now did the conversation begin in earnest.

"My sweet fool, Ardalyon," Varvara began, "is demanding that I write the Princess once more. But why should I write her for nothing! She wouldn't answer or she would answer the wrong thing. We're not all that marvelously close to each other."

Princess Volchanskaya, in whose house Varvara had lived at one time as a domestic seamstress for ordinary chores, might have been able to offer some patronage to Peredonov: her daughter was married to the privy councillor Shchepkin, an important person in the Ministry of Education. In response to Varvara's request, the Princess had already written the previous year that she wasn't about to intercede on behalf of a fiancé of Varvara's, but if it were Varvara's husband that would be a different matter and it would be possible to intercede when the opportunity arose. Peredonov had not been satisfied by that letter: only a vague hope was being offered and it was not directly stated that the Princess would without fail help to secure an inspector's post for Varvara's husband. In order to resolve the confusion, they had recently made a trip to St. Petersburg. Varvara went to see the Princess and then brought Peredonov to visit her, but she deliberately procrastinated over this visit so that they would miss the Princess at home. Varvara understood that at the very best the Princess would confine herself to the advice of getting married as soon as possible and to several vague promises to intercede when the opportunity offered—promises which would have been completely insufficient for Peredonov. So Varvara decided not to show the Princess to Peredonov.

"I'm relying on your rock-solid support," Varvara said. "Help me, Marya Osipovna, honey."

"But how can I help you, Varvara Dmitrievna, sweetheart?" Grushina asked. "You know full well that I'm ready to do anything I can for you. Do you want me to tell your fortune?"

"I know all about your fortune telling," Varvara said with a laugh. "No, you have to help me in a different way."

"How?" Grushina asked in anxious, happy anticipation.

"Very simple," Varvara said smirkingly. "You are going to write a letter as though it came from the Princess, in her handwriting, and I'll show it to Ardalyon Borisych."

"Ai, sweetheart, come now, how can I!" Grushina began, pretending to be frightened. "As soon as people find out about this business, what'll happen to me then?"

Varvara was not in the least dismayed by her answer and she pulled a crumpled letter out of her pocket and said:

"Here I've brought a letter from the Princess for you to use as a model."

Grushina demurred for a long while. Varvara clearly saw that Grushina would agree, but that she wanted to get more for doing it. On the other hand, Varvara wanted to give her less. She carefully increased her promises, pledged various minor gifts, an old silk dress, and finally Grushina saw that Varvara would give absolutely no more. Varvara fairly gushed with words of entreaty. Grushina pretended that she was agreeing merely out of pity and she took the letter.[2]

IV³

I T WAS DENSE with tobacco smoke in the billiard room. Peredonov, Rutilov, Falastov, Volodin and Murin (a landowner of enormous size, stupid in appearance, the owner of a small estate, a man who was resourceful and had money)—all five of them were preparing to leave after finishing the game.

Evening was coming on. On the filthy planked table there was a forest of drained beer bottles. The players, who had drunk a great deal while playing, were flushed in the face and were raising a drunken clamor. Only Rutilov preserved his customary consumptive pallor. He had drunk less than the others, but even after a real drinking bout he would only have turned more pallid.

Vulgar words hung in the air. No one was offended: they were friends.

Peredonov had lost, as was almost always the case. He was a poor billiard player. But he maintained an imperturbable sullenness on his face and paid out the money reluctantly. Murin shouted loudly:

"Fire!"

And he aimed at Peredonov with his billiard cue. Peredonov screamed in terror and cowered. The stupid thought flashed through his mind that Murin wanted to shoot him. Everyone roared. Peredonov muttered with annoyance:

"I can't stand jokes like that."

Murin was already repenting over the fact that he had frightened Peredonov: his son was studying at the gymnasium and for that reason he considered it his responsibility to oblige the gymnasium teachers in any way possible. Now he began to excuse himself to Peredonov and treated him to a wine and seltzer.

Peredonov said sullenly:

"My nerves are a little on edge. I'm not very happy with our headmaster."

"The future inspector has lost," Volodin shouted in his bleating voice. "He begrudges the money!"

"Unlucky at cards, lucky in love," Rutilov said, chuckling and showing his rotten teeth.

It was enough that Peredonov was in a bad mood because of losing and the fright he had received, without the others starting to tease him about Varvara.

He shouted:

"I'll get married and that will fix Varka!"

His friends roared and teased him:

"You wouldn't dare."

"I will so dare. Tomorrow I'm going to propose."

"A bet! Agreed?" Falastov proposed. "For ten roubles."

But Peredonov begrudged the money. If he lost he would have to pay up. He turned away and fell into a sullen silence.

At the gate leading out of the gardens they said goodbye to one another and dispersed in different directions. Peredonov and Rutilov set out together. Rutilov now tried to persuade Peredonov to marry one of his sisters immediately.

"I've fixed everything up, don't worry," he insisted.

"There hasn't been any announcement," Peredonov pleaded.

"I've fixed everything up, I'm telling you," Rutilov tried to convince him. "I've found the right kind of priest: he knows that you're not related."

"There aren't any ushers," Peredonov said.

"It's true there aren't. We'll get the ushers right now, I'll send for them and they'll come straight to the church. Or I'll go and pick them up myself. It was impossible to do it beforehand, your cousin might have found out and interfered."

Peredonov was silent and with a melancholy expression was gazing all around to where the scattered and silent houses grew dark behind sleepy gardens and rickety fences.

"You just stand by the gate," Rutilov said convincingly, "I'll bring out any one that you want. Now listen, and I'll prove it to you. Two times two is four, isn't that right?"

"It is," Peredonov replied.

"Well then, just as two times two is four, it follows that you should marry my sister."

Peredonov was stunned.

"But that's true," he thought. "Of course, two times two is four." And he regarded the sober-minded Rutilov with respect, thinking: "I'll have to get married! You won't get out of anything with him."

By this time the friends had arrived at Rutilov's house and stopped by the gate.

"It can't be done in a rush," Peredonov said angrily.

"You strange fellow, you can't keep people waiting," Rutilov exclaimed.

"But maybe I don't want to."

"No, you don't want to, you queer chap! What then, do you want to live forever as an old bachelor?" Rutilov protested confidently. "Or are you getting ready to go into a monastery? Or hasn't Varya disgusted you enough yet? No, just imagine the kind of mug she'll pull if you bring home a young wife."

Peredonov produced a brief and fitful roar of laughter, but almost immediately frowned and said:

"But maybe they don't want to."

"What do you mean they don't want to, you strange fellow!" Rutilov replied. "I'm giving you my word."

"They're arrogant," Peredonov sought an excuse.

"What do you care! So much the better."

"They make fun of people."

"But not of you," Rutilov tried to convince him.

"How am I to know that!"

"You just believe me, I won't deceive you. They respect you. You're not just any kind of Pavlushka that people can make fun of you."

"Sure, I believe you," Peredonov said mistrustfully. "No, I want to assure myself that they don't make fun of me."

"What a strange fellow," Rutilov said in amazement. "How would they dare to make fun of you? But, nevertheless, how do you want to assure yourself?"

Peredonov thought for a while and then said:

"Have them come outside right now."

"All right, that can be done," Rutilov agreed.

"All three of them," Peredonov continued.

"All right."

"And have each one say how she would try and please me."

"But whatever for?" Rutilov asked in amazement.

"Then I'll see what they want, otherwise you might be leading me around by the nose," Peredonov explained.

"No one is leading you around by the nose."

"Maybe they want to make fun of me," Peredonov reasoned. "But if you have them come out and they want to make fun of me, then I'll be able to make fun of them."

Rutilov thought for a moment, pushed his hat back on his head and then forward on his forehead and finally said:

"Well, wait here, I'll go and tell them. What a strange chap! Only in the meantime you go into the yard, otherwise who knows who the devil might come along the street and see."

"I don't give a damn," Peredonov said, but still he followed Rutilov in through the gate.

Rutilov headed for the house and his sisters while Peredonov remained waiting in the yard.

All four sisters were sitting in the living room, the corner room that faced the gate. They were all the image of each other and resembled the brother. They were all attractive, rosy cheeked and gay: Larisa, married, calm, pleasant and plump; Darya, fidgety, quick, the tallest and most slender of the sisters; Lyudmila, easily amused; and Valeriya, small, delicate and fragile to look at. They were treating themselves to nuts and raisins and obviously were waiting in anticipation of something because they were more excited and laughing more than usual, recalling the latest town gossip and making fun of both people they knew as well as strangers.

As early as the morning they had been ready to head for the altar. All that remained was to put on a dress that was appropriate for getting married in and pin on a veil and flowers. The sisters did not bring up Varvara in their conversations, as though she didn't even exist. But the very fact that they were usually so merciless in their mockery and picked everyone to pieces, and nevertheless hadn't so much as whispered a single word about Varvara all day, that alone proved that the awkward thought was haunting each of the sisters.

"I brought him!" Rutilov announced as he entered the living room. "He's standing at the gate."

The sisters stood up in excitement and started to laugh and talk all at once.

"Only there's a hitch," Rutilov said, chuckling.

"What do you mean?" Darya asked.

Valeriya knitted her beautiful dark brows in annoyance.

"I hardly know whether to tell you," Rutilov said.

"Well, come, come!" Darya rushed him.

It was with some embarrassment that Rutilov explained what Peredonov wanted. The young ladies raised a cry and took turns in abusing Peredonov. But little by little their cries of displeasure were replaced with jokes and laughter. Darya put on a sullenly expectant face and said:

"This is the way he's standing at the gate."

It was an amusingly good imitation.

The young ladies started to peek out the window in the direction of the gate. Darya opened the window slightly and shouted:

"Ardalyon Borisych, may we talk through the window?"

A sullen voice was heard:

"You may not."

Darya hastily banged the window shut. The sisters burst into peals of unrestrained laughter and ran out of the living room into the dining room so that Peredonov would not hear. In this happy family they were capable of switching from the most angry mood to laughter and jokes, and most frequently it was a happy word that settled the matter.

Peredonov stood and waited. He felt sad and frightened. He was thinking about running away but he couldn't bring himself to decide to do even that. The sound of music was borne hither from somewhere far away: it must have been the daughter of the marshal of the nobility playing on the piano. The faint tender sounds wafted through the soft dark air of evening and induced sorrow and aroused sweet dreams.

At first Peredonov's dreams took an erotic direction.

He imagined the young Rutilov ladies in the most seductive situations. But the longer the waiting went on the greater Peredonov's irritation in wondering why they were keeping him waiting. And no sooner had the music affected his deathly vulgar emotions than it died away.

Meanwhile, night, soft, rustling with ominous whispering sounds and people approaching, descended all around. And it seemed all the more dark everywhere because Peredonov was standing in the space which was illuminated by the living room lamp whose light settled in two strips on the yard and widened as it reached out towards the neighboring fence behind which dark log walls were visible. The trees from the Rutilov garden were growing suspiciously dark and whispering about something in the depths of the yard. Someone's slow deliberate steps could be heard for a long while on the boardwalk in the streets. Peredonov began to fear that while he was standing there someone would attack and rob him, or even kill him. He pressed right up against the wall, into the shadows, so that he could not be seen, and there he waited timidly.

But then long shadows flitted through the strips of light in the yard, doors started to bang and voices were heard behind the door to the porch. Peredonov perked up. "They're coming!" he thought joyfully and the pleasant dreams about the lovely sisters began to stir lazily once more in his head—the vile offspring of his pathetic imagination.

The sisters were standing in the entry way. Rutilov came out into the yard towards the gate and looked around to see whether anyone was on the street.

There was no one to be seen or heard.

"There's no one," he said in a loud whisper through his cupped hands to the sisters.

He stayed outside to keep watch on the street. Peredonov followed him out on to the street.

"Well, they're going to tell you now," Rutilov said.

Peredonov stood right by the gate and peered through the crack between the gate and the gate post. His face was sullen and almost frightened. All dreams and thoughts were extinguished in his head and were replaced by a vague, ponderous lust.

Darya was the first to come up to the partially open gate.

"Well, what would you like me to do to please you?" she asked.

Peredonov was sullenly silent. Darya said:

"I'll bake you the tastiest *bliny*, hot ones, only don't choke on them."

From behind her shoulder Lyudmila shouted:

"And every morning I'll go around the town and gather up all the gossip and then tell you. It'll be very amusing."

The capricious and slender face of little Valeriya appeared for an instant between the cheerful faces of the two sisters and her fragile voice said:

"And nothing will make me tell you how I'll please you—guess for yourself!"

Dissolving into laughter, the sisters ran off. Their voices and laughter died away behind the doors. Peredonov turned away from the gate. He was not entirely satisfied. He thought that they had simply babbled something and then left. It would have been better if they had given him notes. But it was already getting late to be standing there and waiting.

"Well, did you see?" Rutilov asked. "Which one for you?"

Peredonov was plunged into meditation. Of course, he realized finally that he had to choose the youngest. What was the point of him marrying an old maid!

"Bring out Valeriya," he said with determination.

Rutilov made his way back to the house while Peredonov went into the yard once more.

Lyudmila was secretly peeking out the window, trying to hear what was being said but she couldn't catch anything. Then suddenly steps were echoing on the pathway in the yard. The sisters fell silent and sat there, excited and embarrassed. Rutilov came in and announced:

"He's chosen Valeriya. He's waiting, standing by the gate."

The sisters began to fuss and laugh. Valeriya turned slightly pale.

"Well, well," she repeated, "a lot I want it, a lot I need it."

Her hands were trembling. They started to dress her up. All three sisters were bustling around her. As always, she fussed and dallied. The sisters hurried her. Rutilov chattered away incessantly, cheerful and animated.

He was pleased by the fact that he had organized the whole business so cleverly.

"Have you got the cab drivers ready?" Darya asked with concern.

Rutilov replied with annoyance:

"Are you serious? The whole town would come running. Varvara would drag him off home by the hair."

"So what will we do?"

"This is what. We'll go as far as the square in pairs and there we'll hire the cabs. It's very simple. First you and the bride, then Larisa with the groom, but not all at once, otherwise someone will see you in town. Lyudmila and I will go and get Falastov, they'll go on together while I go and grab Volodin."

The sisters involuntarily showed that they were envious of Valeriya because of the jokes they made at her expense and because they kept pushing her and scolding her for her finicky ways. Finally she said:

"Really, now, he's nothing to boast about. I still don't want to marry him if you must know."

And she burst into tears. The sisters exchanged glances, scurried to console her with kisses and caresses.

Left by himself, Peredonov plunged into sweet reveries. He dreamed of Valeriya amid the enchantment of the wedding night, undressed, bashful, but joyful. All slender and frail.

He was dreaming, yet all the while he was pulling out the caramels his pocket was stuffed with and sucking on them.

Then the recollection came to him that Valeriya was a coquette. He was thinking that she would demand fine clothes and furniture. That would mean, to be sure, that he wouldn't be able to save money every month and would have to squander what had been saved. This kind of wife would get finicky and wouldn't have anything to do with the kitchen. Or what was more, they would slip him poison in the kitchen—Varya would bribe the cook out of spite. "And what's more," thought Peredonov, "she's far too slender a thing, Valeriya is. How would you treat someone like that? How would you bawl her out? How would you push her around? How would you spit on her? She'd dissolve into tears and ruin your name all over town. No, it'd be terrible to have anything to do with her. Now take Lyudmila, she's simpler. Maybe I should marry her?"

Peredonov went up to the window and knocked with his walking stick on the frame. In half a minute Rutilov stuck his head out the window.

"What do you want?" he asked anxiously.

"I've changed my mind," Peredonov growled.

"What!" Rutilov shouted with fright.

"Bring out Lyudmila," Peredonov said.

Rutilov left the window.

"The square-eyed devil," he grumbled, and went to the sisters.

Valeriya was overjoyed.

"Your good fortune, Lyudmila," she said gaily.

Lyudmila started to laugh. She dropped into an armchair threw herself back and roared and roared.

"What should I tell him?" Rutilov asked. "Do you agree then?"

Lyudmila could not say a single word for laughing and just kept waving her hands.

"Yes, of course she agrees," Darya said for her. "Tell him quickly otherwise he'll be stupid enough to leave without waiting."

Rutilov went out into the dining room and said in a whisper through the window:

"Wait, everything will be ready in a moment."

"Be quick about it," Peredonov said angrily. "What's all the dawdling there!"

Lyudmila was being swiftly attired. She was completely ready in about five minutes.

Peredonov was thinking about her. She was cheerful and full-figured. The only thing was that she loved to laugh. To be sure, she would start to laugh. It would be terrible. Darya, for all that she was quite perky, was the more solid and quiet one. And she was attractive as well. Better to take her. He knocked on the window again.

"He's knocking again," Larisa said. "Maybe he wants to marry you now, Darya?"

"Damnation!" Rutilov swore and ran to the window.

"What now?" he asked in an angry whisper. "Have you changed your mind again, eh?"

"Bring out Darya," Peredonov replied.

"Well, wait," Rutilov said furiously.

Peredonov was standing and thinking about Darya—and once more the short-lived admiration for her in his imagination was replaced with terror. Indeed, she was quick and insolent. She'd pester him to death. Besides, what was the point of standing there and waiting? This is what he was thinking. On top of it all he'd catch a cold. Or maybe someone was hiding in a ditch along the street or in the grass by the fence and they would suddenly leap out and bump him off. A feeling of melancholy overcame Peredonov. After all, they had no dowry, he was thinking. They had no patronage in the Ministry of Education. Varvara would complain to the Princess. Even now the headmaster had it in for Peredonov.

Peredonov felt annoyed with himself. Why was he getting mixed up with Rutilov? It was as though Rutilov had cast a spell over him. Indeed, perhaps he had actually cast a spell over him. He must counteract that spell as quickly as possible.

Peredonov started to circle around on the spot, spitting in all directions and muttering:

"Line to line, circle bright, spirits black, spirits white. Line to line, circle bright, spirits flee, day and night."

A stern concentration was mirrored on his face as though he were performing some important ritual. After this essential action he felt safe from Rutilov's sorcery. He knocked determinedly with his walking stick on the window, muttering angrily:

"I ought to denounce them, they're trying to ensnare me. No, I don't want to get married today," he declared to Rutilov who had thrust his head out.

"Come now, Ardalyon Borisych, everything is ready now," Rutilov tried to convince him.

"I don't want to," Peredonov said with determination. "Let's go and play cards at my place."

"Damnation!" Rutilov swore. "He doesn't want to get married, he's got cold feet," he announced to his sisters. "But I'll get my way with the fool. He's inviting me to play cards at his place."

The sisters started to shout all at once, heaping abuse on Peredonov.

"And you're going to that scoundrel's place?" Valeriya asked in annoyance.

"Of course I'm going and I'll make him pay for it. He's not going to get away from us that easily," Rutilov said, trying to maintain a note of assurance but feeling quite awkward.

The girls' annoyance at Peredonov quickly changed to laughter. Rutilov left. The sisters ran to the windows.

"Ardalyon Borisych!" Darya shouted. "Why are you so indecisive? You mustn't be like that."

"Mr. Sourpuss!" Lyudmila shouted and laughed.

Peredonov felt annoyed. To his mind, the sisters ought to have been weeping from sorrow that he had rejected them. "They're pretending!" he thought as he silently left the yard. The girls were running from window to window facing the street and shouting words of sarcasm after Peredonov until he disappeared in the darkness.

V

PEREDONOV WAS OPPRESSED with melancholy. He no longer had any caramels in his pocket and that saddened and irritated him. Rutilov was talking alone practically the entire way. He went on singing the praises of his sisters. Only once did he join in the conversation. He asked angrily:

"Does a bull have horns?"

"Yes, it does, but what is that supposed to mean?" asked an amazed Rutilov.

"Well, I don't want to be a bull," Peredonov explained.

An irritated Rutilov replied:

"You, Ardalyon Borisych, are a proper ass."

"You're lying!" Peredonov said sullenly.

"No, I'm not lying and I can prove it," Rutilov said with malice.

"Prove it then," Peredonov demanded.

"Just you wait, I'll prove it," Rutilov replied, preserving the same malice in his voice.

Both were silent. Peredonov waited fearfully and he felt oppressed with ill-will towards Rutilov. Suddenly Rutilov asked:

"Ardalyon Borisych, do you have any assets?"

"Yes, I do, but I won't give you any," Peredonov answered spitefully.

Rutilov roared with laughter.

"If you've got assets, then you must be an ass!" he shouted joyfully.

Peredonov seized his head in horror.

"You're lying, I haven't got an ass's head, this is a human noggin," he muttered.

Rutilov was roaring. Gazing at Rutilov with anger and cowardice, Peredonov said:

"Today you purposely led me past some *durman** and drugged me with the smell of it so that you could marry me off to your sisters. As though it weren't

---

*"Durman" (Latin *datura stramonium*) is a member of the nightshade family (*Solanacae*). In England it is known as "thorn apple" and in North America as "jimsonweed." It is a big, hardy annual with large attractive white, trumpet-like flowers. Throughout North America, Europe and Russia it has been known for centuries as a narcotic and poisonous plant. Herbalists have attributed various powers to it, including madness, convulsions and blindness. It has also been recognized as an aphrodisiac.

enough for me to marry one witch, just imagine marrying all three at once!"

"You queer fellow, then how is it that I wasn't drugged as well?" Rutilov asked.

"You know some remedy," Peredonov said. "Perhaps you were breathing through your mouth and didn't take it in through your nose, or you spoke the right kind of words, whereas I have no knowledge of what to do against magic. I'm no magician. Until I cast a counter-spell I was standing there completely drugged."

Rutilov roared.

"How did you cast a counter-spell?" he asked.

But Peredonov was no longer saying anything.

"Why have you latched onto Varvara so firmly?" Rutilov asked. "Do you think everything will be fine for you if you get a position through her? She'll harness you up good."

That was incomprehensible to Peredonov.

After all, she was exerting herself on her own behalf, he thought. It would be better for her when he became an important official and earned a lot of money. It meant that she ought to be grateful to him and not the other way around. And in any event he felt more comfortable with her than with anyone else.

Peredonov had grown used to Varvara. He was attracted to her, perhaps as a result of his becoming pleasantly accustomed to making fun of her. He might not be able to find another woman who was made to order as well as she was.

It was already late. The lamps were burning in Peredonov's apartment, the windows stood out brilliantly against the darkness outside.

Guests were seated around the tea table: Grushina (nowadays she had become a daily visitor to Varvara's), Volodin, Prepolovenskaya, her husband, Konstantin Petrovich, a tall man of close to forty with a dull pallor, dark-haired, and extrordinarily reticent. Varvara was all dressed up, she had put on her white dress. They were drinking tea and chatting. As always, Varvara was upset by the fact that Peredonov hadn't come home for a long while. With a happy bleating laugh, Volodin was relating how Peredonov had gone off somewhere with Rutilov. That increased Varvara's anxiety.

Peredonov finally put in an appearance with Rutilov. They were greeted with shouts, laughter and silly, indecent jokes.

"Varvara, where's the vodka?" Peredonov shouted angrily.

Varvara scurried from the table with a guilty smirk and quickly brought the vodka in a large, ugly cut-glass decanter.

"Let's drink," Peredonov extended the sullen invitation.

"Wait," Varvara said. "Klavdyushka will bring some *zakuski**. Hustle up, you slowpoke," she shouted into the kitchen.

*Zakuski are generally savory cold dishes (meat, sausage, fish, pickled mushrooms and vegetables, etc.) that Russians will eat especially when drinking alcoholic beverages. The Russian word suggests something which is at once more substantial, and perhaps less delicate, than *hors d'oeuvres*. It is more common to eat sweet pastries with tea. The fact that Peredonov is frequently depicted as mixing sweets and vodka probably shows not only his sweet footh, but his utter lack of good taste as well.

But Peredonov had already filled the glasses with vodka and mumbled: "Why wait, time doesn't."

They drank and snacked on the pastries with blackcurrant jam. The only things Peredonov had at his disposal for entertaining guests were cards and vodka. Since they couldn't sit down to cards yet—tea had to be drunk first—then only vodka was left.

In the meanwhile, the *zakuski* were brought in so that it was possible to drink some more. When she went out Klavdiya didn't close the door tightly and Peredonov began to get upset.

"Always close the door tight," he growled.

He was afraid of a draught: he might catch cold. For that reason it was always stuffy and smelly in the apartment.

Prepolovenskaya took an egg.

"Nice eggs," she said. "Where do you get them?"

Peredonov said:

"Those eggs are nothing, on our estate my father had a hen that laid two enormous eggs every day the whole year round."

"That's nothing," Prepolovenskaya replied, "if you really want to brag about something! There was a hen in our village that laid two eggs and a spoonful of butter every day."

"We had the same thing too, we did," Peredonov said without noticing the mockery. "If others did it then ours did it too. It was really an outstanding hen."

Varvara laughed.

"That's just some tomfoolery," she said.

"You talk enough nonsense to make a person's ears wilt," Grushina said. Peredonov gave her a furious look and replied harshly:

"Well if they're going to wilt then they ought to be plucked off!"

Grushina was dismayed.

"Really, Ardalyon Borisych, you're always saying things like that!" she said plaintively.

The rest of the guests laughed sympathetically. Screwing up his eyes and wagging his head, Volodin explained amusingly:

"If your ears are going to wilt, then you must pluck them off, otherwise it wouldn't be nice if they do wilt away and just start drooping back and forth, back and forth."

Volodin used his fingers to show how limp ears would be drooping. Grushina raised her voice at him:

"Really, you just don't know how to make up anything yourself, you're always latching on to something ready-made!"

Volodin was offended and said with dignity:

"I can too, Marya Osipovna, it's just that since we're spending a good time in company then why shouldn't we pick up on someone else's joke! And if you don't care for that, then have it your own way. Just as you bear with us so we'll bear with you."

"Very reasonable, Pavel Vasilyevich," Rutilov gave his laughing approval.

"Pavel Vasliyevich is standing up for himself now," Prepolovenskaya said with a sly grin.

Varvara cut off a piece of bread and while enjoying Volodin's fanciful speeches, went on holding the knife in her hand. The point glistened. Peredonov had a frightening sensation: what if she suddenly slit his throat? He cried:

"Varvara, put the knife down!"

Varvara gave a start.

"What are you shouting for, you afraid?" she said and laid the knife down. "He's so touchy, you know," she explained to the taciturn Prepolovensky, seeing that he was stroking his beard and getting ready to say something.

"It happens," Prepolovensky said in a sweet and sorrowful voice. "I had an acquaintance and he was afraid of needles, constantly afraid that he would be pricked and the needle would disappear into his insides. And he was terribly afraid, you can imagine, whenever he saw a needle . . ."

And once he had started to talk he could no longer stop and kept retelling the very same thing in a variety of ways until someone interrupted him by talking about something else. Then he lapsed once more into silence.

Grushina brought the conversation around to erotic themes. She told the story of how her deceased husband had been jealous of her and how she had been unfaithful to him. Afterwards she told a story that she had heard from a friend living in the capital about the mistress of a certain highly placed person and how she had been riding along the street and had met her benefactor.

"And she just shouted out to him: 'Hello there, mon petit Jean!' And it was right there on the street!" Grushina said.

"And I'm going to denounce you," Peredonov said angrily. "How dare you spread such stupid gossip about those kind of distinguished people?"

Grushina babbled fearfully:

"I didn't mean anything, it's what I was told. I'm just passing it on for what it's worth."

Peredonov was angrily silent and drank tea from his saucer, leaning on the table with his elbows. He was thinking that it was unfitting to speak disrespectfully about the nobility in the house of a future inspector. At one point Peredonov even said to Volodin:

"Well, brother, I expect you're jealous! You'll never be an inspector but I will."

Lending his face an inspired expression, Volodin protested:

"To each his own, Ardalyon Borisych. You are a specialist in your work and I in mine."

"Our Natasha," Varvara informed them, "went straight from us to work for a police official."

Peredonov gave a shudder and terror was expressed in his face.

"Are you lying?" he asked her questioningly.

"And why should I be lying?" Varvara answered. "Why don't you go and ask him yourself."

This unpleasant piece of news was confirmed by Grushina. Peredonov was stunned. Natasha would say something untrue, the police official would fasten on it and likely write to the Ministry. A foul business.

At that very moment Peredonov's eyes came to rest on the shelf above the commode. Several bound books were standing there: the slender ones were by Pisarev and the somewhat thicker ones were *Notes of the Fatherland*.* Peredonov turned pale and said:

"These books must be hidden, otherwise people will denounce me."

Earlier Peredonov had kept these books on display in order to show that he held liberal opinions even though in actual fact he held no opinions whatsoever, nor even possessed any inclination for reflection. Moreover, he merely kept the books, he didn't read them. It had been a long time since he had read a single book. He said that formerly he hadn't subscribed to any newspaper, but had learned his news through conversations. It wasn't that there wasn't anything for him to learn about, it was simply that nothing in the external world interested him. He even made fun of those who subscribed to the newspapers as being people who squandered money and time. His time, one would think, was a precious thing for him!

He went to the shelf grumbling:

"We have the kind of town here where people might denounce you right away. Lend me a hand, Pavel Vasilyevich," he said to Volodin.

Volodin went up to him with a serious and understanding look on his face and carefully held the books that Peredonov handed to him. Peredonov took a smaller packet of books for himself and gave Volodin a larger one and then he went off into the living room with Volodin following behind.

"Where are you going to hide them, Ardalyon Borisych?" he asked.

"Just wait and see," Peredonov said with his customary sullenness.

"What are you carting off there, Ardalyon Borisych?" Prepolovenskaya asked.

"Strictly forbidden books," Peredonov replied without stopping. "People will denounce me if they see them."

In the living room Peredonov squatted down in front of the stove and dumped the books on the iron grating. Volodin did the same. Then Peredonov started forcefully to stuff one book after the other into the small opening. Volodin squatted beside him, a little to the rear, and handed him the books while maintaining an expression of profound concentration and understanding on his sheeplike face, lips puffed out with importance and his steep forehead bowed in a surfeit of understanding. Varvara peeked in on them through the door. She said laughingly:

"He's into his tomfoolery!"

But Grushina stopped her:

Notes of the Fatherland (1839–1884) was one of the most important literary and political journals of nineteenth-century Russia. Published in St. Petersburg, it represented throughout its long and varied history many of the liberal and progressive tendencies in Russia, including Westernism and Populism. Belinsky, Herzen, Turgenev, Saltykov-Shchedrin. Nekrasov, Pisarv, Uspensky and Mikhailovsky were but a few of the most prominent writers to be connected with the journal. It was shut down in 1884 for censorship reasons.

"Oh, Varvara Dmitrievna, sweetheart, you mustn't talk like that, this could cause serious trouble if people found out. Particularly if it's a teacher. The authorities are terribly afraid that the teachers will teach the young kids to revolt."

They drank tea and sat down to play cards, all seven of them around the card table in the living room. Peredonov played recklessly but badly. At the end of each twenty points he had to pay what he owed to his fellow-players, particularly to Prepolovensky. The latter accepted the money for both himself and his wife. The Prepolovenskys won most of the time. They had fixed signals—knocking or coughing—by means of which they exchanged information on their cards. That day Peredonov was unlucky from the start. He was in a hurry to recoup his losses, whereas Volodin was slow in dealing the cards and shuffled them painstakingly.

"Pavlushka, deal," Peredonov shouted impatiently.

Feeling like an important person in the game, Volodin assumed an important expression and asked:

"What do you mean by calling me Pavlushka? Is it on the basis of friendship or what?"

"Friendship, friendship," Peredonov retorted carelessly. "Just deal the cards more quickly."

"Well, if it's on the basis of friendship, then I'm delighted, I'm very delighted," Volodin said with a delighted and silly laugh as he dealt the cards. "You're a fine fellow, Ardasha, and I even love you a great deal. But if it hadn't been on the basis of friendship, then it would have been another matter. But if it is on the basis of friendship then I am delighted. For that I have given you an ace," Volodin said and led with trump.

In actual fact an ace did turn up in Peredonov's hand, but not a trump ace and he had to forfeit it.

"He did deal one!" Peredonov growled angrily. "An ace, but the wrong one. You were fooling me. You should have given me a trump card, but what did you deal? What do I need a chub of spaces for?"

"You hardly need a chub of spaces, your own chubby belly takes up enough space for an ace," Rutilov laughingly rejoined.

"The future inspector is getting his tongue all twisted up—chubby bellies with spaces for aces."

Rutilov nattered on incessantly, gossiping and relating anecdotes that at times were of a rather delicate nature. In order to tease Peredonov he started to insist that the students at the gymnasium behaved themselves badly, particularly those who were living in lodgings: they smoked, drank vodka and chased after girls. Peredonov believed him. And Grushina supported it. These stories afforded her particular satisfaction. After the death of her husband she had wanted at one time to lodge three or four students from the gymnasium in her own home, but the headmaster hadn't given her permission despite. Peredonov's intercession on her behalf. Grushina had a bad reputation in the town. Now she had taken to abusing the landladies in the lodgings where the students were living.

"They bribed the headmaster," she declared.

"Landladies are all bitches," Volodin said with conviction. "Even mine. She and I had an agreement when I took the room that she would give me three glasses of milk every evening. It was fine for the first month or two, she did give me the milk."

"And you didn't drink yourself sick?" Rutilov asked laughingly.

"Why would I drink myself sick!" Volodin protested, taking offense. "Milk is a beneficial substance. I had become used to drinking three glasses for the night. Suddenly I see that I'm being brought only two glasses. Why is that, I asked? The maid said that Anna Mikhailovna begs my pardon that that their cow is giving little milk now. And what does that have to do with me! An agreement is more precious than money. If their cow were to stop giving milk altogether, is that supposed to mean that I'm not given anything to drink? Well, I said to her, I did, tell Anna Mikhailovna that I'm asking her to give me a glass of water as well. I've gotten used to having three glasses, two glasses are too little for me."

"Our Pavlushka is a real hero," Peredonov said. "Tell us, brother, how you grappled with the general."

Volodin repeated his story willingly. But this time it was held up to ridicule. He puffed out his lower lip and took offense.

Everyone drank themselves drunk at dinner, even the women. Volodin suggested that they mess up the walls some more. Everyone was overjoyed! Immediately, without having finished eating, they went to work and amused themselves with a frenzy. They spat on the wallpaper, poured beer over it, threw paper darts with butter-smeared tips at the walls and ceiling, stuck spitballs of chewed bread on the ceiling. Afterwards they came up with the idea of tearing strips off the wallpaper for the sport of it, to see who could tear off the longest strip. The Prepolovenskys won an additional rouble and a half at this game.

Volodin lost. Because he had lost and had gotten drunk he started to complain about his mother. He assumed a reproachful expression and for some reason thrusting his hand downwards, said:

"Why did she have to give birth to me? What was she thinking of at the time? What kind of life have I got now? She's no mother to me, just the woman who gave birth to me. Because a real mother cares about her child, but my mother only gave birth to me and then made a public ward out of me when I was still very young."

"On the other hand you managed to get a training out of it and made your own way in life," Prepolovenskaya said.

With his forehead bowed, Volodin was shaking his head back and forth and he said:

"No, what kind of life is this of mine, it's the very lowest kind of life. And why did she give birth to me? What was she thinking of at the time?"

Peredonov suddenly recalled the *erly* from the day before. "So," he turned his thoughts to Volodin, "he's complaining about the fact that his mother gave birth to him, he doesn't want to be Pavlushka. Apparently he actually is jealous. Perhaps he's already thinking about marrying Varvara and crawling into my skin," Peredonov thought and gazed with melancholy at Volodin.

He'd better marry him to someone else.

That night, in the bedroom, Varvara said to Peredonov:

"You think that all these young wenches that are trailing after you are so young and good-looking? They're nothing but filth, I'm more beautiful than all of them."

She swiftly undressed and with an insolent smirk she showed Peredonov her lightly colored, shapely, attractive and supple body.

Although Varvara was stumbling about from drunkenness and her face would have provoked disgust in any healthy person with its flaccidly lewd expression, nevertheless her body was beautiful, like the body of a tender nymph to which the head of a jaded whore had been affixed by force of some despicable spell. And for those two miserable, drunken and filthy people that exquisite body represented nothing more than the source of vulgar temptation. Such is often the case—and verily in our age it is appropriate for beauty to be scorned and desecrated.

Peredonov roared with sullen laughter as he gazed at his naked girlfriend.

All that night he dreamt of women of all shapes and sizes, naked and vile.

Varvara believed that rubbing herself with stinging nettles, which she had done on the advice of Prepolovenskaya, had helped her. It seemed to her that she immediately began to put on weight. She kept asking all her acquaintances:

"I've really put on weight, haven't I?"

And she was thinking that now, after Peredonov saw how she was putting on weight and when in addition he had received the forged letter, he would marry her without fail.

Peredonov's contemplations were far from being so pleasant. Long ago he had become convinced that the headmaster was hostile to him—and in actual fact the headmaster of the gymnasium considered Peredonov to be a lazy and incapable teacher. Peredonov thought that the headmaster was instructing his students not to have any respect for him—which was, understandably, another nonsensical invention of Peredonov himself. But it implanted the certainty in Peredonov that he had to protect himself against the headmaster. More than once out of spite towards the headmaster, Peredonov had started to revile him in front of the senior classes. That kind of talk appealed to many of the students.

Now, when Peredonov had taken a fancy to becoming an inspector, the hostile attitudes of the headmaster towards him appeared particularly unpleasant. One might suppose that if the Princess wished, she could foil the headmaster's intriguings with her patronage. Nevertheless, the headmaster still presented a danger.

And there were other people in the town (as Peredonov had noted during recent days) who were hostile towards him and wanted to interfere with his promotion to an inspector's post. Volodin, for example. It wasn't by chance that he kept repeating the words "future inspector." After all, there were cases in which people assumed someone else's name and enjoyed their lives. Of course it would be a bit difficult for Volodin to replace Peredonov himself. Still, a fool like Volodin could have the most unseemly designs. Furthermore, there were the Rutilovs and Vershina with her Marta who were partners in jealousy. They would all be delighted to do him harm. And how would they do him harm? Quite simply they would discredit him in the eyes of the authorities and represent him as an unreliable person.

Thus, two concerns arose in Peredonov: to prove his reliability and to make himself secure from Volodin by marrying him off to a rich girl.

And so on one occasion Peredonov asked Volodin:

"Do you want me to propose you for marriage to the young Adamenko lady? Or are you still pining away for Marta? Haven't you been able to console yourself after a whole month?"

"Why should I be pining for Marta!" Volodin retorted. "I proposed to her in good faith and if she doesn't want to then what does it matter to me! I'll find another one—do you think I can't find any brides for myself? There are as many of those goods around as you like."

"Well, but this Marta went and tweaked your nose," Peredonov teased.

"I don't know what kind of husband they were expecting," Volodin said, offended. "If at least there had been a large dowry, but they were only offering a pittance. It's you, Ardalyon Borisych, that she's head over heels in love with."

Peredonov gave his advice:

"If I were you I'd smear tar all over her gate."

Volodin giggled, but immediately settled down and said:

"If I were caught, it might cause trouble."

"Hire someone else to do it. Why do it yourself?" Peredonov said.

"She deserves it, by God, she does," Volodin said with feeling. "Because if she isn't willing to enter into a legal marriage, yet in the meanwhile admits young men into her room through the window, then that's really something! That means a person has neither shame nor conscience."

VI

THE FOLLOWING DAY Peredonov and Volodin set out for the home of the young Adamenko girl. Volodin had dressed himself up. He had put on his new tight-fitting jacket, a clean starched shirt, a gaudy embroidered neckerchief, oiled his hair with pomade, perfumed himself—and his spirits soared.

Nadezhda Vasilyevna Adamenko lived together with her brother in their own little red brick house in the town. She had an estate not far from the town which had been leased out. The year before last she had completed her studies in the local gymnasium and nowadays she was occupying herself by lying on the sofa, reading books of all sorts and tutoring her brother, an eleven-year-old student at the gymnasium who escaped her stern ways only by declaring angrily:

"It was better living with Mama. Mama would only make you stand in the corner."

Only her aunt, a retiring and decrepit creature who had no voice whatsoever in the domestic affairs, was living with Nadezhda Vasilyevna. Natalya Vasilyevna exercised a stern choice in her acquaintanceships. Peredonov had rarely been in her home and this slight acquaintanceship with her served as the sole basis for supposing that this young lady might marry Volodin.

Now she was amazed at the unexpected visit, but she greeted her unbidden guests politely. The guests had to be entertained, and Nadezhda Vasilyevna thought that the most pleasant and comfortable conversation for a teacher of the Russian language would be a conversation about the state of pedagogy, about the reform of the gymnasia, about the raising of children, about literature, about Symbolism and about the Russian journals. She touched on all of those topics, but received nothing in response other than perplexing rebuffs which revealed that her guests were not interested in those questions. She saw that only one conversation was possible: town gossip. Nevertheless, Nadezhda Vasilyevna made one further attempt.

"Have you read Chekhov's 'The Man in the Case'?" she asked. It's really to the point, isn't it?"

Since she had addressed Volodin with this question, he grinned pleasantly and asked:

"What is it, an article or a novel?"

"A story," Nadezhda Vasilyevna explained.

"Pray, did you say Mister Chekhov?" Volodin inquired.

"Yes, Chekhov," Nadezhda Vasilyevna said with a grin.

"Where did it appear?" Volodin continued to express his interest.

"In the journal *Russian Thought*," the young lady replied politely.

"In which issue?" Volodin inquired further.

"I can't quite recall, in one of the summer issues," Nadezhda Vasilyevna responded with the same politeness but with a certain amazement at the same time.

The young student from the gymnasium stuck his head through the door.

"It was printed in the May issue," he said, hanging on to the door with one hand and scanning the guests and his sister with his cheerful, blue eyes.

"It's too early for you to be reading novels," Peredonov said angrily. "You ought to be studying and not reading obscene stories."

Nadezhda Vasilyevna gave her brother a stern look.

"Very nice that is, standing behind the door and listening," she said and raising her two hands made a right angle with the tips of her small fingers.

The student frowned and disappeared. He went to his room, stood in the corner and started to look at the clock. Two small fingers held at an angle was a sign to stand in the corner for ten minutes. "No," he thought with annoyance, "it was better living with Mama. Mama would only stand the umbrella in the corner."

Meanwhile, back in the living room, Volodin was consoling the hostess with his promise to get hold of the May issue of *Russian Thought* without fail and read the story by Mister Chekhov. Peredonov was listening with an expression of obvious boredom on his face. Finally he said:

"I haven't read it either. I don't read rubbish. All sorts of nonsense is being written in stories and novels."

Nadezhda Vasilyevna smiled politely and said:

"You have a very stern attitude towards contemporary literature. But good books are being written now as well."

"I've already read all the good books earlier," Peredonov declared. "I'm not about to read what's being written now."

Volodin looked at Peredonov respectfully. Nadezhda Vasilyevna sighed gently and, since there was no other choice, she started to indulge in idle talk and gossip as best she knew how. Although she had no love for that kind of talk, nevertheless she held up her end with the cleverness and cheerfulness of a lively and self-possessed young lady.

The guests were revived. It was unbearably boring for her, whereas they thought that she was being exceptionally polite with them and ascribed it to a fascination with Volodin's charming appearance.

When they had left, Peredonov congratulated Volodin on the street with his success. Volodin was laughing happily and prancing about. He had already forgotten all the girls who had rejected him.

"Stop kicking up your feet," Peredonov said to him. "You're off and prancing about like a sheep. Just you wait, they'll tweak your nose."

But he said it in jest and he himself fully believed in the success of the intended match-making.

Grushina came running to see Varvara practically every day and Varvara was at her place even more frequently so that they were almost never apart.

Varvara was anxious and Grushina was taking her time, insisting that it was very difficult to copy the letters so that they would look similar.

Peredonov still didn't want to name the wedding day. Once more he was demanding that he be given the inspector's position first. Remembering how many potential brides he had, he threatened Varvara more than once as he had done so during the past winter:

"I'm going to get married right this minute. I'll return in the morning with a wife and out you go. This is the last time you're spending the night here." And with these words he would leave—to play billiards. Sometimes he returned from there by evening, but more frequently he would go carousing in some squalid hangout with Rutilov and Volodin. On nights like that Varvara couldn't fall asleep. For that reason she suffered from migraines. It was good at least if he returned at one or two o'clock in the morning, then she would breathe freely. But if he showed up only the next morning then Varvara would greet the day quite sick.

Finally Grushina had prepared the letter and showed it to Varvara. They examined it for a long while, comparing it with the letter from the Princess the year before. Grushina assured her that it was so similar that the Princess herself would be unable to detect the forgery. Though in fact there was little similarity, nevertheless Varvara believed her. Moreover she understood that Peredonov wouldn't be able to remember the vaguely familiar handwriting of the Princess accurately enough to detect the forgery.

"Well, finally," she said happily."I'd been waiting for so long that I gave up waiting. But what about the envelope? If he asks, what am I to say?"

"Well it's impossible to forge the envelope. There are the postmarks," Grushina said, chuckling and peering at Varvara with her sly and unmatched eyes: the right one was larger and the left one smaller.

"What can I do?"

"Varvara Dmitrievna, sweetheart, you just tell him that you threw the envelope in the stove. What use did you have for the envelope?"

Varvara's hopes were revived. She said to Grushina:

"If only he'd marry me then I wouldn't be running around for him. No, I'd just sit and make him do the running for me."

On Saturday after dinner Peredonov went to play billiards. His thoughts were oppressive and sad. He was thinking:

"It's vile to live in the midst of people who are hostile and envious. But what can I do, they can't all be inspectors! It's a struggle for survival!"

At the intersection of two streets he met the staff police officer. An unpleasant meeting!

Lieutenant-colonel Nikolai Vadimovich Rubovsky, a short solid man with thick eyebrows, cheerful gray eyes and a limping walk that made his spurs jingle loudly and unevenly, was extremely polite and therefore popular in society. He knew all the people in town, knew all their affairs and relations, loved to listen to gossip but was himself modest and as silent as the grave and never caused anyone any unnecessary trouble.

They stopped, exchanged greetings and chatted. Peredonov scowled, looked round to the sides and said cautiously:

"I've heard that our Natasha is living with you, but don't believe whatever she says about me, she's lying."

"I don't collect gossip from a maid," Rubovsky said with dignity.

"She's vile herself," Peredonov continued, paying no attention to Rubovsky's objection. "She's got a lover, a Pole. Perhaps she went to work for you on purpose in order to filch something secret."

"Please, don't worry yourself over that," the lieutenant-colonel objected. "I don't keep the plans to the fortresses in my house."

The mention of fortresses perplexed Peredonov. It seemed to him that Rubovsky was alluding to the fact that he could imprison Peredonov in a fortress.

"Well, hardly a fortress," he murmured. "It's a far cry from that, I just meant that in general people say all sorts of nonsense about me, but it's mostly out of jealousy. Don't you go believing anything of the sort. They're denouncing me in order to deflect suspicion from themselves, but I myself can denounce them."

Rubovsky was puzzled.

"I assure you," he said, shrugging his shoulders and clinking his spurs, "No one has denounced you to me. Apparently someone has threatened you for the sake of a joke, indeed, there's plenty that people will say at times."

Peredonov didn't believe him. He thought that the police officer was being secretive, and he became terrified.

Every time Peredonov passed Vershina's garden, Vershina stopped him and lured him into her garden with her spell-binding movements and words. And he would go in, involuntarily submitting to her gentle sorcery. Perhaps she would succeed sooner than the Rutilovs in achieving her goal. After all, Peredonov was equally distant from all people and why shouldn't he be joined in holy matrimony with Marta? But apparently it was a sticky bog that Peredonov had crept into and no spells would succeed in plopping him from one bog into another.

Thus, even now, when Peredonov had parted with Rubovsky and was walking past, Vershina, dressed as always totally in black, lured him in.

"Marta and Vladya are going home for the day," she said, looking tenderly at Peredonov with her brown eyes through the smoke of her cigarette. "Perhaps you should go and visit with them in the country. A worker has come in the cart for them."

"Too cramped," Peredonov said sullenly.

"What do you mean, cramped," Vershina objected. "You'll be wonderfully comfortable. And it's no misfortune if you're a little cramped, it's not far, only about six versts to go."

Meanwhile Marta had come running out of the house to ask Vershina something. The commotion before leaving had stirred her indolence somewhat and her face was more lively and cheerful than ordinarily. Once again, Peredonov was invited to the country, this time by the two of them.

"There's lots of room for you to be comfortable," Vershina assured him. "You and Marta on the back seat, and Vladya and Ignaty on the front. Here, take a look, the cart is in the yard."

Peredonov followed Vershina and Marta into the yard where the cart stood while Vladya was busy around it packing away something. The cart was spacious. But examining it sullenly, Peredonov declared:

"I won't go. Too cramped. With the four of us and the things as well."

"If you think it's going to be cramped," said Vershina, "then Vladya can go on foot."

"Sure, I can," said Vladya, giving a reserved and tender smile. "I can make it easily on foot in an hour and a half. If I start out right now, then I'll be there before you."

Then Peredonov explained that it would be bumpy and he didn't like bumpiness. They returned to the summer house. Everything had already been packed away, but the worker, Ignaty, was still eating in the kitchen, eating his fill solidly and without haste.

"How is Vladya studying?" Marta asked.

She couldn't think up any other conversation with Peredonov and Vershina had already reproached her more than once for not knowing how to entertain Peredonov.

"Badly," Peredonov said. "He's lazy and doesn't listen."

Vershina liked to grumble. She started to lecture Vladya. Vladya blushed and smiled, shrugged his shoulders as though from cold and, as was his habit, raised one shoulder higher than the other.

"Well, the year has only started," he said, "I've still got time."

"You have to study right from the very start," Marta said in the tone of an elder, but blushing slightly at the same time.

"And he's naughty," Peredonov complained. "Yesterday he was romping about just like the street urchins. And rude, he was insolent to me on Thursday."

Vladya suddenly flushed crimson and spoke heatedly but without ceasing to smile:

"There was nothing insolent, I just said the truth that in other school books you had missed on the average five mistakes each, but you had underlined every one in my book and had given me a two, yet mine was written better than those whom you gave a grade of three to."

"And furthermore you said something insolent to me," Peredonov insisted.

"There was nothing insolent, I just said that I would tell the inspector," Vladya said vehemently, "that you gave me a grade of two for nothing . . ."

"Vladya, don't forget yourself," Vershina said angrily. "You ought to be asking forgiveness and here you are repeating yourself."

Vladya suddenly recalled that he mustn't irritate Peredonov, that he might become Marta's husband. He blushed deeply, tugged at the belt on his long shirt out of embarrassment and timidly said:

"I'm sorry. I only wanted to ask you to remark it."

"Quiet, quiet now, please," Vershina interrupted him, "I can't bear arguments like this, I can't bear them," she repeated and her entire dry body gave an almost imperceptible shudder. "When people are making a remark to you, you keep quiet."

And Vershina heaped a fair amount of abuse on Vladya, smoking her cigarette and smiling crookedly the way she always smiled regardless of what the discussion.

"Your father ought to be told so that he can punish you," she concluded.

"He ought to be whipped," Peredonov decided and looked angrily at Vladya who had offended him.

"Of course," Vershina confirmed. "He ought to be whipped."

"He ought to be whipped," Marta said as well and then blushed.

"When I go to your father's today," Peredonov said, "I'll tell him to whip you, and properly, while I'm there."

Vladya was silent, looked at his tormentors, his shoulders hunched up, and smiled through his tears. His father was a stern man. Vladya tried to console himself by thinking that these were merely threats. Did they really want to spoil his holiday? After all, a holiday is a special day, a noteworthy and happy one, and everything about a holiday was incommensurate with everything connected to school and a weekday.

But Peredonov liked it when boys cried, particularly if he had caused them to cry and then confess. Vladya's embarrassment and the restrained tears in his eyes, and his timid, guilty smile—all that delighted Peredonov. He decided to go with Marta and Vladya.

"Well, fine, I'll go with you," he said to Marta.

Marta was overjoyed, but somehow frightened. Of course she wanted Peredonov to go with them, or, to be more exact, Vershina wanted it for her and had conjured up the realization of this wish for Marta with her quick sorcery. But now, when Peredonov said that he was going, Marta began to feel awkward because of Vladya. She felt sorry for him.

Vladya had an eerie feeling as well. Was Peredonov really going because of him? He felt like trying to gain favor with Peredonov. He said:

"Ardalyon Borisych, if you think that it will be cramped, I can go on foot."

Peredonov glanced at him suspiciously and said:

"Sure, if we let you go alone, you'll run off somewhere. No sir, we better take you to your father, let him give it to you."

Vladya blushed and sighed. He felt so awkward and melancholy and annoyed over this sullen and tormenting person. Nevertheless, in order to soften up Peredonov, he decided to arrange his seat more comfortably.

"I'll fix it up," he showed him, "so that you'll have an excellent seat."

And he hastily made off for the cart. Vershina watched him go, smiling crookedly and smoking, and she said quietly to Peredonov:

"They're all afraid of their father. He's a very stern person."

Marta blushed.

Vladya had wanted to take his new English fishing rod, which he had bought with his savings, to the country with him and he had wanted to take a few other things, but all of that would have taken up a lot of space in the cart. So Vladya carried all his things back into the house.

It wasn't hot. The sun was setting. The road, which had been dampened by the morning rain, wasn't dusty. The cart rolled smoothly along the fine gravel, carrying the four passengers out of the town. The gray, well-fed horse was trotting as though it took no notice of their weight, and the lazy, taciturn worker, Ignaty, controlled the horse's speed by means of movements on the reins which were apparent only to a practiced eye.

Peredonov was sitting beside Marta. They had cleared so much space for him that it was quite uncomfortable for Marta to sit. But he took no notice of that. And even if he had taken notice of it, he would have thought that that was the way it should have been. After all, he was the guest.

Peredonov felt quite good. He decided to have a polite chat with Marta, to joke a bit and amuse her. This is how he began:

"Well, now, are you going to start a revolt soon?"

"Why a revolt?" Marta asked.

"You Poles are always getting ready to revolt, but it won't do you any good."

"I hadn't even considered it," Marta said. "None of us want to revolt."

"Sure, that's just what you're saying, but you hate the Russians."

"No, we aren't considering it," Vladya said, turning to Peredonov from the front seat where he was sitting beside Ignaty.

"We know what you mean when you say you're not considering it. Only we're not going to give you your Poland back. We conquered you. We've done a lot of good deeds for you, and apparently, regardless of how you feed a wolf, it keeps looking at the forest."

Marta didn't protest. Peredonov was silent for a while and then suddenly said:

"The Poles are brainless."

Marta blushed.

"There are all kinds of people like that, both Poles and Russians," she said.

"No, that's not so, it's true," Peredonov insisted. "The Poles are stupid. They only know how to swagger about. Now the Jews, those are smart people."

"The Jews are cheats and not at all smart," Vladya said.

"No, the Jews are a very clever race. The Jew can always dupe a Russian, but a Russian can never dupe a Jew."

"People shouldn't cheat," Vladya said. "Is it really so smart to cheat and dupe people?"

Peredonov glanced angrily at Vladya.

"The smart thing is in studying," he said. "And you aren't studying."

Vladya sighed and again turned and began to watch the regular trot of the horse. Peredonov said:

"The Jews are smart at everything, at learning too, and just everything. If they allowed Jews to be professors, then all professors would be Jews. But the Poles are all slovenly."

He glanced at Marta and noting with pleasure that she had blushed deeply, he said politely:

"Don't go thinking that I'm talking about you. I know that you'll make a good housekeeper."

"All Polish women are good housekeepers," Marta replied.

"Sure," Peredonov protested, "some housekeepers they are, clean on the outside but with dirty petticoats underneath. But then you did have

Mickiewicz.* He's better than our Pushkin. I have a picture of him on my wall. Pushkin used to hang there but I took him out to hang in the out-house. He was a bedchamber lackey."

"But you're Russian," Vladya said, "What does our Mickiewicz mean to you? Pushkin is good and Mickiewicz is good too."

"Mickiewicz is better," Peredonov repeated. "The Russians are fools. The only thing they invented was the samovar and nothing else."

Peredonov glanced at Marta, screwed up his eyes and said:

"You have a lot of freckles. It's not very pretty."

"What can I do," Marta murmured, smiling.

"I have freckles too," Vladya said, turning around on his narrow seat and bumping against the taciturn Ignaty.

"You're a boy," Peredonov said. "It doesn't matter, a man doesn't have to be good-looking, but for you," he continued, turning to Marta, "it's not nice. That's why no one will want you for a wife. You have to wash your face with pickle brine."

Marta thanked him for the advice.

Vladya was looking at Peredonov with a smile.

"What are you smiling for?" Peredonov said. "Just you wait, when we arrive then you'll get a first-rate licking."

Turning around on his seat, Vladya was gazing attentively at Peredonov, trying to guess whether he was joking or telling the truth. But Peredonov couldn't bear it when people stared at him.

"What are you eyeing me for?" he asked rudely. "I haven't stripes on me. Or do you want to give me the evil eye?"

"Excuse me," he said timidly. "I didn't mean anything by it."

"Do you believe in the evil eye?" Marta asked.

"There's no such thing as the evil eye, it's only superstition," Peredonov answered angrily. "Only it's terribly rude to stare and scrutinize."

An awkward silence ensued for a few minutes.

"You're actually poor," Peredonov suddenly said.

"We're not rich," Marta replied. "Still we're not that poor. Each of us has something put aside."

Peredonov looked at her mistrustfully and said:

"Of course I know you're poor. You go around barefoot at home everyday."

"We don't do it because we're poor," Vladya said pertly.

"And I suppose you do it because you're rich or something?" Peredonov asked and abruptly roared.

"It has nothing to do with being poor," Vladya said, blushing. "It's very good for your health. We build up our health and it's nice to do in the summer."

"Well, you're lying there," Peredonov objected rudely. "Rich people don't go around barefoot. Your father has a lot of children, but he only earns a pittance. Not enough money for so many boots."[4]

*Adam Mickiewicz (1798–1855) is the national poet of Poland and was active in the Polish national independence movement. He was forced to live in exile outside of Poland in Russia where he became familiar with both the Decembrists and the works of Alexander Pushkin. Mickiewicz and Pushkin admired each other's work. For reasons both aesthetic and nationalistic, there has always been a critical and emotional debate as to which of the two poets, so similar in many ways, was the greater, and which poet had the greater influence on the other.

VII

VARVARA KNEW NOTHING about where Peredonov had gone. She spent a horribly anxious night.

But even when he returned to town in the morning, Peredonov didn't go home. Rather he had himself taken to church. Mass was beginning at the time. It seemed dangerous to him now not to attend church regularly. To be sure, people could denounce him for that.

As he entered the churchyard he met a cute young male gymnasium student with a rosy and naive face and guileless pale blue eyes. Peredonov said:

"Ah, Mashenka, greetings, you sissy."

Misha Kudryavtsev blushed painfully. Peredonov had already teased him on several occasions by calling him Mashenka. Kudryavtsev couldn't understand why and couldn't bring himself to make a complaint. Several of his friends, silly young boys, immediately got together and began to laugh at Peredonov's words. It made them happy as well to tease Misha.

The Church of the Prophet Ilya, an old church built back during the reign of Tsar Mikhail,* stood on a square opposite the gymnasium. Consequently, on holidays the gymnasium students were obliged to gather here for mass and vespers and stand in rows on the left side by the chapel of St. Ekaterina the Martyr, while one of the school prefects was stationed behind them to supervise. Immediately alongside, closer to the center of the church, stood the teachers from the gymnasium together with the inspector and headmaster and with their families. As a rule, almost all the orthodox students were gathered there, with the exception of a few who received permission to visit their own parish churches together with their parents.

A choir of gymnasium students sang well and for that reason the church was attended by the front-rank merchantry, officials and families of the landed gentry. There weren't many of the simple folk for the additional reason that, in accord with the wishes of the headmaster, mass was celebrated here at a later hour than in other churches.

Peredonov stood in his usual spot. From here he could see all the singers. Screwing up his eyes, he looked at them and thought that they were

---

*Tsar Mikhail Fyodorovich (1596–1645). The first of the Romanov dynasty to rule Russia.

standing in a disorderly fashion and that he would have straightened them out if he had been the inspector at the gymnasium. There was the swarthy Kramarenko, small, slender and fidgety, he kept turning around first one way then the other, whispering something, smiling—and no one stopped him. Just as though no one were concerned.

"A disgrace," Peredonov thought. "These singers are always good-for-nothings. That swarthy lad has a clear and pure soprano, so he thinks that he can go ahead and whisper and smile in church."

And Peredonov frowned. Alongside him stood Sergei Potapovich Bogdanov, the inspector of public schools who had arrived a little later. He was an old man with a brown stupid face which constantly bore the expression of a man who seemingly wanted to explain to someone something that he himself could not comprehend. No one could be as easily amazed or frightened as Bogdanov. No sooner would he hear something new or unsettling then some inner painful effort would bring a frown to his forehead, and confused, perturbed exclamations would fly from his mouth.

Peredonov leaned over to him and said in a whisper:

"One of your lady teachers goes around wearing a red blouse."

Bogdanov took fright. The white goatee on his chin started to shake.

"What, what's that you say?" he whispered hoarsely. "Which one, which one is that?"

"That loud-mouthed one, the fatso, I don't know what her name is," Peredonov whispered.

"The loud-mouthed one, the loud-mouthed one," Bogdanov was distractedly trying to recall. "Yes, that's Skobochkina."

"That's her," Peredonov confirmed.

"But how can it be, how can it be!" Bogdanov exclaimed in a whisper. "Skobochkina in a red blouse, goodness! And did you see her yourself?"

"I did and people say that she's always showing off in school. Or even worse things happen: she puts on a sarafan, and walks around like some ordinary peasant girl."

"You don't say! We really must find out, we really must. That's not allowed, not allowed. She could be dismissed for that, yes, dismissed," Bogdanov babbled. "She was always like that."

Mass ended. They walked out of the church. Peredonov said to Kramarenko:

"Hey, you, you little blackamoor, why were you smiling in church? Just you wait, I'll tell your father."

Peredonov always addressed the students who weren't from the gentry in the familiar fashion; but he used the formal manner of address with the members of the gentry. He always found out at the school office who was from which class and his memory latched firmly onto these differences.

Kramarenko looked at Peredonov in amazement and silently ran past. He belonged to that number of students who found Peredonov to be vulgar, stupid and unfair, and who hated and despised him for that. The majority of students were like that. Peredonov thought that these were the ones whom the headmaster was inciting against him, if not personally, then through his sons.

Once he was outside the churchyard Volodin approached Peredonov with a delighted giggle. He had on what could pass for a blissful birthday face. His derby was on the back of his head and he was shifting his walking stick from one hand to the other.

"Guess what I'm going to tell you, Ardalyon Borisych," he whispered happily. "I've persuaded Cherepnin and in a few days he's going to smear tar all over Marta's gate."

Peredonov was silent for a few moments, weighing something, and then suddenly he roared sullenly. Volodin stopped grinning just as quickly, assumed a modest appearance, straightened his derby, and looking up at the sky and waving his stick said:

"Nice weather, but it's going to rain by evening. Well, what's a little rain, the future inspector and I will sit at home for a while."

"I won't have much time to sit around at home," Peredonov said. "I have things to do today; I have to go into town."

Volodin assumed an understanding face although, of course, he didn't know what things Peredonov had suddenly found to do. Peredonov was thinking that he absolutely had to pay a few visits. Yesterday's chance meeting with the police officer had led him to a thought which seemed entirely sensible: to make the rounds of all the important people in town and assure them of his reliability. If he succeeded in doing that, then, whatever happened, Peredonov would have defenders in the town who could attest to the correct nature of his thoughts.

"Where are you going, Ardalyon Borisych?' Volodin asked, seeing that Peredonov was veering from the path that he always returned by. "Aren't you going home?"

"Yes, I'm going home," Peredonov replied. "Only today I'm afraid to walk along the street,"

"Why?"

"A great deal of *durman* grows there and the fragrance is strong. It has a powerful effect on me, it makes me feel drugged. My nerves are weak today. All kinds of troubles."

Volodin once more assumed an understanding and sympathetic look on his face.

Along the way Peredonov tore off several heads from some thistles and stuck them in his pocket.

"What are you gathering that for?" Volodin asked grinning.

"For the cat," Peredonov replied with a frown.

"To stick them in its fur?" Volodin inquired in a serious tone.

"Yes."

Volodin started to giggle.

"Don't you start without me," he said. "It'll be fun."

Peredonov invited him to come in right then, but Volodin said that he had some business. He suddenly felt that it was somehow indecent never to have any business to do. Peredonov's words about his own affairs had stirred him and he was thinking that it would be a good idea now to drop in on his own to see the young Adamenko lady and to say to her that he had some new and very exquisite drawings to be framed and wouldn't she like to take a look at them. Moreover, Volodin was thinking, Nadezhda Vasilyevna would treat him to coffee.

And Volodin did so. On top of it he came up with a very devious trick. He suggested to Nadezhda Vasilyevna that he give her brother instruction in manual work. Nadezhda Vasilyevna thought that Volodin needed to earn some money and immediately gave her consent. The agreement was for Volodin to give instruction three times a week, two hours each time, and for thirty roubles a month. Volodin was ecstatic. He had both the money and the opportunity of frequent meetings with Nadezhda Vasilyevna.

As always, Peredonov was gloomy when he returned home. Varvara, pale from her sleepless night, started to grumble:

"You might have told me yesterday that you weren't coming home."

Teasing her, Peredonov related how he had made the trip to Marta's. Varvara was silent. She had the Princess's letter in her hands. Even though it was forged, nevertheless . . .

Over lunch she said with a smirk:

"While you were passing the time with Marfushka, I received a reply here from the Princess without you.

"Did you really write her?" Peredonov asked.

His face grew animated with the gleam of dreary anticipation.

"Look at him, indulging in his tomfoolery," Varvara replied with a laugh. "You yourself told me to write."

"Well, what does she write?" Peredonov asked anxiously.

"Here's the letter, read it yourself."

Varvara rummaged around in her pockets as though she were looking for the letter that she had stuffed somewhere and then she pulled it out and handed it to Peredonov. He abandoned his food and pounced hungrily on the letter. He read it and rejoiced. Here, finally, was a clear and positive promise. No doubts arose in him. He quickly finished his breakfast and went to show the letter to his friends and acquaintances.

With sullen animation he quickly entered Vershina's garden. As was practically always the case, Vershina was standing by the gate and smoking. She rejoiced: earlier she had had to lure him, now he had dropped in of his own accord. Vershina was thinking:

"That's what it means to go for a ride with a young lady and to spend some time with her—lo, he's come running! Perhaps he already wants to make a proposal?" she thought, anxiously and joyfully.

Peredonov disenchanted her almost immediately. He showed her the letter.

"There, you were all doubting," he said, "But look, the Princess herself has written. Here read it and see for yourself."

Vershina looked mistrustfully at the letter, quickly puffed tobacco smoke several times in his direction, smiled crookedly and asked quietly and quickly:

"And where's the envelope?"

Peredonov suddenly took fright. He thought that Varvara could have

fooled him with the letter. She might have gone ahead and written it herself. He had to demand the envelope from her as quickly as possible.

"I don't know," he said, "I have to ask."

He said a hasty goodbye to Vershina and quickly went back to his
house. It was essential to ascertain as quickly as possible what the origin of
the letter was. The sudden doubt was so agonizing.

Standing by the gate, Vershina watched him go, smiled crookedly and
puffed rapidly on her cigarette as though she were hurrying to complete a
school lesson that had been assigned for that day.[5]

Peredonov ran home with a frightened and desperate face, and while he
was still in the front hall he shouted in a voice that was hoarse with alarm:

"Varvara, where's the envelope?"

"What envelope?" Varvara asked in a trembling voice.

She gave Peredonov an insolent look and would have turned red in the
face if she hadn't been rouged.

"The envelope, from the Princess, that the letter came in today,"
Peredonov explained, looking spitefully and fearfully at Varvara.

Varvara gave a tense laugh.

"I burned it, what did I need it for?" she said. "What do you expect
me to do, collect envelopes or something, to make a collection out of them?
They don't pay money for envelopes. It's only for bottles that they give you
money in the taverns."

Gloomy, Peredonov walked about the rooms and grumbled:

"There are all kinds of Princesses around. Don't we know it. Perhaps
this Princess even lives here."

Varvara pretended that she had no idea what he was suspicious about,
but she was terribly afraid.

When Peredonov was passing Vershina's garden towards evening,
Vershina stopped him.

"Did you find the envelope?" she asked.

"Varya says that she burned it," Peredonov replied.

Vershina laughed and then white clouds of tobacco smoke undulated
before him in the calm and mild air.

"Strange," she said. "How could your cousin be so careless. A business
letter and suddenly there's no envelope! Still one might have been able to
see from the postmark when and where the letter was dispatched."

Peredonov was terribly annoyed. Vershina was unsuccessful in inviting
him into the garden and was unsuccessful in promising to tell his fortune
with cards. Peredonov left.

Nevertheless he showed the letter to his friends and boasted. And his
friends believed him.

But Peredonov didn't know whether to believe or not to believe. In any
event he decided that beginning on Tuesday he would start out on his visits of self-vindication to the important people in the town. He couldn't start
on Monday—it was a painful day.

VIII

A s SOON AS Peredonov had left to play billiards, Varvara went to Grushina's. They conferred for a long while and finally decided to correct matters with a second letter. Varvara knew that Grushina had acquaintances in Petersburg. By using them it shouldn't be difficult to have the letter, which they were preparing here, sent there and then back again.

As was the case the first time, Grushina pretended to refuse for a long while.

"Oh, Varvara Dmitrievna, sweetheart," she said, "I'm still all atremble and afraid over the one letter. No sooner do I see the policeman near my house than I go completely to pieces thinking that they're coming for me and they want to put me in jail."

Varvara went on trying to convince her for a good hour, pledging all manner of presents, giving her some money in advance. Finally Grushina agreed. They decided to do it in the following manner. First Varvara would say that she had written a reply to the Princess thanking her. Then, after a few days a letter would arrive, supposedly from the Princess. In this letter it would be written even more definitely that there were positions available and if she were to quickly get married, then it would be possible right then to help secure one for Peredonov. The letter would be written by Grushina here, like the first one. Then they would seal it, affix a seven-kopeck stamp, Grushina would put it inside another letter to her friend and the latter would drop it in the post box in St. Petersburg.

And thus Varvara and Grushina went to a shop at the far end of town and there they bought a packet of envelopes, narrow ones with a colored lining, and colored paper. For the envelopes and paper they selected the only remaining ones of that type in the shop—a precaution which Grushina thought of in order to conceal the forgery. The narrow envelopes were chosen because then the forged letter could easily fit into another envelope.

On returning to Grushina's, they composed a letter from the Princess. Two days later when the letter was ready it was perfumed with cypress. They burned the rest of the envelopes and paper so that no evidence would be left.

Grushina wrote to her friend to tell her on precisely which day to post the letter. They calculated so that the letter would arrive on a Sunday, then the postman would deliver it while Peredonov was at home and that would be extra proof that the letter was not forged.

On Tuesday Peredonov tried to return home earlier from the gymnasium. Chance came to his rescue. His final lesson was in a classroom whose door fronted on the corridor close to the spot where the clock hung and the watchman, a dashing non-commissioned reservist who kept vigil by ringing the bell at the appointed hours, was stationed.

Peredonov sent the watchman to the teachers' room to fetch the class register while he himself set the clock a quarter-hour ahead. No one noticed.

At home Peredonov refused lunch and said that dinner should be made later—he had to go out on business.

"They keep trying to get me entangled but I'll untangle it," he said angrily, thinking about the intrigues his enemies were mounting against him.

He put on a dress jacket he rarely used and which now felt tight and uncomfortable on him. With the years he had put on weight and the jacket had shrunk. He was annoyed that he had no medals. Others had them. Even Falastov from the town school had them, but he had none. It was all the doing of the headmaster. Not once had he wanted to recommend Peredonov for any. Promotion through the ranks* continued, the headmaster couldn't stop that, but what did it matter if no one could actually see it. It was good that he would be able to wear epaulettes according to his rank and not according to the type of position he held. That would be important, having epaulettes like a general and one large star. Immediately everyone would see that it was a State Councillor walking down the street. "I better order a new uniform as quickly as possible," Peredonov thought.

He went out into the street and only then did he begin to consider whom to start with.

It seemed that the most indispensable people in his situation were the district police chief and the procurator of the regional court. He ought to start with them. Or with the marshal of the nobility. But Peredonov felt frightened to begin with them. The marshal of the nobility, Veriga, was a general and had aspirations to a governorship. As for the district police chief and the procurator, they were the frightening representatives of the police and the courts.

"To begin with," Peredonov thought, "I must choose the less imposing authorities to get my bearings there and have a sniff around. From them it should be apparent how they regard me and what they say about me." Therefore, Peredonov decided that the smartest thing would be to start with the town mayor. Although the latter was a merchant and had only attended the regional school, nevertheless he had been everywhere. Everyone had been in his home and he enjoyed respect in the town. He had rather important acquaintances in other towns as well, even in the capital.

Peredonov made for the home of the mayor with determination.

The weather was bleak. Leaves were falling from the trees, resigned and tired. Peredonov was a little afraid.

*The "table of ranks" was established by Peter the Great in 1722 and consisted of 14 ranks or grades (with the 1st class being the highest). There were three types of ranking: military, civil and courtly. The "table" was removed after the Russian Revolution. A State Councillor was the fifth rank.

In the mayor's home it smelled of parquet flooring that had recently been polished and of something else barely discernible, something pleasantly savory. It was quiet and humdrum. The host's children, a son from the gymnasium and a young girl in her teens ("she's being tutored by a governess," the father said), spent the time being well-behaved in their rooms. There it was cozy, calm and cheerful, the windows looked out onto the garden, the furniture was comfortable, the games varied in the rooms and in the garden and the voices of children rang brightly.

But in the rooms of the upper floor that fronted on the street and where guests were received, everything was strained and severe. It was as though the mahogany furniture represented a version of toy furniture many times enlarged. It was uncomfortable for ordinary people to sit on it. One felt as though one had fallen on a rock when sitting down. It made no difference to the ponderous host. He would take a place, sit down and be comfortable. The archimandrite who would frequently visit the mayor from the monastery in the town's vicinity called these upholstered chairs and sofas "soul-saving," to which the mayor would respond:

"I don't like those fragile ladies' things you find in other homes. You sit down on springs and you yourself bounce and the furniture bounces—what's good about that? Incidentally, even doctors don't approve of soft furniture."

The mayor, Yakov Anikievich Skuchaev, greeted Peredonov in the doorway to the living room. He was a fat, tall man with shortly cropped black hair. He bore himself with a dignity and a politeness that was not far removed from a certain disdain in his attitude to people who were not well-off.

Sitting erect in a wide chair and replying to his host's polite questions, Peredonov said:

"I've come to you on business."

"My pleasure. How may I help you?" the host inquired politely.

A disdainful light was ignited in the mayor's cunning black eyes. He thought that Peredonov had come to ask to borrow money and he decided that he wouldn't give him more than a hundred and fifty roubles. There were many officials in town who to a greater or lesser extent were in debt to Skuchaev. Skuchaev never reminded them about returning the loan, but on the other hand he wouldn't extend any further credit to delinquent debtors. On the first occasion, however, he would give willingly, according to the cash he had on hand and the financial condition of the suppliant.

"You, Yakov Anikievich, as the mayor, occupy the top position in the town," Peredonov said. "This is why I have to talk with you."

Skuchaev assumed an important look and bowed slightly while sitting in his chair.

"People are cooking up all sorts of nonsense about me in town," Peredonov said sullenly. "They're making up things that aren't true."

"You can't stop people from talking," the host said. "And, any way, as you know, in our Palestines the scandal-mongers have nothing better to do than to wag their tongues."

"They say that I don't attend church, but it isn't true," Peredonov continued. "I do attend. But if I wasn't there on St. Ilya's Day, it was because I had a stomach ache, otherwise I always attend."

"That's true," the host confirmed. "I can say that I have had occasion to see you there. Even though I don't always attend your church. I go more frequently to the monastery. This is a long tradition in our family."

"They cook up all manner of nonsense," Peredonov said. "They say that I supposedly tell the gymnasium students vile things. But that's nonsense. Sometimes, of course, you tell something amusing in a lesson in order to liven things up. Your own son is a student at the gymnasium. He never told you anything of the sort about me, did he?"

"That's true," Skuchaev agreed. "There was nothing of that sort. But then those lads are an exceedingly cunning lot: they won't say what they're not supposed to. My son, of course, is still young, he might have blabbed something out of stupidity. However, he's never said anything of the sort."

"In the senior classes they already know everything," Peredonov said. "But even there I don't say any vulgar words."

"That's the way things are," Skuchaev replied. "As everyone knows, the gymnasium isn't a market square."

"And we have the kind of people," Peredonov complained, "who'll go about bleating things that aren't true. That's why I came to see you. You're the mayor of the town."

Skuchaev was quite flattered by the fact that people came to see him. He didn't quite understand what it was for or what the matter was here, but for the sake of politics, he didn't show that he didn't understand.

"And there's something else bad that people say about me," Peredonov continued. "They say that I'm living with Varvara. They say that she isn't my cousin, but my mistress. But swear to God, she is my cousin, only a distant cousin, a third cousin, and one can marry those. And I am going to get married to her."

"Indeed, indeed, of course," Skuchaev said. "The altar, in any event, would put an end to the business."

"But it was impossible for me to do so earlier," Peredonov said. "I had important reasons. It was just impossible. Otherwise I would have gotten married long ago. You can believe me."

Skuchaev assumed a dignified air, frowned and tapping on the dark table cloth with his white, puffy fingers, said:

"I believe you. If it's so, then it's really a different matter. Now I believe you. Otherwise, it must be admitted, it was doubtful the way you, if I may be allowed to say, were living with your friend without being married. It's doubtful, you know, because the lads are a sharp folk. They imitate anything that's bad. It's difficult to teach them something good, but the bad comes by itself. So, true, it was doubtful. Anyway, regardless of who is involved, that's how I would judge it. But the fact that you have made a complaint, then I feel flattered because even though we're only homespun folk and didn't get beyond the country school, well, nevertheless I have gained the respect I hold through the trust of society. I'm in my third term of office as mayor, so my word is worth something among the townspeople."

Skuchaev was talking and getting more and more entangled in his thoughts and it seemed to him that the rambling speech issuing from his mouth would never come to an end. And he broke off his speech and thought with melancholy:

"Anyway it's like pouring water into a sieve. The trouble with these scholars," he thought, "is that you can't understand what he wants. Everything is clear to him in books, this learned fellow, but soon as you drag his nose away from the book he gets all tangled up and tangles others up."

With melancholy perplexity he stared at Peredonov, his sharp eyes had become glazed, the plump body had sagged and he no longer seemed the same cheerful political figure of late, but simply a rather foolish old man.

Peredonov was also silent for a while as though spellbound by his host's words, and then he said, screwing up his eyes with a vaguely glum expression:

"You are the town mayor, so you can say that all of this is nonsense."

"In what regard do you mean?" Skuchaev inquired cautiously.

"I mean," Peredonov explained, "that if people denounce me to the district officials, saying that I don't attend church or tell them something else there, and then they come here to ask you."

"That we can do," the mayor said. "In any event, of that you can be assured. In a case like that we will stand up for you. Why shouldn't we put in a good word for a good person? We could even present you with a testimonial from the town council if required. We can do all of that. Or, for example, we could give you the designation of a respected citizen. Why not, if it's required. Everything is possible."

"So then I can rely on you," Peredonov said sullenly as though replying to something that wasn't very pleasant for him. "Otherwise the headmaster will go on persecuting me."

"I say!" Skuchaev exclaimed and shook his head sympathetically. "One must suppose that he's doing so only because of the slander. Nikolai Vlasyevich, it seems to me, is a solid gentleman and he wouldn't offend someone for nothing. Indeed, I can see it from my son. A serious gentleman, strict, doesn't spoil anyone and he doesn't show favorites, in short, a solid gentleman. It could only be due to the slander. Why are you and he at odds?"

"We don't share the same views," Peredonov explained. "And I have people who are jealous of me in the gymnasium. They all want to be inspectors. But Princess Volchanskaya promised to help secure an inspector's post for me. So now they're angry out of jealousy."

"I see, I see," Skuchaev said cautiously. "Anyway, why are we having such an official conversation? We ought to have a bite to eat and a drink."

Skuchaev pushed the button on the electric bell near the hanging lamp.

"A handy thing," he said to Peredonov. "Perhaps you ought to transfer into a different department. Dashenka," he said to the comely girl of athletic build who had entered in response to the bell, "bring us something to eat and some hot coffee, understand?"

"Yes, sir," Dashenka replied, smiled and left, walking with amazing lightness, considering her build.

"Go into another department," Skuchaev turned to Peredonov. "Perhaps even the church, for example. If you took holy vows, then you would make a serious, reliable priest. I could lend my aid. I have some very good acquaintances who are bishops."

Skuchaev named seveal diocesan and suffragan bishops.

"No, I don't want to join the priesthood," Peredonov replied. "I'm afraid of the incense. Incense turns my stomach and makes my head ache."

"In that case it might also be a good idea to join the police," Skuchaev advised. "For example, join the district police force. What rank do you hold, if I may ask?"

"I am a State Councillor," Peredonov said pompously.

"Indeed!" Skuchaev exclaimed, "I say, what important ranks you've been given! And is it for teaching children? I say, knowledge really is important! Anyway, even if in our day some gentleman attacks knowledge, nevertheless, you can't manage without knowledge. Even though I myself only studied in a country school, I'm sending my son to university. As you know, you have to lead them by stick and carrot through the gymnasium, but once he gets there everything will be fine. You know, I never give him a whipping. Whenever he gets lazy or slips up, I take him by the shoulders, lead him to the window—we have birch trees standing there in the garden. I show him a birch tree. I say to him, do you see that? Yes, I do, papa, he says, I won't do it any more. And really, it helps, the lad straighten out as though he had actually been whipped. Oh, children, children!" Skuchaev finished with a sigh.

Peredonov sat at Skuchaev's for two hours. After their business conversation came abundant *zakuski*.

Skuchaev's hospitality, like everything that he did, was carried out with gravity, as though he were engaged in some important matter. Moreover, he attempted to do so with some cunning twists. Mulled wine was served in large glasses, just like coffee, and the host called it coffee. The vodka glasses came with the bases broken off and rounded so that it was impossible to set them down on the table.

"I call these glasses 'pour more, drink more'," the host explained.

Another merchant, Tishkov, arrived. He was grayheaded, short, cheerful and sprightly, and wore a long frock coat and boots like barrels. He drank a lot of vodka, spoke all kinds of nonsense in rhymes, quickly and cheerfully, and apparently was quite pleased with himself.

Peredonov finally concluded that it was time to go home and he started to say goodbye.

"Don't be in a rush," the host said, "sit a while."

"Sit down, stay around," Tishkov said.

"No, I have to go," Peredonov replied anxiously.

"He's not to be late, his cousin can't wait," Tishkov said and winked at Skuchaev.

"I have things to do," Peredonov said.

"We'll make much ado for people with things to do," Tishkov retorted instantly.

Skuchaev accompanied Peredonov to the front hall. They embraced and kissed when they parted. Peredonov was pleased with this visit.

"The mayor is for me," he thought confidently.

Returning to Tishkov, Skuchaev said:

"They're gossiping about the fellow for nothing."

"If they gossip forsooth, they don't know the truth," Tishkov rejoined at once as he poured himself a glass of English bitters with a spritely movement.

It was apparent that he didn't think about what people said to him but only caught the words for the sake of rhyme.

"He's alright, a sincere fellow and a good drinker," Skuchaev continued, pouring himself a drink and paying no attention to Tishkov's rhymes.

"If he's a good drinker, he must be a real thinker," Tishkov cried boisterously and tossed the glass off.

"And if he is passing the time with a mam'selle, so what does it matter!" Skuchaev said.

"Bugs in the covers with mam'selles as lovers," Tishkov replied.

"Whoever has not transgressed in the eyes of the Lord is not guilty in those of the Tsar!"

"We always fall into transgression whenever we seek affection."

"But he wants to erase his sin before the altar."

"They who erase their sin before the altar are doomed to fight and falter."

Tishkov always talked like this if it didn't concern his own personal business. He would have bored everyone to death, but they had already grown used to him and no longer took any note of the rhyming patter he uttered so boisterously. It would only affect a decent person at times. But it made no difference to Tishkov whether people listened to him or not. He couldn't help seizing on other people's words for the sake of rhyme and he operated with the steadiness of a cunningly devised mechanical bore. After staring for a long while at his abrupt and distinct movements, one might have thought that this was no living person, that he had already died or had never been alive, and could see nothing in the living world and could hear nothing other than the deadly ring of his own words.

IX

THE FOLLOWING DAY Peredonov went to the public prosecutor, Avinovitsky. Once again the weather was overcast. The wind blew in gusts and swept up dusty whirlwinds along the streets. Evening was approaching and everything was illuminated with a mournful light filtering through the murky overcast and seemingly from a source other than the sun.

A melancholy lull hung over the streets and it seemed that the pitiful buildings, hopelessly decrepit, timidly hinting at the impoverished and boring life lurking within their walls, had originated for nothing. People appeared from time to time and even they were walking slowly as though without motivation, as though they were barely succeeding in overcoming the somnolence that was inducing them to stillness. Only the children, those eternal, tireless vessels of God's delight in the earth, were lively and ran and played. But sluggishness was even settling over them by now, and some faceless and invisible monster, nestling at their shoulder, peered from time to time with eyes full of menace into their faces which were suddenly growing listless.

In the midst of this langour in the streets and in the houses, in the grip of this alienation from the sky, through this sullied and impotent earth strolled Peredonov, languishing from indistinct fears. And for him there was no solace in the heavenly and no joy in the earthly, because even now, as was always the case, he looked at the world through deathly eyes like some kind of demon who was languishing in gloomy solitude out of fear and melancholy.

His sensibilities were dull and his consciousness was an apparatus for corruption and destruction. Everything that reached his consciousness was transformed into something vile and filthy. He was immediately taken with deformities in objects and he rejoiced over them. Whenever he passed an erect and pure column, he wanted to deform it or deface it. He laughed with joy when things were spoiled in his presence. He despised the cleanly washed students at the gymnasium and persecuted them. He called them "goody-goodies." The slovenly ones were more comprehensible to him. He had no objects that he loved just as there were no people he loved. And for that reason nature could influence his sensibilities only in one direction— only to suppress them. It was the same in his encounters with people.

Particularly with strangers and people he didn't know and to whom he couldn't utter any vulgarity. Being happy for him meant doing nothing and, after shutting himself off from the world, gratifying his belly.

"And now," he thought, "like it or not I have to go and explain myself. What a burden! What a bore!" And even if he might have been able to spoil things where he was going, not even that would have consoled him.

The public prosecutor's house strengthened and concentrated in Peredonov those oppressive sentiments into a feeling of melancholy fear. And it was precisely as though that house possessed an angry and spiteful appearance. The high roof hung frowningly over the windows and forced them down towards the ground. Both the wooden trim and the roof had been painted a bright and cheerful color at one time, but time and rain had rendered the paint gloomy and gray. The gates, enormous and heavy, higher than the house itself, seemed to be installed in order to repulse enemy attacks and were bolted at all times. A chain rattled behind the gates and a dog barked at every passerby in a deep bass.

Barren lots and gardens stretched out in all directions around the house while a few hovels sat about lopsidedly. Opposite the public prosecutor's house was a long six-sided square with a depression in the middle, completely unpaved and overgrown with grass. Right next to the house towered a lamp standard, the only one in the entire square.

Slowly and reluctantly Peredonov mounted the four sloping steps onto the porch, which was covered with a two-sided planked roof, and took hold of the darkened bronze handle to the bell. The bell rang somewhere close by, with a piercing and prolonged jarring sound. In a short while he could hear stealthy footsteps. Someone had tiptoed up to the door and stood as quiet as quiet could be. They must have been peering through some invisible crack. Then the iron handle rattled, the door opened—and a dark-haired, sullen, pock-faced girl with suspicious eyes that took everything in was standing on the threshold.

"Whom do you want?" she asked.

Peredonov said that he had come to see Alexander Alexeevich on business. The girl let him in. Peredonov muttered a counter-spell under his breath as he crossed the threshold. And a good thing that he was quick about it—he hadn't managed to take his coat off before Avinovitsky's sharp, angry voice sounded in the living room. The public prosecutor's voice had always been frightening—he never spoke any differently. Such was the case now when from the sitting room in an argumentative and angry voice he shouted out words of greeting and his expression of pleasure that Peredonov had finally come to visit him.

Alexander Alexeevich Avinovitsky was a man of a gloomy exterior, as though he had already been adapted from nature to administer a proper scolding and dressing-down. He was a man of invincible health—he went from one ice-cold bath to the next. However, he seemed rather lean given the fact that he had such a vigorous black beard with a bluish hue. He inspired at the very least a feeling of awkwardness, if not outright fear in everyone because he was tirelessly fulminating against someone or threatening someone with Siberia and penal servitude.[6]

"I've come on business," Peredonov said with embarrassment.

"With a confession? Did you kill a person? Commit arson? Rob the post office?" Avinovitsky shouted angrily, guiding Peredonov into the sitting room. "Or have you yourself become a victim of persecution, which is more than likely in our town? Our town is vile and the police here are even worse. I'm still amazed that dead bodies aren't lying all about on this square every morning. Well, sir, I beg you to sit down. So what is your business? Are you a criminal or a victim?"

"No," said Peredonov, "I haven't done anything of the sort. It's the headmaster who would be happy to put me on trial, but I haven't done anything of that sort."

"So you haven't brought me a confession?" Avinovitsky asked.

"No, nothing of the sort," Peredonov muttered fearfully.

"Well, if you haven't done anything of the sort," the procurator said with fierce stress on the words, "then I can offer you something."

He took a bell from the table and rang. No one came. Avinovitsky grabbed the bell in both hands, raised a furious pealing, then threw the bell on the floor, started to stamp his feet and shout in a wild voice.

"Malanya! Malanya! The devils, the demons, the goblins!"

Unhurried steps were heard and a student from the gymnasium, the son of Avinovitsky, entered. He was a dark-haired, thickset boy of about thirteen with a completely confident and independent manner. He bowed to Peredonov, picked up the bell, put it on the table and only then did he say calmly:

"Malanya has gone to the garden."

Avinovitsky relaxed instantly and looking at his son with an affection that did not in the least suit his heavily bearded and angry face, said:

"Well, my son, you run out to her and tell her to get something for us to eat and drink."

The boy left the room without haste. The father watched him go with a proud and joyful smile. But when the boy had reached the doorway, Avinovitsky suddenly frowned fiercely and shouted in a frightening voice that made Peredonov start:

"And quick!"

The gymnasium student ran off and they could then hear the impetuous opening and slamming of doors. The father listened for a bit, smiled happily with his thick red lips and then once more said in an angry voice:

"My heir. Good, eh? What will become of him, eh? What do you think? A fool, perhaps, but a scoundrel, a coward or a milksop—never!"

"Of course," Peredonov muttered.

"Nowadays people are a parody of the human race," Avinovitsky thundered. "They think that health is a trivial matter. A German devised the undershirt. I would have sent that German off to penal labor. Just imagine an undershirt on my Vladimir! He never once put any boots on the whole summertime at my place in the country, and him in an undershirt! A hundred lashes for that accursed German!"

Avinovitsky switched from the German who had devised the undershirt to other criminals.

"The death sentence, my kind sir, is no barbarity!" he shouted. "Science has recognized the existence of born criminals. And that, old boy, says all. They must be exterminated and not fed at the expense of the state. Here he is a malefactor, yet he will be provided with a warm corner in a penal institution for his entire life. He has committed murder, arson, rape, yet the taxpayer is answerable with his pocket for his upkeep. No sir, hanging is much more fair and inexpensive."

The table was laid in the dining room with a red-bordered white table-cloth and plates with fat sausages and other foods, pickled, smoked and marinaded, as well as decanters and bottles of various sizes and forms with all manner of vodkas, liqueurs and brandies. Everything was to Peredonov's liking and he even found it appealing that there was a certain amount of disorder in the furnishings.

The host continued to fulminate. Using the food as a pretext he attacked the shopkeepers and then started for some reason to talk about heredity.

"Heredity is a marvellous business!" he cried fiercely. "To turn the peasants into aristocracy is stupid, ridiculous, wasteful and immoral. The land is growing impoverished, the towns are filling up with vagrants, there are crop failures, ignorance, suicide—do you like all of that? Teach the peasant as much as you want but don't award him any rank for that. Otherwise the peasantry will lose the best of its members and remain rabble and boodle forever, while the gentry will also suffer damage from the influx of uncultured elements. In his own village he was better than the rest, whereas he is introducing something vulgar, unchivalrous and ignoble into the gentry class. Profit and his own belly occupy the foreground for the peasant. No, sir, old boy, the castes were a clever arrangement."

"In our gymnasium the headmaster is letting all kinds of rabble in," Peredonov said angrily. "Even the children of peasants are there, and there are even a lot of the petite bourgeoisie."[7]

"A fine thing, what can you say!" the host cried.

"There's a circular saying that just any riff-raff shouldn't be allowed in, but he goes his own way," Peredonov complained. "He refuses almost no one. He says that people don't have much money in our town and there are so few students for the gymnasium. What does he mean, so few? He should be letting in even fewer. Otherwise you don't have time to correct some notebooks. And there's no time to read any books. And the students purposely use dubious words in their compositions and you have to keep referring to the dictionary."

"Drink some flavored vodka," Avinovitsky offered. "What's your business with me?"

"I have enemies," muttered Peredonov, despondently examining the glass with yellow vodka before drinking it.

"The pig lived without any enemies," Avinovitsky replied, "and still they went and slaughtered him. Have some, it was a fine pig."

Peredonov took a slice of ham and said:

"People are spreading all sorts of rubbish about me."

"Well, I can certainly say that as far as slander is concerned there is no town worse!" the host cried fiercely. "What a town! Regardless of whatever foul thing is committed, all the pigs immediately start oinking about it."

"Princess Volchanskaya promised to help secure me an inspector's post, and now suddenly everyone is gossiping. It could be harmful to me. And it's all out of jealousy. The headmaster as well has corrupted the gymnasium: the students who live in outside quarters smoke, drink and chase after the girl students. And there are locals who do the same. He himself corrupted them, but here he's persecuting me. Perhaps people have been spreading slander about me to him. And they'll go and spread it further. It'll reach the Princess."

Peredonov's account about his fears was long and incoherent. Avinovitsky listened angrily and exclaimed wrathfully from time to time:

"Scoundrels! Rogues! Herod's offspring!"

"What kind of nihilist am I?" Peredonov said. "That's ridiculous. I have an official cap with a cockade, only I don't always wear it, whereas he only wears an ordinary hat. And if Mickiewicz is hanging on my wall, then it's because of his verses that I put him there and not because he was a revolutionary. I haven't even read his work *The Bell*.*

"Well, you've got your stories mixed up there," Avinovitsky said unceremoniously. "*The Bell* was published by Herzen and not Mickiewicz."

"Then it's a different *The Bell*," Peredonov said. "Mickiewicz also published something called *The Bell*."

"I don't know about that. You ought to publish that. A scientific discovery. You'll be famous."

"It's impossible to publish that," Peredonov said angrily. "I'm not allowed to read forbidden books. Furthermore, I don't read them. I am a patriot."

After protracted lamentations in which Peredonov poured out his soul, Avinovitsky concluded that someone was trying to blackmail Peredonov and to that end was spreading rumors about him with the purpose of frightening him and thereby preparing the groundwork for the sudden demand of money. Avinovitsky explained the fact that these rumors hadn't reached him because the blackmailer very cleverly was operating in the closest proximity to Peredonov, so all Avinovitsky had to do was to bring some influence to bear on Peredonov. Avinovitsky asked:

"Whom do you suspect?"

Peredonov grew thoughtful. By chance, Grushina came to mind because he vaguely recalled the recent conversation with her when he had interrupted her story by threatening to denounce her. The fact that he had threatened Grushina with a denunciation became confused in his mind with a murky conception of denunciation in general. Whether he would

---

* Herzen, Alexander Ivanovich (1812–70). One of Russia's foremost philosophical and socialist thinkers. He was an essayist and writer with strong revolutionary leanings. Forced to leave Russia, he eventually settled in England where he established a Russian press. Beginning in 1857, together with N.P. Ogaryov he published a free Russian weekly newspaper, *The Bell*. It was regularly smuggled into Russia where it was read widely.

carry out the denunciation or whether he himself would be denounced—that was unclear and Peredonov had no wish to make the effort to recall precisely. The one thing that was clear was that Grushina was an enemy. And, what was worst of all, she had seen where he had hidden the Pisarev. He would have to change the hiding place.

Peredonov said:

"There's this person by the name of Grushina here."

"I know, a first-rate rascal," Avinovitsky concluded briefly.

"She's always coming to our place," Peredonov complained. "And she's always trying to sniff things out. She's greedy and she always wants you to give her something. Perhaps she wants me to pay her money so she won't denounce me for having Pisarev. Or perhaps she wants to marry me. But I don't want to pay and I have another fiancée. Let her denounce me, I'm not guilty. Only it would be unpleasant for me if the story became known and that could harm my appointment."

"She is a well-known charlatan," the procurator said. "She wanted to deal in fortune-telling here, she was turning the heads of fools and I told the police that it had to be halted. They were smart that time and obeyed."

"She's still telling fortunes now," Peredonov said. "She read my fortune in the cards and it always came out the same: a long journey and an official letter."

"She knows what to say and to whom. Just wait, she'll be casting her nooses and then she'll go and try to extort money. At that point you come straight to me. I'll deal her a hundred hot ones," Avinovitsky pronounced his favorite saying.

One wasn't supposed to take it literally, it meant simply a proper tongue-lashing.

This was how Avinovitsky promised his protection to Peredonov. But Peredonov was still upset with vague fears when he left. Avinovitsky's threatening talk had strengthened those fears in Peredonov.

Each day Peredonov carried out one visit in this manner before dinner. He couldn't manage more than one because he had to conduct lengthy explanations everywhere he went. As was his habit he would go off to play billiards in the evening.

Vershina went on luring him with her spell-binding invitations. Rutilov went on singing the praises of his sisters. At home Varvara tried to talk him into getting married as quickly as possible, but he made no decision. "Of course," he thought at times, "marrying Varvara would bring the greatest advantage to me, but what if suddenly I find out she's deceiving me? People in town would start to laugh at me." And that would stop him.

The pursuit by prospective wives, the jealousy of his colleagues (more a product of his own imagination than actual fact), the suspected intrigues of others—all that made his life monotonous and mournful like the weather which had been gloomy for several days in a row and frequently culminated in a gentle, monotonous but long and cold rain. Life was taking a vile turn, Peredonov felt, but he thought that soon he would become an inspector and then everything would take a turn for the better.

X

ON THE THURSDAY, Peredonov made his way to the marshal of the nobility.

The marshal's home was reminiscent of a roomy summer home somewhere in Pavlosk or Tsarskoe Selo* that was entirely suitable for winter living. One wasn't struck by any luxury, but the newness of many things seemed exaggerated and superfluous. Alexander Mikhaylovich Veriga was waiting for Peredonov in his study. He pretended that he was supposedly bestirring himself to greet his guest and only by chance hadn't managed to do so earlier.

Veriga held himself extraordinarily erect even for a retired cavalry officer. People said that he wore a corsette. His face, smoothly shaven, was uniformly ruddy as though it had been rouged. His hair had been clipped with an instrument that cut hair very closely—a device that was convenient for minimizing his bald patch. His eyes were gray, polite and cold. He was extremely polite in his treatment of everyone and in his views he was firm and stern. A fine military bearing was apparent in all his movements and at times one had a glimpse of the manners of a future governor.

Peredonov, sitting opposite him at a carved oak table, started to explain:

"There are all sorts of rumors about me afoot, and so, as a member of the gentry, I am turning to you. People are saying all sorts of nonsense about me, Your Excellency. Things that aren't true."

"I have heard nothing," Veriga replied and smiling expectantly and politely, fixed his gray attentive eyes on Peredonov.

Peredonov peered stubbornly into a corner and said:

"I was never a socialist and the fact that at some other time a person might have said something superfluous, well then, who doesn't get a bit excited in their younger years. But now I have none of those thoughts whatsoever."

"So you were really a great liberal?" Veriga asked with a polite smile. "You wanted a constitution, isn't that right? In our youth we all wanted a constitution. Would you care for one?"

Veriga moved a box of cigars towards Peredonov. Peredonov was afraid to take one and declined. Veriga lit one.

*The more fashionable environs of the capital, St. Petersburg.

"Of course, Your Excellency," Peredonov admitted, "at university I, and at the time I alone, wanted a different kind of constitution than the others."

"And precisely what kind was that?" Veriga asked with a hint of incipient displeasure in his voice.

"I wanted a constitution, only one without a parliament, "Peredonov said. "Otherwise they'd only be wrangling in parliament."

Veriga's gray eyes glittered with quiet rapture.

"A constitution without a parliament!" he said dreamily. "You know, that would be practical."

"But that was a long while ago," Peredonov said. "Now I think nothing of the sort."[8]

He looked hopefully at Veriga. Veriga emitted a slender filament of smoke from his mouth, was silent for a while and then said slowly:

"Now you're a pedagogue and given my position in the district I am obliged to come into contact with schools as well. From your point of view, be so good as to tell me which schools you would give your preference to, the church-run parochial schools or these so-called rural council schools?"*

Veriga knocked the ash off his cigar and stared directly at Peredonov with his polite but all-too-attentive eyes. Peredonov frowned, glanced about the corners and said:

"The rural council schools have to be tightened up."

"Tightened up," Veriga repeated in a vague tone of voice. "I see."

And he lowered his eyes to his smouldering cigar as though he were preparing himself to listen to long explanations.

"The teachers there are nihilists," Peredonov said. "And the female teachers don't believe in God. They stand in church and blow their noses."

Veriga glanced quickly at Peredonov, smiled and said:

"Well, you know, it is essential sometimes."

"Yes, but she blows her nose just like a horn so that the singers laugh," Peredonov said angrily. "She does it on purpose. There's this woman by the name of Skobochkina."

"No, that's not nice," Veriga said. "But with Skobochkina it's more a matter of the lack of breeding. She's a girl who's utterly without manners, but still a conscientious teacher. But in any event, it's not nice. She should be told."

"She goes around in a red blouse. And sometimes she even goes barefoot and wears a sarafan. She plays skittles with the young boys. Things are very free in their schools," Peredonov continued. "There's no discipline. They don't want to use any punishment at all. But you can't do that with the children of peasants the way you can with those of the gentry. They have to be whipped."

Veriga gazed calmly at Peredonov. Then, as though experiencing some awkwardness over the absence of tact he had just witnessed, he lowered his eyes and said in a chilly tone almost reminiscent of a governor:

"I must say that I have observed many fine qualities in the pupils of the country schools. There is no doubt that in the vast majority of instances they

*See introduction.

have a completely conscientious attitude to their work. Naturally, as is the case everywhere with children, offences are committed. As a result of poor breeding in the local milieu these offences can assume rather vulgar forms, all the more so because the sentiments of duty, honor and a respect for the property of others are generally poorly developed in the rural population of Russia. The school is obliged to treat these kinds of offences in an earnest and strict fashion. If all measures of reprimand are exhausted or if the offence is great, then, naturally, it would be necessary to seek recourse to extreme measures to avoid dismissing the pupil. Incidentally, this would apply to all children, even to those of the gentry. But in general I am agreed with you that education in this type of school is not organized in an entirely satisfactory manner. Mrs. Shteven, in her really quite interesting book . . . have you, pray, read it?"

"No, Your Excellency," Peredonov said with embarrassment. "I never had the time, there's a great deal of work in the gymnasium. But I will read it."

"Well, it isn't so essential," Veriga said with a polite smile, as though he were giving Peredonov permission not to read the book. "Well then, this Mrs. Shteven relates with great indignation about how two of her pupils, young fellows close to seventeen, were sentenced by the rural court to be whipped. They were arrogant, you see, these young fellows, and we, you understand, were all suffering torments as long as the shameful sentence hung over their heads. It was later repealed. But I'll say to you that in place of Mrs. Shteven I would have been ashamed to spread this story all over Russia. After all, if you can imagine, they were sentenced for the theft of apples. I beg you to note—for theft! On top of it she writes that these were her best pupils. Nevertheless, they stole the apples! So much for education! All that's left is to frankly admit that we are refuting the right of ownership."

In his excitement Veriga had risen from his seat, and taken two steps forward, but he immediately regained possession of himself and sat down again.

"If I become an inspector of public schools I'll conduct matters differently," Peredonov said.

"Ah, you have prospects?" Veriga asked.

"Yes, Princess Volchanskaya has promised me."

Veriga assumed a pleased look.

"I shall be pleased to offer my congratulations. I have no doubt that in your hands matters will improve."

"But the thing is, Your Excellency, people are spreading various bits of nonsense in the town. Furthermore it could happen that someone will make a denunciation to the district authorities and interfere with my appointment, and yet I'm innocent."

"Whom do you suspect of spreading false rumors?" Veriga asked.

Peredonov grew distracted and muttered:

"Whom do I suspect? I don't know. People. I'm concerned because it can do me harm in my career."

Veriga thought that there was no need for him to know who exactly was responsible. After all he wasn't the governor yet. He once again assumed the role of marshal of the nobility and delivered a speech which

Peredonov listened to with fear and melancholy:

"I thank you for the trust which you have rendered to me in seeking recourse to my (here Veriga wanted to say 'patronage', but restrained himself) mediation between you and the society wherein, according to your information, rumors are circulating which are unfavorable to you. These rumors have not reached me and you may console yourself with the fact that the calumny, which is being spread at your expense, does not dare to rise out of the depths of the town's society and, so to speak, is cringing in darkness and secrecy. But I am very pleased that while serving in your appointed position, nevertheless, you value simultaneously the importance of public opinion and the dignity of the position that you occupy in the capacity of an educator of youth, one of those to whose enlightened charge, we, the parents, entrust our most precious property, our children. As an official you have your superior in the person of your exceedingly respected headmaster, but as a member of society and a member of the gentry you always have the right to count on the . . . good offices of the marshal of the nobility in questions concerning your honor, your dignity as a person and as a member of the gentry."

Continuing to speak, Veriga stood up, and balancing himself with the fingers of his right hand on the edge of the desk, looked at Peredonov with that neutrally polite and attentive expression with which people look at a crowd as they pronounce their benevolently overbearing speeches. Peredonov stood up as well and crossing his hands over his stomach, stared sullenly at the carpet under his host's feet. Veriga was saying:

"I am happy that you have turned to me for the further reason that in our time it is particularly useful for the members of the leading class everywhere and always to remember above all that they are members of the gentry, to treasure their membership in this class, not only because of the rights, but also because of the obligations and honor of the gentry. The gentry in Russia, as you of course know, represent what is primarily a service class. Strictly speaking, all civil positions, with the exception of the lowest ones, of course, must be in the hands of the gentry. The presence of the *raznochintsy** in the civil service represents, of course, one of the reasons for the kind of undesirable manifestations which have disturbed your tranquillity. Calumny and defamation are the weapons of people of a lower order who have not been bred in the beneficial traditions of the gentry. But I hope that public opinion will speak out clearly and loudly in your favor and you can count entirely upon all my good offices in this regard."

"I humbly thank you, Your Excellency," Peredonov said. "I shall rely upon it."

Veriga smiled politely and did not sit down, thereby indicating that the conversation was concluded. Having uttered his speech, he suddenly had the feeling that it had ended up by being entirely irrelevant and that Peredonov was nothing other than some coward seeking a good position, haunting doorsteps in search of patronage. He dismissed Peredonov with a

*Intellectual déclassés not belonging to the gentry in the nineteenth century.

chilly condescension which he had become accustomed to feeling towards him for his dishonorable life.

Putting his coat on with the help of a lackey in the front hall and hearing the sounds of a piano coming from somewhere afar, Peredonov was thinking that arrogant people were living the aristocratic life in that home and that they had a high opinion of themselves. "He's aiming for a governorship," Peredonov thought in respectful and envious wonder.

On the stairs he was met by the two young sons of the marshal of the nobility who were returning from a walk with their tutor. Peredonov gave them a look of somber curiosity.

"They're real clean ones," he thought. "Not even a speck of dust in their ears. And so energetic and, likely, self-disciplined. They keep to the straight and narrow. No doubt," he thought, "they're never whipped."

Peredonov stared angrily after them as they quickly went upstairs, chatting happily. And the thing that amazed Peredonov was that their tutor treated them as his equals and didn't scowl and didn't shout at them.

When Peredonov returned home he found Varvara in the kitchen with a book in her hands, something that rarely happened. Varvara was reading a cookbook—the only kind of book that she ever opened. The book was an old and tattered one, in a black binding. Peredonov was struck by the black binding and it made him despondent.

"What are you reading, Varvara?" he asked angrily.

"What? You know what, a cookbook," Varvara replied. "I haven't got time to read silly things."

"Why a cookbook?" Peredonov asked with horror.

"What do you mean, why? So I'll be able to prepare your food, you're always so finicky," Varvara explained, grinning with self-satisfaction and arrogance.

"I'm not going to eat anything that comes out of a black book!" Peredonov declared resolutely, seized the book quickly out of Varvara's hands and carried it off to the bedroom.

"A black book! Just imagine, making dinners out of it!" he thought fearfully. "That was all he needed, namely, to have people trying to openly torment him with black book sorcery! It's essential to destroy this terrible book," he thought, paying no attention to Varvara's noisy grumbling.[9]

On Friday Peredonov was at the home of the president of the district rural council.

Everything in this house spoke of the desire to live simply and well and to work for the common good. The eye was struck by many objects that were reminiscent of country life and simplicity: an armchair with a shaft-bow for the back and axe-handles for arm rests; and inkstand in the form of a horseshoe; a bast shoe for an ashtray. There were a large number of measuring devices in the room—on the walls, tables and floor—with samples of various kinds of grain. And here and there were pieces of "famine bread": nasty blocks resembling peat moss. Drawings and models of agricultural implements hung in the living room. The study was piled high with shelves of books on agricultural and school matters. On the desk were papers, printed reports, boxes with cards of varying size. A lot of dust and not a single picture.

The host, Ivan Stepanovich Kirillov, seemingly, was very anxious on the one hand to be polite, or polite in the European manner, but on the other hand, not to ignore his dignified position as president in the district. He was an entirely strange and contradictory person, as though soldered of two halves. From his surroundings one could see that he worked hard and sensibly. But if you looked at the man himself, then it seemed that all this rural council activity was merely a pastime for him and he was only temporarily engaged in it, whereas his genuine concerns lay in some future direction where his eyes—energetic but seemingly lifeless with a pewter gleam—would focus from time to time. It was as though someone had removed his living soul and put it away on the shelf and then replaced it with a lifeless but agile dynamo.

He wasn't large in stature, but thin and youngish—so youngish and ruddy-faced that at times he looked like a boy who had pasted a beard on and had rather successfully adopted the ways of adults. His movements were precise and quick. Exchanging greetings, he would nimbly bow and shuffle his feet and slide about on the soles of his stylish boots. His clothing might have been called a kind of suit: a gray jacket, an unstarched loose shirt of linen with a turned down collar, a string-like blue tie, narrow trousers and gray socks. And his conversation, always impeccably courteous, seemed likewise ambiguous in nature: he might be talking away gravely—and suddenly he would have a childishly naive smile, a kind of boyish manner. But a moment later you would look—once again he had calmed down and assumed a dignified air. His wife, a quiet and grave woman who seemed older than her husband, came into the study several times while Peredonov was there and each time she would ask her husband for some specific information on district affairs.

Their own household affairs in town were in a confused state. People were constantly coming and going on business and constantly drinking tea. No sooner had he sat down then Peredonov too was brought a glass of lukewarm tea and a roll on a plate.

Another guest had been sitting there before Peredonov. Peredonov knew him. Indeed, who doesn't know whom in our town? Everyone knows one another. It's just that some have broken off acquaintanceships after a falling-out.

It was the rural council doctor, Georgiy Semyonovich Trepetov, a small man (even smaller than Kirillov) with a blotchy face that was pinched and insignificant. He wore blue spectacles and he was always looking down or into a corner as though he found it an effort to look at the person he was talking to. He was unusually honorable and never gave up a single kopeck of his for the good of someone else. He deeply despised everyone working in the civil service—he would still offer his hand on meeting, but he would stubbornly decline to take part in conversation. For this reason he had the reputation of being a lucid mind, as did Kirillov, although he knew little and was a poor doctor. He was always on the verge of living like the ordinary people and to that end he would observe the way peasants blew their noses, scratched the backs of their heads, wiped their lips with the palm of their hands, and he himself would sometimes imitate them in private. But he kept putting off the simple life of the people until the following year.

Here, too, Peredonov repeated all his usual complaints of recent days against town slander and the envious people who wanted to interfere with him getting his inspector's post. Kirillov at first felt flattered by this appeal. He exclaimed:

"Now do you see what a provincial milieu it is? I always said that the sole salvation for thinking people was to rally together and I am delighted that you have come to that very same conviction."

Trepetov gave a grudging and angry snort. Kirillov looked at him fearfully. Trepetov said scornfully:

"Thinking people!" and he snorted again.

Then, after a short silence, he said in a thin, grudging voice:

"I don't know how thinking people can serve such a musty classicism!"

Kirillov said irresolutely:

"But, Georgiy Semyonovich, you are not taking into account that not every person is in a position to choose his occupation."

Trepetov snorted contemptuously and thereby conclusively cut down the polite Kirillov. Then he plunged into a deep silence.

Kirillov turned to Peredonov. When he heard the latter speak about an inspector's post, Kirillov grew anxious. It seemed to him that Peredonov wanted to be the inspector in our district. But at the district rural council a proposal was forthcoming to establish the post of their own inspector of schools, who would be selected by the rural council and confirmed by the education authorities.

Then, inspector Bogdanov, who had the schools of three districts under his authority, would move to one of the neighboring towns and the schools in our district would be transferred to the new inspector. The members of the rural council already had their eye on a person for this post, an instructor from the teachers' seminary in the nearby town of Safata.

"I have patronage there," Peredonov said. "The only thing is that the headmaster and others, too, are up to some nasty tricks here. They're spreading all sorts of rubbish. So, in case there are any inquiries about me I just wanted to forewarn you that it's all nonsense what people are saying about me. Don't you believe these people."

Kirillov replied quickly and energetically:

"Ardalyon Borisych, I don't have the time to particularly involve myself in town relationships and rumors. I am up to my chin in work. If my wife didn't help me, I wouldn't know how to manage. I never go anywhere, see anyone, hear anything. But I am utterly certain that I have not heard all these things that people are saying about you, word of honor. I fully believe that all of this is nonsense. But the position doesn't depend on me alone."

"You might be asked," Peredonov said.

Kirillov looked at him in amazement and said:

"How could they not ask? Of course, they'll ask. But the thing is, we have in mind . . ."

At that moment Mrs. Kirillova appeared in the doorway and said:

"Ivan Stepanovich, just for a moment."

The husband left. Worriedly she said:

"I think that it's better not to tell this character that we have Krasilnikov in mind. This character seems suspicious to me. He could do something nasty to Krasilnikov."

"You think so?" Kirillov whispered quickly. "Yes, yes, it's likely. That wouldn't be nice."

He clutched his head. His wife looked at him with businesslike sympathy and said:

"Best of all is to say absolutely nothing to him about it, just as though there weren't any position."

"Yes, yes, you're right," Kirillov whispered. "But I have to run. It's awkward."

He ran into the study and there he started to shuffle his feet earnestly and to inundate Peredonov with polite words.

"So, if you could . . ." Peredonov began.

"Rest assured, rest assured, I shall bear it in mind," Kirillov said quickly. "We haven't completely decided on it yet, this question."

Peredonov didn't understand what question Kirillov was talking about and he had a fearful and melancholy feeling. Kirillov said:

"We are organizing a school network. We wrote for a specialist from Petersburg. We worked the whole summer. It cost us nine hundred roubles. An amazingly painstaking work. All the distances were calculated and all the school sites indicated."

In a detailed and protracted fashion Kirillov gave an account of the school network, that is, of the divison of the district into the kind of smaller sections where each section would have its own school that would not be far from any village. Peredonov understood nothing and became entangled by the tight thinking in the verbal loops of the network that Kirillov was spinning so energetically and dexterously before him.

Finally he said goodbye and left, with a melancholy feeling of hopelessness. In that home, he thought, no one wanted to understand him or even hear him out. The host was talking some kind of nonsense. Trepetov kept snorting for some reason, the wife came, wasted no time on formalities and then departed. Strange people were living in that house, Peredonov thought. A wasted day!

XI

ON THE SATURDAY Peredonov intended to go to the district chief of police. Although he wasn't a bigwig like the marshal of the nobility, Peredonov thought, nevertheless he could do more harm than all the rest; but if he wanted to, then he could also be a help with his testimonial before the authorities. The police was a serious business.

Peredonov took his official cap with its cockade out of the box. He had decided that he would wear only it from that day on. It was fine for the director to wear an ordinary hat—he was on good terms with the authorities. But Peredonov still had to get his inspector's post. He couldn't rely on patronage alone, he himself had to show his best side. That had been on his mind even a few days back, before he had embarked on his tour of the authorities, but it had always been his ordinary hat that had come to hand. But now Peredonov organized things differently. He flung the ordinary hat up on the stove—to be more certain that it would be harder to come by.

Varvara wasn't at home. Klavdiya was washing the floors in the rooms. Peredonov went into the kitchen to wash his hands. On the table he saw a package of blue paper and a few raisins had spilled out of it. It was a pound of raisins which had been bought for making tea buns (they were baked at home). Peredonov started to eat the raisins, just the way they were, unwashed and uncleaned, and he ate the entire pound quickly and greedily, standing by the table while looking around at the door so that Klavdiya didn't come in unexpectedly. Then he painstakingly rolled up the thick blue wrapper, carried it out into the front hall under his jacket and there he put it into his coat pocket so that once he was out on the street he could throw it away and thereby destroy the evidence.

He left. Klavdiya soon noticed the absence of the raisins, became frightened and started to search for them, but couldn't find them. Varvara returned, found out about the disappearance of the raisins and let loose with abuse against Klavdiya. She was certain that Klavdiya had eaten the raisins.

It was windy and quiet on the street. Only occasional clouds gathered. The puddles had dried up. The sky rejoiced pallidly. But Peredonov felt melancholy at heart.

Along the way he stopped by the tailor's to hurry him up. He wanted him to make as quickly as possible the new uniform that he had ordered two days before.

Passing by the church, Peredonov took off his cap and crossed himself three times, vehemently and vigorously, so that everyone who caught sight of the future inspector passing by the church might see. Earlier he had never done so, but now he had to be on his guard. Perhaps some spy was stealthily trailing him from behind, or someone was lurking behind a tree and observing.

The chief of police lived in one of the distant streets of the town. Peredonov ran into a policeman at the gates which were wide open. This was the kind of meeting which left him feeling despondent of late. In the courtyard several peasants were to be seen, but not the kind one saw everywhere. These were some kind of special, unusually peaceful and taciturn ones. It was muddy in the courtyard. Carts covered with bast matting stood around.

In the dark entry way Peredonov ran into yet another policeman, a short, emaciated man with a diligent but nevertheless despondent look about him. He was standing there motionlessly and holding a book in a black leather binding under his arm. A ragged barefoot girl came running out of a side door, pulled Peredonov's coat off and guided him into the sitting room, repeating several times:

"Please, Semyon Grigoryevich will be out in a moment."

The ceiling was low in the sitting room. It weighed down on Peredonov. The furniture was pressed tightly to the wall. Hemp matting lay on the floor. Both to the left and the right whispering and rustling could be heard through the walls. Pale women and scrofulous boys, all of them with hungry gleaming eyes, kept peeking out of doors. Sometimes questions and answers emerged more distinctly out of the whispering:

"I brought it . . ."

"Where should I take it?"

"Where would you like me to put it?"

"From Ermoshkin, Sidor Petrovich."

The chief of police soon emerged. He was buttoning up his uniform jacket and smiling sweetly.

"Forgive me for keeping you," he said, squeezing Peredonov's hand in his two large and clutching hands. "We had various visitors on business there. Our work is such that it won't tolerate procrastination."

Semyon Grigoryevich Minchukov, a tall solid man, dark-haired with sparse patches in the center of his head, held himself slightly stooped, his hands extended downwards with predatory fingers. He frequently smiled with the kind of expression as though he had just eaten something forbidden but pleasant and was now licking his lips. His lips were a brilliant red and thick, his nose was fleshy, his face lustful, zealous and stupid.

Peredonov was dismayed by everything he heard and saw here. He muttered disconnected words and while sitting in his chair tried to hold his cap so that the chief of police could see the cockade. Minchukov was sitting opposite him, on the other side of the table and his clutching hands were gently moving on his knees, clenching and unclenching.

"People are spreading goodness knows what gossip," Peredonov said. "Things that aren't true. I myself could make a denunciation. I haven't done anything of the sort, but I know what they've done. Only I don't want to. They say all kinds of rubbish behind my back and laugh to my face. You must agree yourself that in my situation it's a ticklish business. I have patronage, but they are playing nasty tricks. They are following me around for absolutely nothing, they're wasting their time but they're embarrassing me. Wherever you go everyone already knows all over the town. So I'm hoping that I will have your support in whatever the case might be."

"But of course, of course, for goodness sake, with the greatest pleasure," Minchukov said, pushing his wide palms forward. "Of course, we the police have to know if there is anything suspect or not about someone."

"I don't give a damn, of course," Peredonov said angrily. "Let them gossip, but I'm just afraid that they'll play dirty tricks on me at work. They're cunning. You don't see the kind of gossip that goes on there, even Rutilov for example. For all you know he could be undermining the State Treasury. And that's why he's trying to switch the blame to someone who's innocent."

At first Minchukov thought that Peredonov had been drinking and was just spinning tales. Then, after listening carefully he concluded that Peredonov was complaining about someone who was slandering him and was asking him to take some kind of action.

"The young people," Peredonov continued, thinking of Volodin, "think highly of themselves. They plot against others, but they themselves are not without blame. As you know, the young people get carried away. Some of them are even working as police and are poking their noses in there as well."

He talked about young people for a long while, but for some reason he didn't want to name Volodin. Peredonov mentioned the young people in the police just in case, so that Minchukov would understand that he possessed a few bits of unfavorable information in regard to the people serving in the police. Minchukov concluded that Peredonov was alluding to two young officials in the police force—they were young, always laughing and chasing after young ladies. Involuntarily, Minchukov felt infected by Peredonov's obvious fear and dismay.

"I shall investigate," he said worriedly, hesitated for a moment and again began to smile sweetly. "I have some young officials who are still wet behind the ears. Believe it or not, his mother made one of them stand in the corner, swear to God."

Peredonov gave a fitful laugh.

Meanwhile, Varvara was passing the time at Grushina's where she found out some staggering news.

"Varvara Dmitrievna, sweetheart," Grushina said hurriedly, no sooner had Varvara crossed the threshold of her house. "You'll just die when you hear the news I'm going to tell you."

"Well, what's the news?" Varvara asked with a smirk.

"No, just imagine the kind of base people there are in the world! The things they won't do in order to get what they want!"

"What's the matter?"

"Well, just you wait, I'll tell you."

But the cunning Grushina treated Varvara to coffee beforehand and then chased her kids out of the house, whereupon the eldest daughter turned stubborn and wouldn't go.

"Oh, you good-for-nothing scum!" Grushina screamed at her.

"You're scum yourself," the impudent daughter replied and stamped her feet at her mother.

Grushina grabbed her daughter by the hair and threw her out of the house into the yard and locked the door.

"The spoiled creature," she complained to Varvara. "It's nothing but trouble with these children. I'm alone and there's no one to manage them. They ought to have a father."

"If you got married, they'd have a father," Varvara said.

"You just don't know what'll come your way, Varvara Dmitrievna, sweetheart. Someone else might start to play the tyrant with them."

At that moment the daughter came running up from the street, threw a fistful of sand through the window and hit her mother all over her head and dress. Grushina stuck her head out the window and screamed:

"You scum, you, I'll thrash you, just you wait till you get home, I'll give it to you, you mangy scum!"

"You're scum yourself, a wicked old fool!" the daughter shouted on the street, jumping up and down on one foot and shaking her filthy little fists at her mother.

Grushina screamed at her daughter:

"Just you wait! You'll get it from me!"

And she closed the window. Then she sat down calmly as though nothing had happened and said:

"I wanted to tell you the news but I hardly know how. You, Varvara Dmitrievna, sweetheart, don't you get upset, they won't get away with it."

"What do you mean?" Varvara asked fearfully and the saucer filled with coffee started to tremble in her hands.

"You see, the other day a student, by the name of Pylnikov and supposedly from Ruban, entered directly into the fifth form because his aunt bought an estate in our district."

"I know," Varvara said. "I saw him pass by with his aunt, such a cute fellow, looks just like a girl and is always blushing."

"Varvara Dmitrievna, sweetheart, how could not he look like a girl—after all, he is really a young girl in disguise!"

"Come now!" Varvara exclaimed.

"They came up with the idea on purpose in order to catch Ardalyon Borisych," Grushina said hurriedly, waving her hands about and getting happily excited because she was passing on such important news. "You see, this young lady has a cousin who is an orphan and he was going to school in Ruban, so the mother of this young lady took him out of the gymnasium and using his papers the young lady has entered school here. And take note that he was put in lodgings where there aren't any other students. He's there alone so that everything would stay hugger-mugger, so they thought."

"But how did you find out?" Varvara asked mistrustfully.

"Varvara Dmitrievna, sweetheart, the ground has ears. Everything became suspicious immediately. All the boys act like boys, but this one just walks gingerly around as though on eggs. One look at the face and you'd think it ought to be a nice-looking lad, rosy-cheeked and big-chested. And so modest, as his classmates found out—barely say a word to him and he blushes. They tease him for being like a girl. Only they think they're doing it just to make fun of him and they don't know that it's true. And just imagine how cunning they are—not even the landlady knows anything."

"But how did you find out?" Varvara repeated.

"Varvara Dmitrievna, sweetheart, what don't I find out! I know everyone in the district. Really, everyone knows that they still have a boy living at home the same age as this one. Why didn't they send them both off to the gymnasium? They say that he was sick in the summer, so he has to recuperate for one year and then he'll go to the gymnasium. But that's all nonsense. The real boy is already in a gymnasium. And again, everyone knows that they had a young girl, but they said that she had gotten married and moved to the Caucasus. Once again they're lying, she did nothing of the sort and she's living here disguised as a boy."

"But why are they doing it?" Varvara asked.

"What do you mean, why?" Grushina said animatedly. "She'll snatch one of the teachers. We've got few enough bachelors, or any other men for that matter. Disguised as a boy she can even come to the apartment and there's hardly anything she couldn't do."

Varvara said fearfully:

"Such a cute girl."

"You're right there, a real picture of beauty," Grushina agreed. "She's only being modest now, but just you wait, she'll get used to it, let herself go and then she'll have everyone spinning here in town. And just imagine how cunning they are. No sooner did I find out about this business then I immediately tried to meet his landlady, or her landlady—you hardly know what to say any more."

"Phew, a real changeling, God forgive me!" Varvara said.

"I went to vespers in their parish on St. Pantaleimon's Day and she was very devout. I said to her, Olga Vasilyevna, why do you only have one boy from the gymnasium living with you now? It's not very profitable for you, I said. But she said, what do I need more for? There's a lot of bother with them. So I said, other years you always had two or three. But she said— just imagine, Varvara Dmitrievna—she said that they had made it a condition that Sashenka be the only one living with her. She said that they weren't poor people and they would pay more, otherwise they were afraid that he would be corrupted living with other boys. Who do they mean?"

"What sly foxes!" Varvara said maliciously. "What did you say to her, that this was a girl?"

"I said to her, look out, Olga Vasilyevna, they might have slipped you a girl instead of a boy."

"And what did she say?"

"Well, she thought that I was making a joke and she laughed. Then I said more seriously, Olga Vasilyevna, sweetheart, you know, really, people are saying that this is a girl. But she wouldn't believe it. Rubbish, she said, what kind of girl could it be. I'm not blind, you know . . ."

Varvara was struck by the story. She completely believed that it was all true and that a fresh assault from a different direction was being prepared against her future husband. She had to unmask the disguised girl as quickly as possible. They consulted together for a long while on how to do it, but for the time being they couldn't come up with any idea.

At home Varvara was even more upset over the disappearance of the raisins. When Peredonov returned home, Varvara hurriedly and excitedly told him that Klavdiya had done something with the pound of raisins and wouldn't admit it.

"And on top of it she made up the story," Varvara said in an irritated voice, "that perhaps it was the master who had eaten them. She said that he had gone into the kitchen for something when she was washing the floors and according to her had spent a long while there."

"It wasn't long at all," Peredonov said with a frown. "I only washed my hands and I didn't even see the raisins there."

"Klavdyushka, Klavdyushka!" Varvara shouted. "The master here says that he didn't even see the raisins and so it means that you had already hidden them by that time."

Klavdiya poked a reddened face, puffy from tears, out of the kitchen.

"I didn't take your raisins," she cried in a sobbing voice. "I'll pay you back for them, only I didn't take your raisins!"

"You'll pay it back, you certainly will!" Varvara said angrily. "I'm not obliged to feed you on raisins."

Peredonov guffawed and shouted:

"Piggy swiped a pound of raisins!"

"Bullies!" Klavdiya shouted and slammed the door.

At dinner Varvara couldn't restrain herself from passing on what she had heard about Pylnikov. She wasn't thinking of whether it would be harmful or beneficial to her, depending on how Peredonov reacted to it. She was simply talking out of spite.

Peredonov tried to recall Pylnikov, but for some reason he couldn't clearly imagine who the boy was. Up until then he had paid little attention to this new student and despised him because he was good-looking and clean, and furthermore because he acted modestly, studied well and was the youngest in age of all the students in the fifth form. But now Varvara's story ignited a lecherous curiosity in him. Immodest thoughts slowly began to stir in his murky head . . .

"I ought to go to vespers," he thought, "to have a look at this girl in disguise."

Suddenly Klavdiya came running in, and rejoicing, threw the crushed blue wrapper on the table and cried:

"You were blaming me for eating the raisins, and what's that? A lot I need your raisins."

Peredonov guessed what was up. He had forgotten to throw the wrapper out on the street and now Klavdiya had found it in the pocket of his coat.

"Damn it!" he exclaimed.

"What's that, where'd it come from?" Varvara cried.

"I found it in Ardalyon Borisych's pocket," Klavdiya replied maliciously. "He ate them himself and tried to put the blame on me. You know that Ardalyon has a big sweet tooth, but why blame others when he himself . . ."

"Well, that's a good one," Peredonov said angrily. You just keep lying. You put it in my pocket, I didn't take anything."

"Why should I do that? Really, God help you!" Klavdiya said distractedly.

"How dare you go sneaking about in his pockets!" Varvara replied. "Were you looking for money there?"

"I wasn't sneaking about his pockets," Klavdiya said rudely. "I took his coat to clean it, it was all muddy."

"And why did you go into his pockets?"

"It fell out of his pocket. Why should I go sneaking around in his pockets?" Klavdiy tried to justify herself.

"You're lying, piggy," Peredonov said.

"Why are you calling me a piggy, really, what tormentors they are!" Klavdiya cried. "To hell with you, I'll pay you back for your raisins and may you choke on them. You guzzled them yourself and I have to pay for them! Well I'll pay, apparently you don't have any conscience. There's no shame in your eyes, and still you call yourself a gentleman!"

Klavdiya went off into the kitchen, crying and cursing. Peredonov laughed fitfully and said:

"She's really got her back up."

"Let her pay for them," Varvara said. "If you let them get away with anything, they'll be prepared to gobble everything up, the greedy devils."

For a long while afterward they both teased Klavdiya with the fact that she had eaten a pound of raisins. The money for the raisins was deducted from her pay and all the guests were told about the raisins.

The cat, as though attracted by the shouting, came out of the kitchen, crept along the walls and crouched near Peredonov, peering at him with greedy and wicked eyes. Peredonov bent over to pick it up. The cat hissed ferociously, scratched Peredonov's hand, ran away and hid under the cupboard. It peeked out from there and its narrow green pupils glittered.

"Just like a changeling," Peredonov thought with fear.

Meanwhile, still thinking about Pylnikov, Varvara said:

"Instead of going to play billiards every evening, you ought to drop in on the students at their lodgings sometimes. They know that teachers rarely look in on them and they don't expect the inspector to come more than once a year, so all kinds of disgraceful things go on there, like card-playing and drunkenness. You ought to drop in on this girl in disguise. Go a little later when they're getting ready for bed. It wouldn't take much to catch her out or embarrass her."

Peredonov thought about it and guffawed.

"Varvara is a cunning rascal," he thought. "She knows a thing or two."

XII

PEREDONOV WENT OFF to vespers in the gymnasium church. There he stood behind the students and kept an attentive eye on how they behaved. Several of them, it seemed to him, were being naughty, poking each other, whispering and laughing. He took note of who they were and tried to memorize their names. There were a lot of them and he was annoyed with himself because he hadn't thought to take some paper and a pencil from home to write it down. He felt sad that the students were behaving themselves poorly and that no one was paying any attention to that although the headmaster and the inspector were both standing right there in the church with their wives and children.

In actual fact the students were standing there in a well-behaved and modest manner. Some were unconsciously making the sign of the cross, others were thinking about something unconnected with the church and yet others were praying assiduously. Very rarely did anyone whisper something to his neighbor, only two or three words without turning his head, and the other would reply just as briefly and quietly, or even with just a quick movement, a glance, a shrugging of shoulders or a smile. But these small movements, which went unnoticed by the senior class prefect, produced an illusion of extreme disorderliness on the anxiety-ridden, but dull sensibilities of Peredonov. Even in a calm state Peredonov, like all vulgar people, was incapable of precisely evaluating minor events. Either he did not notice them, or he exaggerated their significance. But now, when he was upset by expectations and fears, his sensibilities served him even more poorly and little by little before his very eyes all of reality was becoming enshrouded in a mist of repulsive and wicked illusions.

Besides, what had the students meant to Peredonov even earlier? Had they performed any other function than dragging pen and ink across paper and retelling in stilted language what at one time had been said in a human language! In all of his pedagogical activity Peredonov had sincerely not understood or thought about the fact that the students were just like people, just like adults. Only the bearded students at the gymnasium, with their awakening attraction to women, had suddenly become equals in his eyes.

Having stood in the back for a while and accumulated enough melancholy impressions, Peredonov moved forward to the middle rows. There on

the right, at the end of one of the rows, stood Sasha Pylnikov. He was praying modestly and frequently knelt down. Peredonov kept glancing at him
and it was particularly pleasant for him to see Sasha on his knees, like
someone being punished, and gazing directly in front towards the gleaming
altar doors with an anxious and pleading expression on his face, with
prayerfulness and sorrow in the dark eyes that were overshadowed with
long, almost bluish-black lashes. He was swarthy and shapely and this was
particularly noticeable when he was on his knees, calm and erect, as though
beneath someone's stern and observing eye. With his high and broad chest,
as far as Peredonov was concerned, he looked completely like a girl.

Peredonov firmly decided now to pay him a visit at his lodgings that
very evening after vespers.

People started to leave the church. They noticed that Peredonov was-
n't wearing his ordinary hat, as he always had done before, but rather his
official cap with the cockade. Rutilov asked with a laugh:

"What's this, Ardalyon Borisych, now you're showing off in fancy
dress with your cockade? That's what it means when a person is aiming for
an inspectorship."

"Will soldiers have to salute you now?" Valeriya asked with affected naiveté.

"Come now, what silliness!" Peredonov said angrily.

"You don't understand anything, Valerochka," Darya said. "Soldiers
have nothing to do with it! It's only from the gymnasium students that
Ardalyon Borisych will get much more respect than before."

Lyudmila laughed. Peredonov hastened to say his farewells to them in
order to escape their sarcasm.

It was still early to go to Pylnikov's and he didn't feel like going home.
Peredonov walked along the dark streets, trying to think of where he could
spend an hour. There were a lot of houses, lights were burning in many of
the windows and at times voices could be heard through opened windows.
People who were coming from church walked along the streets and there
was the sound of gates and doors being opened and closed. People who
were alien and hostile to Peredonov lived everywhere and some of them
even now might be plotting ill against him. Perhaps someone was already
wondering why Peredonov was alone at that late hour and where he was
going. It seemed to Peredonov that someone was trailing him and lurking
behind him. He felt melancholy. He hurried along without any purpose.

He was thinking that every house contained its deceased. And all the
people who had lived in these old houses about fifty years before, they had
all died. He could still remember some of the deceased.

"When a person dies, the house should be burned," Peredonov thought
with melancholy. "Otherwise it's very frightening."

Olga Vasilyevna Kokovkina, with whom the gymnasium student Sasha
Pylnikov lived, was the widow of a treasury official. Her husband had left her
a pension and a small house in which she had enough space that she was able
to set aside two or three rooms for lodgers. But she preferred gymnasium students. She was lucky in that she was always given the most modest students

who studied properly and finished the gymnasium. In other lodgings a significant portion were made up of those students who wandered from one
educational institution to the other and ended up as students with a smat-
tering of subjects.

Olga Vasilyevna, a skinny old woman, tall and erect, with a kind face
that she nevertheless tried to make appear stern, and Sasha Pylnikov, who
had been well-fed and sternly controlled by his aunt, were sitting at tea. It
was Sasha's turn today to provide the jam from the country and for that
reason he felt like the host and he was ceremoniously serving Olga
Vasilyevna and his dark eyes were gleaming.

There was a ring, and following that, Peredonov appeared in the dining room. Kokovkina was amazed at such a late visit.

"I've come to have a look at our student," he said. "To see how he's
getting on here."

Kokovkina tried to offer Peredonov some hospitality, but he refused. He
wanted them to finish their tea as quickly as possible so that he could be
alone with the student. They finished their tea and went to Sasha's room, but
Kokovkina wouldn't leave them alone and she kept chattering on endlessly.
Peredonov looked sullenly at Sasha, and the latter was bashfully silent.

"Nothing will come of this visit," Peredonov thought with annoyance.

The maid called Kokovkina for something. She left. With a melancholy
feeling Sasha watched her leave. His eyes lost their glitter and were partially screened by his eyelashes and it seemed as though these eyelashes,
overly long, cast a shadow over his entire face which was swarthy but had
suddenly turned pale. He felt awkward in the presence of this sullen person. Peredonov sat down beside him, put his arm clumsily around him and
without altering the impassive expression on his face, asked:

"Well, Sashenka, did you pray to God nicely?"

Sasha glanced at Peredonov with shame, and fear, then blushed and
was silent.

"Well? What about it? Did you?" Peredonov questioned.

"I did," Sasha said finally.

"Goodness, just look at the blush on those cheeks," Peredonov said.
"Admit it now, you're really a girl? A girl, you rascal!"

"No I'm not a girl," Sasha said and suddenly, getting angry with himself because of his bashfulness, he asked in a ringing voice: "Why do you
say I look like a girl? It's those students of yours at the gymnasium who've
thought it up in order to tease me because I'm afraid of bad words. I'm not
accustomed to saying them and I won't say them for anything. Besides why
should I say such vile things?"

"Will your mama punish you?" Peredonov asked.

"I don't have a mother," Sasha said. "Mama died a long time ago. I
have an aunt."

"Well then, will your aunt punish you?"

"Of course she would if I started to say vile things. What's so nice
about that?"

"But how will your aunt find out?"

"I don't want to say them myself," Sasha said calmly. "My aunt could hardly find out. Perhaps I would tell on myself."

"Who of your comrades says bad words?" Peredonov asked.

Sasha blushed again and was silent.

"Come now, tell me," Peredonov insisted. "You are obliged to tell me, you mustn't hide it."

"No one says them," Sasha said with embarrassment.

"But you yourself were just complaining."

"I wasn't complaining."

"Why are you denying it?" Peredonov said angrily.

Sasha felt caught in some kind of miserable trap. He said:

"I was just explaining to you why some of my comrades tease me like a girl. But I don't want to tattle on them."

"Now is that really the reason?" Peredonov asked spitefully.

"It's not nice," Sasha said with vexed grin.

"Well I'll tell the headmaster so that they'll make you tell," Peredonov said maliciously.

Sasha looked at Peredonov with angrily blazing eyes.

"No! Please don't tell, Ardalyon Borisych," he begged. And it was audible from the impetuous sound of his voice that he was making an effort to beg and that he wanted instead to shout words that were bold and threatening.

"No, I will tell him. Then you'll see what you get for covering up vile things. You ought to have complained right away. Just you wait, you'll get it."

Sasha stood up and started to twist his belt in his dismay. Kokovkina came.

"A fine one your goody-goody is, what can I say," Peredonov said spitefully.

Kokovkina was frightened. She went hastily up to Sasha, sat down beside him. Her legs always gave way in the midst of excitement. She asked timidly:

"But what is it, Ardalyon Borisych? What has he done?"

"Why don't you ask him," Peredonov replied with sullen spite.

"What is it, Sasha, what did you do wrong?" Kokovkina asked, touching Sasha's elbow.

"I don't know," Sasha said and burst into tears.

"But what is it, what's the matter with you that you're crying?" Kokovkina asked.

She laid her hands on the boy's shoulders, pulled him over towards herself and didn't notice that he felt awkward. He stood up, hunched over and covered his eyes with a handkerchief. Peredonov explained:

"They're teaching him bad words in the gymnasium, but he doesn't want to say who's doing it. He mustn't hide it. Otherwise he'll learn vile things himself and conceal the others."

"Oh, Sashenka, Sashenka, how could you do that! It's not possible! Aren't you ashamed!" Kokovkina said in dismay as she released Sasha.

"I didn't do anything," Sasha said, weeping. "I didn't do anything bad. They tease me because I can't say bad words."

"Who's saying bad words?" Peredonov asked again.

"No one is saying them," Sasha exclaimed desperately.

"You see how he's lying," Peredonov said. "He ought to be properly punished. He should be punished so that he'll reveal who is saying vile things, otherwise our gymnasium will be censured and we won't be able to do anything."

"But you must forgive him, Ardalyon Borisych!" Kokovkina said. "How can he tell on his comrades? They won't leave him in peace afterwards."

"He is obliged to tell," Peredonov said angrily. "It can only do him good. We will take measures to punish them."

"But they'll beat him up!" Kokovkina said uncertainly.

"They won't dare. If he's afraid then let him tell in secret."

"Well, Sashenka, tell him in secret. No one will find out that you did."

Sasha wept in silence. Kokovkina drew him to herself, embraced him and for a long while whispered something in his ear. He shook his head negatively.

"He doesn't want to," said Kokovkina.

"When he's reprimanded with a birch rod then he'll start to talk," Peredonov said fiercely. "Bring me a rod and I'll make him talk."

"Olga Vasilyevna, what for?" Sasha exclaimed.

Kokovkina stood up and embraced him.

"Enough bawling now," she said tenderly and sternly. "No one's going to touch you."

"As you like," Peredonov said. "But in that case I'll have to tell the headmaster. I was thinking it would be better for him to keep it within the family. Perhaps your little Sashenka is the rascal. We still don't know why they tease him like a girl. Perhaps it's for a different reason. Perhaps they're not the ones teaching him but he's the one who is perverting the others."

Peredonov left the room angrily. Kokovkina followed him out. She said reproachfully:

"Ardalyon Borisych, how can you upset the boy so much for goodness knows what! It's a good thing that he still doesn't understand what you're saying."

"Well, goodbye," Peredonov said angrily. "Only I will tell the headmaster. This must be investigated."

He left. Kokovkina went to console Sasha. Sasha was sitting sadly by they window and was looking at the starry sky. His dark eyes were already calm and strangely melancholy. Kokovkina silently caressed him on the head.

"I'm to blame myself," he said. "I let it slip why I was being teased and he kept on at me. He's the most vulgar one. None of the students like him."

The following day Peredonov and Varvara were finally moving to a new apartment. Ershova was standing in the gateway and exchanging furious insults with Varvara. Peredonov hid from her behind the carts.

They held a church service immediately in the new apartment. According to Peredonov's calculations it was essential to show that he was a religious man. During the service the fragrance of the incense made him dizzy and induced an obscure mood in him that was almost prayerful.

He was dismayed by one strange circumstance. A small creature of indeterminate profile came running out from somewhere: a small, gray spritely *nedotykomka*. It was tittering, quivering, and twirling around Peredonov. But when he reached his hand out to it, it quickly slipped away, ran off behind the door or under the cupboard, but a minute later it would reappear—and gray, faceless and spritely, it quivered and teased.

Finally, as the service was ending, Peredonov bethought himself and whispered a counter-spell. The *nedotykomka* started to hiss ever so softly, compressed itself into a small ball and rolled away behind the door. Peredonov sighed with relief.

"It would be nice if it rolled away for good. Maybe it's living in this apartment, somewhere under the floor and it'll start to come back again and tease me."

Peredonov had a cold and melancholy feeling.

"Why are there all these unclean spirits in the world?" he thought.

When the service was finished and when the guests had dispersed, Peredonov thought for a long while about where the *nedotykomka* could have hidden. Varvara went off to Grushina's, but Peredonov set out in search and started to rummage through her things.

"Maybe Varvara took it away in her pocket?" Peredonov thought. "Would it need much room? It could hide in her pocket and sit there until it was time to come out."

One of Varvara's dresses drew Peredonov's attention. It was all frills, bows and ribbons, as though it had been sewn on purpose in order to hide something. Peredonov examined it for a long while and then, using a knife, forcefully tore out the pocket after partially cutting it free, threw it into the stove and then started to rip and cut the entire dress into tiny pieces. Obscure and strange thoughts were roaming through his mind, and in his heart he had a feeling of melancholy hopelessness.

Varvara soon returned—Peredonov was still shredding up the remains of the dress. She thought that he was drunk and started to curse. Peredonov listened for a long while and then finally said:

"What are you baying at, you fool! Maybe you're carrying a devil around in your pocket. I have to look into what's going on here."

Varvara was stunned. Satisfied with the impression he had created, he hurried off to find his cap and set out to play billiards. Varvara ran out into the front hall and while Peredonov was putting on his coat, she shouted:

"Maybe it's you who's carrying a devil in your pocket, but there's no devil in mine. Where would I get your devil from? Maybe you want me to order you one from Holland!"*

*This is probably a reference to Peter the Great (1672–1725) who spent six months in Holland, learning about shipbuilding and European civilization which he later forcefully and autocratically introduced into Russia against serious opposition. For the traditionalists in Russia he was seen as the Antichrist.

The young official, Cherepnin, the same one about whom Vershina had told the story of how he had been peeking through the window, wanted to start courting Vershina after she became a widow. Vershina was not opposed to marrying a second time, but Cherepnin seemed too insignificant to her. Cherepnin became resentful. He happily yielded when Volodin tried to persuade him to smear tar over Vershina's gates.

He agreed, but later had afterthoughts. Suppose he was caught? It would be awkward, after all he was an official. He decided to hand the business over to others. Spending twenty-five kopecks to bribe two rowdy youths, he promised them a further fifteen kopecks each if they arranged it. And on one dark night the deed was done.

If someone in Vershina's house had opened the window after midnight, they would have heard in the street the light rustle of bare feet on the wooden sidewalk, a quiet whispering, some more soft noises as though someone were brushing the fence, then a gentle clattering, the quick thudding of the same feet going faster and faster, a distant burst of laughter, the alarmed barking of dogs.

But no one opened the window. And in the morning . . . The gate and the fence by the garden and the yard were criss-crossed with the yellowish brown traces of tar. Rude words were written in tar on the gate. Passers-by oh'ed and ah'ed and laughed. The word spread and the curious came.

Vershina was walking quickly about in the garden, smoking, smiling even more crookedly than usual and muttering angry words. Marta did not even come out of the house and was crying bitterly. The servant, Marya, was trying to wash the tar away and exchanged spiteful curses, with the curious people who were gawking, laughing and causing a ruckus.

On the very same day Cherepnin told Volodin who had done it. Volodin immediately passed it on to Peredonov. Both of them knew the two lads who were famous for their insolent pranks.

On his way to billiards, Peredonov dropped in on Vershina. It was cloudy. Vershina and Marta were sitting in the living room.

"Your gate was smeared with tar," Peredonov said.

Marta blushed. Vershina quickly told the story of how they had gotten up and saw that people were laughing at their fence and how Marya had been trying to wash the tar off the fence. Peredonov said:

"I know who did it."

Vershina gave Peredonov a startled look.

"But how did you find out?" she asked.

"I just found out."

"Who is it, tell me," Marta said angrily.

She had become quite unattractive because now her eyes were angry and tear-stained and her eyelids were red and puffy. Peredonov replied:

"I'll tell you, of course, that's why I came. These scoundrels have to be taught a lesson. Only you must promise that you won't tell anyone who told you."

"But why, Ardalyon Borisych?" Vershina asked in amazement.

Peredonov produced a significant silence and then he said by way of explanation:

"These are the kind of troublemakers who could bash your head in if they found out who betrayed them."

Vershina promised to keep quiet.

"And don't you tell that I was the one who told you," Peredonov turned to Marta.

"Fine, I won't tell," Marta quickly agreed because she wanted to find out the names of the guilty ones as soon as possible.

It seemed to her that they had to be subjected to a painful and shameful punishment.

"No, better you swear an oath," Peredonov said cautiously.

"Well, then, I swear to God that I won't tell anyone," Marta assured him. "Only tell me quickly."

Vladya was listening behind the door. He was glad that he had had the foresight not to go into the living room. He would not be forced to give his promise and he could tell whomever he wanted to. And he smiled with the happy thought that he would take revenge on Peredonov.

"Yesterday I was returning home along your street just after midnight," Peredonov related. "Suddenly I heard someone moving around near your gate. At first I thought that it was thieves. I tried to think what to do. Suddenly I heard them running and right in my direction. I crouched against the wall and they didn't see me, but I recognized them. One of them had a brush and the other a bucket. They were well-known scoundrels, the sons of the locksmith Avdeev. They were running along, and the one said to the other that they hadn't wasted the night, they had earned fifty-five kopecks. I wanted to grab one of them but I was afraid I might get my face smeared, and besides, I had a new coat on."

Peredonov had barely left when Vershina set out for the chief of police with her complaint.

Chief of police Minchukov sent a policeman for Avdeev and his sons.

The boys were bold when they arrived, they thought that they were suspected of previous pranks. Avdeev, a despondent, tall old man, was, on the contrary, completely convinced that his sons had once again committed some vile trick. The chief of police told Avdeev what his sons were accused of. Avdeev muttered:

"I can't manage them. Do what you want with them, I've already worn myself out thrashing them."

"It's none of our doing," declared Nil, the elder brother, a tousled boy with ginger hair.

"We get blamed for whatever anyone else does," said Ilya, the younger brother, also tousled but white-haired, in a whining voice." Just because we once played a trick, now it means we have to answer for everything."

Minchukov smiled sweetly, shook his head and said:

"Better you make a clean breast of it."

"There's nothing to confess," Nil said rudely.

"Nothing? What about the fifty-five kopecks someone gave you for the work, eh?"

Judging from the momentary dismay of the boys that they were guilty, Minchukov said to Vershina:

"Well it's obvious that they're the ones."

The boys began to deny it once more. They were taken off into the wood shed—to be whipped. They couldn't bear the pain and they admitted their guilt. But even though they confessed they weren't about to say who had given them the money to do it.

"We did it on our own."

They were whipped in turn, without hurrying, until they said that Cherepnin had bribed them. The boys were handed over to the father. The chief of police said to Vershina:

"Well, there you go, we've punished them, that is, the father has punished them, and you know who did it to you."

"I'm not going to let this Cherepnin off like that," Vershina said. "I'm going to bring him to court."

"I don't advise that, Natalya Afanasyevna," Minchukov said briefly. "Better to forget about it."

"How can you let these good-for-nothings get away with it? Not on your life!" Vershina exclaimed.

"The main thing is that there isn't any evidence," the chief of police said calmly.

"What do you mean, no evidence, if the boys admitted it themselves?"

"It doesn't matter that they've admitted it, but once they're in front of the court they'll deny it, they won't be giving them a whipping there."

"What do you mean, deny it? The policemen are witnesses," Vershina said with less conviction now.

"What kind of witnesses would they be? If you flay the skin off a fellow then he'll admit anything even if it isn't true. Of course they're scoundrels, they got what was coming to them, but you won't get anything out of them in court."

Minchukov smiled sweetly and gazed calmly at Vershina.

Vershina was very dissatisfied when she left the chief of police, but after thinking it over, she agreed that it would be difficult to convict Cherepnin and the only thing that could come of it would be unnecessary scandal and disgrace.

XIII

As evening set in Peredonov showed up at the headmaster's—to have a serious discussion.

The headmaster, Nikolai Vlasyevich Khripach, possessed a certain set of rules which applied to life so comfortably that it was not burdensome in the least to adhere to them. At work he calmly fulfilled everything that was required by the laws or the directions of the authorities, as well as the rules of a generally accepted moderate liberalism. For that reason, the authorities, parents and students were all equally satisfied with the headmaster. He was a stranger to dubious circumstances, indecisiveness and vacillations, and who needed them anyway? One could always find support either in a resolution of the pedagogical council or in the instructions of the authorities. He was just as correct and calm in his personal dealings. His external appearance revealed an air of good-naturedness and steadfastness. Of medium height, solid, agile, with energetic eyes and a confident manner of speaking, he seemed to be a person who had found a good position for himself and intended to do even better. A great many books stood on the shelves in his study. He was making excerpts out of them. When the excerpts had piled up to a sufficient degree, he would put them in order and render them in his own words—and thus, a text book would be composed, printed and sold out. Not the way the books of Ushinsky* or Evtushevsky** were sold out, but nevertheless they did quite well. Sometimes it was from foreign books that he would put together a compendium that was respected and which no one needed and it would be printed in a journal that was also respected and which no one needed as well. He had a lot of children and all of them, both boys and girls, had already manifested embryonic talents of the most diverse nature: one wrote verses, another sketched, yet another was having rapid success in music.

*Evtushevsky, Vasiliy Andrianovich (1836–1888). A Russian pedagogue and editor of the journal *Narodnaya shkola (Public School)*. Developed a methodology for teaching arithmetic and numbers. Author of widely distributed textbooks in the 1870's and 1880's.

**Ushinsky, Konstantin Dmitrievich (1824–1870). One of Russia's most famous pedagogues and one of the principal founders of pedagogical methodology in Russia's public school system. Author of numerous texts for beginners. These textbooks were used for many decades by millions of school children.

Peredonov said sullenly:

"You're always attacking me, Nikolai Vlasyevich. Perhaps people have been slandering me to you, but I haven't done anything of the sort."

"Excuse me," the headmaster interrupted, "I cannot comprehend what slander you are being so good as to indicate. In the administration of the gymnasium which has been entrusted to me, I am guided by my very own observations and I dare to hope that my official experience is sufficient to enable me to evaluate what I see and hear with the requisite precision, and, moreover, to maintain the attentive attitude to work that I adopt for myself as an invariable rule," Khripach said quickly and distinctly, and his voice had a dry clear ring to it like the crackling sound of zinc bars when they're being bent. "As far as my personal opinion of your is concerned, I still continue to think that distressing flaws are manifesting themselves in your official activity."

"Yes," Peredonov said sullenly, "you have gotten it into your head that I'm not good for anything, yet I am constantly concerned for the gymnasium."

Khripach raised his eyebrows in amazement and gave Peredonov a questioning look.

"You haven't noticed," Peredonov continued, "that a scandal could break out in our gymnasium. No one has noticed, only I have kept an eye out."

"What scandal?" Khripach asked with a dry chuckle and started to pace nimbly around the study. "You intrigue me although I must say frankly that I have little faith in the possibility of a scandal in our gymnasium."

"You see, you don't know whom you've recently accepted," Peredonov said with such malice that Khripach came to a halt and stared attentively at him.

"All the newly accepted students have been examined," he said drily. "Moreover, the ones accepted into the first form haven't been rejected by another gymnasium, whereas the single student who joined the fifth form came to us with the kind of recommendations that would exclude the possibility of any unflattering suppositions."

"Yes, only he shouldn't have been sent to us, but to another institution," Peredonov muttered sullenly, almost unwillingly.

"Explain yourself, Ardalyon Borisych, I beg you," Khripach said. "I hope that you are not wanting to say that Pylnikov ought to be sent to a colony for juvenile delinquents."

"No, this creature should have been sent to a boarding school where they don't teach classical languages," Peredonov said maliciously, and his eyes glittered with spite.

Khripach, sticking his hands into the pockets of his short smoking jacket, looked at Peredonov with extraordinary amazement.

"What kind of boarding school?" he asked. "Are you aware of what institutions have that kind of name? And if you are aware, then why were you determined to make such an indecent comparison?"

Khripach blushed deeply and his voice had an even drier and more distinct ring. At another time these signs of the headmaster's wrath would have caused Peredonov great dismay. But now he wasn't embarrassed.

"You all think that it's a boy," he said, screwing up his eyes sardonically, "but it's no boy, it's a girl, and some girl she is!"

Khripach gave a dry and brief laugh, almost an affected laugh that was clear and distinct—that was the way he always laughed.

"Ha-ha-ha!" he laughed distinctly, and when he finished laughing he sat down in his armchair and threw back his head as though dying from laughter. "You have astounded me, my respected Ardalyon Borisych! Ha-ha-ha! Be so kind as to tell me what you base your proposition on, if the premises which have led you to this conclusion are not a secret! Ha-ha-ha!"

Peredonov related everything that he had heard from Varvara and at the same time enlarged upon the bad qualities of Kokovkina. Khripach listened, bursting forth into a dry, distant laughter from time to time.

"My dear Ardalyon Borisych, your imagination is playing tricks on you," he said, stood up and clapped Peredonov on the arm. "Many of my esteemed colleagues, as is the case with myself, have their own children, we weren't born yesterday and do you really think that we could take a disguised girl for a boy?"

"If that's going to be your attitude, who'll be to blame if something happens?" Peredonov asked.

"Ha-ha-ha!" Khripach laughed. "What consequences are you afraid of?"

"There'll be depravity starting in the gymnasium," Peredonov said.

Khripach frowned and said:

"You're going too far. Everything that you've told me until now does not give me the least cause to share your suspicions."

That same evening Peredonov hastily made the rounds of all his colleagues, from the inspector to the class prefects and he told all of them that Pylnikov was a girl in disguise. Everyone laughed and they wouldn't believe him, but after he left they were overcome with doubt. Almost to a person the wives of the teachers believed it at once.

By the following morning many arrived at classes with the thought that perhaps Peredonov was right. They didn't say so openly, but they no longer argued with Peredonov and restricted themselves to indecisive and ambiguous responses. Each was afraid that he would be thought silly if he started to argue and then suddenly it transpired that it had been true. Many wanted to hear what the headmaster would say about it, but the headmaster, contrary to habit, did not leave his apartment at all on that day. He merely passed by, quite late for his one lesson that day in the sixth form, stayed on an extra five minutes there and then left directly for his own quarters without showing himself to anyone.

Finally, before the fourth lesson, the gray-headed teacher of religion and two other teachers went to the headmaster's study under the pretext of some business or other and the old fellow cautiously brought the conversation around to Pylnikov. But the headmaster laughed so confidently and innocently that all three were overwhelmed at once with the assurance that it was nothing but rubbish. Then the headmaster quickly switched to different topics, related the latest town news, complained of an extremely bad headache and said that, apparently, he would have to call the gymnasium doctor, Evgeniy Ivanovich. Then, in a very good-natured tone he told of how the lesson that day had made his headache even worse, because Peredonov had happened to be in the neighboring classroom and the students there for some reason were often laughing unusually loud. Laughing his dry laugh, Khripach said:

"Fate has been unkind to me this year, three times a week I have to sit beside a classroom where Ardalyon Borisych is teaching and just imagine, nothing but laughter and I do mean laughter. It would appear that Ardalyon Borisych is not a humorous person, but he really does seem to provoke constant glee!"

And without giving anyone the opportunity to say something in this regard, Khripach quickly switched to another topic.

In Peredonov's classes people had truly been laughing a great deal lately —and not because he enjoyed it. On the contrary, Peredonov was irritated by children's laughter. But he couldn't restrain himself from saying something superfluous or indecent. First he would tell a silly anecdote, then he would start to mildly tease someone. In a class one could always find those who were happy for the opportunity to create disorder, and they would produce a furious bout of laughter at every trick of Peredonov's.

Towards the end of the lessons Khripach sent for the doctor while he himself took his hat and went off into the garden which lay between the gymnasium and the bank of the river. The garden was extensive and shady. The young students loved it. They could run about without restriction during the recesses. For that reason the class prefects didn't like the garden. They were afraid that something would happen to the boys. But Khripach required the boys to be there during the recesses. He needed it for aesthetic reasons in his reports.

Passing along the corridor, Khripach stopped by the open door leading into the gymnastics room. He stood there for a while, his head lowered, and then entered. Everyone already knew from his cheerless face and slow walk that he had a headache.

The fifth form had gathered there for gymnastics. They were arranged in a single file and the teacher of gymnastics, a lieutenant from the local reserve battalion, was about to give the command for something, but seeing the headmaster, he went up to greet him. The headmaster shook his hand, gave a distracted look at the students and asked:

"Are you satisfied with them? How are they doing, are they trying hard? They're not getting too tired?"

In his heart the lieutenant deeply despised the students who, in his opinion, neither had nor ever could have any military bearing. If they had been cadets, then he would have said outright what he thought of them. But there was no point in telling the person upon whom his lessons depended what he thought of the bumpkins.

And smiling pleasantly with his thin lips and giving the director an amiable and cheerful look, he said:

"Oh, yes, they're fine lads."

The director took several steps along the front, turned towards the exit and suddenly stopped, as though he remembered something.

"What about our new student, are you satisfied with him? How is he doing, is he making an effort? He's not getting too tired?" he asked sluggishly with a frown and put his hand to his forehead.

For the sake of variety and thinking that after all it was a new student from elsewhere, the lieutenant said:

"A little listless and he quickly tires."

But the director wasn't listening to him any more and left the room.

Apparently the air outside did little to refresh Khripach. He returned after half an hour and once again, standing by the door for half a minute, dropped in on the lesson. Exercises were underway on the atheletic equipment. Two or three students, who weren't involved for the moment and who didn't notice the headmaster, were standing about leaning on the wall, making use of the fact that the lieutenant wasn't looking at them. Khripach went up to them.

"Ah, Pylnikov," he said. "Why are you leaning against the wall?"

Sasha turned a brilliant crimson, straightened up and was silent.

"If you're so tired, then maybe the gymnastics aren't good for you?" Khripach asked sternly.

"I'm to blame, I'm not tired," Sasha said fearfully.

"Take your choice," Khripach continued. "Either don't attend the gymnastics lessons, or . . . Anyway, drop in to see me after classes."

He quickly left and Sasha stood there, embarrassed and frightened.

"You're in for it!" his comrades said to him. "He'll lecture you till evening."

Khripach liked to deliver extended reprimands and more than anything else the students feared his invitations.

After classes Sasha timidly set out for the headmaster's study. Khripach invited him in immediately. He quickly approached Sasha as though he were rolling up to him on his short legs, leaned closely and said while peering attentively right into his eyes:

"Pylnikov, are the gymnastics lessons tiring you out in fact? You're a healthy enough boy to look at, but 'appearances can be deceiving'. You don't have any illness do you? Perhaps it's harmful for you to do gymnastics?"

"No, Nikolai Vlasyevich, I'm healthy," Sasha replied, blushing with embarrassment.

"Nevertheless," Khripach objected, "Alexei Alexeevich is complaining about your listlessness and about the fact that you quickly tire. I too noticed today at the lesson that you had a tired look. Or perhaps I was mistaken?"

Sasha didn't know where to avert his eyes from Khripach's penetrating gaze. He muttered distractedly;

"Excuse me, I won't do it again, it's just that I was being lazy standing there. I'm really healthy. I'll do my gymnastics diligently."

Suddenly, quite unexpectedly for himself, he started to cry.

"There you see," Khripach said. "Obviously you are tired. You're crying as though I had given you a stern reprimand. Calm down."

He laid a hand on Sasha's shoulder and said:

"I didn't summon you here to lecture you but to clarify . . . Never mind, just sit down, Pylnikov, I see that you're tired."

Sasha hastily wiped his damp eyes with a handkerchief and said:

"I'm not tired at all."

"Sit down, sit down," Khripach said and pushed a chair up to Sasha.

"Really, I'm not tired, Nikolai Vlasyevich," Sasha tried to assure him.

Khripach took him by the shoulders, sat him down, and then sat down opposite him and said:

"Let's have a calm talk, Pylnikov. You yourself can't know the genuine state of your health. You're a diligent boy and fine in all respects, therefore it's completely understandable to me that you wouldn't want to ask to be dismissed from gymnastics lessons. Incidentally, I have asked Evgeniy Ivanovich to come and see me today because I'm not feeling well. He can have a look at you while he's here. I hope that you don't have anything against it?"

Khripach glanced at his watch and without waiting for a response started to talk to Sasha about how he had spent the summer.

Evgeniy Ivanovich Surovtsev soon appeared. He was the gymnasium doctor, a small man, dark, spritely, who loved conversations on politics and the news. He didn't possess a great deal of expertise but he exercised an attentive attitude towards his patients, preferring diet and hygiene to medications and for that reason he was successful in his treatments.

Sasha was ordered to undress. Surovtsev examined him carefully and found no defect, but Khripach had been convinced that Sasha wasn't a girl. Even though he had been certain of that earlier, nevertheless he considered it useful so that if he had to respond to inquiries from the district authorities, the gymnasium doctor as a consequence would have the opportunity to certify the fact without any further examinations.

Dismissing Sasha, Khripach said to him affectionately:

"Now that we know that you're healthy, I'll tell Alexei Alexeevich that he's not to spare you."

Peredonov had no doubt that the discovery of a girl in one of the gymnasium students would bring the attention of the authorities to him and that, in addition to promotion, he would be given a medal. That encouraged him to keep a vigilant eye on the behavior of the students. Moreover, for a few days in a row the weather had been cloudy and cold and few people gathered for billiards. All that was left to do was to walk about the town and visit the students who were in lodgings as well as those who were living with their parents.

Peredonov selected parents who were less worldly. He would arrive, complain about the boy, he would be whipped—and Peredonov would be satisfied. That was how he complained most of all about Iosif Kramarenko to his father who owned a beer factory in the town. He said that Iosif was being naughty in church. The father believed him and punished his son. Subsequently the very same fate befell several more students. Peredonov didn't go to the ones who might have interceded on behalf of their sons— they might complain to the district authorities.

Every day he visited at least one student in his lodgings. There he acted in an authoritative fashion: he administered scoldings, gave orders and made threats. But the students who were in lodgings felt more independent and at times they teased Peredonov. However, Flavitskaya, an energetic woman who was tall and clear-voiced, painfully whipped her little lodger, Vladimir Bultyakov, at the request of Peredonov.

Peredonov told about his feats the following day in class. He didn't mention the names, but the victims gave themselves away with their embarrassment.

XIV

T HE RUMORS ABOUT Pylnikov being a girl in disguise spread quickly
through the town. The Rutilovs were among the first to find out.
Lyudmila, always curious, was constantly trying to see anything
new with her own eyes. She was consumed with a burning curiosity about
Pylnikov. Naturally she had to take a look at this masked rogue. She was
even acquainted with Kokovkina. And so, one day towards evening,
Lyudmila said to her sisters:

"I'm going to have a look at this girl."

"Busybody!" Darya shouted angrily.

"She's all dressed up," Valeriya noted, with a restrained snigger.

They were annoyed because they hadn't thought of going—it would be
too awkward for the three of them to go. Lyudmila had gotten more dressed
up than usual. She herself didn't know why. In any event she liked to get
dressed up and usually dressed in a more revealing fashion than her sisters:
there was more naked arm and shoulder, her skirt was shorter, the shoes
lighter, stockings thinner, more transparent and flesh-colored. At home she
liked to go around in just a skirt and barefoot, and to wear shoes without
any stockings. Moreover, her blouse and skirt were always too dressy.

The weather was cold and windy, fallen leaves were floating on rip-
pling puddles. Lyudmila walked quickly and she hardly felt cold at all
under her thick cloak.

Kokovkina and Sasha were drinking tea. Lyudmila took them in with
her perceptive eyes. There was nothing amiss, they were modestly drinking
their tea, eating rolls and chatting. Lyudmila exchanged kisses with the
landlady and said:

"I've come to you on a business matter, dear Olga Vasilyevna. But I'll
tell you later. In the meantime warm me up with some of your tea.
Goodness, just look at the lad sitting here with you!"

Sasha blushed and made an awkward bow. Kokovkina told her guest
Sasha's name. Lyudmila sat down at the table and started to give a lively
account of the news. The townsfolk loved to have her as a guest because she
knew everything and knew how to tell stories nicely and unpretentiously.
Kokovkina, a stay-at-home, was unabashedly happy to see her and greeted her

with warm hospitality. Lyudmila babbled away cheerfully, laughed, jumped up from her place to mimic someone and kept brushing against Sasha. She said:

"You must be bored, my dear, what are you doing sitting at home all the time with this sour little student. You ought to look in on us sometime."

"But how can I?" Kokovkina replied. "I'm too old to go out visiting."

"What do you mean, go out visiting!" Lyudmila objected affectionately. "You come and make yourself right at home and that's all there is to it. There's no need to swaddle this baby."

Sasha assumed an offended look and blushed.

"What a spoiled one he is!" Lyudmila said provocatively, and started to poke Sasha. "Come now, talk with your guests."

"He's still young," Kokovkina said. "He's my modest little boy."

Lyudmila looked at him with a grin and said:

"I'm modest too."

Sasha laughed and protested naively:

"That's a good one! Are you really modest?"

Lyudmila burst into laughter. Her laughter, as always, seemed to be fraught of a mirthfulness both sweet and sensuous. As she laughed she blushed deeply and her eyes assumed a roguishly guilty look and avoided her companions. Sasha was embarrassed, suddenly caught himself and started to justify himself:

"What I really wanted to say was that you're very lively and not modest and not that you're immodest."

But sensing that it wasn't being made as clear in his words as it might in writing, he grew confused and blushed.

"The impudent things he's saying!" Lyudmila cried, laughing and blushing. "It's simply delightful, that's what it is!"

"You've got my little Sasha all flustered," Kokovkina said, gazing affectionately both at Lyudmila and Sasha.

Bending in a feline motion Lyudmila stroked Sasha on the head. He burst into shy and ringing laughter, twisted away from under her hand and ran off to his room.

"Sweetheart, find someone to marry me," Lyudmila said immediately without any transition.

"Really, I'm no matchmaker!" Kokovkina replied with a smile. But it was apparent from her face that she would assume the role of matchmaker with pleasure.

"You can be a matchmaker now, can't you?" Lyudmila protested. "And aren't I a good enough bride? You won't have to be ashamed of finding a match for me."

Lyudmila put her hands on her hips and started to dance in front of the landlady.

"Just look at you!" Kokovkina said. "What a flirt you are."

Lyudmila said laughingly:

"Do it at least for the fun of it."

"What kind of husband do you want?" Kokovkina said with a smile.

"Let him have, yes, let him have brown hair, dearie, brown hair without fail," Lyudmila said quickly. "Dark brown hair. Dark like a pit. And here's a model for you: like your gymnasium student, with the same dark brows and languishing eyes and dark hair with a blue sheen, and ever so thick eyelashes, bluish-black eyelashes. You have a real handsome fellow here, truly, a handsome fellow! That's the kind I want."

Soon Lyudmila was ready to leave. It had already become dark. Sasha went to accompany her.

"Only until we find a cab driver!" Lyudmila grew boisterous once more and started to question Sasha.

"Well, now, are you learning all your lessons? Are you reading any books?"

"I'm reading books," Sasha replied. "I like to read."

"Andersen's fairy tales?"

"Hardly fairy tales, but all kinds of books, I like history and poetry."

"Well, well, poetry. And who is your favorite poet?" Lyudmila asked sternly.

"Nadson,* of course," Sasha replied with the deep conviction that precluded the possibility of any other answer.

"Well, well," Lyudmila said encouragingly. "I like Nadson too, but only in the morning, whereas in the evening, my dear, I like to get all dressed up. And what do you like to do?"

Sasha glanced at her with affectionate dark eyes—and they suddenly grew moist. He said softly:

"I like to cuddle."

"Oh you're an amorous one, you are," Lyudmila said and hugged him around the shoulders. "So you like to cuddle. And do you like to puddle about as well?"

Sasha giggled. Lyudmila questioned him:

"In nice warm water?"

"Both in warm and in cold," the boy said shamefully.

"And what kind of soap do you like?"

"Glycerin."

"And do you like syrup?"

Sasha laughed.

"You're a funny one! They're different things but you're saying words that sound the same. Only you won't fool me."

"As though I needed to fool you!" Lyudmila said, chuckling.

"I already know that you like to make fun of people."

"Where did you get that from?"

"Everybody says so," Sasha said.

"Do tell, what a slanderer he is!" Lyudmila said, pretending to be stern. Sasha blushed.

*Nadson, Semyon Yakovlevich (1862–1887). One of the leading poets representing social consciousness in Russian literature at the end of the 19th century. His emotional "civic idealism" was extremely popular among the liberal intelligentsia and he influenced youthful Russian idealists with his lamentations on social injustices.

"Well, there's a cab driver. Cab driver!" Lyudmila shouted.

"Cab driver!" Sasha cried as well.

With a clatter the driver rode up in his clumsy cab. Lyudmila told him where to go. He thought for a moment and then asked for forty kopecks. Lyudmila said:

"Come now, sweetheart, is it that far? You certainly don't know the way."

"How much will you pay?" the driver asked.

"Take either half of the whole."

Sasha laughed.

"A cheerful young lady," the driver said with a grin. "Add another five kopecks anyway."

"Thank you for accompanying me, my dear," Lyudmila said, firmly shaking Sasha's hand and then she climbed into the cab.

Sasha ran home, thinking cheerful thoughts about this cheerful girl.

A cheerful Lyudmila returned home, smiling and dreaming about something amusing. Her sisters were waiting for her. They were sitting in the dining room at the round table which was illuminated by a hanging lamp. A brown bottle with Copenhagen sherry-brandy stood on a cheerful white table cloth and the wrapping which had stuck to the edges of the bottle-neck glittered brightly. It was surrounded by plates with apples, nuts and halvah.

Darya was intoxicated. Red-faced, dishevelled, half-dressed, she was singing loudly. Lyudmila had already caught the second-to-last stanza of a familiar song.

> O where the dress, O where the pipes!
> He drags her naked to the heights.
> Fears exile shame, shame exiles fears.
> Our shepherdess bewails in tears:
> Forget the things you've seen!

Larisa was there as well, all dressed up, quietly and cheerfully eating an apple which she was slicing up with a knife and chuckling.

"Well, then," she asked, "did you see him?"

Darya fell silent and looked at Lyudmila. Valeriya leaned on an elbow, put out her little finger and tilted her head, mimicking Larisa with a smile. But she was slender, fragile and her smile was restless. Lyudmila poured some of the cherry-red liqueur into a glass and said:

"Nonsense! It's a lad, the genuine variety and very likeable. With dark brown hair and shining eyes and he's young and innocent."

And suddenly she burst into a ringing laughter. Gaping at her, all the sisters started to laugh.

"Well, what can you say, it's all that Peredonov rubbish," Darya said, waving her hand and then she grew thoughtful for a moment, leaning with her elbows on the table and her head bowed over. "Better to sing," she said and started up with a piercing loudness.

A strained, sullen fervor echoed in her wailings. If a corpse had been released from the grave for the sole purpose of singing, then that phantom would have sung in that manner. But the sisters had already long since grown accustomed to Darya's intoxicated bawling and from time to time they would join in with her, making their voices wail on purpose.

"Now she's really let loose with the howling," Lyudmila said with a snicker.

It wasn't that she didn't like the singing, but she would have preferred to give her account and have the sisters listen. Darya cried angrily, interrupting the song in the middle of a line:

"What do you care, I'm not bothering you!"

And starting exactly where she had left off, she began to sing once more. Larisa said affectionately:

"Let her sing."

Poor homeless thing am I,
Nowhere to stay I'll find, —

Darya sang in a wail, distorting the sounds and inserting syllables the way the simple folk singers did for greater sentimentality. It sounded something like this, for example: "Poor-o-poor ho-o-meless thing-oh, am I-I."

When she did it, the unaccented sounds were extended in a particularly unpleasant fashion. One had the extreme impression that this kind of singing could provoke a deathly melancholy in an unjaded person . . .

O, deathly melancholy, resounding over fields and villages, over the broad expanses of our native land! A melancholy embodied in a frenzied din, a melancholy that devours the living word in a corruptive flame, debasing what was once a living song to an insane wail! O, deathly melancholy! O, sweet old Russian song, or are you truly dying? . . .

Suddenly Darya leaped up, put her hands on her hips and started to screech out a merry ditty while she danced and snapped her fingers:

> Beat it, fellow, just beware,
> I can use my knife I swear;
> Robber's daughter proud to be,
> Peasants are no good to me;
> So you're handsome, what the hell,
> I'm to wed a tramp so swell.

Darya sang and danced and the motionless eyes in her face revolved with her gyrations like the revolutions of a dead moon. Lyudmila was laughing loudly and her heart palpitated gently and contracted from a combination of cheerful joy and the cherry-sweet, terrible sherry–brandy. Valeriya was laughing softly, a glassy ringing laugh, and looking enviously at her sisters: she would have liked to feel that kind of cheerfulness, but for some reason she couldn't. She was thinking that she was the final one, the "leftover" and for that reason she was the weak and unfortunate one. And she was laughing just as though she would burst into tears at any moment.

Larisa glanced at her, winked at her and suddenly Valeriya felt cheerful and full of fun. Larisa stood up, shook her shoulders—and in an instant all four sisters were whirling around in a frenzied celebration, suddenly seized by an infectious madness, bawling after Darya the stupid words of more and more ditties, each one more absurd and boisterous than the last. The sisters were young, attractive and their voices had a clear and wild ring to them—the witches on Bald Mountain would have been envious of their ritual dance.

All night long Lyudmila dreamt such sultry, African dreams! First she dreamt that she was lying in a stuffy overheated room and the blanket was slipping off her and baring her hot body—and there was a scaly, ringed serpent who had come crawling into her bedchamber and, raising itself, was creeping along the trunk and the branches of her beautiful legs . . .

Then she dreamt of a lake and a torrid summer evening, beneath the ponderous accumulation of threatening clouds—and there she was lying on the shore, naked, with a smooth golden crown on her head. There was a smell of tepid stagnant water and mire, and the grass wilting from the sultry heat. Over the water, dark and ominously calm, a white swan came swimming, strong, majestically grand. It beat its wings noisily against the water and with a loud hissing sound, drew nearer and embraced her—it grew dark and eerie . . .

It was Sasha's face in both the serpent and the swan bending over Lyudmila, a face that was almost bluish in its pallor, with dark, mysteriously sorrowful eyes. And the bluish-black eyelashes, jealously concealing their spellbinding gaze, sank heavily and frighteningly.

Then Lyudmila dreamt of a magnificent chamber with low, heavy vaults—and thronging with naked, strong and beautiful young boys. And the most beautiful of all was Sasha. She was sitting up high and the naked youths were taking turns whipping one another before her. And when they put Sasha down on the floor, facing Lyudmila, and were whipping him while he laughed and wept in a clear voice, she was laughing the way people laugh at times in their sleep when the heart starts to pound forcefully, laughing for a long while, unrestrainedly, with the laughter of self- obliviousness and death . . .

In the morning after all these dreams, Lyudmila felt that she was passionately in love with Sasha. Lyudmila was gripped by an impatient desire to see him, but she was annoyed to think that she would see him dressed. How stupid that little boys don't go around naked! Or at least barefoot, like the street urchins in the summer at whom Lyudmila loved to look because they were going around barefoot and at times with their legs left bare quite high.

"It's just as though it were shameful to have a body," Lyudmila thought, "so that even little boys hide it."

XV

VOLODIN ATTENDED THE Adamenkos' diligently for lessons. His dreams that the young lady would treat him to coffee were not realized. He was taken each time directly to the small room set aside for the manual work. Misha was usually already standing there in a gray canvas apron by the work bench, having prepared everything necessary for the lesson. He willingly did everything that Volodin asked him, but he did so without any real inclination. In order to work less, Misha tried to draw Volodin into conversation. Volodin wanted to be conscientious and wouldn't give in. He said:

"First of all, Mishenka, you be good enough to work for two hours and then afterwards if you are inclined, we'll have a discussion. Then you can talk as much as you wish, but now, uh-uh, because work comes first."

Misha sighed gently and set to work, but at the end of the lesson he showed no desire for discussion. He would say that he didn't have the time, that he had a lot to do. Sometimes Nadezhda would come to the lesson to have a look at how Misha was working. Misha noticed—and took advantage of it—that Volodin gave in more easily to conversation when she was around. However, Nadezhda, as soon as she would see that Misha wasn't working, would say to him:

"Misha, no laziness now!"

Then she herself would leave after saying to Volodin:

"Forgive me, I was bothering you. When I'm around he's the kind of lad that's not adverse to being lazy if he's given a free rein."

At first Volodin was dismayed by this kind of behavior from Nadezhda. Afterwards he thought that she was embarrassed to treat him to coffee because she was afraid that it might perhaps cause gossip. Then he concluded that she didn't have to come to the lessons at all, and yet she did come, and wasn't that because she was pleased to see Volodin? And Volodin construed it to be in his favor that Nadezhda had willingly agreed from the very first that Volodin should give lessons and she hadn't bargained over the price. Both Peredonov and Varvara had supported him in his thoughts.

"It's clear that she's in love with you," said Peredonov.

"And what other husband could she want!" Varvara added.

Volodin put on a modest face and rejoiced over his success.

Once Peredonov said to him:

"A prospective husband and here you're wearing a grubby tie."

"I'm not a prospective husband yet, Ardasha," Volodin answered discretely, nevertheless trembling all over from joy. "And I can always buy a new tie."

"Buy yourself a patterned one," Peredonov advised, "so that people will see that love is at work inside you."

"A red tie," Varvara said, "and the fancier the better, and a pin. You can buy a pin with a stone cheaply, and it'll be really chic."

Peredonov thought that perhaps Volodin didn't have enough money. Or that he would be too miserly and would buy the most ordinary black one. And that would be vile, thought Peredonov. Adamenko was a young lady of the world. If he went to her with a marriage proposal wearing any old tie, then she might be offended and refuse. Peredonov said:

"Why buy a cheap one? Pavlusha, you won enough for a tie from me. How much do I owe you, a rouble and forty kopecks?"

"You're right about the forty kopecks," Volodin said, baring his teeth and pulling a face. "Only it's not one rouble, but two."

Peredonov knew himself that it was two roubles, but he would have liked better to pay only one rouble. He said:

"You're lying, where do you get two roubles from?"

"Now Varvara Dmitrievna is a witness," Volodin assured him.

With a smirk Varvara said:

"Go on, pay him, Ardalyon Borisych, if you lost. And I do remember that it was two roubles and forty kopecks."

Peredonov thought the fact that Varvara was standing up for Volodin meant that she was switching to his side. He scowled, pulled the money out of his pouch and said:

"Well, alright, so it's two roubles and forty kopecks, it won't ruin me. You're a poor man, Pavlushka, so there you go, take it."

Volodin took the money, counted it, then put on an offended face, bowed his steep forehead, puffed out his lower lip and said in a bleating and reverberating voice:

"As you please, Ardalyon Borisych, you owed me the money and so you have to pay, but the fact that I'm poor, that simply has nothing to do with it. And I'm not asking anyone for bread, and you know that the only poor person is the devil who doesn't have any bread to eat, but since I am still eating bread, and even with butter on it, I am not poor."

And having totally consoled himself, he started to blush with joy that he had answered so successfully and he started to laugh, after unscrewing his lips.

Finally Peredonov and Volodin decided to go and make a marriage proposal. Both of them dressed up in their finest and had a solemn look that was more stupid than usual. Peredonov had put on a white neck scarf, while Volodin wore a gaudy tie that was red with green stripes.

Peredonov reasoned thus:

"I am going to make a marriage proposal, my role is a serious one and it's a distinguished circumstance, so I should be wearing a white tie, whereas you are the prospective husband, you have to show your passionate sentiments."

With tense solemnity they seated themselves: Peredonov on the divan, Volodin in an armchair. Nadezhda was looking at her guests in amazement. The guests chatted about the weather and about the news with the appearance of people who had come on delicate business and who didn't know how to get around to it. Finally, Peredonov coughed and said:

"Nadezhda Vasilyevna, we've come on business."

"On business," Volodin said as well, assuming an important expression and puffing out his lips.

"It concerns him," Peredonov said and pointed his thumb at Volodin.

"It concerns me," Volodin confirmed and also pointed his thumb at himself, at his chest.

Nadezhda smiled.

"Please," she said.

"I will speak for him," Peredonov said. "He's bashful and can't bring himself to do it for himself. But he is a worthy person, a nondrinker and kind. He doesn't earn much, but that doesn't mean a damn. Everyone needs something, some people need money and others need a person. Well, what are you so quiet for," he turned to Volodin, "say something."

Volodin bowed his head and declared in a trembling voice, bleating like a sheep:

"Of course I receive a small salary, but I 'll always have a piece of bread. Of course I was never at university, but I manage as God grant everyone, and I don't know of any faults in myself, and anyway, whoever wants to can judge for himself. Well, really, I'm satisfied with myself."

He spread his hands, bowed his head just as though he were getting ready to butt, and fell silent.

"So there it is, " Peredonov said. "He's a young man, he shouldn't have to live this way. He should get married. In general, it's better for a married man."

"If the wife is of like mind, then what could be better?" Volodin confirmed.

"And you," Peredonov continued, "are a young girl. You ought to get married as well."

Behind the door they could hear a soft rustling, short muffled sounds as though someone were sighing or laughing with their mouth closed. Nadezhda looked sternly at the door and said coldly:

"You are overly concerned about me,"—with a stress of annoyance on the word "overly."

"You don't need a rich husband," Peredonov said. " You're rich yourself. You need the kind of man who will love you and oblige you in everything. And you know such a man, as you may have guessed. He's not indifferent to you. Perhaps you feel the same towards him. So here you are, I've got a buyer and you've got the goods. That is, you yourself are the goods."

Nadezhda blushed and bit her lips to restrain herself from laughing.

The same sounds continued to come from behind the door. Volodin dropped his eyes modestly. It seemed to him that everything was going just fine.

"What goods?" Nadezhda asked cautiously. "Forgive me, I don't understand."

"Come, how can you not understand!" Peredonov said mistrustfully. "Well, I'll say it straight: Pavel Vasilyevich is asking for your hand and heart. And I am asking on his behalf."

Behind the door something fell on the floor and was rolling about, snorting and sighing. Turning red from restrained laughter, Nadezhda regarded her guests. Volodin's proposal seemed to her to be a ridiculous impertinence.

"Yes," Volodin said, "Nadezhda Vasilyevna, I am asking for your hand and your heart."

He blushed, stood up, scraped his foot forcefully over the carpet, bowed and quickly sat down. Then he stood up again, put his hand to his heart and said with a touching smile directed at the young lady:

"Nadezhda Vasilyevna, allow me to explain myself. Since I love you even a great deal, then wouldn't you really like to be of like mind?"

He dashed forward, knelt down in front of Nadezhda and kissed her hand.

"Nadezhda Vasilyevna, believe me! I swear it!" he exclaimed, raised his hand upwards and with full force struck himself in the chest with it so that a hollow sound echoed for a long distance.

"Really, now, please stand up!" Nadezhda said in embarrassment. "Why all this?"

Volodin stood up and with an offended expression returned to his place. There he pressed both hands to his chest and again exclaimed:

"Nadezhda Vasilyevna, believe me! Till the day I die, with all my heart."

"Forgive me," Nadezhda said. "Truly, I can't. I must raise my brother and that's him crying behind the door."

"What do you mean, raise your brother!" Volodin said, offended and puffing out his lips. "I don't believe this would interfere."

"No, in any case, it concerns him," Nadezhda said, hurriedly getting up. "I have to ask him. Wait."

She nimbly ran out of the sitting room, her bright yellow dress rustling, grabbed Misha by the shoulder behind the door, ran with him to his room and there, standing by the door, panting from running and from suppressed laughter, she said in a fitful voice:

"It's quite , quite useless to ask you not to eavesdrop. Is it really essential to seek recourse to the sternest measures?"

Misha, embracing her around the waist and pressing his head to her, was roaring, shaking with laughter and from the attempt to suppress it. His sister shoved Misha into his room, sat down on a chair by the door and started to laugh.

"Did you hear what he's come up with, your Pavel Vasilyevich?" she asked. "Come with me into the sitting room and don't you dare laugh. I'm going to ask you in front of them and don't you dare agree. Understand?"

"Ugh!" Misha lowed and stuck the end of a handkerchief into his mouth so he wouldn't laugh—something which didn't help much anyway.

"Cover your eyes with the handkerchief if you feel like laughing," his sister advised and again she took him by the shoulder into the sitting room.

There she sat him down in an armchair while she herself took a place on a chair next to him. Volodin had an offended look, his head was bowed like that of a sheep.

"Just look," Nadezhda said, pointing to her brother, "I've barely wiped his tears away, the poor boy! I'm like a mother to him and suddenly he thinks that I'm going to leave him."

Misha covered his face with the handkerchief. His whole body was shaking. To hide his laughter he was producing long wailing sounds:

"Boo-hoo, boo-hoo."

Nadezhda put her arms around him and pinched him surreptitiously on the arms and said:

"Now, don't cry, my dear, don't cry."

It was so unexpectedly painful for Misha that tears came to his eyes. He lowered the handkerchief and looked angrily at his sister.

"What if suddenly," thought Peredonov, "the boy gets really angry and starts to bite. They say that people's spittle is poisonous."

He moved closer to Volodin so as to hide behind him in the event of danger. Nadezhda said to her brother:

"Pavel Vasilyevich is asking for my hand."

"Your hand and heart," Peredonov added.

"And your heart," Volodin said modestly but with dignity.

Misha covered himself with the handkerchief and sobbing with suppressed laughter said:

"No, don't marry him, what'll happen to me if you do?"

Volodin spoke in a voice that reverberated with offence and anxiety:

"Nadezhda Vasilyevna, I am amazed that you are asking for permission from your brother, who, moreover, is pleased to be a boy. Even if he were pleased to be a grown up youth, you could decide for yourself even in that event. But now that you are asking his permission, Nadezhda Vasilyevna, well, that amazes me very much and even stuns me."

"Asking permission from young boys, now I find that ridiculous," Peredonov said sullenly.

"But whom am I to ask permission of? It makes no difference to my aunt, but then I have to raise him, so how can I marry you? Perhaps you'll start to treat him cruelly. Isn't that true, Misha, you're afraid of the cruel things he'll do?"

"No, Nadya," Misha said, peeking out with one eye from under his handkerchief. "I'm not afraid of the cruel things he'll do, he's not like that! But I am afraid that Pavel Vasilyevich will spoil me and won't let you make me stand in the corner."

"Believe me, Nadezhda Vasilyevna," Volodin said, pressing his hands to his heart, "I won't spoil Mishenka. I don't believe in spoiling a boy! He'll be fed, dressed and shoed, but spoiled—uh-uh. I can also make him stand in the corner but I'd far from spoil him. I could even do more. Since you are a girl, that is, a young lady, then of course it's not convenient for you, but I could handle the rod."

"Both of them will make me stand in the corner," Misha said in a whining voice, once more covering his face with the handkerchief. "That's the kind of people you are, and the rod on top of it. No. That's no good to me. No, Nadya, don't you dare marry him!"

"Well, there you are, you heard him, I definitely can't," Nadezhda said.

"It seems very strange to me, Nadezhda Vasilyevna, that you're acting in this manner," Volodin said. "I am greatly disposed to you and one might even say passionately so, whereas, among other things, you are doing it because of your brother. If you're doing it now because of your brother, another one will be pleased to do so because of a cousin, a third because of a nephew, and there would even be someone doing it for some relative or other, and in that way no one would ever get married, with the result that the human race would come to a complete end."

"Don't be worried about that, Pavel Vasilyevich," Nadezhda said. "For the time being the world isn't being threatened by that kind of danger. I do not want to get married without Misha's consent, and he, as you heard, does not agree. And it's understandable, you're promising to give him a whipping right off. You might give me a beating as well."

"For goodness sake, Nadezhda Vasilyevna, do you really think that I would allow myself that kind of ignorance!" Volodin exclaimed in despair.

Nadezhda smiled.

"I myself do not have any wish to get married," she said.

"Perhaps you want to become a nun?" Volodin asked in an offended voice.

"Join the Tolstoyans and their sect," Peredonov added, "and manure the ground."

"Why do I have to go anywhere?" Nadezhda asked sternly, getting up from her spot. "I like it just fine here."

Volodin also got up, puffed out his lips offendedly and said:

"After this, if Mishenka displays those kind of feelings towards me, and if things turn out like this when you ask him, then I ought to decline to do the lessons because how can I come now if Mishenka feels like that towards me?"

"But why ever for?" Nadezhda protested. "That's something completely separate."

Peredonov thought that they ought to keep trying to persuade the young lady—perhaps she might agree. He said to her gloomily:

"Nadezhda Vasilyevna, now just think it over well. Why are you acting without rhyme or reason? He's a fine fellow. He's my friend."

"No," Nadezhda said. "There's nothing to think about! I thank Pavel Vasilyevich very much for the honor, but I can't."

Peredonov glanced angrily at Volodin and stood up. He thought that

Volodin was a fool. He wasn't even capable of making the young lady fall in love with him.

Volodin was standing by his chair, his head downcast. He asked in a reproachful voice:

"So that means it's final, Nadezhda Vasilyevna? E-ech! A fellow loved a girl but she didn't love him. God's my witness! Well, then, I'll have a cry and that's that."

"You're scorning a fine fellow, and who knows the kind that might turn up next," Peredonov said insistently.

"E-ech!" Volodin exclaimed once more and was about to head for the door. But suddenly he decided to be magnanimous and returned—to offer his hand by way of farewell to both the young lady and even that offender, Misha.

Out on the street Peredonov was grumbling angrily. Volodin was discussing it the whole way in an offended squealing voice just as though he were bleating.

"Why did you give up the lessons?" Peredonov grumbled. "A real rich man!"

"Ardalyon Borisych, I merely said that if such was the case then I ought to give them up, but she was pleased to say that it wasn't necessary to do so, and since I was pleased not to answer, then it ended up with her begging me. So now it depends upon me: if I wish to, I can refuse; if I wish to, I can continue."

"Why refuse?" Peredonov said. "Just continue as though nothing had happened."

"He may as well make the best of it there," Peredonov thought. "He'll be less envious."

There was a melancholy feeling in Peredonov's heart. Volodin still wasn't fixed up—he'd better keep an eye on both of them so that Volodin wouldn't go and conspire with Varvara. What was more, Adamenko might be angry with him because he had tried to propose Volodin as a husband. She had relatives in Petersburg. She might write them and it could do him harm.

And the weather was unpleasant. The sky was frowning, crows were flying about and cawing. They were cawing right over Peredonov's head, just as though they were teasing him and prophesying fresh and even more terrible troubles. Peredonov wrapped his neck up in his scarf and thought that it wouldn't be difficult to catch a cold in that kind of weather.

"What kind of plant is that, Pavlushka?" he asked, showing Volodin a plant with berries by the fence in someone's garden.

"That's deadly nightshade, Ardasha," Volodin replied mournfully.

There were a lot of plants like that in their own garden, Peredonov recalled. And what a terrible name they had! Perhaps they were poisonous. Suppose Varvara took them, broke off an entire bunch, brewed them up instead of tea and poisoned him, yes, poisoned him when the paper came so that Volodin could take his place. Perhaps they had already agreed to do so. It was hardly a coincidence that Volodin knew what the plant was called.

Volodin said:

"God's her judge! Why did she have to offend me? She's expecting an aristocrat, but she doesn't realize that there are all kinds of aristocrats and she'll have her share of troubles with someone else. But a simple fine fellow might be able to make her happy. Well, I'm going to church, I'll light a candle for her health and I'll pray that God grant her a drunkard for a husband so that he'll beat her, so that he'll squander his money and make a beggar out of her. Then she'll remember me, but it'll be too late by then. She'll be wiping away her tears with her fist and saying: 'What a fool I was that I turned Pavel Vasilyevich down, no one would have beaten me, he was a fine man.'"

Moved by his own words, Volodin's eyes filled with tears and he wiped the tears from his bulging, sheeplike eyes with his hands.

"You ought to break her windows at night," Peredonov advised.

"Well, God help her," Volodin said sorrowfully. "Suppose I get caught. No, but what a boy he is! My goodness gracious, what did I do to him to make him want to harm me? Wasn't I trying to help him, but just look, if you please, at how he was plotting against me. What kind of a child is that, what will become of him, my goodness, tell me then?"

"Yes," Peredonov said angrily. "You can't even manage with a little boy. E-ech! Some prospective husband you are!"

"Come now," Volodin protested. "Of course I'm a prospective husband. I'll find another. She shouldn't think that anyone's going to shed tears over her."

"E-ech, some prospective husband!" Peredonov teased him. "You even put a necktie on. How did you think you were going to get into society lane with that ugly mug of yours? Some prospective husband!"

"Well, I am a prospective husband, whereas you, Ardasha, are the marriage-broker," Volodin said soberly. "You yourself gave me reason to hope, but you were incapable of making a successful match. E-ech, some marriage-broker, you are!"

And they started to tease each other diligently, squabbling for a long while with the appearance of people who might have been consulting over a business matter.

After she saw her guests out, Nadezhda returned to the sitting room. Misha was lying on the divan and laughing. His sister pulled him off the divan by the shoulder and said:

"And you have forgotten that you are not supposed to eavesdrop."

She raised her hands and wanted to join her baby fingers together, but suddenly she started to laugh and the baby fingers never joined. Misha rushed to her—they embraced and laughed for a long while.

"Nevertheless," she said, "into the corner for eavesdropping."

"Don't," Misha said, "I saved you from a prospective husband and you ought to be grateful to me."

"Who saved whom! You heard how they were getting ready to whip you with the rod. Off you go into the corner."

"It'd be better if I stood here like this for a while," Misha said.

He got down on his knees at his sister's feet and laid his head on her knees. She cuddled and tickled him. Misha laughed, crawling about the floor on his knees. Suddenly the sister pushed him away and changed seats to the divan. Misha was left alone. He stood for a while on his knees, looking questioningly at his sister. She seated herself more comfortably, took a book as though she were going to read, but kept looking at her brother.

"Well, I'm tired now," he said plaintively.

"I'm not keeping you, you did it yourself," his sister said, smiling from behind her book.

"Well, I've been punished now, let me go," Misha begged.

"Was I the one who made you get down on your knees?" Nadezhda asked in a voice that feigned indifference. "Why are you pestering me!"

"I won't get up until you forgive me."

Nadezhda laughed, put her book aside and pulled Misha to herself by the shoulder. He shrieked and rushed to embrace her, exclaiming:

"Pavlusha's fiancée!"

XVI

T HE DARK-EYED BOY filled all of Lyudmila's thoughts. She frequently talked about him with her own family and with acquaintances, at times quite irrelevantly. She saw him in her dreams almost every night, sometimes modest and ordinary, but more frequently in some wild or magical setting. The stories of these dreams became quite a habit with her so that soon the other sisters themselves started to ask her first thing in the morning how she had dreamt of Sasha that night. Her daydreams about him occupied all her spare time.

On Sunday Lyudmila persuaded her sisters to invite Kokovkina over after mass and to keep her there as long as possible. She wanted to get Sasha alone at home. She didn't go to church herself. She instructed her sisters:

"Tell her that I slept in."

The sisters laughed at her plot but, of course, they agreed. They lived together very amiably. And it suited them just fine: Lyudmila would be busying herself with a young boy, thus she'd be leaving the real prospective husbands for them. They did as they promised and invited Kokovkina over after mass.

Meanwhile, Lyudmila got herself ready to go. She had dressed up in a cheerful and attractive fashion, perfumed herself with a soft, delicate Atkinson syringe, put a small atomizer and an unopened bottle of perfume into a beaded bag and concealed herself by the window behind the curtain in the sitting room, so that from this place of ambush she could see in time whether Kokovkina was coming. She had thought of taking the perfume with her earlier—to perfume the gymnasium student so that he wouldn't smell of his repulsive Latin, ink and boyishness. Lyudmila loved perfume, ordered it from St. Petersburg and used up a great deal of it. She loved aromatic flowers. Her room was always fragrant with something: flowers, perfume, pine, fresh branches of birch in the springtime.

There were her sisters and Kokovkina was with them. Lyudmila ran joyfully through the kitchen, across the orchard, through the gate and along the alleyway so that she wouldn't come face to face with Kokovkina. She was smiling cheerfully, walking quickly towards Kokovkina's house and playfully twirling her white bag and white umbrella. The warm autumn day made her happy and it seemed as though she were bearing her own characteristic spirit of cheerfulness with herself and spreading it all around.

At Kokovkina's the servant told her that the lady was not at home. Lyudmila laughed noisily and joked with the red-cheeked girl who had opened the door for her.

"Maybe you're fooling me," she said. "Maybe your mistress is hiding from me."

"Hee-hee, why would she be hiding!" the servant answered with a laugh. "Go and take a look for yourself in the rooms if you don't believe me."

Lyudmila peeked into the sitting room and cried out playfully:

"Is anyone alive here? Aha, the student!"

Sasha had glanced out of his room, caught sight of Lyudmila and was overjoyed, and Lyudmila grew even more cheerful at the sight of his joyful eyes. She asked:

"But where is Olga Vasilyevna?"

"She's not home," Sasha replied. She hasn't come back yet. She went somewhere from church. When I got back she wasn't here yet."

Lyudmila pretended that she was surprised. She waved her umbrella and said with annoyance:

"Really, but everyone has come home from church. Everyone is sitting at home, but, how do you like that, there's no one here. Is it you, my young classman, who causes such a ruckus that the old lady can't sit at home?"

Sasha smiled silently. Lyudmila's voice and Lyudmila's ringing laughter made him happy. He was trying to think up some way whereby he could cleverly volunteer to accompany her home, so that he could spend at least a few minutes more with her, to look at her and listen to her.

But Lyudmila had no intentions of going. She gave Sasha a crafty grin and said:

"Well, aren't you going to ask me to sit down a while, my dear young fellow? I say, I am tired! Let me have a little rest at least."

Chuckling, she went into the sitting room, caressing Sasha with her quick, tender eyes. Sasha was embarrassed, blushed and rejoiced—she would be with him for a while!

"Do you want me to atomize you?" Lyudmila asked in a lively tone. "Do you want me to?"

"You're a fine one!" Sasha said. "Right away you want to atomize me! What did I do to deserve such cruelty?"

Lyudmila burst into ringing laughter and threw herself against the back of the chair.

Atomize!" she exclaimed. "Silly! You misunderstood me. I want to atomize you with perfume."

Sasha said with amusement:

"Ah, with perfume! Well, that's a different matter."

Lyudmila took the atomizer out of her purse, and twirled a handsome vessel of dark-red and gold-patterned glass with a gutta-percha bulb and bronze fittings in front of Sasha's eyes, and said:

"You see, yesterday I bought a new atomizer and I went and forgot it in my bag."

Then she pulled out a large bottle of perfume with a dark, variegated label—Pao-Rosa by Guerlain of Paris. Sasha said:

"What a deep bag you have!"

Lyudmila replied cheerfully:

"Well, don't expect anything more, I didn't bring you any spice cakes."

"Spice cakes," Sasha repeated with amusement.

He watched with curiosity when Lyudmila uncorked the perfume and asked:

"How are you going to pour it in there without a funnel?"

Lyudmila said cheerfully:

"You'll give me a funnel."

"But I don't have one," Sasha said with dismay.

"As you like, but you'll still give me a funnel," Lyudmila insisted with a chuckle.

"I'd get one from Malanya, but she uses it for kerosene," Sasha said.

Lyudmila burst into cheerful laughter.

"Ah, what a slow-witted young fellow you are! Give me a piece of paper, if you don't mind—and there's our funnel."

"Ah,of course!" Sasha exclaimed joyfully. "We can roll one out of paper. I'll bring some right away."

Sasha ran off into his room.

"Will it do from a notebook?" he shouted from there.

"It doesn't matter," Lyudmila answered cheerfully. "Even tear it out of a school book, from your Latin Grammar, I don't mind."

Sasha laughed and shouted:

"No, I'd better take it from a notebook."

He found a clean notebook, tore out the middle sheet and was about to run into the sitting room, but Lyudmila was already standing in the doorway.

"May I come into the host's room?" she asked playfully.

"Yes, please do!" Sasha cried cheerfully.

Lyudmila sat down at his table, rolled a funnel out of paper and with a businesslike face started to pour the perfume from the bottle into the atomizer. The paper funnel grew wet and darkened at the bottom and along the side where the rivulet flowed. The aromatic liquid settled in the funnel and drained slowly downwards. A warm, sweet fragrance of roses, mingling with a penetrating smell of alcohol, wafted through the air. Lyudmila poured half of the perfume from the bottle into the atomizer and said:

"Well, that's enough."

And she started to screw on the atomizer. Then she crumpled up the damp paper into a ball and rubbed it between her palms.

"Smell," she said to Sasha and lifted a palm to his face.

Sasha bent over, half closed his eyes and inhaled. Lyudmila laughed, slapped him gently on the lips with her palm and held her hand to his mouth. Sasha reddened and kissed her warm fragrant palm with the delicate touch of his trembling lips. Lyudmila sighed and a rapturous expression passed over her attractive face and once again was replaced with her customary expression of happy cheerfulness. She said:

"Now just hold still while I spray you!"

And she pressed the gutta-percha bulb. A fragrant mist spurted out, vaporized and diffused through the air onto Sasha's shirt. Sasha laughed and turned around obediently as Lyudmila nudged him.

"Smells nice, eh?" she asked.

"Very nice," Sasha replied cheerfully. "What is it called?"

"Some baby you are! Read the label and you'll see," she said in a teasing voice.

Sasha read and then said:

"It smells kind of like rose oil."

"Oil!" Lyudmila said reproachfully and gently slapped Sasha on the back.

Sasha laughed with a squeal and stuck out the tip of his tongue rolled up into a tube. Lyudmila stood up and started to look through Sasha's school texts and notebooks.

"May I look?" she asked.

"Please do," Sasha said.

"Where are your ones and zeroes,* show them to me."

"So far I haven't had anything so delightful," Sasha replied in an offended voice.

"You're telling lies, now," Lyudmila said decidedly. "You're the kind of person who would get bad marks. I imagine you've hidden them."

Sasha smiled silently.

"You're fed up with Latin and Greek I suppose."

"Not really," Sasha replied, but it was apparent that he would be overcome with the usual boredom when the conversation turned to school texts alone. "It's rather boring cramming all the time," he admitted. "But I don't mind, I have a good memory. But I do like to solve problems."

"Come to my place tomorrow after dinner," Lyudmila said.

"Thank you, I will come," Sasha said, blushing.

He felt pleased that Lyudmila had invited him.

Lyudmila asked:

"Do you know where I live? Will you come?"

"I know. Alright, I'll come," Sasha said happily.

"You come for certain now," Lyudmila repeated sternly. "I'll be expecting you, you hear!"

"What if I have a lot of lessons?" Sasha said, more from a sense of conscientiousness than from the actual thought that he wouldn't come because of his lessons.

"Come now, that's nonsense, you just come all the same," Lyudmila insisted. "Or you'll be impaled on a stake."

---

*In the Russian school system grades are assigned from a high of "five" (excellent) to a low of "one" or "zero" (failure).

"But what for?" Sasha asked with a chuckle.

"Just because you deserve it. You come and I'll tell you something and show you something," Lyudmila said, skipping, humming and tugging at her skirt and spreading her rosy fingers. "You just come now, my dear, silver, golden boy."

Sasha laughed.

"Tell me what it is today," Sasha begged her.

"I can't today. And how could I tell you today? You wouldn't come tomorrow then and you'd say what's the point of going."

"Well, alright, I'll come if they let me."

"What else now, of course they'll let you! You're hardly being kept on a chain."

Saying goodbye, Lyudmila kissed Sasha on the forehead and raised her hand to Sasha's lips—he was obliged to kiss it. And it was pleasant for Sasha to kiss that white tender hand once more. Yet it was almost shameful at the same time. How could he not help but blush! As she walked away, Lyudmila kept giving him a sly but tender smile. And she turned around several times.

"How sweet she is!" Sasha thought.

He was left alone.

"How quickly she left!" he thought. "She suddenly made up her mind and gave me no chance to come to my senses before she had already left!" Sasha thought. And he felt ashamed because he had forgotten to volunteer to accompany her.

"I ought to have gone part of the way with her!" Sasha was lost in reverie. "Maybe I could catch up to her? Has she gone far? If I run quickly I could catch her up smartly."

"Is she likely to laugh?" thought Sasha. "Or perhaps I'd just be getting in her way."

Thus he decided not to run after her. He felt somehow bored and at a loss. That tender sensation from the kiss still lingered faintly on his lips and her kiss burned his forehead.

"How tenderly she kisses!" Sasha reminisced dreamily. "Just like a dear sister."

Sasha's cheeks were burning. He had a pleasurable and shameful feeling. Nebulous dreams were being born.

"If she were my sister!" Sasha was daydreaming blissfully, "I could go up to her, embrace her and say something tender to her. I could say to her: Lyudmilochka, my dearest! Or I could use some quite special name for her—Tinkle or Dragonfly. And she would answer me. That would really be happiness."

"But she's a stranger, a dear one, but a stranger. She came and left and I daresay she's not even thinking about me now. All she left behind was the fragrance of lilac and roses and the sensation of two tender kisses—and a vague excitement in my heart that gives birth to a sweet daydream, just as the wave gave birth to Aphrodite."

Kokovkina returned shortly.

"Phew, you smell so strongly!" she said.

Sasha blushed.

"Lyudmilochka was here," he said, "but you weren't at home and she sat for a while, put perfume on me and then left."

"Such tender ways," the old lady said. "You're already calling her Lyudmilochka."

Sasha laughed in embarrassment and ran off to his room. Meanwhile Kokovkina was thinking that those Rutilov sisters were cheerful and affectionate girls—they knew how to flatter both the old and the young with their affection.

From the morning on the following day Sasha felt cheerful to think that he had been invited. He waited impatiently for dinner at home. After dinner, blushing all over from embarrassment, he asked Kokovkina's permission to go off to the Rutilovs' until seven o'clock. Kokovkina was amazed but she let him go. Sasha ran off cheerfully after painstakingly combing and even pomading his hair. He was rejoicing and was slightly excited as though in anticipation of something nice and important. And he was pleased to think that he would arrive, kiss Lyudmila's hand and she would kiss him on the forehead. And later, when he would be leaving, again the same kisses. He dreamt pleasurably about Lyudmila's white tender hand.

All three sisters greeted Sasha while he was still in the front hall. They loved to sit by the window looking out on the street and for that reason had caught sight of him from afar. Cheerful, dressed up and twittering brightly, they surrounded him with their effervescent blizzard of cheerfulness—and he immediately felt pleasant and relaxed with them.

"Here he is, the mysterious young fellow!" Lyudmila exclaimed joyfully.

Sasha kissed her hand and he did so adeptly and with great satisfaction. At the same time he also kissed the hands of Darya and Valeriya. There was no avoiding them and he discovered that this also gave him a distinct pleasure. All the more so because all three kissed him on the cheek: Darya kissed loudly but indifferently, like he was a board; Valeriya did it tenderly with downcast eyes, cunning eyes, giggling softly and gently touching him with her delicate joyful lips, and the kiss fell on his cheek like a fragrant apple blossom; and Lyudmila gave him a smacking kiss, joyfully, cheerfully and firmly.

"This is my guest," she declared resolutely, took Sasha by the shoulders and led him off to her room.

Darya immediately grew angry.

"Your guest, so go ahead and kiss with him all you want!" she cried angrily. "She's found herself a treasure! No one's going to take it away."

Valeriya said nothing, just grinned—it would be very interesting to have a chat with the boy! What does he understand?

In Lyudmila's room it was spacious, cheerful and bright because of two large windows that looked out on the garden and which were lightly curtained with a delicate yellowish lace. There was a sweet fragrance. Everything was smart and bright. The chairs and armchairs were upholstered in a golden-yellow fabric with a barely discernible white pattern. A variety of phials for perfume, toilet waters, jars, tins, fans and several Russian and French books were to be seen.

"I dreamt about you last night," Lyudmila said with a laugh. "You were swimming by the town bridge while I was sitting on the bridge and I caught you with my fishing rod."

"And put me in a jar?" Sasha asked with amusement.

"Why into a jar?"

"But where else?"

"Where else? I plucked you by the ears and tossed you back into the river."

And Lyudmila burst into a long ringing laughter.

"Oh, you're quite a one!" Sasha said. "What did you want to say to me today?"

Lyudmila laughed and didn't reply.

"Obviously you deceived me," Sasha guessed. "And you also promised to show me something," he said reproachfully.

"I'll show you! Do you want to eat?" Lyudmila asked.

"I've already had dinner," Sasha said. "Oh, what a deceiver you are!"

"As though I needed to deceive you. Is that pomade you're reeking of?" Lyudmila suddenly asked. Sasha blushed.

"I can't bear pomade!" Lyudmila said with annoyance. "A little miss with pomade in his hair!"

She ran her hand over his hair, got oil on her hand and slapped him on the cheek with her palm.

"Please, don't you dare use pomade!" she said.

Sasha was dismayed.

"Alright, I won't," he said. "What stern measures! But you use perfume!"

"Perfume is one thing and pomade another, silly! Imagine trying to compare the two," she said with conviction. "I never use pomade. Why stick your hair together! Perfume is not the same thing at all. Here, let me put some perfume on you. Is that appealing to you? I'll put lilac on you, is that appealing?"

"Yes, it is appealing to me," Sasha said with a smile.

It was pleasant for him to think that he would carry the scent home with himself and surprise Kokovkina once more.

"Who finds it appealing?" Lyudmila asked again, took a phial with a syringe and gazed slyly and questioningly at Sasha.

"It really is appealing to me," Sasha repeated.

"Is it appealing to you? A peeling? I see! You think it's a peeling from an orange!" Lyudmila teased him cheerfully.

Sasha and Lyudmila burst into cheerful laughter.

"You're not afraid any more that I'm going to 'atomize' you?"

Lyudmila asked. "Do you remember what a coward you were yesterday?"

"I wasn't any coward," Sasha replied hotly, flaring up.

Lyudmila chuckled and started to apply the perfume, teasing him all the while. Sasha thanked her and kissed her hand once more.

"And please, cut your hair!" Lyudmila said sternly. "What's so nice about wearing long curls, you'll scare horses with your hairdo."

"Well, alright, I'll get it cut, "Sasha agreed. "Such terrible measures! My hair is still quite short, only a half-inch long and the inspector didn't say anything to me about my hair."

"I like young people with their hair cut short, take note of that," Lyudmila said gravely and threatened him with a finger. "And I'm not your inspector, you have to obey me."

From that time Lyudmila got into the habit of going to Kokovkina's for Sasha more and more frequently. Particularly at first she tried to come when Kokovkina wasn't at home. At times she resorted to cunning and lured the old woman out of the house. Darya said to her once:

"E-ech, what a coward you are! You're afraid of the old woman. If she's there when you arrive, then just take him away—for a walk."

Lyudmila obeyed and started to go at whatever the time. If she found Kokovkina at home, then, after sitting with her for a little while, she would take Sasha for a walk. But if that were the case, then she never kept him for long.

Lyudmila and Sasha were quickly drawn into a tender but uneasy friendship. Without noticing it herself, Lyudmila was already arousing in Sasha urges and desires that were precocious and as yet vague. Sasha frequently kissed Lyudmila's hands—those delicate, pliant fingers covered with a tender supple skin—and the meandering blue veins were visible through the yellowish pink membrane. And higher up—the long shapely arms—it was easy to kiss them right up to the elbows after pushing back the wide sleeves.

Sometimes Sasha concealed from Kokovkina that Lyudmila was coming. He didn't lie, he simply said nothing. Besides, how could he lie—the servant herself could tell the truth. And it wasn't easy for Sasha to keep quiet about Lyudmila's visits because her laughter continued to echo in his ears. He wanted to talk about her. But for some reason it was awkward for him to do so.

Sasha quickly became friends with the other sisters as well. He would kiss all their hands and within a short while he even started to call the girls Dashenka, Lyudmilochka and Valerochka.

XVII

ONCE WHEN LYUDMILA met Sasha on the street during the day, she said to him:

"The director's oldest daughter is celebrating her name day tomorrow. Is your old lady going?"

"I don't know," Sasha said.

And a joyful hope stirred in his heart, and it was not so much a hope as a desire that Kokovkina would go and Lyudmila would come and spend time with him precisely at that time. In the evening he reminded Kokovkina of the coming name day.

"I almost forgot," Kokovkina said. "I'll go. She's such a nice girl."

And directly after Sasha returned from the gymnasium, Kokovkina left to go to the Khripach family. Sasha was overjoyed by the thought that he was able to get Kokovkina out of the house. Now he was certain that Lyudmila would find the time to come.

And so it happened that Lyudmila did come. She kissed Sasha on the cheek, let him kiss her hand and she laughed cheerfully while he reddened. A sweet, floral, moist fragrance wafted from Lyudmila's clothing: rose and iris. The fleshly and voluptuous iris dissolved in the sweet reverie of roses. Lyudmila had brought a narrow box wrapped in a fine paper through which a yellowish drawing was visible. She sat down, put the box on her knees and looked slyly at Sasha.

"Do you like dates?" she asked.

"I adore them," Sasha said with a funny face.

"Well, I'm going to treat you," Lyudmila said gravely.

She undid the box and said:

"Eat!"

She herself took one date at a time out of the box and put it into Sasha's mouth and after each one she forced him to kiss her hand. Sasha said:

"My lips have become so sweet!"

"It's hardly a misfortune that they've become sweet, go ahead and kiss to your heart's content," Lyudmila answered cheerfully. "I won't be offended."

"It would be better if I gave you all the kisses afterwards at once," Sasha said with a chuckle. And he was about to reach for a date himself.

"Deceiver, deceiver!" Lyudmila cried, deftly slapped the box shut and struck Sasha on the fingers.

"Come now, I'm honest and I won't deceive you," Sasha assured her.

"No, no, I don't believe you," Lyudmila insisted.

"Well, do you want me to give you all the kisses first?" Sasha offered.

"Now that's more like it," Lyudmila said joyfully. "Kiss me."

She stretched out her hand to Sasha. Sasha took her slender, long fingers, kissed them once and asked with a sly grin without letting her hand go:

"You won't deceive me, Lyudmilochka?"

"As though I weren't honest!" Lyudmila answered cheerfully. "Don't worry, I won't deceive you, you can kiss me without having any doubts."

Sasha bent down over her hand and started to kiss it quickly. He fairly covered the hand with kisses, making loud smacking sounds with his widely parted lips and he felt pleased that he could cover her with so many kisses. Lyudmila counted up the kisses carefully. She counted to ten and said:

"It's awkward for you standing on your feet, you should bend down."

"I'll arrange myself more comfortably," Sasha said.

He got down on his knees and continued zealously with his kisses.

Sasha loved to eat. He liked to have Lyudmila treat him to sweets. He loved her even more tenderly for that reason.

Lyudmila sprayed Sasha with a sickly sweet smelling perfume. Sasha was amazed at the fragrance: sweet but strange, dizzying, murky bright, like the early, goldening, but sinful dawn behind a white mist. Sasha said:

"What strange perfume!"

"Try it on your hand," Lyudmila advised.

She gave him an unattractive rectangular bottle with rounded edges. Sasha peered at the color—a brilliant yellow, cheerful liquid. An enormous colorful label with an inscription in French: cyclamen from Piver's. Sasha took hold of the flat glass stopper, pulled it out and smelled the perfume. Then he did it the way Lyudmila loved to do it: he put the palm of his hand over the mouth of the bottle, quickly inverted it and then turned it right side up, rubbed the drops of cyclamen together on his palms and carefully smelled his palm. The alcohol dissipated and the pure fragrance remained. Lyudmila looked at him with mounting anticipation. Sasha said uncertainly:

"It smells a little like a sugar-coated bedbug."

"Now, now, stop your lying, please," Lyudmila said with annoyance.

She also took some of the perfume on her hand and smelled. Sasha repeated:

"Really, it smells like a bedbug."

Lyudmila suddenly flared up so that little tears glittered in her eyes and she struck Sasha on the cheek and cried:

"Ah, you wicked boy! That's for your bedbug!"

"That was a hefty blow!" Sasha said, laughed and kissed Lyudmila's hand. "Why are you so angry, Lyudmilochka, sweetheart! Well, what do you think it smells of?"

The blow didn't anger him, he was completely enchanted by Lyudmila.

"What does it smell of?" Lyudmila asked and grabbed Sasha by the ear. "I'll tell you right away what it smells of, but first I'm going to pluck your ear off."

"Oi-oi-oi, Lyudmilochka, darling, I won't do it again!" Sasha said, screwing up his face from the pain and doubling over.

Lyudmila let go of the reddened ear, tenderly drew Sasha to herself, sat him down on her knees and said:

"Listen. Three spirits reside in cyclamen. This poor little flower smells of sweet ambrosia and that is for the worker bees. Surely you know that in Russian it is called sowbread."

"Sowbread," Sasha repeated with a chuckle. "What a funny name."

"Don't you laugh, you imp," Lyudmila said, took him by the other ear and continued. "Sweet ambrosia and the bees buzz above it and that is its joy. And it also smells of a delicate vanilla and that is no longer intended for the bees, but for what they are dreaming about. That is its desire—the little flower and the golden sun overhead. And its third spirit, it smells of a delicate sweet body, for the one who is in love, and that is its love—the poor little flower and the heavy midday sultry heat. The bee, the sun, the sultry heat—now do you understand, light of my eye?"

Sasha nodded his head silently. His swarthy face was flaming and his long dark eyelashes were trembling. Lyudmila was gazing dreamily into the distance. She was all flushed and she said:

"It brings joy, that delicate and sunny cyclamen, it beckons to desires that bring sweet and shameful feelings and it excites the blood. You understand, my little sun, when something is sweet, joyful and painful and you feel like weeping? Do you understand? That's the kind of flower it is."

She clung to Sasha's lips with a lingering kiss.

Lyudmila was staring pensively straight ahead. Suddenly a sly grin passed over her lips. She gave Sasha a gentle nudge and asked:

"Do you like dandelions?"

Sasha sighed, opened his eyes, smiled sweetly and whispered gently: "I do."

"What kind?" Lyudmila asked.

"All kinds, big and small," Sasha said enthusiastically and stood up from her knees with an adroit boyish movement.

"So you like dandelions?" Lyudmila asked tenderly and her ringing voice was trembling with concealed laughter.

"I do," Sasha answered quickly.

Lyudmila started to laugh and blushed.

"Silly, you like dandelions, but you've never even been to a zoo," she exclaimed.

They both roared with laughter and blushed.

These stimulations—of necessity innocent—represented the principal delight of their affair for Lyudmila. They excited, yet were far removed from vulgar and repulsive consummation.

They started to argue about who was the stronger. Lyudmila said:

"Well, even if you are stronger, what of it? It's a matter of agility."

"I'm agile too!" Sasha boasted.

"Away with you, agile!" Lyudmila cried in a teasing voice.

They argued for a long while. Finally Lyudmila suggested:

"Come on, let's fight then."

Sasha laughed and said provocatively:

"You won't be able to manage me!"

Lyudmila started to tickle him.

"Oh, you!" he cried with laughter, turned around and seized her about the waist.

A tussle began. Lyudmila saw immediately that Sasha was stronger. She couldn't win by strength, so, cunning as she was, she waited for the right moment and tripped up Sasha. He fell and pulled Lyudmila down with him. Lyudmila twisted around agilely and pinned him to the floor. Sasha cried desperately:

"That's not fair!"

Lyudmila planted her knees on his stomach and pinned him to the floor with her hands. Sasha struggled desperately to break loose. Lyudmila started to tickle him again. Sasha's ringing laughter mixed with hers. Laughter finally forced her to release Sasha. Laughing, she fell to the floor. Sasha leapt to his feet. He was red and piqued.

"*Rusalka!**" he cried.

But the *rusalka* just lay on the floor and laughed.

Lyudmila sat Sasha on her knees. Tired after their struggle they gazed intently and cheerfully into each other's eyes and smiled.

"I'm too heavy for you," Sasha said. "I'll crush your knees, you'd better let me go."

"It doesn't matter, just sit there," Lyudmila replied affectionately. "You yourself said you liked to cuddle, you know."

She stroked his head. He pressed tenderly against her. She said:

"How handsome you are, Sasha."

Sasha blushed and laughed.

"You're just making it up!" he said.

Conversations and thoughts about beauty dismayed him for some reason when they were applied to him. Never before had he been curious enough to find out whether people found him attractive or ugly.

---

*Rusalka is a water-nymph, usually mischievous or even wicked, and frequently encountered in Russian folklore.

Lyudmila pinched Sasha's cheek. Sasha smiled. The cheek turned red at the spot. It was attractive. Lyudmila pinched the other cheek as well. Sasha didn't resist. He simply took her hand, kissed it and said:

"Enough pinching, it hurts, you know, and besides you'll get callouses on your fingers."

"Away with you," Lyudmila said. "It's not painful and some flatterer you've become."

"I don't have any time, I've got a lot of lessons to do. Cuddle me just a little more, for good luck, so that I'll get a five on my Greek."

"Sending me packing!" Lyudmila said.

She grabbed him by the arm and raised his sleeve above his elbow.

"Are you going to wallop me?" Sasha asked, embarrassed and blushing guiltily.

But Lyudmila was admiring his arm, turning it this way and that.

"You have such beautiful arms!" she said loudly and joyfully and suddenly kissed him near the elbow.

Sasha reddened, tried to pull his arm free, but Lyudmila held on to it and kissed it several times more. Sasha grew calm, languid, and a strange expression settled on his brilliant half-opened lips. And beneath the curtain of his thick eyelashes his torrid cheeks started to pale.

They parted. Sasha accompanied Lyudmila to the gate. He would have gone farther, but she didn't bid him to do so. He stopped by the gate and said:

"Come more often, my dearest, bring me some sweeter spice cakes."

This was the first time that he had addressed her in the familiar fashion and for Lyudmila it had the echo of a tender caress. She abruptly embraced him, kissed him and ran off. Sasha stood like one who was stunned.

Sasha had promised to come. The appointed hour came and went— and there was no Sasha. Lyudmila waited impatiently. She was casting about, fretting and looking out the window. As soon as steps could be heard in the street she would peer outside. The sisters were chuckling. She said angrily and excitedly:

"Enough, you! Stop!"

Then she attacked them with stormy reproaches, whereupon they laughed. By then it was obvious that Sasha was not coming. Lyudmila began to weep from annoyance and grief.

"Oh boo-hoo-hoo! Poor, poor little old me!" Darya teased her.

Lyudmila, in a burst of grief forgetting to get angry over the fact that she was being teased, said softly and sobbingly:

"The disgusting old hag wouldn't let him go, she keeps him tied to her apron strings so that he'll study his Greeks."

With a rather vulgar feeling of sympathy Darya said:

"He must be some kind of lout, doesn't even know how to get away."

"You've got yourself involved with a wee babe," Valeriya said scornfully.

Although both sisters were chuckling, nevertheless they felt sorry for Lyudmila. They all loved one another, with a love that was tender, but not strong—and a tender love is a superficial love! Darya said:

"What are you crying for, bawling your eyes out for a babe-in-arms? Must have been the devil that got you mixed up with a kid."

"What devil are you talking about?" Lyudmila cried vehemently and turned a deep crimson all over.

"Well, old girl," Darya replied calmly, "you might be young, but still . . ."

Darya didn't finish to the end and gave a piercing whistle.

"Nonsense!" Lyudmila said in a strangely ringing voice.

A strange and cruel smile illuminated her face through the tears, just the way a brilliantly flaming ray of light shines through the final downpour of an exhausted rain at sunset.

Darya asked her with annoyance:

"Well what's so interesting about him anyway, if you don't mind telling me, please?"

Still wearing the same amazing smile Lyudmila replied pensively and slowly:

"How handsome he is! And how many inexhaustible possibilities he possesses!"

"Well, that's cheap to come by," Darya said conclusively. "All little boys have that."

"No, it isn't cheap to come by," Lyudmila replied with annoyance. "There are vile ones as well."

"And what's he, pure?" Valeriya asked. She drawled out the word "pure" in a scornful fashion.

"A lot you understand!" Lyudmila cried, but she immediately began to talk gently and dreamily: "He's innocent."

"That's a good one!" Darya said sarcastically.

"The very best age for boys," Lyudmila said, "is from fourteen to fifteen. He still can't do anything and doesn't understand in a genuine way, but he's already beginning to have premonitions of everything, definitely of everything. And he hasn't a disgusting beard."

"Some satisfaction that is!" Valeriya said with a disdainful grimace.

She was sad. It seemed to her that she was small, weak, fragile, and she envied her sisters: Darya for her cheerful laughter and even Lyudmila with her weeping. Lyudmila said once more:

"You don't understand anything. I don't love him at all in the way you think I do. It's better to love a boy than to fall in love with a vulgar phiz with a moustache. I love him in an innocent way. I don't want anything from him."

"If you don't want anything from him then why do you keep pestering him?" Darya protested coarsely.

Lyudmila blushed and a guilty expression settled heavily over her face. Darya felt sorry, she went up to Lyudmila, put her arms around her and said:

"Don't get upset, we're not trying to be spiteful."

Lyudmila started to cry again, pressed against Darya's shoulder and said bitterly:

"I know there's nothing to hope for here, but all I want is for him to caress me a little, any old way."

"There's your melancholy for you!" Darya said with annoyance, turned away from Lyudmila, put her hands on her hips and burst into clear song:

> My lover I would leave
> To go to bed every eve.

Valeriya dissolved in a fragile ringing laughter. And Lyudmila's eyes grew cheerful and lascivious. She abruptly went off into her room, sprayed herself with corylopsis—and the fragrance, spicy, sweet and lascivious, put her in the grip of an insinuating seductiveness. She went out on to the street all dressed up, excited, and emanating the immodest delight of that seductiveness.

"Maybe I'll meet him," she thought.

And she did.

"A fine one!" she cried both joyfully and reproachfully.

Sasha felt both dismay and joy.

"I didn't have the time," he said with embarrassment. "Nothing but lessons, I had to study all the while, truly, I had no time."

"You're lying, my dear, let's go right now."

He tried to excuse himself, chuckling, but it was obvious that he was happy that Lyudmila was taking him. Lyudmila brought him home.

"I brought him!" she cried triumphantly to her sisters and guided him by the shoulder off to her own room.

"Just you wait, I'm going to get even with you," she threatened and bolted the door shut. "Now no one will be able to protect you."

With his hands stuck in his belt, Sasha stood awkwardly in the middle of her room. He had a pleasurable but eerie feeling. There was the festive and sweet scent of some new perfume, but something in the scent affected and set his nerves on edge, like the touch of joyful, spritely, rough-skinned little serpents.

XVIII

PEREDONOV WAS RETURNING home from one of the students' lodgings. Suddenly he was caught in a fine shower. He started to ponder where he could stop by so that he wouldn't spoil his new silk umbrella in the rain. Across the road, on a separate, two-storied stone building, he saw a sign: "Office of Notary Gudaevsky." The notary's son was studying in the second form at the gymnasium. Peredonov decided to go in. At the same time he could complain about the student.

He found both the mother and father at home. They greeted him with a fuss. Everything here was done in this fashion.

Nikolai Mikhailovich Gudaevsky was a medium-sized man, solid, dark-haired, balding and with a long beard. His movements were always impetuous and surprising. It was as though he didn't walk but fluttered like a sparrow and it was always impossible to tell from his face and position what he was going to do a moment later. In the midst of a businesslike conversation he would suddenly shoot his knee out, which, rather than seeming ridiculous, would seem perplexing because of any lack of motivation. Whether at home or visiting he might just be sitting there when suddenly he would leap up and without any apparent necessity quickly begin to pace about the room, shouting and banging. On the street he would be walking along and suddenly he would stop, do a squat or make a lunge or some other gymnastic exercise, and then continue on his way. On documents which he drew up or witnessed, Gudaevsky loved to make funny remarks. For example, instead of writing about Ivan Ivanovich Ivanov living on Market Square, in the home of Ermilova, he would write about Ivan Ivanovich Ivanov living on Market Square in the block where it was impossible to breath because of the stench, and so forth. He would even make mention at times of the number of chickens and geese owned by the person whose signature he was witnessing.

For all the dissimilarity in shape, Yuliya Gudaevskaya, a passionate, tall, slender, cruelly sentimental and dry woman, resembled her husband in her manners: she had the same impetuous movements, the same complete disparity with the movements of others. She dressed in a gaudy and youthful fashion and because of her quick movements was constantly fluttering off in all directions with her long variegated ribbons with which she loved to decorate both her dress and hairdo abundantly.

Antosha, a slender, spritely boy, was scraping his feet courteously. Peredonov was seated in the sitting room and he immediately began to complain about Antosha: he was lazy, inattentive, didn't listen in class, talked, laughed and played pranks during recesses. Antosha was amazed— he didn't know that he had turned out to be that bad. He started to defend himself hotly. Both parents were upset.

"Please," the father cried, "tell me precisely what his pranks consist of?"

"Nika, don't defend him," the mother cried, "He mustn't play pranks."

"Well, what pranks?" the father questioned, running around on his short legs just like he was rolling.

"Just pranks in general, romping around, fighting," Peredonov said sullenly. "He's constantly playing pranks."

"I don't fight," Antosha exclaimed with a protest. "Ask whom you like, I've never fought with anyone."

"He's always pestering people," Peredonov said.

"Fine, I'll go to the gymnasium myself and I'll find out from the inspector," Gudaevsky said with determination.

"Nika, Nika, why don't you believe him!" Yuliya cried; "Do you want Antosha to end up as a good-for-nothing? He must be whipped."

"Rubbish! Rubbish!" the father cried.

"I'll whip him, I'll whip him for sure!" the mother cried, seized her son by the shoulder and started to drag him off into the kitchen, "Antosha," she cried, "let's go, sweetheart, I'm going to whip you."

"I won't let you!" the father cried, tearing his son away.

The mother wouldn't give in, Antosha was crying desperately and the parents were shoving each other.

"Help me, Ardalyon Borisych," Yuliya cried. "Hold this monster while I settle things with Antosha."

Peredonov went to her aid. But Gudaevsky tore his son free, pushed his wife away, leapt at Peredonov and cried:

"Stay out of it! When two dogs have a bone to pick, a third one doesn't try to butt in! I'll fix you!"

Red, dishevelled, perspiring, he shook his fist in the air. Peredonov retreated, muttering something indistinctly. Yuliya was running around her husband, trying to snatch Antosha away. The father hid him behind his back, dragging him by the hand first to the right and then to the left. Yuliya's eyes were flashing and she cried:

"He's raising a brigand! He'll get a prison term! He'll end up doing penal servitude!"

"A plague on you for saying such things!" Gudaevsky cried. "Shut up, you wicked fool!"

"Ah, you tyrant!" Yuliya screeched, leapt at her husband, struck him in the back with her fist and dashed impetuously out of the sitting room. Gudaevsky clenched his fists and leapt at Peredonov.

"You came to stir things up!" he cried. "Antosha is playing pranks? You're lying, he's not playing any pranks. If he had been, I would have known about it without you coming and I don't wish to talk to you. You're going around the town, deceiving fools, whipping young boys. You want to get a diploma as a master of the whipping trade. Well, you've come to the wrong place. My gracious sir, I request you to remove yourself!"

Saying that he leapt at Peredonov and forced him into a corner. Peredonov was frightened and was happy to flee, but Gudaevsky hadn't noticed, in the heat of his exasperation, that he was blocking off the exit. Antosha grabbed his father from behind by his coattails and pulled him towards himself. The father angrily tried to hush him and kicked out at him. Antosha adroitly jumped to the side, but wouldn't release his father's coat.

"Hush!" Gudaevsky shouted. "Antosha, mind yourself."

"Papa," Antosha cried, continuing to pull his father back. "You're preventing Ardalyon Borisych from getting by."

Gudaevsky quickly leapt back. Antosha barely had a chance to get out of the way.

"Excuse me," Gudaevsky said and showed him the door. "Here's the way out, I wouldn't presume to detain you."

Peredonov left the sitting room hastily. Gudaevsky cocked a snook with his long fingers and then he jerked his knee up in the air as though he were kicking his guest out. Antosha started to giggle. Gudaevsky cried angrily at him:

"Antosha, mind yourself! Beware, tomorrow I'm going to the gymnasium and if it turns out to be true, I'll hand you over to your mother to be disciplined."

"I didn't play any pranks, he's lying," Antosha said in a plaintive and squeaking voice.

"Antosha, mind yourself!" the father cried. "You mustn't say he's lying, but that he's mistaken. Only young people lie, whereas adults are mistaken."

Meanwhile, Peredonov had made his way into the semi-darkness of the entry way, somehow found his coat and started to put it on. He couldn't get his arms into the sleeves from fear and excitement. No one came to help him. Suddenly Yuliya came running from somewhere out of a side door, rustling her fluttering ribbons, and she heatedly whispered something, waving her hands and jumping up and down on her toes. Peredonov couldn't understand right away.

"I'm so grateful to you," he finally made out. "It was so noble on your part, so noble, such concern. Everyone is so indifferent, but you understand the role of a poor mother. It's so difficult to raise children, so difficult, you can't imagine. I have two and it makes my head spin. My husband is a tyrant, he's a terrible, terrible man, isn't he? You saw for yourself."

"Yes," Peredonov muttered. "Your husband . . . how could he, he shouldn't do that, I am concerned, whereas he . . ."

"Ah, don't say it," Yuliya whispered, "He's a terrible man. He'll drive me to my grave and be glad of it, and he'll pervert my children, my little

Antosha. But I am a mother, I won't let him, I'll give him a whipping in any case."

"He won't let you," Peredonov said and nodded his head in the direction of the other rooms.

"When he goes off to the club. He won't take Antosha with him! He'll go off and until then I'll keep silent as though I agreed with him. But as soon as he goes, I'll give him a whipping and you'll help me. You will help me, won't you?"

Peredonov thought for a moment and then said:

"Fine, only how will I know?"

"I'll send for you, I will," Yuliya whispered joyfully. "You be waiting. As soon as he goes off to the club, then I'll send for you."

In the evening Peredonov received a note from Gudaevskaya. He read:

"Most Esteemed Ardalyon Borisych! My husband went off to the club and now I am free of his barbarity until one a.m. Be so kind as to come as quickly as possible to render me assistance in dealing with my criminal son. I realize that he must be rid of his vices while he's still young, whereas afterwards it will be too late.

With sincere respect, Yuliya Gudaevskaya. P.S. Please come quickly, otherwise Antosha will go to bed and he'll have to be awakened."

Peredonov dressed in haste, wrapped his neck up with his scarf and set out.

"Ardalyon Borisych, where are you off to for the night?" Varvara asked.

"On business," Peredonov replied sullenly, hurrying off.

Varvara had the melancholy thought that once again she wouldn't get much sleep. If only she could get him to marry her as soon as possible! Then she could sleep day and night—now that would be bliss!

Out on the street Peredonov was overcome with doubt. What if it were a trap? And suddenly it turns out that Gudaevsky is at home and they grab him and start to beat him? Wasn't it better to turn back?

"No, I have to go to their house and I'll see how things are there."

Night, quiet, cool and dark, had set in from all sides and forced him to slow his steps. A fresh breeze was blowing from the distant fields. Gentle rustling sounds and noises came from the grass along the fences and all around everything seemed suspicious and strange. Perhaps someone was lurking behind him on his trail. All things were strangely and surprisingly concealed behind the darkness as though a different nocturnal life, that was incomprehensible and hostile to man, had awakened in them. Peredonov walked softly along the streets and muttered:

"You're wasting your time following me. I'm not going to do anything bad. Brother, I'm only concerned about the good of my work. Really."

Finally he arrived at the dwelling of the Gudaevskys. There was only light to be seen in one window facing the street, the other four were dark. Peredonov went up on the porch just as quietly as he could, stood for a while, pressed his ear to the door and listened—everything was quiet. He gently tugged the bronze handle of the bell. A weak reverberating sound echoed somewhere far off. But however weak it was, it frightened Peredonov as though all the hostile forces ought to be awakened after the bell and hasten to these doors. Peredonov quickly ran off the porch and cowered against the wall, hiding behind a column.

A few brief moments passed. Peredonov's heart went faint and then started to pound heavily.

Light steps were heard, the sound of a door being opened—and Yuliya peered out on the street, her black passionate eyes flashing.

"Who's there?" she asked in a loud whisper.

Peredonov moved slightly away from the wall and peering up into the narrow opening of the door where it was dark and quiet, he asked in a whisper as well—and his voice was trembling:

"Has Nikolai Mikhailovich gone?"

"He's gone, he's gone," Yuliya whispered joyfully and nodded.

Looking timidly around, Peredonov followed her into the dark entry way.

"Excuse me," Yuliya said. "I don't have a light, otherwise someone might see and gossip."

She proceeded Peredonov up the staircase and into a corridor where a small lamp hung, casting a murky light on the top steps. Yuliya was laughing softly and joyfully and her ribbons were trembling convulsively from the laughter.

"He's gone," she whispered joyfully, looking around and giving Peredonov the once-over with her passionately burning eyes. "I was almost afraid that he would stay at home today because he had put up such a fierce struggle. But he couldn't get by without playing cards. I sent the servant away. Only Liza's nurse is left. We don't want to be disturbed. You know the kind of people there are today."

Heat emanated from Yuliya and she was all hot and dry like a piece of kindling. At times she would grab Peredonov by the sleeve and it was as though these quick dry touches made quick dry fires run up and down his entire body. As quietly as could be, on tip-toe, they walked along the corridor past several closed doors and stopped by the last one—the door into the nursery . . .[10]

Peredonov left Yuliya at midnight when she was beginning to expect her husband to return soon. He walked along the dark streets, sullen and gloomy. It seemed to him that someone was still standing near the house and was following him now. He muttered:

"I went on official business. I'm not guilty. She wanted to do it herself. You won't pull one on me, you've got the wrong person."

Varvara still wasn't asleep when he returned. The cards were spread out in front of her.

It seemed to Peredonov that someone might have snuck in when he entered. Perhaps Varvara herself had let the enemy in. Peredonov said:

"I want to go to bed and you're casting spells conjuring with your cards. Give me the cards here, otherwise you'll be casting a spell on me."

He took the cards away and hid them under his pillow. Varvara smirked and said:

"You and your tomfoolery. I don't know how to cast spells. As though I needed it."

It annoyed him and frightened him that she was smirking: he thought it meant that she could do it without cards. Then the cat squeezed under the bed and flashed its green eyes—one could cast spells on its fur by rubbing it the wrong way to make sparks leap up. And there was the gray *nedotykomka* flitting under the commode again—maybe it was Varvara summoning it at nights with a soft whistle resembling a snore?

Peredonov had a foul and terrible dream. Pylnikov had come, stood in the doorway, beckoned to him and smiled. It was as though someone were drawing Peredonov on and Pylnikov led him through the dark, filthy streets while the cat ran alongside with shining green pupils . . .[11]

XIX

THE ECCENTRICITIES IN Peredonov's behavior worried Khripach more and more from day to day. He consulted with the gymnasium doctor to see whether Peredonov had gone crazy. With a laugh the doctor replied that nothing would make Peredonov crazy but that he was simply acting foolishly out of stupidity. Complaints came as well. First was Adamenko who sent the director her brother's workbook in which he had received a grade of one for work that was well done.

During one of the recesses the director invited Peredonov into his study.

"He really does look like a madman," Khripach thought when he caught sight of the traces of perturbation and terror in the dull gloomy face of Peredonov.

"I have a complaint to make against you," Khripach began in his dry rapid speech. "Every time I have to give a lesson next to you, my head literally splits—there's such laughter coming out of your class. Could I ask you not to give lessons that are so humorous in content? 'Joking, always joking. When will you ever stop?'"*

"I'm not to blame," Peredonov said angrily. "They laugh by themselves. And it's impossible to go on talking about orthography and the satires of Kantemir** all the time. Sometimes you say something and they immediately start grinning. They're badly disciplined. They need to be reined in."

"It's desirable and even essential that classroom work possess a serious character," Khripach said. "And there's something else."

Khripach showed Peredonov two notebooks and said:

"Here are two notebooks in your subject, both are by students in the same class, Adamenko and my son. I have been obliged to compare them and I am forced to take the opinion that you do not have a sufficiently attentive attitude towards your work. The last piece of work by Adamenko,

*A paraphrase of a famous line from A.S. Griboedov's play Woe from Wit (1822–24).
**Kantemir, Prince Antioch Dmitrievich (1708–1744). Chiefly known as Russia's first satirist and a leading figure in literary classicism of 18th-century Russia. He was also responsible for important stylistic innovations in the development of the Russian literary language.

which was executed with complete satisfaction, was given the grade of one, whereas the work of my son, which was more poorly written, earned a four. Obviously you made a mistake: you gave the grade of one student to the other and vice versa. Although a person is bound to make mistakes, nevertheless I request you to forego similar mistakes. They provoke a well-grounded dissatisfaction in the parents and the students themselves."

Peredonov muttered something indistinct.

With renewed vigor he spitefully started to tease the young boys who had been recently punished because of his complaints.

He especially attacked Kramarenko. The latter was silent and grew pale beneath his dark suntan and his eyes were glittering.

Emerging from the gymnasium, Kramarenko was in no hurry to get home that day. He stood by the gates, and kept glancing at the entrance. When Peredonov came out, Kramarenko followed him at some distance, waiting for the rare passers-by to disappear.

Peredonov was walking slowly. The gloomy weather had induced a melancholy feeling in him. During recent days his face had assumed more and more of a dull expression. Either his gaze would be fixed on something far off, or it would wander strangely. It seemed as though he were constantly scrutinizing an object. This caused the objects to double before his eyes, freeze and then pulsate.

Whom was he trying to discover? Denouncers. They were hiding behind all objects, speaking in hushed whispers and laughing. His enemies were besieging Peredonov with an entire army of denouncers. Sometimes Peredonov tried to catch them unawares. But they always managed to flee in time, just as though the earth had swallowed them up . . .

Peredonov caught the sound of quick, bold steps along the wooden sidewalk behind him and he looked around in fear—Kramarenko was coming up abreast of him and was staring at him spitefully and resolutely with burning eyes, pale, slender, like a young savage ready to pounce on his enemy. That look frightened Peredonov.

"What if he suddenly bites me?" he thought.

He walked faster, but Kramarenko didn't fall back. Peredonov stopped and said angrily:

"What are you hanging about for, you scruffy black imp! I'll take you off to your father right this minute."

Kramarenko also stopped and still went on staring at Peredonov. Now they were standing opposite each other on the rickety wooden sidewalk in the deserted street beside a gray fence that was indifferent to everything living. Trembling all over, Kramarenko said in a hissing voice:

"You scoundrel!"

He grinned and turned around to leave. He took about three steps, stopped, looked back and repeated more loudly:

"What a scoundrel! A foul reptile!"

He spat and set off. Peredonov sullenly watched him go and then headed home as well. Vague, fearful thoughts slowly filed through his mind.

Vershina hailed him. She was standing behind the fence of her garden by the gate, wrapped up in a large black kerchief and smoking. Peredonov did not recognize Vershina at once. In her figure he had the illusion of something ominous: a black witch standing there, emitting a spellbinding smoke and casting spells. He spat and uttered a counter-spell. Vershina laughed and asked:

"What's the matter, Ardalyon Borisych?"

Peredonov looked at her dully and finally said:

"Oh, it's you! I didn't recognize you."

"That's a good sign. It means that I'm going to be rich soon," Vershina said.

Peredonov didn't like that. He felt like getting rich himself.

"Sure," he said angrily. "What do you need to get rich for! You've got enough as it is."

"I'm going to win two hundred thousand," Vershina said with a crooked smile.

"No, I'm going to win the two hundred thousand," Peredonov argued.

"I'll win in one lottery and you'll win in another one," Vershina said.

"Well, you're lying," Peredonov said rudely. "It never happens that there are two winners in one town. I'm the one who'll win."

Vershina noticed that he was getting angry. She stopped arguing. She opened the gate and lured Peredonov, saying:

"What are we standing here for? Come in, please, Murin is here."

Murin's name had a pleasant association for him: food and drink. He went in.

In the sitting room which was somewhat dark because of the trees, sat Marta, with contented eyes and a red kerchief tied around her neck, Murin, more dishevelled than usual, seemingly pleased about something, and the grown-up gymnasium student, Vitkevich, who was courting Vershina, thinking that she was in love with him and dreaming of leaving the gymnasium, marrying Vershina and managing her estate.

Murin stood up to greet Peredonov, who was entering the room, with exaggeratedly joyful exclamations. His face grew even sweeter, his little eyes turned oily—and none of it suited his hefty body with his tousled hair wherein pieces of straw were visible here and there.

"I'm cultivating my business," he said in a loud and hoarse voice. "I have business everywhere, but my dear hostesses here decided to treat me to tea as well."

"Business, sure," Peredonov answered angrily. "What kind of business do you have! You don't have official business, you just make money. I'm the one who has business."

"Well, business is business—it's all other people's money," Murin protested with a loud burst of laughter.

Vershina smiled crookedly and sat Peredonov down at the table. The round table in front of the divan was covered with glasses and cups of tea, rum, cloudberry jam, an open-work silver basket covered with a woven napkin and filled with sweet rolls and homemade almond spice cake.

Murin's glass smelled strongly of rum, whereas Vitkevich had put a lot of jam on his glass plate which was in the shape of a crab. Marta was eating a sweet roll in small pieces with obvious pleasure. Vershina wanted to treat Peredonov as well, but he refused tea.

"They might have poisoned it," he thought. "It'd be the easiest thing of all to poison it—you'd drink it and you wouldn't notice it, there are sweet-tasting poisons, but once you got home you'd kick the bucket."

He was annoyed over the thought of why they had put jam out for Murin, but when he had come they hadn't bothered to bring a fresh jar with better jam. They had more than cloudberry jam because they made all sorts of jam.

As for Vershina, it was certain that she was chasing after Murin. Seeing that there wasn't much hope for Peredonov, she was trying to round up other prospective husbands for Marta. Now she was luring Murin. This landowner, who had sunk to a semi-civilized state in his pursuit of profits that were not easily come by, was willingly going for the bait: he liked Marta.

Marta was happy. After all it had been her constant dream that a prospective husband would be found for her, she would get married and she would have a fine household and live in plenty. She looked at Murin with eyes of love. This forty-year-old, enormous man with a coarse voice and with an ingenuous expression seemed to her the very model of male strength, bravado, handsomeness and goodness.

Peredonov noted the loving looks which Murin and Marta were exchanging. He noted them because he was expecting admiration from Marta for himself. He said angrily to Murin:

"You're sitting there just like a prospective husband, your whole phiz is glowing."

"It's because of happiness," Murin said in a cheerful voice. "I've settled my business well here."

He winked at the hostesses. They both smiled happily. Peredonov asked in an angry voice, screwing up his eyes scornfully:

"Have you found yourself a bride, or something? Are they giving much of a dowry?"

Murin spoke as though he hadn't heard the questions:

"Natalya Afanasyevna, may God grant her everything nice, has just agreed to give lodgings to my Vanyushka. He'll be living here as though in the bosom of Christ and my heart will rest in peace that he won't be corrupted."

"He'll play pranks together with Vladya," Peredonov said sullenly. "They'll burn the house down."

"He wouldn't dare!" Murin cried resolutely. "You, my dear old Natalya Afanasyevna, need not worry about that. He'll keep to the straight and narrow with you."

In order to interrupt this conversation Vershina said with a crooked smile:

"I feel like something tart to eat."

"Would you like some bilberries and apple? I'll bring it," Marta said, quickly getting up.

"Yes, please bring some."

Marta ran out of the room. Vershina didn't even watch her go. She had grown so accustomed to calmly accepting Marta's obliging ways as something to be expected. She sat calmly and deeply sunk into the divan, exhaled blue puffs of smoke and compared the men who were talking. Peredonov was angry and dispirited, Murin was cheerful and animated.

She liked Murin much more. He had a good-natured face whereas Peredonov didn't even know how to smile. She liked everything about Murin: he was big, fat, attractive, spoke in a pleasant low voice and was very respectful towards her. There were even times when Vershina thought that maybe she ought to turn things around so that Murin proposed not to Marta but to her. But she always concluded her musings by magnanimously giving him to Marta.

"Everyone," she thought to herself, "will be proposing to me once I have money and then I can choose whom I wish. Maybe I'll take this youth," she thought and fixed her gaze with a certain pleasure on the greenish, rude, but nevertheless attractive face of Vitkevich who was not saying much, eating a great deal and glancing at Vershina with an insolent smile all the while.

Marta brought the bilberries with apple in a clay bowl and started to relate what she had dreamt that night. She had been with friends at a wedding and was eating pineapple and *bliny* with honey when she found a hundred rouble note in one of the *bliny*. The money had been taken from her and she had wept. She had woken up in tears.

"You should have hid it on the sly so that no one would see," Peredonov said angrily. "If you couldn't hang on to the money in your dream, what kind of lady of the house are you!"

"There's no point in feeling sorry about that money," Vershina said. "That's the least of what people see in their dreams."

"But I felt so terribly sorry about the money," Marta said naively. "A whole hundred roubles!"

Tears started to well up in her eyes and she gave a forced laugh so that she wouldn't start to cry. Murin fussed in his pocket, exclaiming:

"Dear mother, Marta Stanislavovna, now don't you go on feeling sorry, we'll fix that right now!"

He pulled a hundred rouble note out of his wallet, laid it on the table in front of Marta, slapped his palm on it and cried:

"If you please! No one will take that away."

Marta was on the verge of rejoicing, but then she turned a brilliant crimson and said with embarrassment:

"Ah, really, now, Vladimir Ivanovich, I just couldn't! I won't take it, goodness, really I can't!"

"No, now if you please, don't be offended," Murin said, chuckling but not withdrawing the money. "Go ahead, it means that your dream has come true."

"No, really, I'm ashamed, I couldn't take it for anything," Marta kept making excuses while gazing at the hundred rouble note with greedy eyes.

"Why kick up such a fuss if someone's giving it to you," Vitkevich said. "Here's good luck falling right into a person's lap," he said with an envious sigh.

Murin stood up in front of Marta and exclaimed in a persuasive voice:

"My dear Marta Stanislavovna, believe me, I mean it from the bottom of my heart, take it, please! And if you can't just accept it for nothing, then it's for looking after my Vanyushka. What Natalya Afanasyevna and I agreed on, that still stands, but this would be for you, for supervising him."

"But really, it's so much," Marta said indecisively.

"For the first half year," Murin said and bowed to Marta from the waist. "Now, don't be offended, just take it and you can take the place of an older sister for my Vanyushka."

"Well, go on, Marta, take it," Vershina said. "Thank Vladimir Ivanovich."

Blushing with shame and joy, Marta took the money. Murin started to thank her warmly.

"Make a marriage proposal right away, it'll be cheaper," Peredonov said wrathfully. "What a fuss you've made!"

Vitkevich roared with laughter, while the rest of them pretended not to hear. Vershina was about to give an account of her dream, but Peredonov didn't let her finish and stood up to say goodbye. Murin invited him to come to his place for the evening.

"I have to go to vespers," Peredonov said.

"Since when has Ardalyon Borisych become such a zealous churchgoer," Vershina said with a dry and quick chuckle.

"I always have been," he replied. "I believe in God, not like other people. Perhaps I'm the only one in the gymnasium like that. That's why I'm being persecuted. The director is an atheist."

"When you're free, then you name the time," Murin said.

Cramming his cap on, Peredonov said:

"I don't have time to go visiting."

But almost immediately he recalled that Murin always fed people well and gave them good things to drink, and he said:

"Well, I could come on Monday."

Murin was ecstatic and started to invite Vershina and Marta. But Peredonov said:

"No, we don't need the ladies. Otherwise people will get tight and just blurt something out without any precautionary censorship, so it's awkward with ladies present."

When Peredonov left, Vershina grinned ironically and said:

"Ardalyon Borisych is being eccentric. He very much wants to be an inspector, but Varvara must be leading him around by the nose. Look at the way he's acting up."

Vladya, who had been hiding away during Peredonov's visit, came out and said with a malicious grin:

"The locksmith's sons found out from someone that it was Peredonov who turned them in."

"They'll break his windows!" Vitkevich exclaimed with a joyful roar of laughter.

Out on the street everything seemed hostile and ominous to Peredonov. A sheep was standing at the crossroads and gazing dully at Peredonov. This sheep was so reminiscent of Volodin that Peredonov took fright. He thought that perhaps Volodin had turned himself into a sheep in order to follow Peredonov.

"How do we know," he thought, "perhaps it is possible. Science hasn't gotten that far yet, but maybe someone already knows how. After all, there you have the French, an educated people, yet magicians and magic established themselves in Paris," Peredonov thought. And he felt terrified. "What if this sheep starts to kick," he thought.

The sheep bleated and it resembled Volodin's laugh, sharp, penetrating and unpleasant.

Once again he ran into the police staff officer. Peredonov went up to him and said in a whisper:

"You'd better get on the trail of Adamenko. She's corresponding with socialists and she's one herself."

Rubovsky gave him a silent and surprised look. Peredonov went on and thought with melancholy:

"Why does he keep turning up? He keeps following me and has stationed policemen everywhere."

The muddy streets, the overcast sky, the miserable little houses, the ragged dispirited children—they all had an air of melancholy, barbarity and ineradicable sorrow.

"It's not a good city," Peredonov thought. "And the people here are wicked and vile. I ought to move to another city as soon as possible where all the teachers will bow down low and all the school children will be afraid and whisper in terror: the inspector is coming. Yes, authorities live completely differently in the world."

"Mister Inspector of the second district of the Ruban Guberniya," he muttered to himself under his breath. "His grace, State Councillor Peredonov. That's the way! Recognition! His excellency, mister director of public schools of the Ruban Guberniya, Actual State Councillor, Peredonov. Hats off! Hand in your resignation! You, leave! I'll straighten you out!"

Peredonov's face grew haughty; in his impoverished imagination he was receiving his share of power.

When Peredonov arrived home, he heard, while removing his coat, a sharp sound carrying from the dining room—it was Volodin laughing. Peredonov's heart fell.

"He's already managed to run over here," he thought. "Perhaps he and Varvara are hatching some plot on how to make a dunce out of me. That's why he's laughing, he's happy that Varvara is on his side."

Melancholy and spiteful he went into the dining room. It was already laid out for dinner. Varvara greeted Peredonov with a concerned face.

"Ardalyon Borisych!" she exclaimed, "We've had a real adventure! The cat has run off."

"Well!" Peredonov cried with an expression of terror on his face. "Why did you let it go?"

"What am I supposed to do, sew it by the tail to my skirt?" Varvara asked with annoyance.

Volodin giggled. Peredonov thought that perhaps the cat had gone off to the police station and was purring everything out that it knew about Peredonov and about why and where Peredonov went out at night. It would reveal everything and on top of it it would miaow about things that weren't true. Nothing but trouble! Peredonov sat down on a chair at the table, lowered his head and while kneading the edge of the tablecloth, fell into sorrowful contemplation.

"Cats always run off to their old homes," Volodin said, "because cats get accustomed to a place and not to their master. You have to turn a cat in circles when you take it to a new apartment and not show it the way, otherwise it'll run away for sure."

Peredonov was relieved.

"So you think, Pavlushka, that he ran off to the old apartment?" he asked.

"For certain, Ardasha," Volodin replied.

Peredonov stood up and cried:

"Well, let's drink to it, Pavlushka!"

Volodin giggled.

"Don't mind if I do, Ardasha," he said. "I don't mind having a drink any time at all."

"We have to get the cat back from there!" Peredonov decided.

"A real treasure!" Varvara replied with a smirk. "I'll send Klavdyushka after dinner."

They sat down to eat. Volodin was cheerful, rambled on and laughed. For Peredonov his laughter sounded like the bleating of the sheep on the street.

"What evil plot is he hatching?" Peredonov thought. "Does he need a plot?"

And Peredonov was thinking that perhaps he might succeed in gaining Volodin's favor.

"Listen, Pavlushka," he said. "If you won't go and do me any harm, then I'll buy you a pound of fruit drops every week, the very best sort and you can suck away on them to my health."

Volodin laughed, but immediately assumed an offended expression and said:

"Ardalyon Borisych, I am agreed not to do you any harm, only I don't need any fruit drops because I don't like them."

Peredonov was dejected. Varvara said with a smirk:

"Enough of your tomfoolery, Ardalyon Borisych. How could he do you any harm?"

"Any fool can ruin things," Peredonov said dejectedly.

Offended, Volodin puffed out his lips, shook his head and said:

"Ardalyon Borisych, if that's the way you feel about me, then there's only one thing I can say: I thank you humbly. If that's what you feel about me, then what am I supposed to do after this? How am I supposed to understand this, in what sense?"

"Drink up your vodka, Pavlushka, and pour me one," Peredonov said.

"Don't pay any attention to him, Pavel Vasilyevich," Varvara tried to console Volodin. "You know he just talks that way, his heart doesn't know what his tongue is babbling."

Volodin fell silent, and preserving his offended look, started to pour vodka from the decanter into the glasses. Varvara said with a smirk:

"What's this, Ardalyon Borisych, you're not afraid to drink vodka from him? He might have put a curse on it, look at him moving his lips."

Terror formed on Peredonov's face. He grabbed the glass that Volodin had filled, tossed the vodka out of it on to the floor and cried:

"Fend, forfend, fend, forfend. Plot upon the plotter, let his tongue wither, let his black eye burst. Death upon the offender. Fend, forfend, fend, forfend."

Then he turned to Volodin with a malicious face and thumbed his nose at him and said:

"There you go, try your teeth on that. You're cunning, but I'm even more cunning."

Varvara roared with laughter. Volodin said in an offended reverberating voice just as though he were bleating:

"You're the one, Ardalyon Borisych, that knows all kinds of magic words and pronounces them, whereas I have never, if you please, been involved in magic. I am not giving my consent to putting a curse on your vodka or anything else, whereas, perhaps you are the one who is bewitching all my prospective wives away from me."

"That's a good one!" Peredonov said angrily. "A lot I need your prospective wives. I can find better ones myself."

"You uttered a curse so that my eye would burst," Volodin continued. "Only just beware that your own spectacles don't burst first."

Peredonov made a frightened grab for his spectacles.

"What are you trying to stir up!" he grumbled. "You've got a tongue like a broom."

Varvara gave Volodin a look of caution and said angrily:

"Don't be so malicious with your tongue, Pavel Vasilyevich. Eat your soup or it'll get cold. Goodness, what a viper!"

She was thinking that quite likely Ardalyon Borisych had pronounced this counter-spell without meaning it. Volodin started to eat his soup. Everyone was silent for a while and then Volodin said in an offended voice:

"It's no coincidence that in a dream I had last night I was being smeared with honey. You were trying to smear me, Ardalyon Borisych."

"That's not the way you should be smeared," Varvara said angrily.

"What for, may I ask? It seems that I haven't done anything," Volodin said.

"Because you have a vile tongue," Varvara explained. "You shouldn't blab everything that comes into your head—there's a right time for everything."[12]

XX

I N THE EVENING Peredonov went to the club—he had been invited to play cards. The notary, Gudaevsky, was there as well. Peredonov took fright when he saw him. But Gudaevsky was acting peacefully and Peredonov relaxed.

They played for a long while and drank a great deal. Late at night in the buffet Gudaevsky suddenly leaped at Peredonov, struck him in the face several times without any explanation, smashed his glasses and briskly left the club. Peredonov didn't put up any resistance, pretended to be drunk, collapsed on the floor and started to snore. They shook him awake and took him home.

Everyone in town was talking about the fight the following day.

That evening Varvara found the opportunity to steal the first forged letter back from Peredonov. It was essential for her to do so—as Grushina had stipulated—so that subsequently if the two forgeries were compared, no difference would be noted. Peredonov usually carried this letter around with himself, but on that day for some reason he accidentally left it at home. When he was changing from his official uniform into his jacket, he took it out of his pocket, stuck it under a textbook on the commode and forgot it there. Varvara burned it with a candle at Grushina's.

Late that night, when Peredonov returned home and Varvara saw his broken glasses, he told her that they had burst on their own. She believed him and decided that Volodin's wicked tongue had been to blame. Peredonov himself believed that it had been his wicked tongue. In any event, the following day Grushina gave Varvara a detailed account of the fight in the club.

In the morning when he was getting dressed, Peredonov missed the letter, couldn't find it anywhere and was terrified. He started to shout in a wild voice:

"Varvara, where's the letter?"

Varvara was flustered.

"What letter?" she asked looking at Peredonov with her frightened, wicked eyes.

"The letter from the Princess!" Peredonov cried.

Somehow or other Varvara plucked up her courage. With an insolent smirk she said:

"How should I know where it is! You must have thrown it among your waste paper and Klavdyushka burned it. Look in your room and see if it's still around."

Peredonov left for the gymnasium in a gloomy mood. He recalled the troubles of the day before. He was thinking about Kramarenko: what had made that vile boy decide to call him a scoundrel? It meant that he wasn't afraid of Peredonov. Maybe he already knew something about Peredonov? He knew something and wanted to denounce him.

In class Kramarenko kept staring at Peredonov and smiling and that frightened Peredonov even more.

During the third recess Peredonov was once more invited to the director's office. He went with the vague apprehension of something unpleasant.

Rumors about Peredonov's feats were coming to Khripach from all directions. That morning he had been told about the episode the day before in the club. Volodya Bultyakov, who had been punished by his landlady a few days before on the basis of Peredonov's complaints, put in an appearance before Khripach after classes the day before as well. Fearing a second visit from Peredonov with the same consequences, the boy had made a complaint to the headmaster.

In a dry, sharp voice Khripach communicated to Peredonov the rumors that had reached him—from reliable sources, he added—about how Peredonov was visiting students in their lodgings and communicating incorrect information about the achievements and behavior of the children to either the parents or guardians and demanding that the boys be whipped, in consequence of which enormous troubles were provoked among the parents at times, such as, for example, the evening before in the club with the notary, Gudaevsky.

Peredonov listened, resentful and cowardly. Khripach fell silent.

"Really now," Peredonov said angrily, "he's the one who's picking a fight and is that actually allowed? He had no right whatsoever to let me have it in the face. He doesn't go to church, he worships a monkey and is corrupting his son into the same sect. He ought to be denounced, he's a socialist."

Khripach looked attentively at Peredonov and said in an imposing voice:

"All of that does not concern us and I am completely at a loss to understand what you comprehend with the original expression of 'he worships a monkey.' In my opinion there is no reason to enrich the history of religion with newly invented cults. As regards the insult which has been perpetrated against you, you ought to bring him before the courts. But the best thing for you would be to leave our gymnasium. That would be the very best expedient for both you personally and for the gymnasium."

"I'm going to be an inspector," Peredonov protested angrily.

"Until that time," Khripach continued, "you ought to refrain from these strange escapades. You yourself must agree that such behavior is unseemly for a pedagogue and lowers the dignity of a teacher in the eyes of his pupils. Going around houses to whip boys—that, you must admit your-self . . ."

Khripach didn't finish and shrugged his shoulders.

"Really," Peredonov protested again, "I was doing it for their own good."

"Please, we will not argue," Khripach interrupted sharply. "In the most resolute fashion I am demanding that you not repeat any of this in the future."

Peredonov looked angrily at the director.

That evening they decided to hold a housewarming. They invited all their acquaintances. Peredonov walked around the rooms and looked to see that everything was in order and to make certain there wasn't anything people could denounce him for. He was thinking:

"Well, everything seems fine. No forbidden books to be seen, the icon lamps are lit, the royal portraits are hanging on the wall in the place of honor."

Suddenly Mickiewicz winked at Peredonov from the wall.

"He's going to play tricks on me," Peredonov thought with fear, quickly took the portrait down and dragged it off to the outhouse to change places with Pushkin and to hang Pushkin back up.

"All the same, Pushkin was a courtier," he thought, hanging him on the wall in the living room.

Then he remembered that they were going to play cards that evening and he decided to examine the cards. He took an unsealed deck which had only been used once and started to sort through the cards as though he were looking for something in them. He didn't like the expressions on the face cards: they were so goggle-eyed.

Lately while playing cards it had always seemed to him that the cards were smirking like Varvara. Even the six of spades displayed an insolent appearance and wobbled about obscenely.

Peredonov gathered up all the cards there were and with the sharp ends of the scissors pricked through the eyes of the face cards so they couldn't spy. At first he did it with the used cards, but then he unsealed new decks as well. He did all of this while looking over his shoulder, as though fear-ing that someone would catch him. To his good luck Varvara was busy in the kitchen and didn't peek into the other rooms—besides, how could she leave unguarded such an abundance of food supplies—Klavdiya had come in handy at that particular moment. When she needed something in the other rooms, she would send Klavdiya there. Every time Klavdiya entered, Peredonov would shudder, hide the scissors in his pocket and pretend that he was laying out the cards for solitaire.

While Peredonov was thus depriving the kings and queens of any possibility of annoying him with their spying, trouble was approaching him from a different direction. The hat, which Peredonov had thrown on top of the stove in the other apartment so that it wouldn't come so easily to hand, was discovered by Ershova.

She reckoned that the hat had not been left behind accidentally. Her archenemies—the tenants who had moved out—very likely, thought Ershova, had cast a spell in the hat out of spite so that no one would rent the apartment afterwards. In fear and annoyance she took the hat to a wise woman. The latter examined the hat, sternly and mysteriously made whispering sounds over it, spat in all four directions and said to Ershova:

"They tried to play a dirty trick on you, but you can turn the trick against them. A powerful wizard has cast a spell, but I am more cunning: I will cast a counter-spell against him so that he himself will be crushed."

And for a long while she worked a spell over the hat, and after receiving generous gifts from Ershova, she ordered her to give the hat to a red-haired fellow so that he would take the hat back to Peredonov, give it to the first person he met there and then run away without looking back.

It transpired that the first red-headed fellow that Ershova met was one of the locksmith's sons who were furious with Peredonov for revealing their nocturnal prank. He agreed with pleasure to fulfill the commission for five kopecks and on the way kept spitting into the hat on his own behalf. At Peredonov's apartment, he ran smack into Varvara in the dark entry way, slipped her the hat and ran away so nimbly that Varvara didn't manage to make out who it was.

And thus, Peredonov had barely had time to blind the final jack when Varvara, amazed and even frightened, entered the room and said in a voice trembling with agitation:

"Ardalyon Borisych, have a look at this."

Peredonov looked and almost fainted from terror. That very same hat that he had tried to get rid of was now in Varvara's hands, crumpled, covered in dust and barely preserving the traces of its former magnificence. He asked, choking with terror:

"Where, where did it come from?"

Varvara told him in a frightened voice how she had gotten the hat from a spritely boy who almost seemed to have risen up out of the ground before her eyes, only then seemingly to be swallowed up by the ground again. She said:

"It couldn't be anyone but that old hag Ershova. She's the one who put a spell in the hat, that's for certain."

Peredonov muttered something indistinct and his teeth were chattering with fear. Gloomy fears and apprehensions were tormenting him. He walked around frowning, while the gray *nedotykomka* ran about under the chairs and giggled.

The guests came early. They brought a lot of pies, apples and pears to the housewarming. Varvara accepted it all joyfully, and kept repeating for the sake of decorum:

"Goodness, why did you bother? You needn't have bothered yourself for nothing."

But if it seemed to her that people brought something cheap or bad, then she became angry. Nor did she like it if two guests brought the same thing.

Losing no time they sat down to play cards. They played cards at two tables.

"Ah, goodness gracious!" Grushina exclaimed. "What's this, my king is blind!"

"My queen hasn't any eyes either," Prepolovenskaya said, examining her cards. "And the jack as well."

Laughing, the guests started to examine the cards.

Prepolovensky said:

"Well, well, there I was thinking what the matter was, the cards seem rough—and that's why. I kept fingering them all the while, thinking what's wrong, the back is kind of rough, but then it turns out that it's because of these holes. Well-well, it's the back of the card and it's rough."

Everyone was laughing, only Peredonov alone was sullen. Varvara, smirking, said:

"You know how eccentric my Ardalyon Borisych is always acting. He's always coming up with fresh tricks."

"Why did you do it?" Rutilov asked with a loud burst of laughter.

"What do they need eyes for?" Peredonov said sullenly. "They don't have to look."

Everyone roared with laughter while Peredonov remained sullen and taciturn. It seemed to him that the blinded figures were making faces, smirking and winking at him with the gaping holes in their eyes.

"Perhaps," Peredonov thought, "they've contrived some way to look with their noses now."

As was almost always the case he was unlucky and he imagined an expression of ridicule and malice on the faces of the kings, queens and jacks. The queen of spades was even grinding her teeth, apparently furious at the fact that she had been blinded. Finally, after one enormous loss, Peredonov grabbed the pack of cards and furiously started to tear them to pieces. The guests roared with laughter. Smirking, Varvara said:

"That's the way my fellow is all the time—he has a drink and starts to act strange."

"When he's drunk, you mean?" Prepolovenskaya said poisonously. "Ardalyon Borisych, do you hear what your cousin thinks about you?"

Varvara blushed and said angrily:

"What are you doing pouncing on my words?"

Prepolovenskaya smiled and was silent.

They took a fresh deck of cards in place of the torn one and continued the game.

Suddenly a crash was heard—the glass window was smashed and a stone fell on the floor near the table where Peredonov was sitting. Under

the window they could hear someone softly talking, laughter, then the
sound of feet disappearing quickly into the distance. Everyone leapt up
from their places in great commotion. The women, as usual, started to
shriek. They picked up the stone, examined it fearfully, but no one could
make up their mind to go to the window. First they sent Klavdiya out on
the street and only after she had reported that it was deserted outside did
they begin to examine the shattered window.

Volodin concluded that students from the gymnasium had thrown the
stone. The conjecture seemed likely and everyone gave Peredonov a significant look. Peredonov frowned and muttered something unintelligible. The
guests started to talk about what brazen and illdisciplined boys there were.

Of course it hadn't been students from the gymnasium but the sons of
the locksmith.

"It's the headmaster who put the students up to it," Peredonov suddenly declared. "He keeps finding fault with me, he doesn't know how to
get at me and so he thought this up."

"Some trick he's pulled!" Rutilov cried with laughter.

Everyone burst into laughter, only Grushina said:

"And what do you think, he's the kind of poisonous person that you
might expect anything from. He didn't do it himself, he'd keep to the side.
He'd put them up to it through his sons."

"It doesn't matter that they're aristocrats," Volodin bleated in an
offended voice. "You can expect anything from aristocrats."

Many of the guests thought that it was likely true and they stopped
laughing.

"You don't have any luck with glass, Ardalyon Borisych," Rutilov said.
"First they broke your spectacles and then they smashed the window."

That provoked a fresh fit of laughter.

"Broken glass means a long life," Prepolovenskaya said with a
restrained smile.

When Peredonov and Varvara were getting ready to go to bed, it
seemed to Peredonov that Varvara had something wicked on her mind. He
took the knives and forks away from her and hid them under the bed. He
was babbling with a sluggish tongue:

"I know you. As soon as you marry me, then you're going to denounce
me so that you can get rid of me. You'll get my pension while they'll be
grinding me to bits in the mill in Petropavlovsky Prison."

That night Peredonov was delirious. Indistinct, frightening figures were
roaming about noiselessly—kings and jacks shaking their staffs. They were
whispering and trying to hide from Peredonov, and stealthily crept up
under his pillow. But soon they became bolder and started to walk, run and
fuss about all around Peredonov, on the floor, the bed and the pillows.
They whispered in hushed voices, teasing Peredonov, sticking their tongues
out at him, making strange faces in front of him, distorting their mouths
hideously. Peredonov saw that they were all small and mischievous, that

they wouldn't kill him, but were only mocking him, auguring ill. But he was frightened. First he muttered some incantations, scraps of spells that he had heard in his childhood. Then he started to scold them and chase them away, waving his arms and crying in a hoarse voice.

Varvara woke up and asked angrily:

"What are you yelling for, Ardalyon Borisych? You won't let me sleep."

"The queen of spades keeps pestering me inside the mattress covering," muttered Peredonov.

Varvara got up, and grumbling and cursing, she administered some kind of drops to Peredonov.

In the local provincial newspaper an article appeared on the subject of how supposedly in our town a certain Mrs. K. was whipping young gymnasium students, the sons of the best local gentry families, who were lodging in her apartment. The notary, Gudaevsky, swept through the entire town with this news and was indignant.

Various other awkward rumors as well were circulating through the town about the local gymnasium. People were talking about the young girl who was dressed up as a boy student. Then the name of Pylnikov gradually came to be associated with Lyudmila's. At first he hardly reacted to these jokes, but then he began to flare up at times and defend Lyudmila, insisting that nothing of the sort was true.

For this reason he felt ashamed to go to Lyudmila's, but he had an even stronger urge to do so. His ardent, confused feelings of shame and attraction were a source of agitation to him and his imagination was filled with vaguely passionate visions.

XXI

O N SUNDAY WHEN Peredonov and Varvara were having breakfast, someone entered the front hall. Varvara, as was her habit, crept stealthily up to the door and glanced through it. Just as softly she returned to the table and whispered:

"It's the postman. We ought to give him some vodka, he's brought another letter."

Peredonov nodded his head in silence. What did it matter, he didn't begrudge a glass of vodka. Varvara shouted out:

"Postman, come in here!"

The letter carrier entered the room. He rummaged around in his bag and pretended that he was searching for a letter. Varvara poured some vodka into a large glass and cut off a piece of pie. The letter carrier watched her activity lasciviously. Meanwhile, Peredonov kept thinking of whom the postman reminded him. Finally he remembered—it was that very same red-headed, pimply-faced knave who not long ago had tricked him into such an enormous loss.

"He's likely to pull another trick," Peredonov thought with melancholy and made a rude sign to the letter carrier from his pocket.

The red-headed knave handed the letter over to Varvara.

"For you, Madame," he said respectfully, thanked her for the vodka, drank it down, grunted, grabbed the pie and left.

Varvara turned the letter over and over in her hands and without unsealing it handed it to Peredonov.

"Go on, read it. Looks like it's from the Princess again," she said, smirking. "She's written plenty, but what's the point. Rather than writing, she ought to give you a post."

Peredonov's hands were trembling. He tore open the envelope and quickly read the letter. Then he leapt up from his place, waved the letter and started to whoop:

"Hurray! There are three inspector's posts, any one can be chosen. Hurray, Varvara, we've won!"

He started to dance and whirled around the room. With his impassive red face and dull eyes he seemed like a strangely large doll that had been wound up to dance. Varvara was smirking and looking joyfully at him. He shouted:

"Now it's decided, Varvara. We're getting married." He grabbed Varvara by the shoulders and started to whirl her around the table stamping his feet.

"A Russian dance, Varvara!" he cried.

Varvara put her hands on her hips and glided out in a dance, while Peredonov crouched down to dance in front of her.

Volodin came in and bleated joyfully:

"The future inspector is stomping out a *trepak!*"

"Dance, Pavlushka!" Peredonov cried.

Klavdiya peered out from behind the door. Volodin shouted to her, laughing and clowning:

"Dance, Klavdyushka, you too! Everyone together. Let's entertain the future inspector!"

Klavdiya gave a squeal and glided into dance, shaking her shoulders. Volodin twirled dashingly in front of her—he crouched down on his haunches, spun around, sprang up and down, clapped his hands. It made a particularly dashing impression when he raised his knee and clapped his hands under the knee. The floor vibrated beneath their heels. Klavdiya rejoiced at the fact that she had such an agile young fellow.

They grew tired and sat down at the table while Klavdiya ran off to the kitchen with a cheerful laugh. They drank vodka, beer, broke bottles and glasses, shouted, roared with laughter, waved their arms about, embraced and kissed. Then Peredonov and Volodin ran off to the Summer Gardens—Peredonov was in a hurry to brag about his letter.

They came upon the usual company in the billiard room. Peredonov showed his friends the letter. It created a big impression. Everyone looked it over trustingly. Rutilov grew pale, and mumbling something, sputtered.

"The postman delivered it while I was at home!" Peredonov exclaimed. "I unsealed it myself. So that means there's no deception here."

And his friends regarded him with respect. A letter from a Princess!

From the Summer Gardens Peredonov hurried to Vershina's.

He walked with a quick and regular motion, waving his arms uniformly and muttering something. It seemed as though there were no expression on his face—it was impassive like the face of a doll that had been wound up. Only some hungry fire was reflected in the deathly glimmer of his eyes.

It turned out to be a clear hot day. Marta was sitting in the summer house. She was knitting a stocking. Her thoughts were vague and devout. At first she was thinking about vices, then she directed her thoughts to something more pleasant and started to contemplate the virtues. Her thoughts were enshrouded in drowsiness and became graphic. The clarity of their dreamlike outlines increased in proportion to the progressive deterioration of their abstract verbal intelligibility. The virtues became represented before her as large beautiful dolls in white dresses, radiant and fragrant. They promised her rewards, keys were jingling in their hands and wedding veils fluttered on their heads.

In their midst was one strange doll that was dissimilar. It promised nothing but gave reproachful looks and its lips were moving in soundless threat. It seemed that if she were to say anything, it would be terrible. Marta guessed that it represented conscience. She was all in black, this strange eerie visitor with her black eyes and black hair. And suddenly she started to talk about something, quickly, rapidly, clearly. She started to resemble Vershina completely. Marta roused herself, answered something to her question, answered almost unconsciously—and once again was overcome with drowsiness.

Either it was her conscience or it was Vershina sitting opposite her and saying something quickly and distinctly, but unintelligibly, and smoking something strange smelling. Decisive Vershina, quiet, demanding that everything be as she wished. Marta wanted to look directly into the eyes of this importunate visitor, but for some reason or other she couldn't. And the visitor was smiling strangely, grumbling, and her eyes were wandering off somewhere and fastening on distant unfamiliar objects that were terrible for Marta to look at. . . .

A loud conversation woke Marta up. Peredonov was standing in the summer house and speaking loudly, exchanging greetings with Vershina. Marta looked around in fright. Her heart was pounding while her eyes were still stuck together and her thoughts were still confused. Where was conscience? Or had it never existed? And shouldn't it have been there?

"You were deep in sleep here," Peredonov said to her. "You were snoring your head off. She was lumbering."

Marta didn't understand his pun, but she smiled, guessing from the smile on Vershina's lips that something had been said that was supposed to be humorous.

"You ought to be called Kitty," Peredonov continued.

"Why?" Marta asked.

"Because you were having a catnap."

Peredonov sat down on the bench beside Marta and said:

"I have news and very important it is."

"What news do you have, do share it with us," Vershina said and Marta immediately felt envious of her because she was able to express the simple question of "What news?" with such a large quantity of words.

"Guess," Peredonov said in a sullenly solemn voice.

"How can I guess what news you have," Vershina replied. "You tell us and then we'll know what your news is."

Peredonov didn't like it that they didn't want to guess what his news was. He fell silent and sat there, hunched over, dull and heavy and gazed impassively directly in front. Vershina was smoking and smiling crookedly, showing her dark yellow teeth.

"How can we guess what your news is," she said and was silent for a while. "Let me divine it for you from the cards. Marta, bring the cards from the room."

Marta stood up, but Peredonov stopped her angrily:

"Sit, don't bother, I don't want them. You guess yourselves, but leave me alone. You're not going to stump me with your fortune-telling. Here I'm going to show you something that will make you gape."

Peredonov smartly pulled his wallet out of his pocket, fetched the letter out with its envelope and showed it to Vershina without letting go of it.

"You see," he said, "an envelope. And here's the letter."

He pulled out the letter and read it slowly, with a dull expression of satisfied malice in his eyes. Vershina was taken aback. Up until the final moment she had never believed in the Princess, but now she understood that the business with Marta was totally lost. She grinned with an annoyed, crooked expression and said:

"Well, really, congratulations."

Marta was sitting there with a surprised and frightened look on her face and smiling distractedly.

"What do you think of that?" Peredonov said maliciously. "You took me for a fool, but I've turned out to be smarter than you. You were talking about the envelope, well there's your envelope. This business of mine is certain now."

He banged his fist on the table, not hard and not loudly, and this motion and the sound of his words remained somehow indifferent, as though he were alien to and far removed from his affairs.

Vershina and Marta exchanged looks that were distastefully perplexed.

"What are you exchanging looks for!" Peredonov said rudely. "There's nothing to exchange looks for: now everything is settled, I'm marrying Varvara. There were a lot of young ladies here who were trying to catch me."

Vershina sent Marta off for cigarettes and Marta ran joyfully out of the summer house. Out on the sandy paths, which were brilliantly colored with faded leaves, she felt free and easy. She met the barefooted Vladya near the house and she felt even more cheerful and joyful.

"He's marrying Varvara, it's decided," she said animatedly, lowering her voice and drawing her brother into the house.

Meanwhile, Peredonov suddenly started to say goodbye without waiting for Marta.

"I don't have any time," he said. "Getting married is no sewing bee."

Vershina didn't try to detain him and parted coldly with him.[13] She was terribly annoyed: up until this time she had still had a feeble hope of fixing Marta up with Peredonov, while she herself would take Murin. But now the final hope had faded.

And Marta would be in for it that day! She would have to shed some tears.

Peredonov left Vershina's and had an urge to smoke. He suddenly caught sight of a policeman—he was standing by himself on a corner and cracking sunflower seeds. Peredonov had a melancholy feeling.

"Another spy," he thought. "They keep looking to find fault with something."

He didn't dare light up the cigarette he had pulled out. He went up to the policeman and asked timidly:

"Mister policeman, is it allowed to smoke here?"

The policeman made a salute and inquired respectfully:

"Excuse me, sir, what do you mean?"

"A cigarette," Peredonov explained, "Am I allowed to smoke just this one cigarette?"

"An order hasn't been issued on this matter," the policeman replied evasively.

"There hasn't?" Peredonov asked again with melancholy in his voice.

"None whatsoever. So, no order has been received to stop gentlemen from smoking, but I cannot say whether specific information has been issued on the matter."

"If there wasn't anything, then I won't do it," Peredonov said submissively. "I am a loyal person. I'll even throw the cigarette away. I'm a State Councillor you know."

Peredonov crushed the cigarette, threw it on the ground, and already fearing that he might have said something superfluous, hastily went home. The policeman watched him go in perplexity, and finally decided that the gentleman had had a few "for the road", and satisfied by that, he started once more to peacefully crack his sunflower seeds.(a)

"The street is getting its back up," Peredonov muttered.

The street rose to a low hill and then descended on the other side, and the bend in the street between two hovels was etched against a sky that was blue, mournful and turning to evening. This quiet district of miserable life was shut up in itself and deep in sorrow and languor. The trees spread their branches over the fence and scrutinized and prevented people from passing. Their whisperings were scornful and threatening. A sheep stood at the crossroads and gazed dully at Peredonov.

Suddenly a bleating laughter came from around the corner—Volodin emerged into sight and came up to say hello. Peredonov looked at him gloomily and thought about the sheep that had just been standing there and suddenly had disappeared.

"That means of course," he thought, "that Volodin has turned into a sheep. It isn't by chance that he resembles a sheep so much and it's impossible to distinguish whether he's laughing or bleating."

He was so preoccupied by these thoughts that he didn't hear in the least what Volodin said by way of greeting.

"What are you kicking about, Pavlyushka!" he said with melancholy. Volodin bared his teeth, bleated and protested:

"I'm not kicking, Ardalyon Borisych, but greeting you with a handshake. Perhaps where you come from people kick with their hands, but where I come from people kick with their feet, and it's not people that do it, if I may say so, but horses."

"I expect you'll be butting next," Peredonov said with a grumble. Volodin was offended and in a reverberating voice said:

"Ardalyon Borisych, as of yet I haven't grown any horns, but perhaps you might grow horns before I do."

"You have a long tongue, it's always babbling something it shouldn't," Peredonov said angrily.

"If that's what you think, Ardalyon Borisych," Volodin immediately objected, "then I might as well be silent."

And his face assumed an utterly sorrowful expression, while his lips were all puffed out. However, he walked on alongside Peredonov—he still hadn't eaten dinner and was counting on dining at Peredonov's that day. He had been invited that morning to his joy at morning mass.

An important piece of news was awaiting Peredonov at home. While still in the entry way it was possible to guess that something extraordinary had happened—a commotion and frightened exclamations could be heard from the other rooms. Peredonov thought that things weren't ready for dinner yet, but they had seen him coming, had become frightened and were hurrying. He felt good—about the way they were afraid of him! But it turned out that something else had happened. Varvara ran out into the front hall and cried:

"They brought the cat back!"

Frightened, she didn't notice Volodin right off. As usual, her dress was slovenly: a greasy blouse over a gray filthy skirt and battered shoes. Her hair was uncombed and dishevelled. She said excitedly to Peredonov:

"It's that Irishka! Out of spite she's come up with a fresh trick. A boy ran up again, brought the cat and dumped it. And the cat had rattles on its tail and it's making a racket. The cat's crawled under the divan and won't come out.

Peredonov felt terrified.(b)

"What should we do now?" he asked.

"Pavel Vasilyevich," Varvara asked, "you're younger, chase him out from under the divan,"(c)

"We'll chase him out, yes we will," Volodin said with a giggle and went into the front room.

Somehow or other they dragged the cat out and removed the rattles from its tail. Peredonov searched for some burdocks and once more started to stick them on the cat. The cat hissed ferociously and ran off into the kitchen.(d) Tired from the commotion over the cat, Peredonov sat down in his usual pose: elbows on the arms of an easy chair, fingers intertwined, one leg crossed over the other, his face impassive and sullen.(e)

Peredonov guarded the second letter from the Princess more zealously than the first. He always carried it around with himself in his wallet, but he showed it to everyone and assumed a mysterious look when he did so. He watched, sharp-eyed, to see whether anyone was about to take the letter away and he wouldn't hand it over to anyone. After each showing he would hide it in his wallet, stuff his wallet into his jacket, in the inner side pocket, button up his jacket and sternly and significantly regard his companions.

"Why are you running around with it like that?" Rutilov once asked with a laugh.

"Just in case," Peredonov explained sullenly. "Who knows what you'll do! You might try and snatch it."

"This business of yours is pure Siberia," Rutilov said, roared with laughter and slapped Peredonov on the back.

But Peredonov preserved an imperturbable pompousness. In general he had begun of late to act more pompously than was customary. He frequently boasted:

"I'm going to be an inspector. The rest of you here will be rotting away, but I'll have two regions under my authority. Or even three. Oh-ho-ho!"

He was completely convinced that in the very shortest time he would get an inspector's post. He said more than once to the teacher, Falastov:

"I'll get you out of here, brother."

And the teacher, Falastov, became very respectful in the way he treated Peredonov.

XXII

PEREDONOV STARTED TO attend church regularly. He would stand in an obvious spot and either cross himself more often than necessary, or suddenly grow rigid as a post and gaze dully in front of himself. It seemed to him that some spies were hiding behind the columns, peeking out from there and trying to make him laugh. But he didn't give in.

Laughter, with quiet chuckling, giggling and whispering from the Rutilov girls, rang in Peredonov's ears, growing at times to extraordinary proportions. It was just as though those sly girls were laughing right in his ears so that they would make him laugh and ruin him. But Peredonov didn't give in.

The *nedotykomka*, smoky and bluish, would appear from time to time amid the puffs of incense smoke. The little eyes gleamed with fires and it sometimes floated around through the air, but not for long. Most frequently it scurried about at the feet of the parishioners, making fun of Peredonov and tormenting him relentlessly. Of course, it wanted to frighten Peredonov so that he would leave the church before the end of mass. But he realized what its devious plan was and didn't submit.

The church service, not in its words and rites, but in its innermost movement which was so dear to such a multitude of people, was incomprehensible to Peredonov and therefore frightened him. The swinging of the censers terrified him like superstitious spells.

"What's he swinging it around for?" he thought.

The priests' attire seemed like coarse, annoyingly colorful rags, and when he looked at a priest in his sacerdotal robes he felt like tearing up the robes and smashing the holy vessels. He imagined the rites and mysteries of the church to be a wicked form of sorcery that was directed towards the enslavement of the simple folk.

"He dropped crumbs from the holy wafer into the wine," he thought angrily of the priest. "It's the cheapest wine and they turn the heads of the people so that they bring more money for the offerings."

The mystery of the eternal transformation of impotent matter into a force that annulled the bonds of death was forever veiled from him. A walking corpse! He was possessed of an incongruous combination of non-belief in the living God and Christ with a belief in sorcery!

People started to leave the church. The village teacher, Machigin, an unassuming young man, went up to the girls, smiled and chatted energetically. Peredonov thought that it was unseemly of him to act so freely in front of a future inspector. Machigin was wearing a straw hat. But Peredonov recalled that at some time during the summer he had seen him outside the town wearing an official cap with a cockade. Peredonov decided to complain. In the event, inspector Bogdanov was there as well. Peredonov went up to him and said:

"Your Machigin wears a cap with a cockade. He's playing the aristocrat."

Bogdanov was frightened, started to tremble, and shook his grayish little beard.

"He has no right, no right whatsoever does he have," he said with concern, blinking his little red eyes.

"He doesn't have the right, but he wears one," Peredonov complained. "They have to be reined in, I've told you that long ago. Otherwise any uncouth peasant will start wearing a cockade and then what'll happen!"

Bogdanov, who had already been frightened by Peredonov earlier, became even more overwrought.

"How could he dare to do it, eh?" he said in a whining voice. "I shall summon him immediately, immediately I say, and I shall forbid it most sternly."

He took leave of Peredonov and hastily trotted off home.

Volodin walked alongside Peredonov and said in a reproachfully bleating voice:

"He's wearing a cockade. Do tell, for goodness sake! As though he's been awarded ranks! How could it be!"

"Neither are you allowed to wear a cockade," Peredonov said.

"Not allowed and not necessary," Volodin protested. "Only sometimes I too put a cockade on—but I alone know where and when it's allowed. If I go off by myself outside the city then I put it on there. It gives me a lot of pleasure and no one would forbid it. If you run into a peasant, all the same there's more respect."

"A cockade doesn't suit your mug, Pavlushka," Peredonov said. "And move away from me—you're getting me dusty with your hooves."

Volodin fell into an offended silence, but continued to walk alongside. Peredonov said with concern:

"Those Rutilov girls still ought to be reported. They only go to church to gossip and laugh. They powder themselves up, get all dressed up and off they go. But they're stealing the incense and making perfume out of it— they always reek of it."

"Do tell, for goodness sake!" Volodin said, shaking his head and rolling his dull eyes.

A shadow from a cloud crept swiftly over the ground and provoked an attack of fear in Peredonov. The gray *nedotykomka* flitted from time to time through the puffs of dust in the air. If the grass started to rustle in the wind, it would seem to Peredonov as though the *nedotykomka* was running around in it, biting it and eating its fill.

"Why do they have grass in the town?" he thought. "A disgrace! It ought to be pulled out."

A branch on a tree started to rustle, shrank into itself, turned black, cawed and flew off into the distance. Peredonov shuddered, cried wildly and ran off home. Volodin trotted along behind him anxiously with a perplexed expression in his goggling eyes, holding his bowler hat on his head and waving his stick.

On that very same day Bogdanov summoned Machigin. Before entering the inspector's apartment, Machigin stood in the street with his back to the sun, removed his hat and used his shadow to comb his hair with his fingers.

"What are you up to, young man, eh? What's this you've contrived, eh?" Bogdanov let loose at Machigin.

"What's the matter?" Machigin asked in an unduly free manner, playing with his straw hat and shuffling his left foot.

Bogdanov didn't sit him down, because he intended to give him a tongue-lashing.

"What are you up to, what's this you're up to, young man, wearing a cockade, eh? How could you bring yourself to commit such an infringement, eh?" he asked, assuming an air of severity and vehemently shaking his little gray beard.

Machigin blushed, but he replied pertly:

"What's wrong, am I not in the right?"

"Well are you really an official, eh? An official?" Bogdanov grew more agitated. "What kind of official are you, eh? An ABC registrar, eh?"

"It's a sign of the teaching profession," Machigin said pertly and suddenly smiled sweetly, recollecting the importance of his teaching profession.

"You carry a stick in your hands, a stick, that's your sign of the teaching profession," Bogdanov advised, shaking his head.

"For goodness sake, Sergei Potapovich." Machigin said with injury in his voice. "What good is a stick! Anyone can carry a stick, but a cockade is for prestige."

"For what kind of prestige, eh? For what kind of prestige, what kind?" Bogdanov flew at the young man. "What kind of prestige do you require, eh? Are you one of the authorities?"

"For goodness sake, Sergei Potapovich," Machigin attempted to prove in a reasonable fashion, "in the uncultured peasant class it immediately arouses a wave of respect—this year they're bowing down much lower."

Machigin smoothed his reddish moustache with self-satisfaction.

"It's not allowed, young man, not allowed at all," Bogdanov said, dolefully shaking his head.

"For goodness sake, Sergei Potapovich, a teacher without a cockade is the same as the British lion without a tail," Machigin sought to persuade him. "Nothing but a caricature."

"What's a tail got to do with this, eh? What's this about a tail, eh?"

Bogdanov said with agitation. "Why are you starting up on politics, eh? Is it any of your affair to start making judgments on politics, eh? No, you be so kind as to take that cockade off, young man. It's not allowed, how could you! Heaven forfend, the number of people that could find out!"

Machigin shrugged his shoulders, wanted to protest further, but Bogdanov interrupted him. What he considered to be a brilliant idea had flashed through his mind.

"Here you've come to see me without a cockade, eh? Without a cockade? You yourself feel that it isn't allowed."

Machigin almost faltered, but this time he found a reason for protest:

"Because we're country teachers, we need a country privilege, whereas in the town we're considered to be second-class members of the intelligentsia."

"No, just you understand, young man," Bogdanov said angrily, "that is not allowed and if I hear once more of this, then we'll dismiss you."

From time to time Grushina organized parties for young people from whose number she was hoping to catch herself a husband. As a decoy she would invite family friends as well.(f)

This was one of those kinds of parties. The guests arrived early.

Paintings that were completely covered over with muslin hung on the walls of Grushina's sitting room. In any event there was nothing indecent in them. When Grushina lifted the muslin coverings with a sly and immodest little grin, the guests would admire the poorly painted naked women.

"What's this, a crooked woman?" Peredonov said sullenly.

"There's nothing crooked about her," Grushina defended the painting vehemently. "She's just bent over like that."

"She's crooked," Peredonov repeated. "And her eyes don't match, like yours."

"Well, a lot you understand!" Grushina said in an offended voice. "These paintings are very fine and expensive. Artists have to paint those kind of pictures."

Suddenly Peredonov burst into laughter. He had remembered the advice which he had given to Vladya the other day.

"What are you neighing for?" Grishina asked.

"Nartanovich, a student at the gymnasium, is going to set fire to his sister Marta's dress," he explained. "I advised him to do so."

"If he does that, then you've found a fool!" Grushina objected.

"Of course he will," Peredonov said confidently, "Brothers and sisters are always fighting. When I was little, that's how I always played nasty tricks on my sisters. I beat up the young ones and I ruined the clothing of the older ones."

"Not all of them fight," Rutilov said. "I don't fight with my sisters."

"What do you do with them, make up to them, or something?" Peredonov asked.

"You, Ardalyon Borisych, are a swine and a scoundrel, and I'm going to slap your face," Rutilov said very calmly.

"Well, I don't care for those kinds of jokes," Peredonov replied and moved away from Rutilov.

"Otherwise," he thought, "he'll really do it, there's something ominous in his face."

"She only has the one black dress," he continued, in reference to Marta.

"Vershina will sew her a new one," Varvara said with malicious envy. "She'll make her entire dowry for her wedding. Some beauty, even horses are spooked," she grumbled softly and looked maliciously at Murin.

"It's time for you to get married," Prepolovenskaya said. "What are you waiting for, Ardalyon Borisych?"

The Prepolovenskys had seen by now that after the second letter Peredonov had firmly decided to marry Varvara. They themselves had believed the letter. They had begun to say that they had always been in favor of Varvara. There was nothing for them to gain by embroiling Varvara and Peredonov—it was advantageous for them to go on playing cards. As for Genya, there was nothing to be done, let her wait. They'd have to look for another prospective husband.

Prepolovensky started to speak:

"Of course, you have to get married. You'll be doing the good deed and obliging the Princess. The Princess will be pleased that you're getting married, so you'll be obliging her and doing the good deed, and that'll be good, otherwise, in general, you'll be doing the good deed and the Princess will be pleased."

"That's what I would say as well," Prepolovenskaya said.

But Prepolovensky couldn't stop and seeing that everyone was already moving away from him, he sat down beside a young official and started to expound on the same topic to him.

"I've made up my mind to get married," Peredonov said. "Only Varvara and I don't know what's necessary to get married. Something has to be done, but I don't know what."

"Well, it's not a tricky business," Prepolovenskaya said. "But if you wish, my husband and I will arrange everything for you, you just sit quiet and don't think about a thing."

"Fine," Peredonov said. "I'm agreed. Only make sure that everything will be nice and decent. I don't begrudge the money."

"Everything will be just fine, don't you worry," Prepolovenskaya assured him.

Peredonov continued to set down his conditions:

"Out of miserliness others buy thin wedding rings, silver ones with gold plating, but I don't want that, I want real gold ones. And instead of wedding rings I even want to order wedding bracelets—that would be more expensive and prestigious."

Everyone laughed.

"You can't have bracelets," Prepolovenskaya said, grinning slightly. "You have to have rings."

"Why can't I?" Peredonov asked with annoyance.

"Because it's not done like that."

"Well maybe it is done," Peredonov said mistrustfully. "I'm going to ask the priest about it as well. He knows better."

Giggling, Rutilov advised:

"Ardalyon Borisych, better you order wedding belts."

"Well, I don't have enough money for that," Peredonov replied without noticing the sarcasm. "I'm not a banker.(g) But just the other day I had a dream in which I was getting married. I had a satin dress coat on and Varvara and I were wearing gold bracelets. And two headmasters were standing behind us, holding wedding wreaths over our heads and singing hallelujah."

"I had an interesting dream last night," Volodin declared. "But I don't know what the meaning of it was. Supposedly I was sitting on a throne and wearing a golden crown. In front of me was grass and there were sheep on the grass, nothing but sheep and more sheep—baa-baa-baa. So all the sheep were walking around doing this with their heads, and going baa-baa-baa all the while."

Volodin went strolling through the rooms, shaking his forehead, puffing out his lips and bleating. The guests laughed. Volodin sat down on the spot, gazed blissfully at everyone, screwed up his eyes with pleasure and then he gave his sheeplike bleating laugh.

"Well, what happened next?" Grushina asked, winking at the guests.

"Well, nothing but sheep and more sheep, and at that point I woke up," Volodin concluded.

"Sheep dreams for a sheep," Peredonov grumbled. "Big deal being king of the sheep."

"I had a dream," Varvara said with an insolent grin. "But I can't tell it in front of men, I'll tell it to you alone."

"Ach, my dear Varvara Dmitrievna, in a word the same thing happened to me," Grushina replied, giggling and winking at everyone.

"Tell us, we're modest men, sort of like women," Rutilov said.

The rest of the men begged Varvara and Grushina to tell their dreams. But the latter exchanged looks, laughed foully and wouldn't tell.(h)

They sat down to play cards. Rutilov assured Peredonov that he was playing excellently. Peredonov believed him. But that day, as usual, he was losing. Rutilov was winning. That made him extremely happy and he talked with greater animation than usual.

The *nedotykomka* was teasing Peredonov. It was hiding somewhere close by. It would show itself at times, popping out from behind the table or from behind someone's back and then hiding again. It seemed as though it were waiting for something. It was frightening. The very look of the cards frightened Peredonov. There were two queens together on each card.

"But where's the third one?" Peredonov wondered.

He dully examined the queen of spades, then he turned it over—maybe the third one was hiding on the back.

Rutilov said:

"Ardalyon Borisych is looking at the backside of his queen."

Everyone burst into laughter.

Meanwhile, two young police officials were playing skat off to the side. They played their hands in a lively fashion. The one who won laughed with joy and made a long nose at the other. The loser got angry.

It began to smell of food. Grushina invited the guests into the dining room. Everyone went, jostling one another and affecting civilized manners. They distributed themselves at the table in a haphazard fashion.(i)

"Eat, ladies and gentlemen," Grushina invited. "Eat, my friends, stuff yourselves from nose to toes."

"If you fill your plate, the hostess feels great," Murin cried joyfully. It made him cheerful to look at the vodka and think that he was winning.

Volodin and the two young officials helped themselves more zealously than all the rest. They selected the better and more expensive items and devoured the caviar greedily. Grushina said with a strained laugh:

"Our Pavel Vasilyevich is sharp-eyed and high—straight past the bread and directly to the pie."

She hadn't bought the caviar for him! And under the pretext of serving the ladies, she moved all the better things away from him. But Volodin didn't lose heart and satisfied himself with what was left. He had already managed to eat many of the good things at the very start and now it made no difference to him.

Peredonov gazed at the people chewing and it seemed to him that they were all laughing at him. Why? What for? He ate everything that came his way with a frenzy, he ate slovenly and greedily.(j)

After supper they played cards again. But soon Peredonov got fed up. He threw his cards down and said:

"To hell with you! No luck. I'm fed up! Varvara, let's go home."

The other guests followed suit.

In the entry way Volodin saw that Peredonov had a new walking stick. Grinning, he turned it around for examination and asked:

"Ardasha, why are the fingers curled up here? What does it mean?"

Peredonov angrily took the stick out of his hand, raised the knob with its carved depiction of a rude gesture in dark wood to Volodin's nose and said:

"A fig to you with butter on it."

Volodin produced an offended expression.

"If you please, Ardalyon Borisych," he said, "I eat my bread with butter and I don't wish to eat a fig with butter."

Without listening to him, Peredonov was assiduously wrapping his neck up in his scarf and buttoning his coat up with all the buttons. Rutilov said laughingly:

"What are you wrapping yourself up for, Ardalyon Borisych? It's warm."

"Health is the most precious thing of all," Peredonov replied.

Out on the street it was quiet. The street had settled down in the gloom and was softly snoring. It was dark, melancholoy and damp. Heavy clouds were wandering overhead. Peredonov grumbled:

"Why has it turned dark?"

But he wasn't afraid now—he was walking with Varvara and wasn't alone.

Soon it started to rain, a fine, rapid and prolonged rain. Everything had turned still and only the rain was babbling something that was insistent, rapid and breathless—inaudible, monotonous and melancholy words.

Peredonov sensed the reflection of his melancholy and fear in the guise of nature's hostility towards him. But that interior life in nature that defied exterior definition, that life which alone could create genuine relations, profound and manifest, between man and nature—no, he had no sense whatsoever of that kind of life. For that reason, all of nature seemed to him to be replete with petty human emotions. Blinded by the delusions of the individual and of separate being, he did not comprehend the Dionysian elemental ecstasies that were exultant and rampant in nature. He was blind and pitiful, like many of us.

XXIII

THE PREPOLOVENSKYS ASSUMED the responsibility for organizing the wedding. They decided to have the marriage in a village about six versts from the town—it was awkward for Varvara to appear before the altar in the town after they had been living together for so many years and pretending to be relatives. They concealed the date the wedding was set for. The Prepolovenskys circulated the rumor that the wedding was taking place on a Friday, but in actual fact the wedding was to be on a Wednesday afternoon. They did this so that the curious would not show up from town. More than once Varvara repeated to Peredonov:

"Ardalyon Borisych, don't you go blabbing when the wedding's to take place, otherwise people will get in the way."

Peredonov unwillingly produced the money for the wedding expenses, making fun of Varvara. Sometimes he would bring his walking stick with the rude gesture on the knob and say to Varvara:

"Kiss my fig and I'll give you the money, if you don't, then I won't."

Varvara would kiss the fig.

"So what, my lips won't split from it," she would say.

They kept the date of the wedding secret even from the ushers right up until the very day so that they wouldn't go blabbing it. First they invited Rutilov and Volodin to be ushers. Both agreed willingly: Rutilov was anticipating an amusing story; Volodin was flattered to play such an important part in such an outstanding event in the life of such a respected person. Then Peredonov got it into his head that he needed another usher. He said:

"You'll have one, Varvara, but I need two, one isn't enough. It'll be difficult to hold the wreath over my head, I'm a tall person."

And Peredonov invited Falastov to be his second usher. Varvara grumbled:

"Why the devil him, there are two already, why another one?"

"He's got golden spectacles, it'll look more important with him there," Peredonov said.

The morning of the wedding day, Peredonov washed in warm water, as always, so that he wouldn't catch cold and then he asked for some rouge, explaining:

"Now I have to do myself up every day, otherwise people will think that I'm decrepit and I won't be appointed inspector."

Varvara begrudged her rouge, but she had to give way. And Peredonov rouged his cheeks. He muttered:

"Veriga himself puts rouge on so that he'll seem younger. I can't get married with white cheeks."

Afterwards, when he had locked himself in the bedroom, he determined to mark himself up so that Volodin couldn't change places with him. He smeared the letter "P" in ink on his chest, his stomach, his elbows and on various other parts.

"I ought to have marked up Volodin as well, but how could I do it? If he saw it he'd wipe it off," Peredonov thought with melancholy.

Then the thought entered his head that it wouldn't be a bad idea to put on a corset, otherwise he might be taken for an old man if by chance he had to bend over. He asked Varvara for a corset. But Varvara's corsets proved to be too tight, no one would do up.

"Should have bought one earlier," he grumbled angrily. "No one thinks of anything."

"What men wear corsets?" Varvara protested. "No one does."

"Veriga wears one," Peredonov said.

"So Veriga is an old man, whereas you, Ardalyon Borisych, are a man in his prime, thank God."

Peredonov smiled with self-satisfaction, looked in the mirror and said:

"Of course, I'll live for another hundred and fifty years."

The cat sneezed under the bed. Varvara said with a smirk:

"There's the cat sneezing, it means it's true."

But Peredonov suddenly frowned. He had already grown frightened of the cat and its sneezing seemed a wicked ruse to him.

"It'll go sneezing out something here it shouldn't," he thought, crawled under the bed and started to chase the cat. The cat miaowed frantically, crouched against the wall and suddenly with a loud and sharp miaow, darted through Peredonov's hands and scampered out of the room.

"The Dutch devil!" Peredonov cursed it angrily.

"It certainly is a devil," Varvara agreed, "That cat has become completely wild, it won't let you stroke it, just as though the devil has settled in it."

The Prepolovenskys sent for the ushers early in the morning. Around about ten o'clock everyone had gathered at Peredonov's. Grushina came with Sofiya and her husband. Vodka and snacks were served. Peredonov didn't eat much and was thinking with melancholy of how he could differentiate himself even more from Volodin.

"He's curled his hair like a sheep," he thought spitefully and suddenly had the idea that he could comb his hair in a special way. He got up from the table and said:

"You go ahead and eat and drink, I don't begrudge it, but I'm going to the hairdresser's to get a Spanish hairdo."

"What's a Spanish hairdo?" Rutilov asked.

"Just wait, you'll see."

When Peredonov had gone to have his hair cut, Varvara said:

"He's always thinking up all kinds of fresh tricks. He fancies he's seeing devils all the time. He ought to be knocking back less raw brandy, the damned sponge!"

Prepolovenskaya said with a cunning grin:

"Soon as you get married, Ardalyon Borisych will get his post and he'll calm down."

Grushina giggled. She was amused by the secretiveness of this marriage and she was incited by an urge to arrange some kind of shameful spectacle, but to do it in a way so that she wouldn't be implicated. The evening before she had told some of her friends on the sly about the time and place of the wedding. This morning she had summoned the younger of the locksmith's sons, given him five kopecks and had put him up to waiting outside town for the arrival of the newlyweds towards evening so that rubbish and paper could be thrown into their carriage. The locksmith's son agreed happily and gave a solemn oath not to betray her. Grushina reminded him:

"But you betrayed Cherepnin as soon as they started to whip you."

"We were fools," the locksmith's son said. "But now even if they hanged us it wouldn't matter."

And by way of sealing his oath, the locksmith's son ate a fistful of earth. Grushina gave him a further three kopecks for that.

At the hairdresser's Peredonov asked for the owner himself. The owner, a young man who had finished the town school not long before and who had read books from the rural council library, was just finishing some landowner whom Peredonov didn't know. He soon finished and came up to Peredonov.

"First let him go," Peredonov said angrily.

The landowner paid up and left. Peredonov sat down in front of the mirror.

"I need a haircut and I want my hair styled," he said. "I have some important business today, very special business, so I want you to give me a Spanish hairdo."

A youthful apprentice standing by the door snorted in amusement. The owner gave him a stern look. He had never been obliged to give a Spanish hairdo, and he didn't know what a Spanish hairdo was or even if there were such a hairdo. But if the gentleman was asking for one, then one had to suppose that he knew what he wanted. The young hairdresser did not wish to reveal his ignorance. He said respectfully:

"It's quite impossible to do so with your hair, sir."

"And why can't you?" Peredonov asked in an offended voice.

"You have poorly nourished hair," the hairdresser explained.

"What should I do, soak it in beer or something?" Peredonov grumbled.

"Gracious me, why beer!" the hairdresser replied politely with a smile. "The only thing is that bearing in mind that a sparse area is already showing up on your head, if any amount is cut off, then there just wouldn't be sufficient left for a Spanish hairdo."

Peredonov felt defeated by the impossibility of having a Spanish haircut. He said despondently:

"Well, cut it as you will."

"They've probably already bribed this hairdresser," he thought, "so that he wouldn't give me a distinctive haircut. I shouldn't have said anything at home." Obviously, while Peredonov was walking properly and gravely along the streets, Volodin had run through the back alleys and connived with the hairdresser.

"May I spray your hair?" the hairdresser asked after he had finished his work.

"Spray me with mignonette, and plenty of it," Peredonov demanded. "Since you've gone and chopped up my hair in any old fashion, at least spice it up with mignonette."

"Forgive me, we don't keep mignonette," the hairdresser said with embarrassment. "Would you care for some balsam?"

"You can't do anything right," Peredonov said woefully. "Go ahead and spray with what you have."

He returned home annoyed. The day had become windy. The wind was causing the gates to bang, hang gaping and laugh. Peredonov looked at them with melancholy. How were they supposed to get there? But everything took care of itself.

Three large carriages had been provided—they just had to get in and go, otherwise the carriages would attract attention and the curious would gather. People might ride up or come running to have a look at the wedding. They arranged themselves in the seats and departed: Peredonov with Varvara, the Prepolovenskys with Rutilov, and Grushina with the rest of the ushers.

Dust rose on the square. Peredonov could hear the pounding of axes. Barely visible through the dust, a wooden wall rose and grew erect. They were hewing out a fortress. There were glimpses of fierce, taciturn peasants in their red shirts.

The carriages rolled past—the frightening vision flashed for a moment and then disappeared. Peredonov looked around in terror, but nothing could be seen now and he determined to tell no one about his vision.

Peredonov was tormented by sorrow the whole day. Everything gazed at him with hostility, threatening omens emanated from everything. The sky was frowning. The wind blew directly into their faces and moaned about something. The trees were unwilling to provide shade—they had gathered it all in for themselves. The dust rose up in a long transparently gray serpent behind them. For some reason the sun kept hiding behind the clouds. Was it spying on him?

The road was like a camel's back. Bushes, groves, fields, streams beneath the hollow-sounding wooden tunnel bridges would suddenly arise unexpectedly from behind the low hills.

"An eyebird flew past," Peredonov said sullenly, peering into the misty off-white depths of the sky. "One eye and two wings, nothing else."

Varvara grinned. She thought that Peredonov was drunk from the morning. But she wasn't arguing with him—otherwise, she thought, he might get angry and refuse to go through with the wedding ceremony.

All four Rutilov sisters were already at the church, standing in a corner, hiding behind a column. Peredonov didn't see them at first, but later, during the actual ceremony itself when they came out of their place of ambush and moved forward, he caught sight of them and took fright. In any event they didn't do anything bad, and—what he had feared at first—they didn't demand that he get rid of Varvara and marry one of them. All they did was laugh the whole while. And their laughter, which at first was quiet, resounded more and more loudly and wickedly in his ears, like the laughter of the implacable Furies.

There were almost no outsiders in the church, only two or three old ladies who had appeared from somewhere. And a good thing too because Peredonov behaved stupidly and strangely. He gawked, grumbled, nudged Varvara, complained that it reeked of incense, wax and peasantry.

XXIV

PEREDONOV'S CAT WAS turning wild, snorting, not responding when called. It had gotten completely out of hand. It frightened Peredonov. Sometimes Peredonov would say a counter-spell against the cat.

"I wonder if it really helps?" he thought. "That cat has powerful electricity in its fur, that's the trouble."

Then once he came up with the idea that he ought to have the cat cropped. No sooner said than done. Varvara wasn't at home. She had gone off to Grushina's after slipping a bottle of cherry brandy into her pocket, so there was no one to interfere. Peredonov tied the cat to a cord after making a collar out of a handkerchief and took it off to the hairdresser's. The cat was miaowing frantically, darting back and forth and resisting. In desperation it would sometimes attack Peredonov, but Peredonov kept it away with his walking stick. Little boys were running behind him in a mob, hooting and roaring with laughter. Passers-by stopped. People peered out of windows at the racket. Peredonov was sullenly pulling the cat by the cord, undismayed at anything.

In any event he arrived with the cat and he said to the hairdresser:

"Sir, shave the cat and as short as possible."

The young boys were thronging the door on the outside, roaring with laughter and clowning about. The hairdresser was offended and blushed. He said in a slightly trembling voice:

"Excuse me, sir, we do not perform that kind of work! Nor have I ever been obliged to see any shaven cats. This must be the very latest style and it hasn't reached us yet."

Peredonov listened to him in dull perplexity. He shouted:

"Go ahead and say you don't know how, you charlatan!"

And he left, dragging the frantically miaowing cat behind. On the way he thought with melancholy that people everywhere were just laughing at him constantly and no one wanted to help him. A melancholy feeling weighed on his heart.

Together with Volodin and Rutilov, Peredonov arrived at the Gardens to play billiards. An embarrassed billiard-marker announced to them:

"You can't play today, gentlemen."

"Why is that?" Peredonov asked spitefully. "Why can't we?"

"Excuse me, because there aren't any billiard balls," the billiard-marker said.

"He was caught napping, the gawker," the threatening cry of the bartender was heard from behind the partition.

The billiard-marker shuddered, wriggled his ears which had suddenly turned red—it was almost a rabbit-like movement—and whispered:

"They were stolen."

Peredonov cried out in fright:

"What! Who stole them?"

"No one knows," the billiard-marker informed him. "It was as though no one was there and suddenly, you look, and no balls."

Rutilov was giggling and exclaiming:

"Now there's a story!"

Volodin assumed an offended expression and upbraided the billiard-marker:

"If people are allowed to steal the billiard balls here while you are in a different spot at the time, and the balls are gone, then you have to produce more balls in good time so that we'll have something to play with. We came here, we wanted to play, but if there aren't any balls, then how can we play?"

"Stop whining, Pavlushka," Peredonov said. "It's revolting enough without you. Marker, go and find some balls, we really have to play and in the meantime bring a couple of beers."

They started to drink the beer. But it was boring. No balls could be found. They cursed among themselves and scolded the billiard-marker. The latter felt guilty and kept silent.

Peredonov espied fresh chicanery from his enemies in this theft.

"Why?" he thought with melancholy and couldn't understand.

He went off into the Gardens, sat down on a bench overlooking the pond. He had never sat there before and he stared dully at the expanse of green water. Volodin sat down beside him, shared his mournfulness and gazed at the same pond with his sheep-like eyes.

"Why is there a dirty mirror here, Pavlushka?" Peredonov asked and pointed his finger in the direction of the pond.

Volodin bared his teeth and replied:

"That's not a mirror, Ardasha, that's a pond. And since there's no breeze now, the trees are reflected in it and that's why it looks as though it's a mirror."

Peredonov raised his eyes. Beyond the pond the Gardens were set off from the street by a fence. Peredonov asked:

"But why is there a cat on the fence?"

Volodin glanced in the same direction and said with a giggle:

"If there was one it's disappeared completely."

There wasn't any cat. Peredonov had only fancied he had seen it. A cat with wide green eyes, his cunning and tireless enemy.

Once again Peredonov started to think about the billiard balls. Who needed them? Had the *nedotykomka* gobbled them up? To be sure, there had been no sign of it that day, Peredonov thought. It had stuffed itself, had collapsed in bed somewhere and was, he expected, sleeping right then.

Peredonov meandered homeward in a despondent mood.

The west was dying out. A cloud wandered across the sky, roaming and stealing along—clouds have soft footwear—and spying. A dark sheen was smiling mysteriously around its dark edges. The shadows of houses and bushes wavered, whispered, sought someone over the river that flowed between the Gardens and the town. Meanwhile on this earth, in this dark and eternally hostile town, all the people he met were wicked and scornful. Everything was united in a general antagonism towards Peredonov. The dogs were roaring with laughter at him while the people greeted him with barking.

The town ladies began to return Varvara's visits. It was with a happy curiosity that several of them hastened to see what Varvara was like at home the very next day or the day after. Others put it off for a week or more. Yet others didn't come at all. For example, Vershina didn't come.

Each day the Peredonovs expected return visits with nervous impatience. They would reckon up who hadn't come yet. It was with particular impatience that they waited for the director and his wife. They waited and grew inordinately anxious. What if suddenly the Khripaches didn't come?

A week passed. Still no Khripaches. Varvara began to lose her temper and curse. The waiting plunged Peredonov into a decidedly depressed state. Peredonov's eyes grew utterly vacant as though they had been extinguished and at times it seemed as though these were the eyes of a dead person. He suffered from absurd fears. Without any obvious pretext he suddenly began to fear objects of one type or another. For some reason or other he got the idea in his head, and was tormented by it for several days, that he was going to have his throat slit. He feared everything that was sharp and hid the knives and forks.

"Perhaps," he thought, "they've been charmed and had a spell cast over them. A person could cut himself on a knife."

"What do we need knives for?" he said to Varvara. "The Chinese eat with sticks."

Because of this they didn't cook meat for a whole week and made do with cabbage soup and buckwheat porridge.

Taking revenge on Peredonov for the fears she had experienced before their marriage, Varvara sometimes supported and encouraged him in the conviction that his whims were justified. She would tell him that he had many enemies and why shouldn't they be jealous of him? More than once she teased Peredonov by saying that people had probably already denounced him and defamed him before the authorities and the Princess. And she rejoiced that he was obviously frightened.

It seemed clear to Peredonov that the Princess was displeased with him. Could she really not have sent him an icon or a cake for the wedding? He thought that he ought to gain her favor, but how? With a falsehood, perhaps? By maligning someone, spreading slander and making denunciations? All women loved gossip, so maybe he ought to make up something amusing and immodest about Varvara and write the Princess. She would laugh and give him a post.

But Peredonov didn't know how to write that kind of letter and he grew frightened at the thought of writing to the Princess herself. Afterwards he forgot about this venture.

Peredonov treated his ordinary guests to vodka and the cheapest port. But he bought madeira at three roubles a bottle for the director. Peredonov considered this wine to be extremely expensive, kept it in the bedroom and would only show it to his guests, saying:

"This is for the headmaster."

Once Rutilov and Volodin were sitting at Peredonov's. Peredonov showed them the madeira.

"What's so nice about looking at the outside!" Rutilov said with a giggle. "Treat us to some of the expensive madeira."

"You're a fine one, what next!" Peredonov replied angrily. "And what will I serve the headmaster?"

"The headmaster will drink a glass of vodka," Rutilov said.

"The headmaster mustn't drink vodka, the director is supposed to have madeira," Peredonov said earnestly.

"But what if he likes vodka?" Rutilov insisted.

"Well, what next, a general* isn't about to like vodka," Peredonov said confidently.

"Treat us to some all the same," Rutilov insisted.

But Peredonov hastily carried the bottle off and there was the sound of the lock being snapped in the wardrobe where he hid the wine. Returning to his guests he started to talk about the Princess in order to change the subject. He said sullenly:

"The Princess! She used to deal in rotten apples in the market, but she seduced a prince."

Rutilov roared with laughter and cried:

"Do princes really go around markets?"

"She certainly knew how to lure them," Peredonov said.

"You're making up a cock-and-bull story to our faces," Rutilov argued. "The Princess is a distinguished lady."

Peredonov gave him a spiteful look and thought: "He's defending her, obviously he and the Princess are in it together. Obviously the Princess has bewitched him, it doesn't matter that she lives far away." Meanwhile the *nedotykomka* was bustling about, laughing soundlessly and shaking with laughter all the while. It reminded Peredonov of various frightening circumstances. He looked around timidly and whispered:

"There's a secret non-commissioned police officer in every town. He wears civilian dress, sometimes he works in the civil service, sometimes in a business,

*This would be Khripach's corresponding military rank.

or does whatever else there is, but during the night, when everyone is asleep, he puts on a pale blue uniform and, presto, he turns into a police officer."

"But why the uniform?" Volodin inquired in a serious way.

"You can't put in an appearance before the authorities without a uniform, you'd be whipped," Peredonov explained.

Volodin started to giggle. Peredonov leaned over closer to him and whispered:

"Sometimes he even leads the life of a changeling. You think it's just a cat, but it's a lie! That's the policeman running along. No one can hide from a cat, and it can eavesdrop on everything."

Finally, after about a week and a half, the headmaster's wife returned Varvara's visit. She arrived with her husband on a weekday at four o'clock, all dressed up, gracious and scented with sweet violet. And it was totally unexpected for the Peredonovs. For some reason they had been expecting the Khripaches to come sooner, and on a holiday. They were in a dither. Varvara had been in the kitchen, half-dressed, filthy. She dashed to change while Peredonov received the guests and he seemed as though he had only just woken up.

"Varvara will be right here," he mumbled. "She's getting dressed. She was cooking. We have a new servant and she doesn't know how to cook the way we like it, an utter fool."

Varvara emerged in a short while with a red frightened face and haphazardly dressed. She stuck a sweaty rather dirty hand at the guests and said in a voice trembling with agitation:

"Forgive me, for making you wait. We didn't know that you went visiting on weekdays."

"I rarely go out on a holiday," Mrs. Khripach said. "The drunks are in the streets. Let the servant have that day to herself."

Somehow or other the conversation got underway and the politeness of the headmaster's wife cheered Varvara up somewhat. The headmaster's wife treated Varvara with a certain amount of disdain, yet was kindly—the way one would treat a repentant sinner to whom one had to show kindness, but with whom one might get soiled by contact. As though in passing she made several critical remarks about clothing and the household.

Varvara tried to oblige the headmaster's wife and the fearful trembling never left her red hands and her cracked lips. The headmaster's wife was embarrassed by this. She tried to be even more polite, but she was overcome with an involuntary loathing. She tried to make Varvara understand by her entire behavior that no close friendship would ever be established between them. But since this was done with utter courtesy, Varvara did not understand and she flattered herself with the thought that she and the headmaster's wife would be great friends.

Khripach had the look of a person who was out of place but he concealed it with courage and skill. He refused the madeira. He had not become accustomed to drinking alcohol at that hour. He chatted about town news, about the impending changes in the makeup of the district court. But it was too apparent that he and Peredonov moved in different circles in local society.

They didn't stay for long. Varvara was overjoyed when they left. They had come and gone quickly. She said joyfully as she got undressed once more:

"Well, thank God, they've gone. Otherwise I wouldn't have known what to say to them. That's the way it is with people you don't know very well. You don't know how to deal with them."

Suddenly she remembered that as the Khripaches were saying goodbye, they hadn't invited them to come for a visit. That dismayed her at first, but then she realized what it meant:

"They'll send a card with a timetable of when to come. Everything has its time with these kind of people. Now I suppose I have to learn how to be witty in French, otherwise I don't know my p's and q's in French."

Returning home, the headmaster's wife said to her husband:

"She's pitiful and hopelessly vulgar. There isn't the slightest possibility of being on equal terms with her. There's nothing in her that corresponds to her position."

Khripach replied:

"She corresponds completely to her husband. I'm waiting impatiently for the moment when they remove him from here."

After the wedding Varvara started to drink from joy, particularly often with Grushina. Once, when she was tipsy and Prepolovenskaya was sitting in her place, Varvara let slip about the letter. She didn't tell everything, but made a fairly clear hint. That was plenty for the cunning Sofiya. It suddenly seemed to dawn on her and she mentally reproached herself: how could she not have guessed it right away! She told Vershina in secret about the forged letters, and from there it made the rounds of the entire town.

Whenever she met Peredonov, Prepolovenskaya couldn't help but make fun of his gullibility. She said:

"How naive you are, Ardalyon Borisych."

"I'm not naive at all," he replied. "I'm a university graduate."

"You might be a graduate, but anyone who wishes can make a fool of you."

"I make a fool of everyone myself," Peredonov argued.

Prepolovenskaya would smile craftily and leave. Peredonov would be dully perplexed: what was she doing that for? For spite! he thought. Everyone was his enemy.

And he made a rude gesture behind her back.

"You won't get away with it," he thought, consoling himself. But fear tormented him.

Prepolovenskaya's hints seemed insufficient. She didn't want to tell him the whole truth in straightforward words. Why embroil him with Varvara? From time to time she would send Peredonov anonymous letters in which the hints were made clearer. But Peredonov misinterpreted them.

Sofiya once wrote him:

"Why don't you look to see whether the Princess that sent you the letters doesn't live here?"

Peredonov thought that truly the Princess herself had come there to keep an eye on him. "Obviously," he thought, "she's madly in love with me and wants to get me away from Varvara."

These letters terrified and angered Peredonov. He started in on Varvara:

"Where's the Princess? People say that she's come here."

Taking revenge for the past, Varvara tormented him with intimations, taunts and cowardly, spiteful circumlocutions. Smirking insolently, she would speak in the false kind of voice that people used when they were deliberately lying and had no hope of being believed:

"How should I know where the Princess is living now?"

"You're lying; you know!" Peredonov said in horror.

He didn't understand what he was supposed to believe: the sense of her words, or the tone of her voice that betrayed the falsehood. This too, like everything else that he couldn't understand, induced a feeling of horror in him. Varvara protested:

"What next! Maybe she left St. Petersburg to go somewhere, she's hardly going to ask me."

"But maybe in fact she has come here?" Peredonov asked timidly.

"Maybe she did," Varvara said in a taunting voice. "She's madly in love with you and has come here to feast her eyes."

Peredonov exclaimed:

"You're lying! But what if she is madly in love with me?"

Varvara laughed maliciously.

From that time Peredonov started to keep a close eye out for the whereabouts of the Princess. At times it seemed to him that she was peeking through a window, eavesdropping at the door and speaking in hushed whispers with Varvara.

Time passed and the document bearing the inspector's appointment, which was anticipated daily, still didn't arrive. Nor was there any private information about the post. He didn't dare make inquiries to the Princess herself—Varvara was constantly frightening him with the fact that she was a distinguished lady. And it seemed to him that if he himself had taken it into his head to write to her, then very serious troubles might have ensued. He had no precise idea of what might be done to him on the basis of a complaint from the Princess, but that was particularly frightening for him. Varvara said:

"Don't you know aristocrats? Just wait, they'll do what has to be done. And if you go reminding them then they'll be offended and it'll be worse. They have so much honor! They're proud people, they like people to believe them."

And for the time being Peredonov still believed. But he was furious with the Princess. Sometimes he even thought that the Princess was denouncing him in order to evade her promises. Or she was denouncing him because she was angry at him for marrying Varvara whereas the Princess herself was in love with him. That was why, so he thought, she had surrounded him with spies who followed him everywhere and who assailed him from all sides to such a degree that there was no longer either air or light. It was not for nothing that she was a distinguished lady. She could do everything she wanted.

Out of spitefulness he made up absurd lies about the Princess. He told Rutilov and Volodin that he had once been her lover and that she had paid him a great deal of money.

"Only I wasted it on drink. What the devil was I supposed to do with it! She also promised to pay me a pension till the day I died, but she duped me."

"Would you have taken it?" Rutilov asked with a giggle.

Peredonov was silent for a moment. He didn't understand the question, but Volodin responded gravely and soberly on his behalf:

"Why not take it if she's rich. If she profited by her pleasures then she ought to pay for it."

"If at least she had been beautiful!" Peredonov said with melancholy. "She was pockmarked and stub-nosed. The only thing was that she paid well, otherwise I wouldn't have given a damn for her, the devil. She ought to carry out my request."

"You're lying, Ardalyon Borisych," Rutilov said.

"So I'm lying, am I? And did she pay me for nothing, then? She's jealous of Varvara, that's why she hasn't given me the position for so long."

Peredonov experienced no shame when he was telling how the Princess had supposedly paid him. Volodin was a trusting listener and didn't notice the absurdities and contradictions in his stories. Rutilov would object, but he thought that where there was smoke there was fire—there had been something between Peredonov and the Princess, he thought.

"She's older than a priest's dog," Peredonov said with conviction, as though it bore some relation. "Just mind, though, that you don't go blabbing that to anyone. If it were to reach her, it could be bad. She smears herself with makeup and injects a piggy's youthfulness into her veins. And you wouldn't know that she's old. But she's already a hundred."

Volodin nodded his head and smacked his lips. He believed everything.

It happened that on the day following this conversation Peredonov had to read Krylov's fable "The Liar"* in one of his classes. And for several days afterwards he was afraid to walk over the bridge. He would take a boat and cross over, otherwise the bridge might be apt to collapse. He explained to Volodin:

"I was telling the truth about the Princess, only what if suddenly the bridge doesn't believe me and it collapses all to hell?"

---

*Ivan Andreyevich Krylov (1769–1844) was Russia's most famous author of fables. "The Liar" concerns a traveler who is constantly boasting about the many marvellous things he has seen in other lands. One of his listeners tells him of a local curiosity in his town, namely a bridge that is reputed to dump all liars into the river. The traveler is afraid to cross the bridge and chooses to ford the river.

XXV

THE RUMORS ABOUT the forged letters circulated through the town. Conversation on the subject occupied the townsfolk and made them happy. Almost all praised Varvara and were happy about the fact that Peredonov had been made a fool of. And all those who had seen the letters were vocal in their assurances that they had guessed at once.

The feeling of malice was particularly great in the home of Vershina. Even though Marta was going to marry Murin, nevertheless she had been rejected by Peredonov; Vershina had wanted to take Murin for herself, but had been forced to give him up to Marta; Vladya had his own appreciable reasons for hating Peredonov and rejoiced over his misfortune. Although he was annoyed that Peredonov was still going to remain at the gymnasium, nevertheless this annoyance was outweighed by the joy over the fact that Peredonov had been made a fool of. Moreover, a stubborn rumor persisted lately among the students at the gymnasium that the headmaster had supposedly reported to the district educational trustee that Peredonov had gone mad and that supposedly he would soon be sent for an examination and thereafter would be removed from the gymnasium.

Whenever acquaintances met Varvara they would begin to talk more or less directly about her ruse and wink insolently. She would produce a brazen smirk, but she would neither confirm nor deny it.

Others hinted to Grushina that they knew about her participation in the forgery. She took fright and went to Varvara to reproach her for blabbing. Varvara said to her with a smirk:

"Why all the tomfoolery, it never entered my mind to tell anyone."

"Then from whom did everyone find out?" Grushina asked vehemently. "I certainly would never tell anyone, I'm not that kind of a fool."

"And I didn't tell anyone," Varvara tried to convince her brazenly.

"Give me the letter back," Grushina demanded. "Otherwise he'll start to examine it and see from the signature that it's a forgery."

"Well, let him find out!" Varvara said with annoyance. "I'll look the fool in the face."

Grushina's uneven eyes flashed and she cried:

"It's fine for you to say, you've got what you wanted, but they'll put me in jail because of you! No, you do as you like, but give me the letter back. Otherwise it's possible to have the marriage annulled."

"Well, that's a good one. Just forget it," Varvara replied, putting her hands on her hips. "Even if you go and publicize it on the town square, the marriage will still stand."

"Don't tell me to forget it!" Grushina cried. "There's no law that says you can get married by deceit. If Ardalyon Borisych takes the whole matter to the authorities and it goes to the Senate, then they can annul the marriage."

Varvara took fright and said:

"What are you getting angry for, I'll get the letter for you. There's nothing to be afraid of, I won't give you away. Do you think I'm that kind of a brute? I do have a soul after all."

"What kind of soul are you talking about!" Grushina said rudely. "All a person has is his breath, same as a dog, and there's no soul. When you die, you're gone."

Varvara decided to steal the letter although it was going to be difficult. Grushina pressed her. There was one hope: to pinch the letter from Peredonov while he was drunk. And he was drinking a great deal. It wasn't rare for him to show up at the gymnasium tight and to deliver shameless speeches that induced revulsion even in the most wicked boys.

Once Peredonov returned from the billiard room drunker than usual. They had been celebrating the acquisition of new billiard balls. Nevertheless, he still didn't part company with his wallet. Somehow, while undressing, he slipped it under his pillow.

He slept restlessly but deeply and was delirious, and in his delirium all his words were about something terrible and ugly. They induced an eerie terror in Varvara.

"Well, no matter," she tried to bolster her spirits, "as long as he doesn't wake up."

She tried to wake him up and kept poking him. He would mutter something, curse loudly, but he wouldn't wake up. Varvara lit a candle and set it up so that the light wouldn't fall in Peredonov's eyes. Rigid with fear, she got out of bed and carefully crept under Peredonov's pillow. The wallet lay close by, but it kept eluding her fingers for a long while. The candle threw a murky light. The flame wavered. Tremulous shadows—wicked little devils darting about—flitted over the walls and bed. The air was stuffy and motionless. There was a smell of raw vodka. The entire bedroom was filled with the sound of snoring and a drunken delirium. The whole room was like a delirium that had materialized.

With trembling hands Varvara pulled the letter out and slipped the wallet back into its former place.

In the morning Peredonov missed the letter; he couldn't find it. He took fright and started to shout:

"Where's my letter, Varya?"

Varvara, horribly afraid, but concealing it, said:

"How should I know, Ardalyon Borisych? You're always showing it to everyone, you must have dropped it somewhere. Or it got pinched. You have a lot of friends and acquaintances with whom you go carousing at night."

Peredonov thought that his enemies had stolen the letter, most likely Volodin. Now Volodin had the letter and later he could get his claws on all the documents and the appointment and join the ranks of the inspectors, while Peredonov would remain a miserable tramp here.

Peredonov made up his mind to defend himself. Every day he compiled one denunciation against his enemies: Vershina, the Rutilovs, Volodin, and his fellow teachers, who, so it seemed to him, were aspiring for the very same position as he. In the evenings he took these denunciations to Rubovsky.

The chief of police lived in a prominent place on the square, near the gymnasium. From their windows many people noticed how Peredonov would enter the chief of police's home through the gates. But Peredonov thought that no one had an inkling. After all, it wasn't for nothing that he chose the evenings to bring the denunciations and used the back entrance by way of the kitchen. He would hold the paper under his coat flap. It was immediately noticeable that he was holding something. If he had to take his hand out to greet someone, he would hold the paper under his coat with his left hand and think that no one could guess. If the people he met asked him where he was going, then he would lie quite inexpertly, yet he himself would be satisfied with his unskilled inventions.

He explained to Rubovsky:

"They're all traitors. They pretend to be friends, but they're actually trying to deceive me. But they don't think that I know the kind of things about them all that would make Siberia too good a place for them."

Rubovsky would listen to him in silence. He sent the first denunciation, which was obviously absurd, to the headmaster. He did likewise with several others. Yet others he kept just in case. The director wrote the educational trustee that Peredonov was displaying obvious signs of mental depression.

At home Peredonov was constantly hearing rustling sounds that were incessant, tiresome and mocking. He said with melancholy to Varvara:

"Someone is tiptoing about there, spies are hanging around everywhere here. Varka, you're not guarding me."

Varvara didn't understand the meaning of Peredonov's delirium. First she would make fun of him, then she would be frightened. She said in a voice that was both spiteful and cowardly:

"Who knows what you fancy you see when you're drunk."

The door into the front hall seemed particularly suspicious to Peredonov. It wouldn't close solidly. The crack between the two halves of the door suggested the presence of something lurking outside. Could it be a knave spying there? Someone's eye, wicked and sharp, was flashing.

The cat followed Peredonov everywhere with its wide green eyes. Sometimes it would blink, sometimes it would miaow frighteningly. It was immediately obvious that it wanted to catch Peredonov out in something and that was the only reason it didn't lose its temper. Peredonov would spit in disgust at the cat but it wouldn't leave him.

The *nedotykomka* ran about under the chairs and in the corners and squealed. It was filthy, repulsive, frightening and reeked. By that time it was clear that it was hostile to Peredonov and had come specifically on his account, because earlier it had never existed anywhere. They had created it and then cast a spell over it. And now, to his terror and ruin, it was living right here, magic and omnipresent, following him, deceiving him and laughing. First it would roll around the floor, then it would pretend to be a rag, a ribbon, a branch, a flag, a cloud, a dog, a column of dust in the street. And it crept and ran everywhere after Peredonov, exhausting him and wearing him out with its vacillating dance. If only someone could get rid of it, either with a word or a solid whack. But he had no friends there, no one would come to save him and he himself would have to extricate himself before the malicious thing ruined him.

Peredonov conceived a means: he smeared the entire floor with glue so that the *nedotykomka* would stick to it. But the soles of Varvara's shoes and the hems of her dresses also got stuck, while the *nedotykomka* rolled around freely and laughed shrilly. Varvara swore spitefully.

Relentless notions of persecution held constant sway over Peredonov and terrified him. More and more he became plunged into a world of wild fantasies. It was reflected in his face: it had become a frozen mask of terror.

By this time Peredonov no longer went to play billiards in the evenings. After dinner he would lock himself up in the bedroom, barricade the door with articles—a chair on the table—and diligently circumscribe himself with crosses and counter-spells and sit down to write his denunciations against everyone he could remember. He wrote denunciations not only against people, but against the queens on the playing cards. Once he finished writing he would immediately take it to the chief of police. And that was how he spent every evening.

Playing card figures—the kings, queens and knaves—walked around everywhere before his eyes as though they were alive. Even the ordinary cards were walking around. These were people with bright buttons: the students at the gymnasium, the town police. The ace was a fat person with a puffed-out belly, almost nothing more than a belly. At times the cards turned into familiar people. Live people and these strange changelings became all mixed up.

Peredonov was certain that a knave was standing behind the door and that the knave had some kind of power and authority, something like a policeman: he could take him away to some terrible police station.

Meanwhile the *nedotykomka* sat under the table. Peredonov was afraid to peer under the table or behind the door.

The fidgety little boy-eights teased Peredonov. These were the changeling students at the gymnasium. They picked up their legs in a strange, lifeless motion, like the arms of a pair of dividers, only their feet were shaggy, with hooves. Instead of tails they had grown whipping rods. The young boys were brandishing them about with a whistling sound and they themselves were squealing with each swing. From under the table the *nedotykomka* was grunting while it chuckled at the antics of the eights. Peredonov thought spitefully that the *nedotykomka* wouldn't dare try to reach any authority. "I expect it would never be admitted," he thought with malice. "The lackeys would flay it with mops."

Finally Peredonov couldn't put up with its spiteful, insolently shrill laughter any longer. He brought an axe from the kitchen and chopped up the table under which the *nedotykomka* was hiding. The *nedotykomka* gave a plaintive and spiteful squeak, dashed from under the table and rolled away. Peredonov shuddered. "It'll bite," he thought, shrieked and cowered. But the *nedotykomka* disappeared peacefully. But not for long . . .

Sometimes Peredonov would take playing cards and with a ferocious expression on his face he would chop off the heads of the playing card figures with a pen knife. Particularly the queens. While beheading the kings he would look around to make sure that no one saw him and accused him of a political crime. But even these kinds of reprisals didn't help for long. Guests came, fresh cards were brought and wicked spies would once more establish themselves in the new cards.

By this time Peredonov had begun to consider himself a secret criminal. He imagined that he had been under police surveillance since his student years. For some reason he concluded that they too were following him. This terrified him and made him feel important at the same time.

The wind was making the wallpaper stir. It whispered with a soft, ominous, rustling sound, and faint semi-shadows slithered over its colorful patterns. "A spy is hiding there, behind the wallpaper," Peredonov thought. "The wicked people!" he thought with melancholy. "It's not for nothing that they put up the wallpaper so unevenly and so badly that a villain, resourceful, flat and patient, could crawl behind it and hide there. After all there were similar examples of that even earlier."

Vague recollections stirred in his head. Someone had hidden behind the wallpaper, someone had been stabbed either with a dagger or an awl. Peredonov bought an awl. When he returned home, the wallpaper started to stir fitfully and anxiously—the spy sensed danger and perhaps wanted to crawl somewhere farther off. The gloom leapt about and sprang to the ceiling. From there it threatened and made faces.

Malice welled up in Peredonov. He swiftly plunged the awl into the wallpaper. A convulsion ran over the wall. Peredonov howled in victory and started to dance, flourishing the awl. Varvara came in.

"What are you doing dancing alone, Ardalyon Borisych?" she asked, dully and insolently, with her usual smirk.

"I killed a bedbug," Peredonov explained sullenly.

His eyes were glittering with savage victory. Only one thing was bad: it smelled vilely. The stabbed spy behind the wallpaper was rotting and

217 THE PETTY DEMON

reeking. Peredonov was shaken by terror and triumph: he had killed an enemy! The performance of this murder had hardened his heart completely. There was no actual murder committed, but for Peredonov it was the same as committing a murder. The insane terror inside him had fashioned a willingness to commit crime. His depraved will was being oppressed by this state of primitive malevolence, by the depressing urge for murder, by the dark notion of some future murder lurking in the nethermost regions of his spiritual being. Though still constrained—many generations had settled over the ancient Cain—it found satisfaction for itself in the fact that he broke and spoiled things, chopped things with an axe, cut and hacked down trees in the garden so that spies couldn't peek out from behind them. And in the destruction of things the ancient demon established itself, the spirit of prehistoric confusion, decrepit chaos, while the savage eyes of an insane man reflected the terror which resembled the terrors of monstrous torments on the periphery of death.

The same illusions repeated themselves ceaselessly and tormented him. Varvara, amusing herself at Peredonov's expense, sometimes crept up stealthily to the doors of the room where Peredonov was sitting and from there she would speak in strange voices. He was terrified and he would quietly approach so as to catch the enemy—and he'd find Varvara.

"Who are you talking to in whispers here?" he asked with melancholy.

Varvara would smirk and reply:

"You're only imagining it, Ardalyon Borisych."

"I'm not imagining everything," Peredonov mumbled. "There is some truth in the world."

Yes, Peredonov was striving for the truth after all, according to the general law of every conscious life and he was oppressed by that striving. He himself was not conscious of the fact that like all people he was striving for the truth, and for that reason his anxiety was obscure. He couldn't find the truth for himself and became muddled and was perishing.

His acquaintances had by now begun to tease Peredonov over the deception. With the rudeness towards the weak that was customary in our town, they talked about the deception in his presence. Prepolovenskaya wou ld ask with a sly little grin:

"Really now, Ardalyon Borisych, why aren't you off to your inspector's post?"

Varvara would answer Prepolovenskaya on Peredonov's behalf with restrained malice:

"As soon as we get the document, then we'll go."

These questions made Peredonov feel melancholy.

"How can I live if they don't give me the post?" he thought.

He kept devising fresh plans of defense against his enemies. He stole the axe from the kitchen and hid it under the bed. He bought a Swedish knife and always carried it around in his pocket. He was constantly locking himself up. He set out traps for the night around the house and inside in the rooms. Afterwards he would look them over. Of course, these traps were set in such a fashion that no one could have been caught in them. They might pinch, but they wouldn't hold, and it was possible to get out of them. Peredonov had no technical knowledge and no keen wit. Every morning when he saw that no one had fallen into the traps, Peredonov thought that his enemies had spoiled the traps. That frightened him again.

Peredonov paid particular attention to Volodin. From time to time he would go to Volodin's place when he knew that Volodin wasn't at home, and he would rummage around to see whether he had seized any papers.

Peredonov began to suspect that what the Princess wanted was for him to love her again. She was repulsive to him, a decrepit woman. "After all, she's a hundred and fifty," he thought spitefully. "She may be old," he thought, "but what a powerful woman she is for all that." And revulsion became intermingled with fascination. Peredonov imagined that she would be barely lukewarm and would smell like a corpse, and he almost fainted from a savage lust.

"Perhaps I could get intimate with her and she would take pity. Should I write her a letter?"

This time Peredonov composed a letter to the Princess without giving it much thought. He wrote:

"I love you because you are cold and distant. Varvara sweats, it's hot sleeping with her, she throws off heat like a stove. I want to have a lover who is cold and distant. Come and be responsive to me."

He finished writing it, sent it off—and regretted it. "What if something comes of it? Maybe I shouldn't have written," he thought. "I ought to have waited until the Princess herself came."

So this letter was produced haphazardly, the way Peredonov did many things haphazardly. He was like a corpse activated by external forces and it was as though these forces had no desire to spend much time with him. One of them would play with him for a while and then toss him to another.

The *nedotykomka* soon reappeared. For a long while it rolled around Peredonov as though it were on a lasso and kept teasing him all the while. Now it made no sound and its laughter was expressed only in the trembling of its entire body. But it would flare up in murky gold sparks, wicked and shameless. It threatened and burned with unbearable triumph. The cat, too, was threatening Peredonov, flashing its eyes and miaowing brazenly and threateningly.

"What are they rejoicing at?" Peredonov thought mournfully and suddenly understood that the end was approaching, that the Princess was already there, close by, quite close by. Perhaps right in that deck of cards.

Yes, no doubt she was the queen of spades or hearts. Perhaps she was hiding in a different deck or behind other cards, but just which one he couldn't tell. The trouble was that Peredonov had never seen her. It wasn't worthwhile asking Varvara—she'd lie.

Finally Peredonov came up with the idea of burning the entire deck of cards. Let them all burn. If people were creeping into his cards to spite him, then they themselves were to blame.

Peredonov bided his time until Varvara wasn't at home and the stove in the front room had been stoked up, and then he tossed the cards into the stove, the whole deck.

With a crackling sound, mysterious, pale red flowers blossomed and burned, charring along the edges. Peredonov gazed in terror at these fiery blossoms.

The cards warped, twisted and moved, just as though they wanted to leap out of the stove. Peredonov grabbed a poker and struck away at the cards. Fine, brilliant sparks scattered in all directions. Suddenly, in a brilliant and wicked flurry of sparks, the Princess arose out of the fire: a small, ashy gray woman all strewn with fading little fires. She gave a piercing wail in a thin voice, then hissed and spat on the fire.

Peredonov collapsed backwards and started to howl with terror. The gloom embraced him, tickled him and laughed in cooing voices.

XXVI

ASHA WAS ENCHANTED with Lyudmila, but something prevented him from talking about her with Kokovkina. It was as though he were afraid. And he even started to fear her visits. His heart would skip a beat and his brows pull together in a frown whenever he caught sight of the quick flash of her pinkish yellow hat under the window. Nevertheless he would wait for her with anxiety and impatience and he would be melancholy if she didn't come for a long while. Contradictory feelings were all mixed up in his heart, because they were dark and vague feelings: feelings that were wanton because they were premature, and feelings that were sweet because they were wanton.

Lyudmila hadn't come either the day before or today. Sasha had languished in anticipation and had already ceased waiting for her. Then suddenly she came. He grew radiant and rushed to kiss her hands.

"You disappeared," he upbraided her vexedly. "I didn't see you for two whole days."

She laughed and rejoiced, and the sweet, langorous and heady scent of Japanese fuchsia emanated from her just as though it were streaming from her reddish-brown curls.

Lyudmila and Sasha went for a walk outside town. They invited Kokovkina—but she didn't go.

"Where's an old lady like me to go for a walk!" she said. "I'll only hold you back. You'd better go for a walk on your own."

"But we'll get into mischief," Lyudmila laughed.

The warm air, melancholy and motionless, caressed them and reminded them of what was irrevocable. The sun, like an invalid, spread a murky light and turned crimson against a pallid, tired sky. Dry leaves lay submissive and dead on the dark earth.

Lyudmila and Sasha descended into a ravine. There it was cool, fresh, almost damp—a delicate autumn weariness reigned between its shadowed slopes.

Lyudmila walked in front. She raised her skirt. Delicate shoes and flesh-colored stockings were revealed. Sasha was looking downward so that he wouldn't trip over roots and he caught sight of the stockings. It seemed to him that she was wearing the shoes without any stockings. A shameful and passionate feeling arose in him. He turned red. His head was spinning. "If only I could fall down at her feet, as though by accident," he was dreaming, "and pull off her shoes and kiss her tender foot."

It was as though Lyudmila had sensed Sasha's burning gaze on herself, his impatient desire. Chuckling, she turned around to Sasha and asked:

"Are you looking at my stockings?"

"No, not really," Sasha mumbled in embarrassment.

"Ach, the kind of stockings I have," Lyudmila said, laughing and not heeding him. "It's terrible, the kind they are! One might think that I had put shoes on bare feet, they're such a flesh color. It's true, isn't it, they really are terribly funny stockings?"

She turned around to face Sasha and raised the edge of her dress.

"Funny?" she asked.

"No, beautiful," Sasha said, red with embarrassment.

With feigned surprise Lyudmila raised her eyebrows and exclaimed:

"Do tell! What do you understand about beauty?"

Lyudmila laughed and continued on. Burning with embarrassment, Sasha awkwardly picked his way along after her and kept stumbling every minute.

They made it across the ravine. They sat down on the stump of a birch that had been broken by the wind. Lyudmila said:

"I've got so much sand in my shoes that I can't go any farther."

She took her shoes off, shook out the sand and glanced slyly at Sasha.

"A pretty foot?" she asked.

Sasha blushed even more and no longer knew what to say. Lyudmila pulled off her stockings.

"Nice little white feet?" she asked once more, with a strange and sly smile. "On your knees! Kiss them!" she said sternly and an imperious cruelty settled over her face.

Sasha deftly got down on his knees and kissed Lyudmila's feet.

"It's nicer without stockings," Lyudmila said, hid the stockings in a pocket and stuck her feet into her shoes.

Once again her face grew calm and cheerful, as though Sasha hadn't just been kneeling down before her, caressing her naked feet.

Sasha asked:

"Dearest, won't you catch cold?"

His voice had a tender and quivering ring to it. Lyudmila laughed.

"Hardly, I'm used to it. I'm not such a sissy."

Once Lyudmila came to Kokovkina's towards evening and summoned Sasha:

"Let's go and hang a new shelf at my place."

Sasha loved to hammer nails and had once promised Lyudmila to help her with the organization of her furnishings. So now he agreed, happy over the fact that there was an innocent pretext for being with Lyudmila and going to Lyudmila's place. And the innocent, somewhat tart fragrance of extra-muguet that wafted from Lyudmila's greenish dress, had a tender, calming effect on him.

Lyudmila changed clothing for work behind a screen and appeared to Sasha in a short, dressy skirt, her arms bare and scented with sweet, languid, heady Japanese fuchsia.

"Just look at you, all dressed up!" Sasha said.

"Well, hardly dressed up. You see," Lyudmila said, grinning "bare feet." She pronounced the words with a shamefully provocative drawl.

Sasha shrugged his shoulders and said:

"You're always all dressed up. Well, then, let's start hammering. Do you have the nails?" he asked seriously.

"Just wait a little bit," Lyudmila replied. "Sit down with me at least for a little, otherwise, it's as though you're just coming on business and you find it boring to talk with me."

Sasha blushed and said tenderly.

"Dearest Lyudmilochka, I'd sit with you for as long as you like, until you chased me away, only I have to do my lessons."

Lyudmila sighed gently and slowly said:

"You get better looking all the time, Sasha."

Sasha turned red, laughed and stuck out the end of his tongue rolled up like a tube.

"You're just making it up," he said. "As though I were a young lady. Better looking, really!"

"You have a beautiful face, and your body! Show it to me at least down to the waist," Lyudmila said, cuddling up to Sasha and embracing him by the shoulder.

"Really, the things you think of!" Sasha said with shame and annoyance.

"What's the matter?" Lyudmila asked in a light-hearted voice. "You'd think you had something to hide!"

"Someone might come in," Sasha said.

"Who's going to come in?" Lyudmila said just as easily and carefreely. "We'll lock the door, then no one can surprise us."

Lyudmila deftly went up to the door and locked it with the bolt. Sasha guessed that Lyudmila was not joking. He said, turning red all over, so that beads of sweat stood out on his forehead:

"Don't, Lyudmila."

"Silly, why not?" Lyudmila asked in a persuasive voice.

She pulled Sasha to herself and started to unbutton his blouse. Sasha struggled free, gripping on to her hands. His face grew frightened and a shame that was akin to fright took hold of him. And it suddenly seemed to weaken him. Lyudmila knitted her brows and was undressing him with determination. She removed his belt, pulled his blouse off somehow. Sasha struggled even more desperately to break free. They scuffled and circled their way around the room, bumping into tables and chairs. The heady scent wafting from Lyudmila was intoxicating Sasha and enervating him.

With a quick shove to his chest, Lyudmila toppled Sasha onto the divan. A button popped off the undershirt that she was tearing at. Lyudmila quickly bared Sasha's shoulder and started to pull his arm out of the sleeve. Breaking free, Sasha inadvertently struck Lyudmila on the cheek with the palm of his hand. He didn't mean to hit her, of course, but the blow, strong and ringing, fell solidly on Lyudmila's cheek. Lyudmila shuddered, stumbled, and turned red with a bloody glow on her cheek but she didn't let go of Sasha.

"You wicked boy, fighting!" she cried in a choking voice.

Sasha was horribly dismayed, lowered his hands and peered guiltily at the whitish stripes, the traces of his fingers, imprinted on Lyudmila's left cheek. Lyudmila took advantage of his distraction. She quickly pulled the undershirt from both shoulders down to his elbows. Sasha regained his senses, tore free from her, but it turned out for the worse. Lyudmila deftly yanked the sleeves off his arms—and the shirt fell down to his waist. Sasha felt the cold and a fresh attack of shame that was clear and merciless and that made his head spin. Now Sasha was bared down to the waist. Lyudmila took firm hold of his arm and with her trembling hand patted him on his bare back, peering into his dazed, strangely glowing eyes beneath the bluish-black eyelashes.

And suddenly these eyelashes trembled, the face twisted into a pitiful, childish grimace—and he began to sob, suddenly and violently.

"Wicked girl!" he cried in a sobbing voice. "Let me go!"

"He's whimpering! The little baby!" Lyudmila said with anger and dismay and pushed him away.

Sasha turned away, wiping away the tears with his palms. He felt ashamed because he was crying. He tried to restrain himself. Lyudmila gazed hungrily at his naked back.

"So much delight in the world!" she thought. "People hide so much beauty from themselves, but why?"

Hunching his shoulders up in shame, Sasha was trying to put on his undershirt, but it only got balled up and strained under his trembling hands and there was no way he could get his arms into the sleeves. Sasha grabbed his blouse—let the undershirt stay as it was for the time being.

"Ach, you're afraid for your property. I won't steal it!" Lyudmila said in a voice that was spiteful and ringing with tears.

She tossed him his belt impetuously and turned away to the window. A lot she needed him, wrapped up in his gray blouse, a vile young boy, a revolting, affected creature.

Sasha quickly put his blouse on, somehow or other straightened out the undershirt and looked at Lyudmila timidly, uncertainly and shamefully. He saw that she was wiping her cheeks with her hands, timidly went up to her and looked into her face—and the tears that were flowing down her cheeks suddenly poisoned him with a tender pity for her, and he was no longer ashamed or annoyed.

"Why are you crying, dearest Lyudmilochka?" he asked softly.

And suddenly he turned red—he had remembered his blow.

"I struck you, forgive me. I didn't do it on purpose," he said timidly.

"You think you'll melt, silly boy, if you sit a while with bare shoulders?" Lyudmila said in a plaintive voice. "You're afraid you'll get sunburnt. Your beauty and innocence will get tarnished."

"But why are you doing it, Lyudmilochka?" Sasha asked with a shameful grimace.

"Why?" Lyudmila said passionately. "I love beauty. I'm a pagan, a sinner. I ought to have been born in ancient Greece. I love flowers, perfume, brilliant clothes, the naked body. They say there's a soul. I don't know, I've never seen it. And what do I need it for? Let me die completely, like a *rusalka*, I'll melt like a cloud beneath the sun. I love the body, strong, dexterous, naked, which is able to take its own pleasure."

"And which is able to suffer," Sasha said softly.

"And suffer, that's good too," Lyudmila whispered passionately. "It's sweet even when it's painful—as long as one can feel the body, as long as one can see the body's nakedness and beauty."

"But isn't it shameful without clothing?" Sasha said timidly.

Lyudmila fell abruptly on her knees before him. Breathlessly she kissed his hands and whispered:

"Dearest, my idol, my godlike youth, if only I could feast my eyes on your dear shoulders for a single moment."

Sasha sighed, lowered his eyes, blushed and awkwardly removed his blouse. Lyudmila seized him with burning hands and showered kisses over his shoulders that were convulsed with shame.

"See how submissive I am!" Sasha said, smiling with an effort so that he could banish his embarrassment with a jest.

Lyudmila was hastily kissing Sasha's arms from the shoulders to the fingers, and Sasha, plunged into a passionate and cruel reverie, did not attempt to remove them. Lyudmila's kisses were infused with the warmth of adoration, and it was as though her burning lips were kissing not a boy, but a god-youth in some thrilling and mysterious ritual of the blossoming Flesh.

Meanwhile Darya and Valeriya were standing behind the door, pushing each other, and taking turns looking through the key-hole and almost fainting from passionate and searing excitement.

"It's time to get dressed," Sasha said finally.

Lyudmila sighed and with the same reverential expression in her eyes she put his undershirt and blouse on him, waiting on him carefully and respectfully.

"So you're a pagan?" Sasha asked in puzzlement.

Lyudmila laughed cheerfully.

"What about you?" she asked.

"What next!" Sasha replied confidently. "I know the entire catechism thoroughly."

Lyudmila laughed. Eyeing her, Sasha smiled and asked:

"If you're a pagan, then why do you go to church?"

Lyudmila stopped laughing, grew pensive.

"Well," she said, "one has to pray. You have to pray, weep, light a candle, commemorate the dead. And I love all of it, the candles, the icon lamps, the incense, the vestments, the singing—if the singers are good—the icons, their mountings, the ribbons. Yes, it's all so beautiful. And I also love . . . Him . . . you know . . . the One who was crucified . . ."

Lyudmila uttered the last words quite softly, almost in a whisper, blushed like one who was guilty and lowered her eyes.

"You know, sometimes I dream about Him—He's on the cross and there are little drops of blood on his body."

From that time on, Lyudmila more than once would start to unbutton his jacket when she took him off to her room. At first he was embarrassed to tears, but he soon grew used to it. And then he would gaze clearly and calmly as Lyudmila pulled down his undershirt, bared his shoulders, fondled and patted his back. And finally, he himself started to undress himself.

It was pleasant for Lyudmila to hold him half-naked on her knees, her arms around him and kissing him.

Sasha was alone at home. He was reminiscing about Lyudmila and his naked shoulders under her burning eyes.

"What does she want?" he was thinking. And suddenly he turned a deep crimson and his heart began to pound ever so painfully. He was seized with an impetuous cheerfulness. He turned several somersaults, collapsed on the floor, leapt up on the furniture—thousands of crazy movements threw him from one corner to the other, and his cheerful, clear laughter resounded through the house.

Kokovkina had returned home at the time, heard the extraordinary noise and went into Sasha's room. She stood on the threshold in perplexity and shook her head.

"What are you doing acting like you're raving mad, Sashenka!" she said. "At least act silly with your comrades, or else you'll be raving by yourself. Dear father, shame on you, you're not a little boy."

Sasha stood there and it was as though his arms, heavy and awkward, were frozen, whereas his entire body was still shaking with excitement.

Once Kokovkina came home to find Lyudmila there—she was feeding sweets to Sasha.

"You're spoiling him," Kokovkina said affectionately. "My boy loves to eat sweet things."

"Well, he calls me a wicked girl," Lyudmila complained.

"Ai, Sashenka, how could you!" Kokovkina said with affectionate reproach. "Why would you do such a thing?"

"Well, she pesters me," Sasha said, stammering.

He gave Lyudmila an angry look and turned crimson. Lyudmila burst into laughter.

"Rumor-monger," Sasha whispered to her.

"How could you be insulting, Sashenka!" Kokovkina upbraided him. "You mustn't be insulting!"

Sasha looked at Lyudmila with a grin and softly murmured:

"I won't do it any more."

Every time when Sasha came now, Lyudmila would lock herself in with him and start to take his clothes off and dress him up in different outfits. Their sweet shame was dressed up in laughter and jokes. Sometimes Lyudmila would truss Sasha up in a corset and put her dress on him. When he was wearing a low-necked dress, Sasha's arms, full and delicately rounded, and his round shoulders seemed very beautiful. His skin was of a yellowish hue, and, as was rarely the case, it was of an even and delicate color. Lyudmila's skirt, shoes and stockings all proved to be just right for Sasha and they all suited him. After he had put on a woman's entire wardrobe, Sasha would sit there submissively and fan himself. When he was wearing this attire he actually did resemble a girl and tried to act like a girl. Only one thing was awkward: Sasha's cropped hair. Lyudmila didn't want to put a wig on him or tie a braid to Sasha's head—that would be repulsive.

Lyudmila was teaching Sasha to perform curtseys. At first he would squat awkwardly and self-consciously. But he possessed a gracefulness even though it was mixed with a boyish angularity. Blushing and laughing, he studied diligently how to perform a curtsey and he flirted recklessly.

Sometimes Lyudmila would take his arms, naked and shapely, and kiss them. Sasha didn't resist and would look at Lyudmila with a chuckle. Sometimes he himself would put his arms to her lips and say:

"Kiss them!"

But best of all he liked the other clothing that Lyudmila sewed herself: a fisherman's outfit with bare legs and the chiton of an Athenian barelegged boy.

Lyudmila would dress him up and admire him. At the same time she would grow pale and melancholy.

Sasha was sitting on Lyudmila's bed, picking at the folds of the chiton and dangling his naked legs. Lyudmila stood in front of him and gazed at him with an expression of happiness and perplexity.

"How silly you are!" Sasha said.

"There's so much happiness in my silliness!" a pale Lyudmila babbled, crying and kissing Sasha's arms.

"Why are you crying?" Sasha asked, smiling carefreely.

"My heart has been smitten with joy. My breast has been pierced with the seven swords of happiness. How can I help but cry?"

"You're a fool, really a fool!" Sasha said with a chuckle.

"And you're smart!" Lyudmila replied with sudden annoyance, wiped the tears away and sighed. "Try to understand, silly," she said in a soft persuasive voice. "Happiness and wisdom can only be found in madness."

"Really now!" Sasha said mistrustfully.

"You have to forget, forget yourself, and then you'll understand everything," Lyudmila whispered. "In your opinion, then, do wise men think?"

"What else?"

"They just know. It's bestowed upon them immediately: one look and all is revealed . . ."

The autumn evening lingered softly on. From time to time a barely audible rustling sound carried from beyond the window when the wind in flight would make the branches of the trees shake. Sasha and Lyudmila were alone. Lyudmila had dressed him up as a bare-legged fisherman in a blue outfit out of fine linen. Then she laid him down on a low couch and sat down on the floor, barefooted and in just her chemise, beside his naked legs. And over his body and his clothing she sprinkled a perfume with a dense, herbaceous and brittle scent, like the motionless breath of a strangely flowering valley enclosed by mountains.

Large, brilliant beads gleamed on Lyudmila's neck; intricate golden bracelets tinkled on her wrists. Her body gave off the scent of iris—a cloying, sensual and irritating fragrance that induced drowsiness and languor and was sated with the miasma of turgid waters. She was languishing and sighing, gazing at his swarthy face, at his blue-tinged eyelashes and midnight eyes. She laid her head on his naked knees, and her light curls caressed his swarthy skin. She kissed Sasha's body and her head began to spin from the fragrance, strange and potent, that intermingled with the smell of his youthful skin.

Sasha was lying there and smiling a soft, uncertain smile. Vague desire was being born inside him and it tormented him sweetly. When Lyudmila was kissing his knees and feet, the tender kisses aroused languid, somnolent reveries. He had the urge to do something to her, something nice or painful, something tender or shameful—but what? Kiss her feet? Or beat her, hard and at length, with long, supple branches? So that she would laugh for joy or cry from pain? Perhaps she would desire both of those things, but it wouldn't be enough. What did she need? There they were the two of them, half-naked, and both desire and prescriptive shame were attendant on their liberated flesh. Yet what did that mystery of the flesh consist of? How could he offer his blood and his body in sweetest sacrifice to her desires and his own shame?

Meanwhile, Lyudmila fretted and languished alongside his legs, pale with impossible desires, first fiery, then turning cold. She whispered passionately:

"Am I not beautiful! Aren't my eyes burning! Don't I have luxuriant hair! Caress me! Caress me! Tear my bracelets off, undo my necklace!"

Sasha grew frightened and he was oppressed by impossible desires.

XXVII

PEREDONOV AWOKE TOWARDS morning. Someone was looking at him with enormous, turbid, rectangular eyes. Was it Pylnikov? Peredonov went up to the window and doused the ominous spectre.

Everything was spellbound and enchanted. The wild *nedotykomka* went on shrilling, both man and beast regarded Peredonov with spite and deceit. Everything was hostile towards him, he was alone against everyone.

In his classes at the gymnasium Peredonov spread malignant gossip about his fellow teachers, the headmaster, parents and students. The students listened to him in perplexity. Some inherently uncouth students were to be found who sought favor with Peredonov and expressed their sympathy to him. Yet others were strictly silent or, when Peredonov made fun of their parents, defended them vehemently. Peredonov would give the latter a sullen look and move away from them, muttering something.

In some classes Peredonov would entertain the students with his absurd interpretations.

Once he read the following verses by Pushkin:

> With labor's clamor held at bay
> As dawn arises out of morn,
> The wolf sets out upon his way
> With wolf-bitch hungry and forlorn.

"Stop a moment," Peredonov said. "One should understand this properly. The allegory is hidden here. Wolves go in pairs: a male wolf and a hungry wolf-bitch. The male wolf is full, whereas she is hungry. The wife is always supposed to eat after the husband. The wife is supposed to submit to her husband in everything."

Pylnikov was cheerful. He smiled and looked at Peredonov with his deceptively pure, black, unfathomable eyes. Sasha's face tormented and tempted Peredonov. The accursed boy was casting a spell over him with his perfidious smile.

And was he even a boy? Or perhaps there were two of them: a brother and sister. And it was impossible to figure out who was where. Or perhaps he even knew how to transform himself from a boy into a girl. It was hard-

229 THE PETTY DEMON

ly a coincidence that he was such a clean little thing—when he was transforming himself he must have rinsed himself in various magical solutions, otherwise it would have been impossible, one couldn't become a changeling. And he always smelled so much of perfume.

"What perfume did you put on, Pylnikov?" Peredonov asked. "Eau de skunk?"

The boys broke into laughter. Sasha blushed from the insult and was silent.

Peredonov could not comprehend the pure desire to be liked, not to be repulsive. He considered any manifestation of that sort, even on the part of the boy, as an attempt to trap him. If someone got dressed up, it meant that the person was plotting to flatter Peredonov. Otherwise why get dressed up? Smart dress and cleanliness were repulsive to Peredonov and perfume seemed foul-smelling. He preferred the smell of a manured field to any kind of perfume—in his opinion the former was beneficial to health. To get dressed up, to clean oneself, to wash—all of these things required time and labor. And the thought of labor induced a melancholy and frightening feeling in Peredonov. It would be nice to do nothing, just to eat, drink and sleep—and nothing more!

His schoolmates teased Sasha because he perfumed himself with "eau de skunk" and because Lyudmilochka was in love with him. He would flare up and protest vehemently. Nothing of the sort, he would say, she wasn't in love with him, all that was just the invention of Peredonov. He was the one who had proposed to Lyudmilochka, but Lyudmilochka had tweaked his nose and so he was angry at her and was spreading ugly rumors about her. His schoolmates believed him. It was Peredonov, as everyone knew, but still they didn't stop teasing him. It was so pleasant to tease people.

Peredonov persisted in telling everyone about Pylnikov's depravity.

"He's mixed up with Lyudmilochka," he said. "They kiss so zealously that she's already given birth to one prep student and now she's carrying another around."

The talk in the town about Lyudmila's love for a student at the gymnasium was exaggerated and filled with stupid and unseemly details. But few people believed it—Peredonov had overdone it. However the dilettantes—of whom there were a great many in our town—asked Lyudmila teasingly:

"What are you doing falling madly in love with a young boy? That's insulting to the rest of the eligible young bachelors."

Lyudmila laughed and said:

"Rubbish!"

The townsfolk gave Sasha looks of vile curiosity. The widow of General Poluyanov, a rich woman from a merchant background, made inquiries about his age and discovered that he was still too young, but that in about two years she could invite him and concern herself with his development.

By now Sasha had begun to reproach Lyudmila at times because people were teasing him over her. It even happened at times that he would beat her—in response to which Lyudmila would merely laugh.

However, in order to put an end to the silly gossip and to protect Lyudmila from an unpleasant business, all the Rutilovs and their numerous friends, relatives and relations took energetic action against Peredonov and tried to prove that all these stories were just the fantasy of a madman. Peredonov's wild antics forced many people to believe the explanations.

At the same time the district educational trustee was beset by denunciations against Peredonov. An inquiry was sent to the headmaster from the district officials. Khripach referred to his previous reports and added that Peredonov's continuing presence in the gymnasium was becoming positively dangerous inasmuch as his mental illness was noticeably progressing.

By now Peredonov was totally in the power of his wild notions. Spectres had divorced Peredonov from the world. His eyes, crazed and dull, wandered without pausing on objects, just as though he were constantly seeking to look beyond them, beyond the objective world, and was searching for the apertures.

When he was left on his own he would talk to himself, shouting out senseless threats at someone:

"I'll kill you! I'll slit your throat! I'll caulk you up!"

Varvara would listen and smirk.

"Go ahead and fly into a rage!" she thought maliciously.

It seemed to her that it was only anger because he had guessed that he had been deceived and was furious. He wasn't losing his mind, a fool had nothing to lose. And if he were to lose his mind, what did it matter? Madness cheers up the stupid!

"You know, Ardalyon Borisych," Khripach once said, "You look very unhealthy."

"I have a headache," Peredonov said sullenly.

"You know, my esteemed sir," Khripach continued in a cautious voice, "I would advise you not to come to the gymnasium for the time being. You ought to recuperate, take care of your nerves which, apparently, are really rather disturbed."

"Not go to the gymnasium! Of course," thought Peredonov. "That would be the best thing. Why didn't I think of it earlier! Pretend to be sick, sit at home, watch and see what comes of this."

"Yes, yes, I won't come. I'm sick," he said joyfully to Khripach.

Meanwhile, the director wrote once more to the district officials and was waiting from one day to the next for them to appoint the doctors who would carry out the examination. But the officials were in no hurry. That was why they were officials.

Peredonov didn't go to the gymnasium and was also waiting for something. Lately he had been sticking to Volodin. It was frightening to let him out of his sight—he might do some harm. From the morning on, as soon as he awoke, Peredonov would think of Volodin with a melancholy feeling. Where was he then? What was he doing? Sometimes he fancied that he was seeing Volodin: the clouds flying through the skies like a flock of sheep and Volodin was running along in their midst with his bowler hat on his head

231 THE PETTY DEMON

and producing his bleating laughter; or sometimes he would fly swiftly past, in the smoke rising out of chimneys, making grotesque faces and leaping up and down in the air.

Volodin thought, and related to everyone with pride, that Peredonov loved him a great deal—he simply couldn't live without him.

"Varvara has tricked him," Volodin said, "and he sees that I'm his only true friend and that's why he's sticking to me."

Peredonov would be coming out of the house to go and see Volodin, but the latter would already be coming to greet him, wearing a bowler hat, carrying a walking stick, springing cheerfully up and down and happily bursting with his bleating laughter.

"What are you wearing a bowler for?" Peredonov once asked him.

"Why shouldn't I wear a bowler, Ardalyon Borisych?" Volodin replied cheerfully and reasonably. "It's modest and proper enough. I'm not supposed to wear an official cap with a cockade, and as far as a top hat is concerned, let the aristocrats indulge in that practice, it doesn't suit us."

"You'll boil in that pot," Peredonov said sullenly.

Volodin giggled.

They went to Peredonov's.

"What a lot of walking to do," Peredonov said angrily.

"Ardalyon Borisych, it's beneficial to get yourself moving," Volodin tried to convince him. "You work a little, walk a little, eat a little—and you'll be healthy."

"Sure," Peredonov objected. "You think that in two or three hundred years people will be working?"

"What else? If you don't work, then you won't eat. You get bread for money and you have to work for money."

"I don't want bread."

"There won't be any rolls or pies either," Volodin said with a giggle. "And you won't be able to buy vodka and there won't be anything to make brandy out of."

"No, people won't be doing the work themselves," Peredonov said. "There'll be machines for everything: you turn a handle, like the hand organ, and it's ready. But it'll be boring to turn the handle for long."

Volodin grew pensive, bowed his head, puffed out his lips and said musingly:

"Yes, that will be very good. Only we won't be there any more."

Peredonov gave him a spiteful look and grumbled:

"You won't be there, but I'll live that long."

"God willing," Volodin said cheerfully. "May you live two hundred years and crawl around on all fours for three hundred years."

Peredonov no longer pronounced his counter-spells—let come what may. He would conquer everyone, he only had to keep his eyes peeled and not give in.

At home, sitting in the dining room and drinking with Volodin, Peredonov told him about the Princess. In Peredonov's imagination there wasn't a day that went by that she didn't grow even more decrepit and even more terrible: yellow, wrinkled, hunched over, long in the tooth and wicked—that was how Peredonov invariably fancied he saw her.

"She's two hundred years old," Peredonov said and stared straight ahead in a strange and melancholy fashion. "And she wants us to get cozy with each other again. Until then she doesn't want to give me the post."

"You don't say, the things she wants!" Volodin said, shaking his head. "What an old matriarch!"

The murder was making Peredonov rave. He said to Volodin, knitting his brows ferociously:

"There's already one hidden there behind my wallpaper. And there's another one I'm going to clobber under the floor."

But Volodin wasn't afraid and giggled.

"Do you smell it behind the wallpaper?" Peredonov asked.

"No, I don't," Volodin said, giggling and clowning.

"Your nose is stuffed," Peredonov said. "It's no coincidence that your nose has turned red. It's rotting over there behind the wallpaper."

"The bedbug!" Varvara cried and burst into laughter. Peredonov looked on, dully and gravely.

Plunging ever deeper into his derangement, Peredonov began to write denunciations: against the figures in the playing cards; against the *nedotykomka*; and against the sheep who was an imposter and who was pretending to be Volodin and was aiming to get a high position, but in fact was just a sheep; against the wood-poachers—they had chopped down all the birch, there was nothing left for the steam baths and it was difficult to educate the children, but they had left the aspen and what good was the aspen?

When he met students from the gymnasium on the street Peredonov would terrify the younger ones and amuse the older ones with his shameless and absurd words. The older ones would walk in a crowd behind him, scattering whenever they caught sight of any other teacher. But the younger ones would run away from him of their own accord.

Peredonov fancied he saw spells and enchantments in everything. He was terrified by his hallucinations and they wrung an insane howling and shrieking out of his breast. The *nedotykomka* would appear before him bloody at one moment and fiery the next. It would moan and howl and its howling made Peredonov's head burst with an unbearable pain. The cat grew to frightening proportions, stomped around in boots and pretended to be a grown man with a red moustache.

XXVIII

S ASHA LEFT AFTER dinner and didn't return at the appointed time: by seven o'clock. Kokovkina grew worried. God forfend that he should run into any of the teachers on the street at the forbidden time. They would punish him and it would be awkward for her. She had always had modest boys living with her, they didn't roam around at night. Kokovkina went to look for Sasha. Naturally enough, where else should she go than to the Rutilovs.

As bad luck would have it, Lyudmila had forgotten to lock the door that day. Kokovkina entered and what did she see? Sasha was standing in front of a mirror in a woman's dress and fanning himself. Lyudmila was roaring with laughter and straightening the ribbons on his brightly colored sash.

"Ach, goodness gracious me!" Kokovkina exclaimed in horror. "What is going on! I'm worrying and looking while he's here clowning about. For shame, he's outfitted himself in a dress! And you, Lyudmila Platonovna, you should be ashamed!"

At first Lyudmila was dismayed at the surprise, but she quickly regained her senses. With a cheerful laugh, embracing Kokovkina and sitting her down in a chair, she told her a story that she made up on the spot:

"We want to put on a play at home. I'll be the boy and he'll be the girl, and it'll be terribly amusing."

Sasha stood there all red, frightened, with tears in his eyes.

"I never heard of such nonsense!" Kokovkina said angrily. "He has to do his lessons and not perform plays. A fine idea! Pray, get dressed immediately, Alexander, and march straight home with me."

Lyudmila's laughter was cheerful and ringing. She kept kissing Kokovkina—and the old woman was thinking that this cheerful girl was acting just like a child whereas Sasha, out of stupidity, was happy to carry out all her ventures. Lyudmila's cheerful laughter made the incident look like a simple childish prank which only demanded a proper rebuke from her. And she grumbled, putting on an angry face, but already her heart was at ease.

Sasha nimbly changed behind the screen where Lyudmila's bed stood. Kokovkina took him away and scolded him the entire way back. Sasha, ashamed and frightened, didn't even try to excuse himself. "What else is going to happen at home?" he wondered timidly.

But at home Kokovkina started off by treating him sternly and ordering him to stand on his knees. Sasha was barely on his knees for a few minutes when she let him go, disarmed by his guilty face and his silent tears.
She said grumpily:

"A fine dandy you are, you smell of perfume a mile away!"

Sasha deftly scraped his feet, kissed her hand—and she was even more
touched by the politeness of the boy who had been punished.

Meanwhile a storm was gathering over Sasha. Varvara and Grushina wrote
an anonymous letter to Khripach which said that the student Pylnikov had been
enticed by a Rutilov girl and was spending entire evenings with her and indulging
in depravity. Khripach recalled a recent conversation. A few days before at a
reception at the home of the marshal of the nobility, someone had made an allusion which escaped everyone about a young woman who had fallen in love with
a juvenile. The conversation immediately went on to other matters: everyone, by
virtue of the unspoken accord of people who were accustomed to better society,
considered this an entirely awkward topic for conversation in Khripach's presence and pretended that the conversation was unsuitable for ladies and that the
subject itself was insignificant and unlikely. Naturally, Khripach noted all of this,
but he was not so naive as to ask anyone. He was utterly certain that he would
soon find out everything, that all the news would arrive of its own accord, one
way or another, and would always do so with proper timeliness. This very letter
was in fact the piece of news he had been expecting.

Not for a moment did Khripach believe in Pylnikov's depravity or that
his acquaintance with Lyudmila possessed any unseemly aspects. "This,"
he thought, "is all the result of that same stupid fiction of Peredonov's and
is being nourished by the jealous spitefulness of Grushina. But this letter,"
he thought, "shows that undesirable rumors are circulating which might
cast a shadow on the dignity of the gymnasium which has been entrusted
to me." And for that reason it behove him to take measures.

First of all, Khripach invited Kokovkina in order to discuss with her
the circumstances which might have given rise to the undesirable rumors.

Kokovkina already knew what it was about. People had informed her
in even plainer terms than they had the headmaster. Grushina had been
lying in wait for her on the street and had started up a conversation and
said that Lyudmila had already completely corrupted Sasha. Kokovkina
was stunned. At home she showered reproach on Sasha. She was all the
more annoyed because it had been taking place almost before her eyes and
Sasha had been going to the Rutilovs with her consent. Sasha pretended
that he understood nothing and asked:

"But what have I done that's bad?"

Kokovkina faltered.

"What do you mean, bad? You don't know yourself? Was it that long
ago I found you in a skirt? Have you forgotten, you shameless boy?"

"You found me like that, but what was particularly bad about that?

Anyway you punished me for that! What's the matter, you'd think I had put on a stolen skirt!"

"My goodness, the way he reasons!" Kokovkina said distractedly. "I punished you, but obviously it wasn't enough."

"Well, punish me some more," Sasha said obstinately, with a look of someone who is being unjustly offended. "You yourself forgave me then, but now it's not good enough. I didn't beg your forgiveness then, I would even have stayed on my knees the whole evening. Otherwise, why do you keep reproaching me!"

"Dear father, they're already talking about you and your Lyudmila in town," Kokovkina said.

"What are they saying?" Sasha asked in an innocently curious voice.

Kokovkina faltered again.

"What are they saying—you know what! You know yourself what people might say about you. They won't be saying much that's good. You're getting into a lot of mischief with your Lyudmila, that's what they're saying."

"Well, I won't get into mischief," Sasha promised as calmly as though the conversation concerned a game of tag.

He put on an innocent face, but his heart was heavy. He kept asking Kokovkina what people were saying and he was afraid of hearing any vulgar words. What could they say about them? The windows in Lyudmila's room look out on the garden, there was nothing visible from the street and Lyudmila always lowered the curtains. But if someone had been spying, then what could they have said about that? Perhaps their words only expressed annoyance and insult? Or were they only talking about the fact that he frequently went there?

Then on the following day Kokovkina received an invitation to see the headmaster. The old lady was completely unnerved by it. She didn't say anything to Sasha, quietly got ready and set out at the appointed time. Khripach politely and gently informed her about the letter he had received. She started to weep.

"Calm yourself, we aren't blaming you," Khripach said. "We know you well. Of course, you'll have to keep a closer eye on him. But now you just tell me what in fact happened."

Kokovkina came home from the director with fresh reproaches for Sasha.

"I'll write your aunt," she said, weeping.

"I'm not guilty of anything, let my aunt come, I'm not afraid," Sasha said and also cried.

The following day Khripach invited Sasha to his office and questioned him dryly and sternly:

"I wish to know which acquaintances you've taken up in the town."

Sasha gazed at the headmaster with his falsely innocent and calm eyes.

"What acquaintances?" he said. "Olga Vasilyevna knows that I only go to my schoolmates and to the Rutilovs."

"Yes, precisely," Khripach continued his interrogation. "What do you do at the Rutilovs?"

"Nothing in particular, just things," Sasha replied with the same innocent look. "Mainly we read. The Rutilov ladies like poetry very much. And I'm always home by seven o'clock."

"Perhaps not always?" Khripach asked, fastening on Sasha a gaze which he tried to make penetrating.

"Yes, I was late once," Sasha said with the calm frankness of an innocent boy. "But I caught it from Olga Vasilyevna and then I was never late."

Khripach was silent. Sasha's calm replies had put him in a dilemma. In any case he would have to administer an admonition, a reprimand, but how and why? In order not to put any bad ideas (which Khripach believed hadn't been there earlier) into his head, and in order not to offend the boy and in order to eliminate those troubles which might occur in the future because of this acquaintance. Khripach thought that the work of the pedagogue was a difficult and responsible work, particularly if one had the honor of presiding over an educational institution. The difficult and responsible work of the pedagogue! This banal definition gave wings to Khripach's thoughts that were on the verge of becoming paralyzed. He started to speak—quickly, distinctly and casually. Sasha listened with half an ear:

". . . your first obligation as a student is to study . . . you mustn't get carried away with the company of others even though it may be pleasant and completely irreproachable . . . in any event, it must be said that the company of boys your own age is much more beneficial for you . . . You must value both your own reputation and that of the educational institution . . . Finally—and I'll say it to you outright—I have reason to believe that your relations with the young ladies possess a loose nature that is inadmissible at your age, and completely inappropriate with the generally accepted rules of seemliness."

Sasha started to weep. He felt sorry that people could talk about his dear Lyudmilochka as about a person with whom it was possible to act in a loose and unseemly fashion.

"Word of honor, there wasn't anything bad," he tried to convince him. "We only read, went for walks and played—well, ran around a bit—there was nothing loose."

Khripach patted him on the shoulder and said in a voice that he tried to make warm, but which remained nevertheless dry:

"Just listen now, Pylnikov . . ." (Why not call the boy Sasha! Was it because it wasn't formal and there hadn't been a circular from the Ministry on the matter as yet?)

"I believe you that nothing bad happened, but nevertheless you'd better curtail these frequent visits. Believe me, it would be better to do so. It's not just your tutor and your superior talking to you, but your friend as well."

There was nothing left for Sasha to do but to bow, thank him and then be obliged to obey. And Sasha started to hurriedly drop in on Lyudmila for very short visits. But still he tried to be there every day. It was annoying that they had to meet for such short periods and Sasha vented his anger on Lyudmila herself. More frequently now he called her Lyudmilka, a silly little fool, a Siamese donkey and beat her. But Lyudmila only laughed at all of that.

A rumor spread through the town that the actors of the local theatre were organizing a masquerade with prizes for the best costumes, both male and female, that was to be held in the town hall. Exaggerated rumors circulated about the prizes. It was said that the woman would receive a cow, and the man a bicycle. The townspeople were excited by the rumors. Everyone wanted to win: the prizes were such substantial ones. Costumes were hurriedly sewn. The money spent was not begrudged. People concealed the costumes they devised from their closest friends so that no one would filch a brilliant idea.

When the printed notice about the masquerade appeared—large posters pasted on fences and distributed to important citizens—it turned out that a cow and bicycle weren't being given as prizes at all, but only a fan for the lady and an album for the man. That disappointed and irritated everyone who was getting ready for the masquerade. People started to grumble. They said:

"As though it were worth wasting money on!"

"It's simply ridiculous, prizes like that."

"They should have announced it at once."

"It's only in our town that the public can be treated in such a fashion."

Nevertheless, the preparations continued. Whatever the prize, it would still be flattering to win it.

Darya and Lyudmila didn't care about the prize, neither before nor after. A lot they needed a cow! Some wonder, a fan! And who was going to be the judge for the prizes? What kind of taste would they have, the judges! But both sisters grew enthused over Lyudmila's dream of sending Sasha to the masquerade in a woman's costume, to deceive the entire town in this way and to arrange it so that he won the prize. Valeriya, too, pretended that she was agreed. Jealous and weak like a child, she was annoyed—it was Lyudmila's little friend and after all he didn't come to visit her. But she couldn't bring herself to argue with her two older sisters. She merely said with a scornful little smile:

"He wouldn't dare."

"But listen," Darya said determinedly, "we'll do it so that no one will know."

And when the sisters told Sasha about their venture and Lyudmilochka said to him: "We'll dress you up like a Japanese lady," Sasha started to leap about and squeal ecstatically. Let come what may—and especially if no one found out—he was agreed. How could he not be! After all it would be terribly hilarious to fool everyone.

It was immediately decided that Sasha would be dressed up as a geisha girl. The sisters kept their venture a strict secret. They didn't even tell Larisa or their brother. Lyudmila herself created the costume for the geisha girl from a label on a bottle of corylopsis: a dress of yellow silk on red satin, long and wide; a colorful pattern sewn onto the dress and large flowers of marvellous design. The girls themselves created the fan out of bamboo sticks and delicate Japanese paper with drawings and the umbrella was fashioned of delicate pink silk on a bamboo handle as well. For the feet—pink stockings and flat wooden sandals. The masterful Lyudmila painted the mask for the geisha girl: a yellowish, but sweet, rather thin face with a passive gentle smile, slit eyes, and a narrow and small mouth. It was only the wig that they had to order from Petersburg: a black one with smooth, combed hair.

Time was required for measuring the costume, but Sasha could only drop by for short periods and then not every day. Still, the time was found. Sasha would run off at night through the window after Kokovkina was already asleep. It worked out happily.

Varvara was also getting ready for the masquerade. She bought a mask with a stupid face and there was no problem with the costume—she got dressed up as a cook. She hung a ladle from her belt, put a black bonnet on her head, bared her arms to above the elbows and rouged them heavily— a cook straight from the hearth—and thus, her costume was ready. If she won the prize, fine; if not, she didn't need it.

Grushina came up with the idea of dressing as Diana. Varvara laughed and asked:

"Really, are you going to put a collar on?"

"What do I need a collar for?" Grushina asked in amazement.

"Sure," Varvara explained. "You thought of dressing yourself up like the dog Dianka."

"Well, that's a good one!" Grushina replied with a laugh. "Not Dianka, but the goddess Diana."

Varvara and Grushina got dressed for the masquerade together at Grushina's place. Grushina's costume turned out to be extremely flimsy: naked arms and shoulders, a naked back, naked chest, feet in light slippers without any stockings and naked to the knees, and a light dress out of white linen with a red border and her body naked underneath. It was a short dress but at the same time wide and with a multitude of pleats. Varvara said with a smirk:

"A bit bare."

Grushina replied with an insolent wink:

"On the other hand all the men will be especially attracted to me."

"But why so many pleats?" Varvara asked.

"So I can stuff them with sweets for my little devils," Grushina explained.

It was attractive to see everything left so courageously bare on Grushina—but what contradictions. There were flea bites on her skin, her movements were vulgar, her words unbearably uncouth. Once more physical beauty had been profaned.

Peredonov thought that the masquerade had been planned on purpose in order to trap him in something. Nevertheless he went, not in costume, but in his jacket. In order to see for himself what plots were being hatched.

Sasha was amused for several days by the thought of the masquerade. But then doubts began to assail him. How would he find the time to sneak

239 THE PETTY DEMON

out of the house? And particularly now after all those problems? The trouble was that he would be expelled if they found out at the gymnasium.

Not long ago the class prefect—a young person who was so liberal that he couldn't simply call his cat Vaska, but said "Vasily the cat"—had made a significant remark to Sasha as he passed out the grades:

"Be careful, Pylnikov, you have to pay attention to your work."

"But I don't have any two's," Sasha said carefreely.

But his spirits sank—what else was he about to say? No, nothing, he was silent. He just gave Sasha a stern look.

On the day of the masquerade it seemed to Sasha that he couldn't make up his mind to go. He was frightened. The only problem was that his costume had been finished at the Rutilovs—how could he fail them? Would all those dreams and the labor be in vain? And Lyudmilochka would cry. No, he had to go.

It was only the habit of being secretive that he had acquired during the past weeks that enabled Sasha to hide his agitation from Kokovkina. Fortunately, the old woman usually went to bed early. Sasha, too, went to bed early. In order to divert attention he undressed, laid his outer clothing on a chair by the door and put his shoes outside the door.

All that remained was to get away and that was the most difficult part. The path had already been mentioned earlier—through the window—as he had done earlier for the fittings. Sasha put on a light-colored summer blouse (it was hanging in the wardrobe in his room), light house slippers and carefully crawled out the window onto the street after biding his time for when there was no sound of any voices or steps in the proximity. There was a fine drizzle, it was muddy, cold and dark. But he kept thinking that he would be recognized. He took off his cap, slippers, threw them back into his room, rolled up his trousers and skipped barefoot along the rickety boardwalk that was slippery from the rain. In that darkness a face was poorly visible, particularly that of a person who was running, and whoever met him would take him for an ordinary boy who had been sent to the shop.

Valeriya and Lyudmila had sewn intricate but colorful costumes for themselves: Lyudmila was dressing up as a gypsy, and Valeriya as a Spaniard. Lyudmila had on brilliant red rags of silk and velvet, whereas Valeriya, delicate and fragile, was wearing black silk and lace, and carried a black lace fan in her hand. Darya hadn't sewn herself a new costume—she still had her Turkish costume from the year before and she put it on, saying determinedly:

"It's not worth trying to make something up!"

When Sasha arrived, all three sisters started to put his costume on. Sasha was disturbed most of all by the wig.

"But what if it falls off?" he kept repeating fearfully.

Finally they fastened the wig on with ribbons tied under his chin.

XXIX

THE MASQUERADE WAS being held in the town hall, a two-storied, stone building resembling an army barracks, painted a brilliant red color, located in the market square. Gromov-Chistopolsky, an entrepreneur and actor in the local town theatre, was organizing it.

Glass lamps were burning at the entrance which was covered over with a canvas curtain. Out on the street a crowd was greeting the arrivals at the masquerade with critical remarks that for the most part expressed disapproval. This was mainly because the costumes were almost invisible beneath the outerwear on the street and the crowd was judging primarily on intuition. Policemen were keeping order on the street with sufficient diligence, while the chief of police and the district superintendent of police were inside the hall in the capacity of guests.

Upon entering, every visitor received two tickets: a pink one for the best female costume; the other one green, for the best male costume. They were to be given to the most worthy participants. Some people inquired:

"Can people keep them for themselves?"

At first the cashier asked in puzzlement:

"Why for themselves?"

"If, in my opinion, my costume is the very best," the guest replied.

Afterwards the cashier was no longer surprised by such questions and said with a sarcastic smile (he was a young man who liked to make fun):

"As you wish. Keep the two of them if you like."

It was rather filthy in the rooms and right from the beginning a significant portion of the crowd seemed to be drunk. Crooked chandeliers were burning in the cramped rooms with sooty walls and ceilings. The chandeliers seemed enormous, heavy and consumed a great deal of air. The discolored curtains by the doors looked as though they would be repulsive to the touch. Crowds gathered first in one spot, then another. Sounds of laughter and exclamations could be heard—these came from the people who were following the costumed guests attracting the general interest.

The notary, Gudaevsky, was depicting an American savage: rooster feathers in his hair, a copper-red mask with grotesque green designs, a leather jacket, a checked plaid over his shoulder and high leather boots with green tassels. He was waving his arms, leaping up and down, and walking with a gymnastic step, energetically pumping his bent, naked knee out in front of himself. His wife was dressed as a wheat sheaf. She had on a gaudy dress of green and yellow rags; sheaves of wheat that had been stuck in everywhere projected out in all directions. They brushed against everyone and pricked them. People tugged and plucked at her. She was cursing spitefully:

"I'll scratch you!" she shrieked.

People laughed all around. Someone asked:

"Where did she collect so many wheat sheaves?"

"She saved them up from summer," came the reply. "She used to go out into the fields every day to steal them."

Several officials without moustaches, who were in love with Gudaevskaya, and therefore informed by her beforehand as to what she would be wearing, accompanied her. They were collecting tickets for her—practically by force and rudeness. They simply took them away from some people who were not particularly brave.

There were other costumed ladies as well who were zealously collecting tickets through their admirers. Some gazed hungrily at tickets that hadn't been given away yet and asked for them. They were greeted with insolent remarks.

One despondent lady, dressed up as night—a blue costume with a glass star and a paper moon on her forehead—said timidly to Murin:

"Give me your ticket."

Murin's response was rude:

"Are you kidding? Give my ticket to you! Beat it!"

Night grumbled something angrily and went away. She only wanted to show two or three tickets at home so that she could say she won them here. Modest dreams can be in vain.

The schoolteacher, Skobochkina, was dressed up as a bear, that is, she had simply thrown a bearskin over her shoulders and put the bear's head on her own like a helmet above the customary demi-mask. In general it was grotesque, but nevertheless it suited her solid build and stentorian voice. The bear walked around with heavy steps and roared through the entire hall so that the flames in the chandeliers fluttered. Many people liked the bear. She received a fair number of tickets. But she didn't know how to hang on to them herself and she didn't have any shrewd partner like the others. More than half the tickets were stolen from her when the shop owners bought her drinks. They sympathized with the ability she displayed for depicting the movements of a bear. People in the crowd would cry:

"Take a look here, the bear is belting back vodka!"

Skobochkina couldn't bring herself to refuse the vodka. It seemed to her that a bear ought to drink vodka once it was offered.

One person, dressed as an ancient German, stood out because of his size and full limbs. A lot of people liked the fact that he was so hefty and that his arms were visible—powerful arms with excellently developed muscles. For the most part, women were following him around and he was surrounded by an affectionate and laudatory whispering. People recognized the actor

Bengalsky in the ancient German. Bengalsky was very popular in our town. For that reason many people gave him their tickets.

The reasoning of many went as follows:

"If I can't get the prize then better an actor (or actress) get it. Otherwise, if one of our people wins it, then we'll be tortured with the boasting."

Grushina's costume also enjoyed success—a scandalous success. Men followed her around in a dense crowd, roared with laughter, made immodest remarks. The ladies turned their heads away with indignation. Finally, the chief of police went up to Grushina and, licking his lips sweetly, declared:

"Madame, you must cover yourself up."

"What do you mean? You can't see anything indecent on me," Grushina replied pertly.

"Madame, the ladies are offended," Minchukov said.

"To hell with your ladies!" Grushina cried.

"I'm afraid not, Madame," Minchukov requested. "You must take pains to at least cover your breast and back with a handkerchief."

"And what if I've blown my nose in it?" Grushina protested with an insolent laugh.

But Minchukov was insistent:

"As you wish, Madame, only if you don't cover yourself, we will be obliged to make you leave."

Cursing and spitting, Grushina went off into the toilet and there, with the help of a maid, fixed the pleats of her dress over her breast and back. Returning to the hall, she continued with the same zeal to look for admirers, although now displaying a more modest appearance. She flirted rudely with all the men. Afterwards, when their attention was drawn off in another direction, she went off to the buffet to steal sweets. She soon returned to the hall, showed Volodin a pair of peaches, and said with an insolent smirk:

"I worked for them myself."

And she immediately hid the peaches in the pleats of her costume. Volodin happily bared his teeth.

"Well!" he said. "I'll go too, if that's how it is."

Soon Grushina had gotten tipsy and was acting recklessly—she was shouting, waving her arms and spitting.

"A cheerful lady, that Dianka!" people said of her.

This was the kind of masquerade to which those extravagant girls had dragged the frivolous student from the gymnasium. Climbing into two cabs, the three sisters set out rather late with Sasha. They were late because of him. Their arrival at the hall was noted. A lot of people liked the geisha girl in particular. A rumor had it that Kashtanova, an actress and a favorite of the male contingent of the present public, was dressed up as the geisha girl. Therefore, Sasha was given many tickets. But Kashtanova wasn't even at the masquerade. Her small son had fallen seriously ill the eve before.

Sasha, intoxicated with his new situation, became the complete coquette. The more tickets that were thrust into the geisha's hand, the more cheerfully and provocatively glittered the eyes through the narrow slits in the mask of the coquettish Japanese. The geisha would curtsey, raise her delicate little fingers, titter in a suppressed voice, wave her fan, tap one man or the other on the shoulder and then hide behind her fan. Every minute she was opening and closing her pink umbrella. They might not have been clever devices, but in any event they were sufficient for seducing all those who were devotees of the actress Kashtanova.

"For the lady I have voted to whom I am devoted," Tishkov said, and handed over his ticket to the geisha with a youthful bow.

He had already drunk a great deal and was flushed. His passive, smiling face and his torpid body made him resemble a doll. And he was still making his rhymes.

Valeriya watched Sasha's success and felt an annoying jealousy. Now she wanted people to recognize her so that the crowd would like her costume and her slender, shapely figure, and she would be given the prize. But she immediately recalled with annoyance that it was not in the least possible: all three sisters had agreed to get tickets just for the geisha. Any that they received would still be handed over to their Japanese girl.

People were dancing in the hall. Volodin, who had quickly become intoxicated, started to do Russian dances. The police stopped him. He said in a cheerfully obediant voice:

"Well, if it's not allowed, then I won't do it."

But two landowners, who, following his example, had started to stamp out a *trepak* folk dance, didn't want to comply.

"What right have you got? We paid our fifty kopecks!" they exclaimed and were ushered out.

Volodin accompanied them, pulling faces, grinning and dancing.

The Rutilov girls hurried to search out Peredonov so that they could make fun of him. He was sitting alone, by a window, and looking at the crowd with aimless eyes. All people and objects appeared senseless to him, but hostile at the same time. Lyudmila, as the gypsy, went up to him and said in an altered husky voice:

"My dear *barin*, let me tell your fortune."

"Go to hell!" Peredonov cried.

The gypsy's sudden appearance had frightened him.

"My *barin*, so fine, so golden, o, *barin* mine, give me your hand. I see from your face that you will be rich, you will be a big official," Lyudmila kept pestering him and took Peredonov's hand anyway.

"Well, just mind that you tell my fortune well," Peredonov grumbled.

"Ai, *barin*, my precious *barin*," Lyudmila predicted his fortune, "you have many enemies, they will denounce you, you'll weep and die under a fence."

"Ach, you bitch!" Peredonov cried and tore his hand away.

Lyudmila darted nimbly into the crowd. Valeriya came to replace her, sat down beside Peredonov and softly whispered to him:

I'm a girl who's young and Spanish,
Men like you I adore.
Skinny wives like yours I'd banish,
You can't hope, dear sir, for more.

"You're lying, you fool!" Peredonov grumbled. Valeriya whispered:

Sweeter than the night my kisses,
Hotter than the day my embrace.
Lay your eyes upon your missus
Spit right in her stupid face.
Your Varvara made you marry,
You are handsome, Ardalyón.
As a pair you look contrary,
You are wise as Solomón.

"You're right in what you say," Peredonov said. "Only how am I going to spit in her face? She'd complain to the Princess and I wouldn't get the post."

"What do you need a post for? You're nice even without a post," Valeriya said.

"Sure, but how am I supposed to live if I'm not given a post," Peredonov said despondently.

Darya slipped a letter sealed in a pink envelope into Volodin's hand. Volodin unsealed it with a joyful bleating, read it through, became pensive—then suddenly grew proud. But then was seemingly dismayed. The note was brief and clear:

"My dearest, come to a rendez-vous with me tomorrow at eleven o'clock in the evening at Soldier's Bath. Your completely unknown Zh."

Volodin believed the letter. But this was the question: was it worthwhile going? And who was this "Zh."? Some Zhenya or other? Or did the surname begin with the letter Zh.?

Volodin showed the letter to Rutilov.

"Go, by all means, go!" Rutilov incited him. "See what comes of it. Perhaps it's a rich bride who's fallen in love with you, but her parents are standing in the way, so she wants to declare herself to you like this."

But Volodin thought and thought, and then decided that it wasn't worth going. He said gravely:

"They're all running after me, but I don't want such depraved ones."

He was afraid that he would get beaten up there: Soldier's Bath was situated in a desolate area on the outskirts of the town.

By now a dense, raucous and exaggeratedly cheerful crowd was crammed into all the rooms of the club, while in the main hall, by the entrance, one could hear a din, laughter and exclamations of approval.

Everyone pressed in that direction. It was passed on from one to another that a terribly original costume had arrived. It was a skinny, tall person in a patched, soiled robe, with a besom under his arm, a wash basin in his hand, and he was picking his way through the crowd. He was wearing a cardboard mask—a stupid face with a narrow little beard and side-whiskers—and a cap with a round civil cockade on it. He kept repeating in a surprised voice:

"I was told there was a masquerade here, but no one's washing themselves here.*

And he waved his wash basin despondently. The crowd followed him, oohing and aahing, and naively ecstatic over his complicated improvisation.

"He'll get the prize, I expect," Volodin said enviously.

He was envious, like many of the people, even though he himself wasn't even in costume. So what did he have to be envious of? And here was Machigin. He was extraordinarily ecstatic. The cockade had particularly delighted him. He laughed happily, clapped his hands and said to acquaintances and strangers alike:

"A fine bit of criticism! Those quill-pushers act pompous a lot, they love to wear their cockades and uniforms. They've got their criticism now—and very cleverly done."

When it became hot, the official in the robe started to wave his besom all around, exclaiming:

"Now it's a real bathhouse!"

Those surrounding him roared with laughter. Tickets fell in a shower into his wash basin.

Peredonov gazed at the besom wavering about in the crowd. It seemed to him that it was the *nedotykomka*.

"The rascal has turned green," he thought in horror.(n)

*In Russian the words for "bathing" or a "bathhouse" ("kupan'e" and "banya") are jokingly used to refer to a masquerade.

XXX

A T LAST THE COUNT began of the tickets received for the costumes. The club elders made up the committee. A tensely expectant crowd gathered by the doors into the judges' room. For a short while it grew quiet and monotonous in the club. No music was being played. The guests had fallen silent. Peredonov felt eerie. But within a short while conversation, impatient grumbling and then a clamor rose in the crowd. Someone was trying to convince people that both prizes had been won by actors.

"You just see," someone's irritated and hissing voice was heard.

Many people believed it. The crowd grew restless. Those who had received only a few tickets were already angered by the fact. Those who had received a large number were upset in anticipation of a possible injustice.

Suddenly a bell gave a delicate and nervous tinkle. The judges had emerged: Veriga, Avinovitsky, Kirillov and the other elders. A wave of commotion ran through the room and suddenly everyone fell silent. Avinovitsky's stentorian voice rang out over the entire hall:

"The prize, an album, for the best male costume has been awarded, on the basis of the majority of tickets received, to the gentleman in the costume of the ancient German."

Avinovitsky raised the album up high and angrily looked at the thronging guests. The strapping German started to pick his way through the crowd. People were looking at him with hostility. They wouldn't even let him pass.

"Don't push, please!" cried the despondent woman in a dark blue costume with glass star and paper moon on her forehead—"Night"—in a plaintive voice.

"He won the prize so he's already imagining that the ladies ought to stretch themselves out in front of him," a spitefully hissing voice was heard from the crowd.

"If you're not willing to let me pass yourselves," the German replied with restrained annoyance.

Finally he somehow reached the judges and took the album from Veriga's hands. The music played a fanfare. But the sounds of the music were drowned in a scandalous racket. Curses flew. People surrounded the German, jostled him and shouted:

"Take off the mask!"

The German was silent. It wouldn't have been difficult for him to beat his way through the crowd, but obviously he was loathe to exercise his strength. Gudaevsky made a grab for the album and at the same time someone quickly tore the mask off the German. People in the crowd started to yell:

"It is an actor!"

Their suppositions had been proven correct: it was the actor Bengalsky. He cried angrily:

"So I'm an actor, what of it! After all, you yourselves gave me the tickets!"

Spiteful cries echoed in response:

"You could have slipped a few in yourself."

"You probably printed the tickets yourself."

"There were more tickets distributed than there were people in the audience."

"He brought fifty tickets in his pocket."

Bengalsky turned crimson and cried:

"It's vile to talk like that. Check it whoever wants, it can be checked against the number of guests."

Meanwhile, Veriga said to the people closest to him:

"Gentlemen, calm down, there hasn't been any deception, I can vouch for that. The number of tickets has been checked against the number of people present."

With the help of several reasonable guests, the elders somehow managed to calm the crowd down. Besides, everyone was now curious to see who would be given the fan. Veriga announced:

"Gentlemen, the greatest number of tickets for the female costume has been received by the lady in the costume of the geisha to whom is awarded the prize of the fan. Geisha, come here please, the fan is yours. Gentlemen, I beg you most humbly, be good enough and let the geisha through."

The music played a fanfare for the second time. The frightened geisha would have been happy to run away. But she was urged on, a path was made for her and she was led forward. Veriga, with a polite smile, handed her the fan. Something colorful and smart-looking flashed before Sasha's eyes which were clouded with fear and embarrassment. He had to express his thanks, he thought. The accustomed politeness of a well-bred boy came to the fore. The geisha curtsied, said something that was inaudible, giggled, raised her little fingers—and once more a furious din arose in the hall as jeering and curses were heard. Everyone strained towards the geisha. A fierce, bristling Wheat Sheaf was crying:

"Curtsey, you vile creature! Curtsey!"

The geisha made a dash for the doors, but they wouldn't let her pass. Spiteful cries echoed through the crowd which had grown agitated around the geisha:

"Make her take her mask off!"

"Off with the mask!"

"Grab her, hold her!"

"Take the fan away!"

The Wheat Sheaf cried:

"You know who they gave the prize to? To the actress, Kashtanova. She took someone else's husband away and they gave her the prize! They won't give it to decent women, but they gave it to that vile creature!"

And she rushed at the geisha, screaming shrilly and clenching her dry fists. Others followed her—mostly her gentlemen admirers. The geisha desperately fought her way free. A savage persecution began. They smashed the fan, tore it to pieces, threw it on the floor and stomped on it. The crowd, with the geisha in its midst, hurtled about the hall in a frenzy, knocking bystanders off their feet. Neither the Rutilov sisters, nor the elders could force their way through to the geisha. The geisha, spritely and strong, was screaming shrilly, scratching and biting. She firmly held on to her mask, first with her right hand, then with her left.

"They all should be beaten!" some infuriated woman shrieked.

A drunken Grushina, hiding behind the others, kept inciting Volodin on together with the rest of her acquaintances.

"Pinch her, pinch the vile creature!" she cried.

Machigin, holding himself by the nose, was dripping blood as he leapt out of the crowd and complained:

"She gave it to me right in the nose with her fist."

Some fierce young man had fastened onto the geisha's sleeve with his teeth and had torn it in half. The geisha screamed:

"Help me!"

Others started to tear at her costume as well. Her body was bared in a few spots. Darya and Lyudmila were pushing and shoving desperately, trying to squeeze through to the geisha, but to no avail. Volodin was tugging at the geisha, screeching and clowning around with such energy that he was even getting in the way of others who were less drunk and more furious than he. It was more out of cheerfulness than spite that he was expending such energy, imagining that a very entertaining amusement was being performed. He ripped the sleeve cleanly off the geisha's dress and wrapped it around his head.

"This is handy!" he cried shrilly, making faces and roaring with laughter.

Making his way out of the crowd where it seemed too cramped for him, he fooled around in the open space and with a wild shriek danced over the remnants of the fan. There was no one around to remove him. Peredonov looked at him in terror and thought:

"He's dancing, he's happy over something. That's the way he'll be dancing on my grave."

Finally the geisha tore free—the men surrounding her couldn't withstand her nimble fists and sharp teeth.

The geisha dashed out of the hall. In the corridor the Wheat Sheaf once again fell on the Japanese girl and grabbed her by the dress. The geisha was about to tear free, but once more she was surrounded. The persecution was renewed.

"The ears, they've got her by the ears," someone shouted.

Some lady grabbed the geisha by the ear and tugged at it, emitting loud triumphant cries. The geisha started to howl and somehow broke free, striking the spiteful woman with her fist.

Finally, Bengalsky, who meanwhile had managed to change into his ordinary dress, forced his way through the crowd to the geisha. He took the trembling Japanese girl in his arms, and using his enormous body and his arms as much as possible to protect her, quickly carried her off, deftly scattering the crowd with his elbows and feet. People in the crowd were crying:

"Scoundrel! Rogue!"

They tugged and pounded at Bengalsky's back. He cried:

"I won't let you tear the mask off the lady. Do as you will, but I won't let you."

In this fashion he carried the geisha through the entire corridor. The corridor ended at a narrow door into the dining room. Here Veriga managed to restrain the crowd for a short while. With the determination of a military man, he stood before the door, blocking it off with his body, and said:

"Gentlemen, you will not proceed any farther."

Gudaevskaya, rustling the remains of her bedraggled wheat sheaves, kept leaping at Veriga, showing him her fists and screamed shrilly:

"Out of the way, let us through."

But the intimidatingly cold face of the general and his determined gray eyes restrained her from taking any action. In an impotent fury she started to shout at her husband:

"You ought to have given her a slap in the face, what were you gaping over, you nitwit!"

"It was awkward to get through," the Indian tried to excuse himself, waving his arms senselessly about. "Pavlushka kept getting in the way."

"You should have given Pavlushka one in the teeth and her one in the ear, what were you mincing about for!"

The crowd started to press in against Veriga. Foul language could be heard. Veriga stood calmly before the door and tried to convince those closest to him to stop their rowdiness. A kitchen boy opened the door slightly behind Veriga and whispered:

"They've left, Your Excellency."

Veriga moved off. The crowd tore into the dining room then into the kitchen. They were looking for the geisha, but they couldn't find her any longer. Bengalsky had carried the geisha at a run through the dining room into the kitchen. She lay calmly in his arms and was silent. It seemed to Bengalsky that he could hear the powerful pounding of the geisha's heart. On her naked arms, tightly pressed together, he noticed several scratches and a bluish-yellow spot from a bruise near the elbow. Bengalsky said in an excited voice to the menials crowded together in the kitchen:

"Quickly, a coat, a robe, a sheet, anything, we have to save the young lady."

Someone's coat was thrown over Sasha's shoulders. Somehow or other Bengalsky wrapped the Japanese girl up and carried her out into the court-yard by way of a narrow staircase that was illuminated with smoking kerosene lamps. And from there through a gate and into an alleyway.

"Take off your mask, it'll be harder for them to recognize you in the mask, anyway it's dark now," he said rather inconsistently. "I won't tell anyone."

He was curious. He probably knew that it wasn't Kashtanova, but who was it? The Japanese girl obeyed. Bengalsky caught sight of a swarthy, unfamiliar face on which fear had been replaced with an expression of joy at having escaped from the danger. The eyes, provocative and cheerful now, rested on the actor's face.

"How can I thank you!" the geisha said in a sonorous voice. "The things that would have happened to me if you hadn't dragged me out of there!"

"The girl's no coward, an interesting little wench!" the actor thought. "But who is she? Obviously, she's a newcomer." Bengalsky knew the local ladies. He said softly to Sasha:

"We have to get you home as quickly as possible. Tell me your address and I'll get a cab."

The Japanese girl's face clouded over once more with fear.

"I mustn't!" she babbled. "I'll go by myself, just leave me."

"How are you going to get there in this kind of mire and in your wood-en sandals, we need a cab," the actor protested confidently.

"No, I'll run, for God's sake, let me go," the geisha implored him.

"I swear on my honor that I won't tell anyone," Bengalsky tried to convince her. "I can't let you go, you'll catch cold. I've taken responsibility for you and I can't let you do it. You'd better tell me quickly, they might give you a licking right here. You saw for yourself that these are utterly sav-age people. They're capable of anything."

The geisha gave a shudder. Quick tears suddenly welled up in her eyes. Sobbingly she said:

"They're horribly, horribly wicked people! Take me to the Rutilovs for the time being, I'll spend the night at their place."

Bengalsky hailed a cab. They got in and rode off. The actor was peer-ing into the swarthy face of the geisha. It seemed curious to him. The geisha kept turning away. A vague inkling flashed through his head. He recollect-ed the town gossip about the Rutilovs, about Lyudmila and her student from the gymnasium.

"Aha, you're a boy!" he said in a whisper so the cab driver wouldn't hear.

"For God's sake," the boy begged, pale with terror.

And his swarthy arms reached out in an imploring gesture to Bengalsky from beneath the coat which sat haphazardly on him. Bengalsky laughed quietly and said just as quietly:

"Well, I won't tell anyone, don't worry. My business is to get you home and I don't know any more than that. But you're a desperate one. Won't they find out at home?"

"If you don't let it slip then no one will know," Sasha said in an entreatingly tender voice.

"You can rely on me, I'll be as quiet as the grave," the actor replied. "I was a young lad once myself, I got into enough mischief."

By now the scandal at the club had begun to subside. But the evening was crowned with a fresh disaster. While the geisha was being persecuted in the corridor, a fiery *nedotykomka*, leaping about the chandeliers, laughed and relentlessly tried to inspire Peredonov with the idea that he ought to light a match and set this fiery, but captive *nedotykomka* loose on these dreary, filthy walls and then, having had its fill of destruction after devouring the building where such terrible and incomprehensible things were taking place, it would leave Peredonov in peace. And Peredonov could not resist its persistent provocation. He went into the small sitting room beside the dance hall. There was no one in it. Peredonov looked around, struck a match, put it to the bottom of the window curtain, right at the very edge, and waited until the curtain caught fire. The fiery *nedotykomka* crept like a spritely little serpent along the curtain, squealing softly and cheerfully. Peredonov left the sitting room and bolted the door behind him. No one noticed the arson.

The fire was first seen from the street after the entire room was in flames. The fire spread quickly. The people were saved but the building burned down.

The following day the only talk in the town was about the scandal over the geisha the evening before and the fire. Bengalsky kept his word and told no one that it had been a boy dressed up as the geisha.

Changing clothes that same night at the Rutilovs and once more becoming the simple, barefooted boy, Sasha had run off home, crawled through the window and calmly fallen asleep. Even in a town that was seething with gossip and where everyone knew everything about everyone else, Sasha's nocturnal escapade thus remained a secret. For a long while, but of course, not forever.

XXXI

EKATERINA IVANOVNA PYLNIKOVA, Sasha's aunt and guardian, received two letters at once concerning Sasha: from the headmaster and from Kokovkina. These letters alarmed her terribly. In the midst of the wet autumn season she dropped all her work and hastily set out from the village for our town. Sasha gave his aunt a joyous welcome—he loved her. She had come bearing ill-will towards Sasha in her heart. But he flung himself so joyously around her neck and covered her hands with so many kisses that she couldn't adopt a stern tone right at the beginning.

"Dear Auntie, how kind you are that you've come!" Sasha said and gazed joyfully at her full, rosy face with the kindly dimples on her cheeks and with her sternly businesslike brown eyes.

"You just hang on a moment with your rejoicing, I'm still going to take you in hand," the aunt said with an uncertain voice.

"That doesn't matter," Sasha said carefreely. "Take me in hand for whatever the reason, but still you've made me terribly happy."

"Terribly!" the aunt repeated in a dissatisfied voice. "Well, the things I've found out about have made me terribly unhappy."

Sasha raised his eyebrows and looked at his aunt with innocent uncomprehending eyes. He protested:

"There's a teacher here, Peredonov, who's invented the idea that I'm supposedly a girl, he kept pestering me, and then afterwards the headmaster bawled me out because I had become acquainted with the young Rutilov ladies. Just as though I were going there to rob them. What concern is it of other people?"

"Still the utter babe that he was," the aunt was thinking in perplexity. "Or has he already been corrupted to such a degree that he can deceive me with his face?"

She locked herself up with Kokovkina and chatted for a long while with her. She was sad when she emerged. Then she went to the headmaster. She returned utterly upset. His aunt's weighty reproaches rained down on Sasha. Sasha wept, but he vehemently tried to assure her that they were all fabrications, that he hadn't ever indulged in any loose behavior with the young ladies. His aunt didn't believe him. She scolded and scolded him, started to weep, threatened to whip Sasha, to whip him painfully, that very moment, that very day, only first she was going to see these girls. Sasha sobbed and continued to try and assure her that nothing bad whatsoever had happened, that it was all terribly exaggerated and invented.

Angry and tear-stained, the aunt set out for the Rutilovs.

Ekaterina Ivanovna was in turmoil as she waited in the Rutilovs' sitting room. She wanted to descend immediately on the sisters with the most cruel reproaches, and she already had her words of anger and reproof prepared— but their peaceful, attractive sitting room intimidated her, despite her wishes, and calm thoughts began to pacify her annoyance. The needlework which someone had begun and then discarded there, the keepsakes, the etchings on the walls, the carefully tended plants by the windows, no dust anywhere, and moreover a kind of special atmosphere of domesticity which was something that didn't exist in disorderly homes and was always appreciated by housewives—now could this really have been the setting for the seduction of her modest boy by the thoughtful mistresses of this kind of room? All those assumptions which she had read and heard about Sasha seemed somehow terribly exaggerated, and, on the other hand, Sasha's explanations of what he had been doing at the home of the Rutilov ladies—reading, chatting, joking, laughing, playing cards and trying to organize a house, play, which Olga Vasilyevna wouldn't allow,—seemed so like the truth.

But the three sisters were thoroughly frightened. They still didn't know whether Sasha's costume was a secret. But after all, there were three of them, and they all supported one another. That made them more courageous. All three of them gathered in Lyudmila's room and conferred in a whisper. Valeriya said:

"We have to go out to her, it's not polite. She's waiting."

"It doesn't matter, let her cool off a little," Darya said carefreely. "Otherwise she'll vent her anger on us."

All the sisters perfumed themselves with the sweetly moist scent of clematis—and they emerged calm, cheerful, attractive, well dressed, as always, and filled the sitting room with their lovable babble, affability and cheerfulness. Ekaterina Ivanovna was immediately enchanted with their darling and seemly appearance. "Some libertines they've found," she thought with annoyance of the pedagogues at the gymnasium. But then she had the thought that perhaps they were only adopting a modest appearance. She determined not to give in to their charms.

"Excuse me, ladies, I must have a serious discussion with you," she said, trying to lend a dry business-like tone to her voice.

The sisters sat her down and babbled on cheerfully.

"Which of you?" . . . Ekaterina Ivanovna began uncertainly.

Lyudmila said cheerfully and with the kind of expression as though she, the polite hostess, were helping a guest out of a difficulty:

"I was the one who spent most time with your nephew. It turned out that he and I shared many of the same views and tastes."

"He is a darling boy, your nephew," Darya said, as though certain that her praise would make their guest feel overjoyed.

"Truly, he is a dear and so amusing," Lyudmila said.

Ekaterina Ivanovna felt increasingly awkward. She suddenly understood that she had no meaningful reasons for reproach. That began to make her angry. And Lyudmila's last words afforded her the opportunity to express her annoyance. She began angrily:

"It might be amusing to you, but for him . . ."

But Darya interrupted her and said in a sympathetic voice:

"Ah, now we see that these stupid fabrications of Peredonov have reached you. But you know, he's quite mad. The headmaster won't let him into the gymnasium. They're only waiting for the psychiatrist to make the examination and then he'll be dismissed from the gymnasium."

"But, I dare say," Ekaterina Ivanovna interrupted in her turn, growing more and more irritated, "I am not interested in that teacher, but in my nephew. I heard, you will please forgive me, that you are perverting him."

And having flung this decisive word at the sisters in the heat of the moment, Ekaterina Ivanovna immediately realized that she had gone too far. Exchanging among themselves a look of perplexity and indignity that was so well performed that not only Ekaterina Ivanovna would have been deceived, the sisters blushed and exclaimed all at once:

"That's nice!"

"Terrible!"

"That's news!"

"Madame," Darya said coldly, "Your expressions are ill-chosen. Before uttering rude words, you ought to find out how appropriate they are."

"Alas, it's quite understandable!" Lyudmila began animatedly with the look of a darling girl who had been offended but who forgave the offense. "After all he's no stranger for you. Of course, all these silly rumors couldn't help but upset you. Unrelated as we were, we still felt sorry for him because we had been nice to him. But everyone in our city would make a crime out of anything. If only you knew what terrible, terrible people there are here!"

"Terrible people!" Valeriya repeated softly in her sonorous, fragile voice and trembled all over, just as though she had touched something unclean.

"You ought to ask him," Darya said. "Take a look at him. After all he's terribly a child. Perhaps you've become accustomed to his naiveté, but for others it's even more obvious that he's not a perverted boy, not in the least."

The sisters lied so confidently and calmly that it was impossible not to believe them. Indeed, a falsehood often seems more like the truth than the truth itself. Almost always. Whereas the truth, of course, doesn't seem like the truth.

"Of course it is true that he was here too frequently," Darya said. "But we won't let him cross the threshold any more if you wish it so."

"And I'll go this very day to Khripach," said Lyudmila. "What has he gone and fabricated? Does he really believe in such an absurdity?"

"No, it seems that he himself doesn't believe it," Ekaterina Ivanovna admitted. "Only he says that ugly rumors are circulating."

"Well, there, you see!" Lyudmila exclaimed joyfully. "Of course he doesn't believe it himself. What's all the fuss about?"

Lyudmila's cheerful voice was seducing Ekaterina Ivanovna. She thought:

"What actually happened? The headmaster did say, after all, that he didn't believe any of it."

The sisters went on for a long while vying with one another as they chirped away, trying to convince Ekaterina Ivanovna of the absolute innocence of their acquaintanceship with Sasha. For greater authenticity they were about to tell in extreme detail precisely when and what they did with Sasha, but in the midst of this recitation they soon digressed: they were all such innocent simple things that there was no way of remembering every one of them. And, finally, Ekaterina Ivanovna quite believed that her Sasha and the dear Rutilov girls were the innocent victims of silly slander.

Taking her leave, Ekaterina Ivanovna exchanged affectionate kisses with the sisters and said to them:

"You are darling, simple girls. At first I thought—forgive me for the rudeness—that you were hussies."

The sisters laughed cheerfully. Lyudmila said:

"No, we're only cheerful girls with sharp little tongues and that's why the other geese around here have no liking for us."

Returning from the Rutilovs, the aunt said nothing to Sasha. He was frightened and embarrassed as he greeted her and kept looking at her closely and cautiously. The aunt went to see Kokovkina. They talked for a long while and finally the aunt decided:

"I'll go and see the headmaster once more."

On that very day Lyudmila set out to see Khripach. She sat for a while with Varvara Nikolaevna in the sitting room, then she announced that she had business with Nikolai Vlasyevich.

An animated conversation took place in Khripach's study—not for the reason that the two actually had a great deal to say to each other, but rather because both loved to talk. They inundated each other with their rapid talk: Khripach with his dry crackling quick speech; Lyudmila with her sonorous, tender babbling. Her semi-false story about her relations with Sasha Pylnikov washed smoothly over Khripach with the irresistible persuasiveness of falsehood. Her main motives had been, of course, sympathy towards the boy who had been insulted by such vulgar suspicion, and a desire to take the place of Sasha's absent family. And, finally, he himself was such a marvellous, cheerful and simple-hearted boy. Lyudmila even began to weep and the quick little tears ran down her rosy cheeks with such marvellous beauty and then onto her lips that were smiling with embarrassment.

"True, I did love him as a brother. He's such a marvellous and kind boy, he appreciates affection so much and he used to kiss my hands."

"Of course, that is very nice on your part," Khripach said, somewhat embarrassed. "It does honor to your kind feelings, but it's pointless for you to take so much to heart the simple fact that I considered it my duty to inform the boy's relatives in regard to the rumors that had reached me."

Without listening to him, Lyudmila continued to babble, switching now to a tone of mild rebuke:

"Tell me, please, what's bad about the fact that we took pity on a boy who was being attacked by that vulgar insane Peredonov of yours, and when will he be removed from our town anyway! You yourself must see that this Pylnikov of yours is still a complete child, well really—a complete child!"

She clasped her small beautiful hands together, made a tinkling noise with her fine gold bracelets, laughed tenderly as though she were crying, pulled out a handkerchief to wipe her tears away—and a tender scent wafted over Khripach. Suddenly Khripach felt like saying that she was "delightful, like a heavenly angel"* and that this entire woeful incident "was not worth a single moment of her dear sorrow."* But he restrained himself.

And Lyudmila's tender rapid babbling purled on and on, and the chimerical construct of Peredonov's falsehood dispersed in smoke. One only had to compare: the insane, vulgar, filthy Peredonov—and the cheerful, radiant, well-dressed, fragrant Lyudmilochka. Whether Lyudmila was telling the complete truth or fibbing, it made no difference to Khripach, but he felt that if he were not to believe Lyudmilochka, if he were to argue with her, allow any after-effects—if nothing more than an exacted promise from Pylnikov—it would have meant that he was putting his foot right into it and would bring shame on himself throughout the entire pedagogical district. All the more so because it was tied up with the business of Peredonov whom everyone, of course, considered to be out of his mind. Khripach, smiling politely, said to Lyudmila:

"I am very sorry that this has upset you so much. Not for a single moment did I allow myself to have any evil thoughts whatsoever in regard to your acquaintance with Pylnikov. I prize highly those kind and dear motives which inspired your actions, and not for a single moment did I regard the rumors circulating about the town and reaching me as anything other than stupid and insane slander which afforded me profound indignation. I was obliged to inform Mrs. Pylnikova, all the more so because even more distorted reports might have reached her, but I did not intend to upset you in any way and I did not think that Mrs. Pylnikova would address her reproaches to you."

"Well, we've come to a peaceful arrangement with Mrs. Pylnikova," Lyudmila said cheerfully. "Only don't you take it out on Sasha because of us. If our home is so dangerous for students, then we won't admit him, if that's what you wish."

"You are very kind to him," Khripach said uncertainly. "We can't have anything against the fact that in his free time, with his aunt's permission, he visits his acquaintances. It is far from our intention to turn student lodgings into places of some form of incarceration. In any event, until the business with Peredonov is resolved, it would be better if Pylnikov stayed at home."

The persuasive falsehood of the Rutilovs and Sasha gained support in a short while by a terrible occurrence in the home of the Peredonovs. Once and for all it convinced the townspeople that all the rumors about Sasha and the Rutilov girls had been the ravings of a madman.

*These are famous lines taken from the Romantic poem "The Demon" by Mikhail Yurievich Lermontov (1814–1841).

XXXII

I T WAS AN OVERCAST, cold day. Peredonov was returning from Volodin's. Melancholy oppressed him. Vershina lured Peredonov into her garden. He submitted once more to her spellbinding summons. Together they walked to the summer house along the damp footpaths that were covered with dark, rotting, fallen leaves. There was a smell of despondent dampness in the summer house. The house, with closed up windows, was visible beyond the bare trees.

"I want to reveal the truth to you," Vershina muttered, quickly glancing at Peredonov and again averting her black eyes.

She was wrapped in a black jacket, wound up in a black shawl and was exhaling thick clouds of black smoke through lips that were clamped on a cigarette holder and blue from the cold.

"I don't give a damn for your truth," Peredonov replied. "I don't give the slightest damn."

Vershina smiled crookedly and objected:

"Don't say that! I feel terribly sorry for you, you've been deceived!"

There was the sound of malice in her voice. Spiteful words spewed from her mouth. She said:

"You were hoping for protection, only you acted too trustfully. You were deceived and you believed it so easily. It's easy for anyone to write a letter. You ought to have known whom you were dealing with. Your spouse is an unscrupulous person."

Peredonov had difficulty understanding Vershina's mumbling speech. For him there was hardly any discernible sense in her circumlocution. Vershina was afraid to speak loudly and clearly: if she spoke loudly, someone might overhear, it would be passed on to Varvara and troubles could ensue. Varvara wouldn't be loathe to create a scandal. If she spoke clearly, then Peredonov himself might get angry. He might even strike her. She had to make hints so that he himself would guess. But Peredonov couldn't guess. It had been the case even earlier that he had been told straight to his face that he was being deceived, but he was totally incapable of taking the hint that the letters had been forged and he kept thinking that it was the Princess herself who was deceiving him, leading him around by the nose.

Finally, Vershina said straight out:

"Do you believe that the Princess wrote those letters herself? By now the entire town knows that Grushina fabricated them on the request of your spouse. The Princess doesn't know a thing. Ask whomever you wish, everyone knows. They let it out of the bag themselves. Then later Varvara Dmitrievna filched the letters from you and burned them so there wouldn't be any trace."

Ponderous, dark thoughts were churning about in Peredonov's brain. He understood one thing: he had been deceived. But the fact that the Princess supposedly didn't know—no, she certainly knew. It wasn't by chance that she had gotten out of the fire alive.

"You're lying about the Princess," he said. "I burnt the Princess, but I didn't finish the job and she thumbed her nose at me."

Suddenly Peredonov was seized with an insane frenzy. They had deceived him! He struck the table ferociously with his fist, tore away from the spot and without taking leave of Vershina quickly went home. Vershina joyfully watched him go and the black clouds of smoke flew quickly out of her dark mouth and were borne away and shredded on the wind.

Peredonov was being consumed with frenzy. But when he caught sight of Varvara, a tormenting fear took hold of him and wouldn't let him say a word.

First thing in the morning the following day Peredonov got a knife ready, a small one in a leather sheath, and he carried it around cautiously in his pocket. He sat through the entire morning, right up until his lunchtime, at Volodin's. Gazing at his work, he made ridiculous remarks. Volodin was happy as before that Peredonov was spending time with him and his stupidities seemed amusing to Volodin.

The whole day long the *nedotykomka* bustled around Peredonov. It wouldn't let him fall asleep after lunch. It completely exhausted him. By the time it was getting on to evening, he was on the verge of falling asleep when some crazy wench from God knows where woke him up. She was stub-nosed and ugly, and she came up to his bed and mumbled:

"The kvass needs pressing, the pies filling and the roast roasting."

She had dark cheeks, whereas her teeth glistened.

"Go to hell!" Peredonov cried.

The snub-nosed wench disappeared just as though she had never existed.

Evening set in. A mournful wind wailed in the chimney. A placid rain pattered softly and insistently at the windows. It was quite dark on the other side of the windows. Volodin was at the Peredonovs'. Earlier in the morning Peredonov had invited him for tea.

"Don't let anyone in. Do you hear, Klavdyushka?" Peredonov cried.

Varvara smirked. Peredonov muttered:

"There are some kind of wenches hanging around here. Have to keep an eye out. One of them forced her way into my bedroom, looking for work as a cook. What do I need a snub-nosed cook for?"

Volodin laughed just as though he were bleating and said:

"Idaresay that wenches go walking along the street, but they don't have any business to do with us and we won't let them sit at our table."

The three of them sat down at the table. They started to drink vodka and eat small meat-pies. They drank more than they ate. Peredonov was gloomy. By now everything seemed like a delirium to him, senseless, disconnected and surprising. He had a torturous headache. One notion kept repeating itself with persistence—the one about Volodin as an enemy. It alternated with oppressive fits in which he was assailed by the insistent idea that he had to kill Pavlushka before it was too late. Then all the enemy's ruses would be laid bare. Meanwhile, Volodin quickly got drunk and was babbling something incoherent to Varvara's amusement.

Peredonov was alarmed. He muttered:

"Someone's coming. Don't let anyone in. Tell them that I've gone off to pray at the Cockroach Monastery."

He was afraid that any guests would interfere. Volodin and Varvara found it funny—they thought that he was just drunk. They kept exchanging winks, going off one at a time, knocking at the door and speaking in different voices:

"Is General Peredonov at home?"

"I have a diamond-studded star for General Peredonov."

But Peredonov wasn't tempted by the diamond-studded star that day. He cried:

"Don't let them in! Throw them out by the collar. Let them bring it in the morning. This isn't the time now.

"No," he thought, "today I have to be firm." Today everything would be revealed, but meanwhile his enemies were still prepared to assail him with all sorts of things so as to ruin him more assuredly.

"Well, we chased them off, they'll bring it tomorrow morning," Volodin said, sitting down once more at the table.

Peredonov fixed his murky eyes on him and asked:

"Are you my friend or an enemy?"

"A friend, a friend, Ardasha!" Volodin replied.

"A friend from the heart is like a cockroach at the hearth," Varvara said.

"Not a cockroach, but a sheep," Peredonov corrected her. "Well, you and I are going to drink, Pavlushka, just the two of us. And Varvara, you drink—the two of us will drink all together."

Volodin, giggling, said:

"If Varvara Dmitrievna drinks with us, then there won't be two of us drinking, but three."

"The two of us," Peredonov repeated sullenly.

"A man and his woman are like a single demon," Varvara said and roared with laughter.

Up until the very last moment Volodin did not suspect that Peredonov wanted to slit his throat. He bleated, played the fool, uttered stupidities, amused Varvara.But Peredonov spent the whole evening thinking about his knife. When Volodin or Varvara approached from the side where the knife was hidden, Peredonov would cry fiercely for them to go away. Sometimes he would point to his pocket and say:

"Right here, brother, I have a little something that'll make you croak, Pavlushka."

Varvara and Volodin laughed.

"Croak, Ardasha, I can always, do that," Volodin said. "Cro-o-ak, cro-o-ak. It's even quite simple."

Red-faced, and dazed from the vodka, Volodin kept croaking and puffing out his lips. He grew even more insolent with Peredonov.

"You were made a fool of, Ardasha," he said with disdainful sympathy.

"I'll make a fool of you!" Peredonov snarled ferociously.

Volodin seemed frightening and threatening to him. He had to defend himself. Peredonov quickly pulled the knife out, flung himself on Volodin and slit his throat. The blood spurted out in a stream.

Peredonov took fright. The knife dropped out of his hand. Volodin kept bleating and trying to clutch at his throat with his hands. It was obvious that he was mortally frightened, growing weaker and unable to lift his hands to his throat. Suddenly he stiffened and tumbled over on Peredonov. He emitted a gasping whine—just as though he had choked—and then fell silent. Peredonov was screeching in terror as well, and Varvara followed suit.

Peredonov shoved Volodin away. Volodin slumped heavily onto the floor. He wheezed, moved his legs and soon died. His opened eyes turned glassy and stared straight upwards. The cat came out of the neighboring room, smelled the blood and miaowed wickedly. Varvara stood there as though frozen. Klavdiya came running in response to the noise.

"Dear father, they've slit his throat!" she wailed.

Varvara came to her senses and with a screech ran out of the dining room together with Klavdiya.

The news of the occurrence spread rapidly. Neighbors gathered in the street and in the yard. Some of the more courageous entered the house. They couldn't bring themselves to enter the dining room for a long while. They kept peeking in and exchanging whispers. Peredonov gazed with insane eyes at the corpse and listened to the whisperings on the other side of the door . . . A dull melancholy oppressed him. He had no thoughts.

Finally, the people gathered their courage and entered. Peredonov was sitting downcast and mumbling something incoherent and senseless.

June 19, 1902

TEXTUAL VARIANTS

THE FIRST SET of textual variants which follow are numbered with Arabic numerals. These variants were first published after Sologub's death when they were appended to the edition of *The Petty Demon* issued by "ACADEMIA" (Moscow-Leningrad) in 1933. These thirteen variants are reproduced in the Bradda Books edition of *The Petty Demon* (1966).

A second set of textual variants, listed alphabetically, follows the first. This second set represents a more or less unified episode which has not been published, to our knowledge, since 1912 and has not appeared in any edition of Sologub's novel either in the original or in translation. These latter fragments are preceded by a more detailed explanation which has been provided by Stanley Rabinowitz who very kindly brought them to the attention of the translator.

—S.D.C.

1.   Natashka, in fact, did want to steal a sweet pastry and eat it in secret, but it was impossible. First of all, Varvara was hovering around her and she couldn't get rid of her for anything. Secondly, even if she did leave and a pastry was removed from the pan, then she would count them up afterwards from the traces left on the pan—and there would be fewer pastries than required. So it was impossible to steal even one. Nata[shka] was angry. Meanwhile, Varvara, in her customary fashion, was cursing and pestering the servant for various acts of carelessness and for what she considered to be her lack of efficiency. On a wrinkled yellow face that preserved some traces of a former attractiveness lay a querulously voracious expression.

"You lazy creature," Varvara shouted, in her reverberating voice. "Have you lost your wits, or something, Natashka! You've barely started and already you hardly want to do anything. You vile sluggard!"

"And who can live with you?" Natasha replied rudely.

It was true. A servant never lasted long at Varvara's: Varvara fed her servants poorly, cursed them ceaselessly, tried to delay paying them, and if she came across one that wasn't very alert, then she would push her around, pinch her and slap her on the cheeks.

"Shut up, you bitch!" Varvara cried.

"Why should I shut up, everyone knows that nobody will live with you, Madame, you don't think anyone's good enough. Well, you're not all that wonderful yourself. You're a fine one to be finicky."

"How dare you, you beast!"

"Well I'm saying it. And who could live with a harpy like you, who'd want to!"

Varvara grew furious, started to scream and stamp her feet. Natashka didn't give way. A furious shouting match ensued.

"You hardly feed me and you demand work," she cried.

"There's not enough trash in a rubbish dump to satisfy you," Varvara replied.

"You know who else is a rubbish dump. That's where all the filth belongs . . ."

"I may be filth, but I'm from the gentry, whereas you're my servant. What a bitch! Here, I'll give you a poke in the kisser," Varvara cried.

"I can deal it out myself!" Natashka replied rudely, looking scornfully down at little Varvara from the height of her size. "In your kisser! It's that master of yours that goes around whacking you in the kisser. I'm not his mistress and no one's going to yank me by the ears."

Meanwhile, a woman's noisome and drunken voice was heard coming from the yard through the open window:

"Hey, you, Madame! Hey, young lady, or something! What am I supposed to call you anyway? Where's your beau?"

"And what business is it of yours, you frenzy?" Varvara shouted, running to the window.

Down below stood the owner of the house, Irinya Stepanovna, a cobbler's wife, bare-headed, and in a filthy cotton dress. She and her husband lived in an annex in the yard and rented out the house. Lately Varvara had frequently been getting into arguing matches with her—the landlady kept appearing half-drunk and pestering Varvara because she had the idea that they wanted to move out.

Now they launched into a fresh swearing match. The landlady was calmer whereas Varvara was beside herself. Finally the landlady turned her back to Varvara and raised her skirt. Varvara immediately responded in kind.

These kinds of scenes and the eternal screaming matches caused Varvara to suffer from migraines afterwards, but she had already grown accustomed to a disorderly and vulgar life and couldn't restrain herself from indecent escapades. She had long since ceased to have any respect for herself or for others.

2.   The following day, after dinner, while Peredonov was still asleep, Varvara went off to the Prepolovenskys. She had sent off an entire bundle of nettles earlier with her new servant, Klavdiya. It was frightening, but nevertheless Varvara went.

Sitting in a circle around the oval coffee table in Prepolovenskys' dining room were Varvara, the hostess and her cousin Zhenya, a tall, plump and red-cheeked girl with indolent movements and deceptively innocent eyes.

"Here, you see what a ruddy-faced fatty of ours she is," said Sofiya. "It's all because her mother used to whip her with nettles. And I whip her too."

Zhenya turned a deep crimson and laughed.

"Yes," she said in a lazy, low voice, "as soon as I start to get thin, I'm treated to a good stinging right away and I fill out once more."

"But isn't it painful for you?" Varvara asked with cautious surprise.

"So what if it hurts, it's still healthy," Zhenya replied. "We've gotten used to it. Even my younger sister was whipped when she was still a girl."

"But aren't you afraid?" Varvara asked.

"What can you do, no one asks me," Zhenya replied clamly. "They just whip me and I don't notice it for long. It's not my idea."

Sofiya said quickly and persuasively:

"What's there to be afraid of, it's not all that painful. I know from myself."

"And does it work well?" Varvara asked once more.

"Really now," Sofiya said with annoyance. "Can't you see, you've got a living example right before your eyes. First you lose a bit of weight, but the very next day you start to put on weight."

Finally the assurances and persuasive efforts of the two cousins overcame Varvara's final doubts.

"Well, alright," she said with a smirk. "Go ahead. Let's see what happens. No one will see?"

"There's no one to see, all the servants have been sent off," Sofiya said.

They led Varvara to the bedroom. She was about to waver at the threshold, but Zhenya gave her a shove in—she was a strong girl—and locked the door.

The curtains were lowered and it was semi-dark in the bedroom. Not a sound could be heard from there. On two chairs lay several bundles of nettles, the stems wrapped up in handkerchiefs so that the person holding them wouldn't get stung.

Varvara took fright.

"Perhaps not," she began indecisively. "My head seems to be aching, better tomorrow . . ."

But Sofiya raised her voice:

"Come on, get undressed quickly, there's nothing to be finicky about."

Varvara dallied and started to back towards the door. The cousins flung themselves on her and undressed her by force. She didn't have time to regain her senses before she was lying in nothing more than her chemise on the bed. Zhenya grabbed both her hands in her one powerful hand and with the other she took the bundle of nettles from Sofiya and started to whip Varvara with them. Sofiya held Varvara's feet firmly and kept repeating:

"Stop squirming—what a squirmer you are!"

Varvara couldn't hold out for long—and she started to screech with pain. Zhenya gave her a long and powerful whipping, replacing the bundles several times. So that Varvara's sceeching couldn't be heard far away she pushed her head into the pillows with her elbow.

Finally they let Varvara go. She stood up, sobbing with the pain. The cousins started to console her. Sofiya said:

"Well, what are you bellowing about? It's hardly anything to speak of. It'll just smart a little and then stop. It's hardly anything yet, it should be repeated in several days."

"Oi, sweetheart, are you serious!" Varvara exclaimed dolefully. "Being tortured once is enough."

"Come now, how were you being tortured," Sofiya soothed her. "Of course, it ought to be repeated from time to time. Both of us were whipped from childhood, and more than once. Otherwise it wouldn't do any good."

"Cream-puff nettles!" Zhenya said, chuckling.

Having had a sleep after dinner, Peredonov set out for the Summer Gardens to play billiards in the restaurant. He met Prepolovenskaya on the street. After having walked Varvara home, she was going off to her friend, Vershina, to tell her secretly about the adventure. They were going in the same direction and they walked together. At the same time Peredonov invited her and her husband to play cards for low stakes in the evening.

Sofiya brought the conversation around to why he wasn't getting married. Peredonov was sullenly silent. Sofiya made allusions to her cousin—after all, Ardalyon Borisych liked those kind of amply endowed girls. It seemed to her that he agreed with her: he looked just as gloomy as usual and didn't argue.

"I know what your tastes are," Sofiya said. "You don't care for those skinny ones. You have to choose a suitable person for yourself, a girl with substance."

Peredonov was afraid to speak—they might be baiting him. And he kept glancing in angry silence at Sofiya.

3.   On the way Peredonov told Volodin that Zhenya, Sofiya's cousin, was Prepolovensky's lover.

Volodin immediately believed it: he was angry at Zhenya who had turned him down long ago.

"She ought to be reported to the ecclesiastical council," Peredonov said. "After all, she comes from a church background, she's a bishop's daughter."

They ought to denounce her so that they'd send her off to a convent to do penance and they'd whip her there!

Volodin was wondering whether to denounce her. But he decided to be gracious—and forget about her. Otherwise he could be drawn into it and they'd tell him to prove it.

4.   In the midst of conversations of this sort they arrived in the village. The house where the lessee lived, Marta's and Vladya's father, was low and wide, with a high gray roof and carved shutters on the window. It wasn't new, but it was solid, and hiding behind a row of birch trees it seemed comfortable and nice—at least it seemed that way to Vladya and Marta. But Peredonov didn't like the birch trees in front of the house. He would have chopped them down or had them broken off.

Running out with cries of joy to greet the arrivals were three barefooted children from about eight to ten: a girl and two boys, blue-eyed and freckle-faced. The host, a broad-shouldered, powerful and big Pole with a long graying moustache and an angular face, greeted the guests at the threshold. The face was reminscent of one of those composite photographs where several similar faces were printed at once on a single plate. All the particular features of a single person were lost in photographs of this sort and only the general aspect remained, namely, what was common to all or many faces. Thus it seemed that in Nartanovich's face there weren't any particular features, but merely what existed in every Polish face. For this reason one of the town wits had nicknamed Nartanovich the four-and-forty Pole. Nartanovich behaved in keeping with this: he was polite, even too polite in his manner of address, never losing the sense of his honor as a Polish gentleman and saying only the most essential things, as though afraid of revealing by way of frivolous conversation anything that pertained only to himself.

Obviously he was happy for the guest and greeted him with village extravagance. When he spoke, his voice boomed with sudden loudness, as though it meant to contend with the noise of the wind. It deafened everything that had just been uttered, and then abruptly broke off and fell. And afterwards, the voices of other people seemed weak and pitiful.

In one of the rooms, which were rather dark and low, where the host could easily have touched the roof with his hand, a table was quickly laid out. A spritely wench brought different kinds of vodka and *zakuski*.

Vershina particularly liked Marta and Vladya for the reason that she could give them orders, grumble at them and sometimes punish them. Vershina loved power and she was very flattered when Marta, after committing some fault, would unquestioningly get down on her knees at Vershina's order.

Peredonov quickly drank some vodka, had a bite to eat and started to complain about Vladya. Nartanovich looked fiercely at his son, kept offering food and drink laconically but insistently to Peredonov. However, Peredonov determinedly refused to eat anything more.

"No," he said. "I came to see you on business. You listen to me first."

"Ah, on business," the host cried. "You mean a reason."

Peredonov started to blacken Vladya from all sides. The father grew more and more furious.

"Aha, the sluggard!" he exclaimed slowly and with impressive accents. "You need your hide tanned. I'll give you a lashing. You're going to get a hundred hot ones."

Vladya started to cry.

"I promised him," Peredonov said, "that I would come on purpose to see you so that you would punish him in my presence."

"I am grateful to you for that," Nartanovich said. "I'll give the lazybones such a licking with the rod that he'll certainly remember it, the sluggard!"

Gazing fiercely at Vladya, Nartanovich got up—and it seemed to Vladya that he was enormous and had forced all the air out of the room. He grabbed Vladya by the shoulder and dragged him off to the kitchen. The children huddled against Marta and looked in terror at the sobbing Vladya. Peredonov followed Nartanovich.

"What are you standing there for?" he said to Marta. "You go on too, have a look and help, you'll have your own children one day."

Marta flared up and, gathering all three children in her arms, she nimbly ran off with them out of the house, as far as possible so that they wouldn't hear what was going to happen in the kitchen.

When Peredonov went into the kitchen, Vladya was undressing. The father was standing in front of him and slowly uttering threatening words:

"Lay down on the bench," he said when Vladya had completely undressed.

Vladya obeyed. Tears were streaming out of his eyes, but he tried to restrain himself. His father didn't like any cries of entreaty. It would be worse if he cried out. Peredonov looked at Vladya, at his father, examined the kitchen and started to worry when he didn't see any whipping rods anywhere. Could Nartanovich really be doing it just for show: he would frighten his son and then let him go unpunished. It was not by chance that Vladya was acting strangely, not at all as Peredonov had expected. He wasn't rushing about, sobbing, bowing down at his father's feet (all Poles were grovellers) begging for forgiveness, running to Peredonov with his entreaties. Had Peredonov come all this way just to watch the preparations for punishment?

Meanwhile, Nartanovich, taking his time, tied his son to the bench. He fastened the hands over his head with a belt, each foot was fastened separately to the bench with a rope, with the feet spread out, one on one side of the bench, the other on the other side. And he also tied him down around the waist. Now Vladya couldn't even move and he lay there, trembling with terror, certain that his father would whip him half to death, since earlier he had punished him for small transgressions without tying him up.

Completing this business, Nartanovich said:

"Now, to break off some switches and whip the sluggard if the gentleman won't find it repulsive to watch your hide getting whipped."

Nartanovich gave a sidelong glance at the sullen Peredonov, grinned, stroked his long moustache and went to the window. A birch tree grew under the window.

"No need even to go out," Nartanovich said, breaking off some stocks.

Vladya closed his eyes. It seemed to him that he was going to faint right away.

"Give a listen, you lazybones," his father shouted in a frightening voice over his head. "For doing it the first time this year I'll give you twenty and the next time you'll get more."

Vladya felt relieved—that was the least number that his father recognized and Vladya didn't find that kind of punishment unusual.

The father started to whip him with long and strong switches. Vladya clenched his teeth and didn't cry out. The blood showed through in drops as delicate as dew.

"Now that's fine," the father said, completing the punishment. "A firm lad!"

And he started to untie his son. It seemed to Peredonov that it hadn't been very painful to Vladya.

"It was hardly worthwhile tying him up for that," he said angrily. "For him it was like water off a duck's back."

Nartanovich looked at Peredonov with his calm blue eyes and said:

"The next time, thank you very much, he'll get more. But that's enough for today."

Vladya put on his shirt and, crying, kissed his father's hand.

"Kiss the switch, you blackamoor," the father cried. "And get dressed."

Vladya got dressed and ran barefoot off into the garden—to cry his heart out in peace.

Nartanovich took Peredonov around the house and the buildings to show him the farm. Peredonov didn't find it in the least engrossing. Although he often thought that he would save his money and buy himself an estate, now, when he was looking at everything that was being shown to him, he saw only rough and untidy objects, he had no feeling for their life and did not understand their connection and meaning for the farm.

They sat down to supper after half an hour. Vladya was called as well. Peredonov made up jokes at Vladya's expense. They seemed vulgar and stupid. Vladya blushed and practically cried, but the others didn't laugh and that distressed Peredonov. And he was annoyed that Vladya hadn't cried out earlier. It must have been painful for him. The blood hadn't spurted for nothing. But he had been silent, the little brat. "The inveterate Polish brat!" Peredonov thought. And by then he was beginning to think that it hadn't been worth the trip.

Peredonov got up early in the morning and said that he was leaving immediately. They tried in vain to persuade him to be their guest for another day. He refused with determination.

"I only came on business," he said sullenly.

Nartanovich grinned slightly, stroking his long graying moustache, and he said in a stentorian voice:

"What a pity, what a pity!"

Peredonov started to tease Vladya again on several occasions. But Vladya was happy that Peredonov was leaving. Now, after the punishment of the evening before, he knew that he could do what he wanted to at home and father wouldn't scold him. He would have responded willingly with some impertinence to Peredonov's pestering. But lately Vershina had repeated to him more than once that if he wanted to do good for Marta, then he ought not to anger Peredonov. And so he took zealous pains to seat Peredonov even more comfortably than the evening before.

Peredonov regarded the troubles taken by Vladya while standing on the porch and questioned him:

"Well, brother, was it hot enough for you?"

"Yes it was," Vladya replied, smiling shamefully.

"You won't forget it till the next thrashing?"

"No I won't."

"Was it a good whipping?"

"Very good."

And the conversation went on in that vein all the while the cart was being hitched up. Vladya was already starting to think that it wasn't always possible to be completely polite. But Peredonov left—and Vladya breathed freely.

Today his father treated him as though nothing had happened the evening before. Vladya's day passed happily.

At dinner Nartanovich said to Marta:

"That teacher of theirs is stupid. He doesn't have any children of his own and he travels around giving whippings to other people's. The tyrant!"

"There was no need to whip him this first time," Marta said.

Nartanovich gave her a stern look and said imperiously:

"It's not out of place at all to give a whipping to a person at your age. Bear that in mind. Besides, he deserved it."

Marta blushed . . . Vladya said with a restrained smile:

"It'll heal in time for my wedding."

"As for you Marta," Nartanovich said, "after dinner you'll get a hiding. Don't try and teach your father. I'll give you twenty hot ones."

5. Peredonov walked quickly, almost ran. He was annoyed by all the policemen he met and frightened by them. "What did they want!" he thought. "Just like spies."

6. He knew an amazing lot about the townspeople. And actually, if every illegal trick could have been exposed with sufficient clarity for communication to the courts, then the town would have had the opportunity to see the kind of people on trial who enjoyed general respect. Several of the court cases would have been curious ones at that!

7. In the entire gymnasium there were now 177 students: 28 from the petty bourgeoisie, 8 from the peasantry, and only 105 from the gentry and civil servants.

8. "So you mean that now you're not a liberal, but a conservative?"

"A conservative, Your Excellency."

9. When Peredonov returned home, he found Varvara in the dining room with a book in her hands, something that rarely happened. Varvara was reading a cookbook, the only one that she ever opened.

There was a great deal in the book that she didn't understand, and everything that she read out of it and attempted to adopt met with failure. It was impossible for her to come to terms with the relative amounts of the constituent parts of the dishes, because the amounts in the book were given for 6 or 12 people, whereas she had to prepare them for two or three people, rarely more. But nevertheless she still made dishes from time to time out of the book. The book was an old one, tattered and in a black cover. The black cover immediately leapt to Peredonov's eyes and drove him to despondency.

"What are you reading, Varvara?" he asked angrily.

"What? You know what, a cookbook," Varvara replied. "I haven't time to read stupid books."

"Why a cookbook?" Peredonov asked in terror.

"What do you mean, why? I'm going to prepare a dish, for you, you're always so finicky," Varvara explained, grinning with a haughty and self-satisfied expression.

"I'm not going to eat anything out of a black book!" Peredonov declared determinedly, quickly seizing the book out of Varvara's hands and carrying if off into the bedroom.

"A black book! And on top of it all, making meals out of it!" he thought with fear. All he needed was for them to try and do him in openly with black magic! It was essential to destroy the book, he thought, not paying any attention to the reverberating complaints of Varvara.

But how to destroy it? Burn it? But it's apt to go ahead and start a fire. Drown it? Of course it would come back to the surface and fall in someone else's hands! Throw it away? It would be found. No, the best thing would be to rip a page out at a time and quietly sneak off with it as occasion dictated, and then later, when it was all finished, burn the black cover. With this in mind he relaxed. But what to do about Varvara? She'd produce a fresh book of sorcery. No, Varvara had to be properly punished.

Peredonov went off into the garden, broke off some birch switches there and, glancing sullenly at the windows, brought them into the bedroom. Then he shouted into the kitchen through the partially opened door:

"Klavdyushka, call the lady into the bedroom and you come yourself."

Varvara and Klavdiya soon came. Klavdiya was the first to catch sight of the whipping rods and started to giggle.

"Lie down, Varvara!" Peredonov ordered.

Varvara gave a squeal and dashed for the door.

"Hold her, Klavdyushka!" Peredonov shouted.

The two of them laid Varvara out on the bed. Klavdiya held her while Peredonov thrashed her. Varvara wept desperately and begged forgiveness.

10. There was the soft sound of children's voices behind the door and Liza's silvery laugh could be heard.

Gudaevskaya whispered:

"You stand here for the moment, behind the door, so he won't know you're here yet."

Peredonov stepped into the far end of the corridor and pressed against the wall. Gudaevskaya flung the door open impetuously and entered the nursery. Through the narrow crack in the door frame, Peredonov saw Antosha sitting at a table with his back to the door, beside a little girl in a white frock. Her curls were touching his cheek and seemed dark because Peredonov was seeing only the side of her that was in the shadow. Her hand was lying on Antosha's shoulder. Antosha was cutting something out of paper for her and Liza was laughing with joy. Peredonov was annoyed that people were laughing here: the lad ought to be thrashed but there he was amusing his sister instead of being penitent and crying. Then he was seized with a feeling of malice: "You'll be howling in just a moment," he thought about Antosha and was consoled.

Antosha and Liza turned around at the sound of the door opening. From his hiding place Peredonov caught sight of Liza's rosy cheek and stubby little

nose underneath the long and straight strands of hair. He also saw the look of
ingenuous surprise on Antosha's face.

The mother walked impetuously up to Antosha, tenderly embraced him
around his little shoulders and said in a brisk and determined voice:

"Antosha, darling, let's go. Maryushka, you stay with Liza," she said,
turning to the nurse whom Peredonov couldn't see.

Antosha stood up unwillingly, while Liza started to snivel that he hadn't
finished yet.

"Afterwards, he'll cut them out for you afterwards," her mother said to her
and she led her son out of the room, holding on to his shoulders all the while.

Antosha still didn't know what was up, but his mother's determined look
had already frightened him and made him suspect something terrible.

When they came out into the corridor and Gudaevskaya had closed the
door, Antosha caught sight of Peredonov, took fright and tried to dash back.
But his mother seized him firmly by the hand and quickly dragged him down
the corridor, repeating all the while:

"Let's go, let's go, darling, I'll give you some nice little whipping rods.
Your father the tyrant isn't at home and I'm going to punish you with some
nice little whipping rods, sweetheart, it'll be good for you, darling."

Antosha started to weep and cried out:

"But I didn't get into mischief, what are you punishing me for!"

"Quiet, quiet, darling!" the mother said, slapped him with her hand on the
back of his head and shoved him into the bedroom.

Peredonov followed them, muttering something quietly and angrily.

In the bedroom the whipping rods were lying ready. Peredonov didn't like
the fact that they were thick and short.

"Whipping rods for ladies," he thought angrily.

The mother quickly sat down on a chair, stood Antosha in front of herself
and started to undo his buttons. All red, his face covered in tears, Antosha cried
out as he twisted about in her hands and kicked with his feet:

"Mamochka, mamochka, forgive me, I won't do anything like that again!"

"Never mind, sweetheart, never mind," the mother replied. "Get
undressed quickly, it'll be very good for you. Never mind, don't worry, it'll
soon heal," she consoled him and deftly undressed Antosha.

The half-undressed Antosha resisted, kicked out with his feet and cried.

"Help me, Ardalyon Borisych," Yuliya Petrovna said in a loud whisper.
"He's such a little bandit, I really didn't know whether I could handle him alone."

Peredonov took Antosha by the feet while Yuliya Petrovna started to whip him.

"Don't be lazy, don't be lazy!" she kept repeating.

"Don't kick, don't kick" Peredonov repeated after her.

"Oi, I won't, oi, I won't!" Antosha cried.

Gudaevskaya worked so zealously that she soon tired.

"Well, that's enough, darling!" she said, letting Antosha go. "Enough, I
can't do any more, I'm tired."

"If you're tired, then I could whip him some more," Peredonov said.

"Antosha, thank him," Gudaevskaya said. "Thank him, scrape your foot.
Ardalyon Borisych is going to whip you some more with the nice little rods.
Lay down on my knees, darling."

She handed a bundle of whipping rods to Peredonov, pulled Antosha back
to herself and buried his head in her knees. Peredonov suddenly took fright: it

seemed to him that Antosha might tear free and bite him.

"Well, that'll do for this time," he said.

"Antosha, do you hear?" Gudaevskaya asked, raising Antosha up by the ears. "Ardalyon Borisych is forgiving you. Thank him, scrape your foot, scrape it. Scrape your foot and get dressed."

Sobbing, Antosha scraped his foot, got dressed and his mother led him out into the corridor by the hand.

"Wait," she whispered to Peredonov. "I still have to have a talk with you."

She took Antosha off to the nursery where the nurse had already put Liza to bed and ordered him to go to bed. Then she returned to the bedroom. Peredonov was sitting sullenly on the chair in the middle of the room. Gudaevskaya said:

"I am so thankful to you, so thankful, I can't possibly say. You have acted so nobly, so nobly. It ought to have been my husband who did it, but you took my husband's place. He deserves to be cuckolded by me. If he lets other people fulfill his responsibilities, then let others have his rights as well."

She impetuously flung herself around Peredonov's neck and whispered:

"Kiss me, darling!"

And then she said a few other unprintable words. Peredonov was dully amazed. However, he grabbed her in his hands, kissed her on the lips and she fastened on his lips with a long voracious kiss. Then she tore free from his hands, dashed to the door, locked it with a key and quickly started to undress.

11. Antosha Gudaevsky was already asleep when his father returned from the club. In the morning when Antosha Gudaevsky was leaving for the gymnasium, his father was still asleep. Antosha saw his father only later in the day. He stole quietly away from his mother into his father's study and complained about being whipped. Gudaevsky became furious, started to run around his study, threw several books from his desk onto the floor and shouted in a terrifying voice:

"Vile! Foul! Base! Abominable! Curses! Villainy! Guards!"

Then he rushed to Antosha, pulled his trousers down, examined his slender little body mottled with pink narrow stripes, and he screamed in a piercing voice:

"Geography of Europe, seventeenth edition!"

He swept Antosha up in his arms and ran off to his wife. Antosha felt embarrassed and ashamed and he whined dolefully.

Yuliya Petrovna was immersed in reading a novel. Hearing from afar her husband's cries, she guessed what the matter was, leapt up, threw the book down on the floor and started to run around the room, clenching her dry fists and making her gaudy ribbons flutter.

Gudaevsky burst stormily in on her, kicking open the door with his foot.

"What's this?" he cried, setting Antosha on the floor and showing her his uncovered body. "Where did this painting come from!"

Yuliya Petrovna started to shake with spite and stamped her feet.

"I whipped him, I whipped him!" she cried. "There, I whipped him!"

"Vile! Most vile!" Vile beyond all belief of desecration!" Gudaevsky cried. "How could you dare without my permission?"

"I'll whip him again, I'll whip him again to spite you!" Gudaevskaya cried. "I'll whip him every day!"

Antosha tore free and buttoned himself up as he ran off, while his father and mother remained behind to abuse each other. Gudaevsky leapt at his wife and slapped her face. Yuliya Petrovna screeched, started to cry and shouted:

"Monster! Miscreant of the human race! You want to drive me to the grave!" She made a deft move, leapt at her husband and whacked him on the cheek.

"Revolt! Betrayal! Guards!" Gudaevsky shouted.

And they fought for a long time, attacking each other all the while. Finally they grew tired. Gudaevskaya sat down on the floor and started to cry.

"Villain! You ruined my youth," she lamented in a plaintive, extenuated wail.

Gudaevsky stood in front of her, intending to smack her in the face, but he changed his mind, sat down on the floor as well, facing his wife, and shouted:

"Fury! Shrew! Tailless witch! You've worn out my life!"

"I'm going to mama's," Gudaevskaya said whiningly.

"Go, by all means," Gudaevsky replied angrily. "I'd be very happy, I'd even take you. I'll beat on the pots and pans, I'll play a Persian march with my lips."

Gudaevsky trumpeted a sharp and wild melody through his fist.

"And I'll take the children!" Gudaevskaya shouted.

"I won't give you the children!" Gudaevsky cried.

They both leapt simultaneously to their feet and shouted as they waved their arms:

"I won't leave you Antosha," his wife cried.

"I won't let you have Antosha," her husband cried.

"I'll take him!"

"I won't let you!"

"You'll pervert him, spoil him, ruin him!"

"You'll tyranize him!"

They clenched their fists, threatened each other and ran off in different directions: she to the bedroom and he to his study. The sound of two doors being slammed echoed through the entire house.

Antosha was sitting in his father's study. It seemed to him to be the most opportune and secure place. Gudaevsky was running around the study and repeating:

"Antosha, I won't let your mother have you, I won't."

"Give her Lizochka," Antosha advised.

Gudaevsky stopped, slapped himself on the forehead with his palm and cried: "A good idea!"

He ran out of his study. Antosha peeked timidly into the corridor and saw his father run into the nursery. From there he could hear Liza's weeping and the nurse's frightened voice. Gudaevsky dragged a violently sobbing, frightened Liza out of the nursery by the hand, took her into the bedroom, threw her at her mother and cried:

"Here's your daughter for you, take her, but our son stays with me on the basis of the seven articles of the seven sections of the code of all codices."

And he ran off to his study, exclaiming along the way:

"The joke's on you! Be satisfied with the little one, whip her a little! Ho-ho-ho!"

Gudaevskaya seized her daughter, sat her down on her knees and started to soothe her. Then she suddenly leapt up, grabbed Liza by the hand and quickly dragged her off to her father. Liza started to cry again.

The father and son heard the sound of Liza's howling approaching along the corridor. They looked at each other in perplexity.

"What does she want?" the father whispered. "She won't take her! She'll try and get at you!"

Antosha crawled under the desk. But at that moment Gudaevskaya ran into the study, threw Liza at her father, pulled her son out from under the desk, struck him on the cheek, grabbed him by the hand and pulled him after herself, crying:

"Let's go, sweetheart, your father is a tyrant."

But the father gathered his wits immediately, grabbed the boy by the other hand, struck him on the other cheek and cried:

"Darling, don't be afraid, I won't give you to anyone."

The mother and father pulled Antosha in different directions and ran quickly around in a circle. Antosha whirled like a top between them and cried in terror:

"Let me go, let me go, you're tearing my arms off!"

Somehow or other he managed to free his hands so that his mother and father were left holding only the sleeves to his jacket. But they didn't notice it and continued to swing Antosha in a furious circle. He shouted all the while in a desperate voice:

"You're tearing me apart! It's cracking in my shoulders! Oi-oi-oi, you're tearing me, you're tearing me! You've torn me apart!"

And, in fact, the father and mother suddenly tumbled in opposite directions on to the floor, each holding a sleeve from Antosha's jacket in their hands. Antosha ran off with a desperate scream:

"They've torn me apart, what's happened!"

The father and mother both imagined that they had torn off Antosha's arms. They started to wail with fear as they lay on the floor:

"We tore Antosha apart!".

Then they leapt up and, shaking the empty sleeves at each other, started to vie with each other in shouting;

"Get the doctor! He's run away! Where are his arms! Look for his arms!"

They both crawled around on all fours on the floor. They couldn't find the arms. They sat down opposite each other and, wailing from fear and pity for Antosha, they started to flail at each other with the empty sleeves, then they fought and rolled around on the floor. The maid and the nurse came running and separated the gentlefolk.

12. After dinner Peredonov lay down to sleep, as was his custom if he didn't go off to play billiards. While asleep he dreamt that he saw nothing but sheep and cats which were walking around him, bleating and miaowing distinctly, but their words were all foul, and everything they did was even more shameless.

After his sleep, he went off to the merchant Tvorozhkov, the father of two students at the gymnasium, in order to complain about them. He had already whetted his appetite with the success of his previous visits, and it seemed to him that he would again enjoy success. Tvorozhkov was a simple person. Schooled on a pittance, he himself had acquired wealth. He had a stern look, spoke little, conducted himself with severity and gravity. His boys, Vasya and Volodya, feared him like fire. Of course, he would give them the kind of flogging that would turn the devil's own stomach.

And when he saw how sternly and taciturnly Tvorozhkov listened to all his complaints, Peredonov grew more and more certain of his own confidence. The boys, the fourteen-year-old Vasya and the twelve-year-old Volodya, stood erect like soldiers in front of their father, but Peredonov was surprised and annoyed by the fact that they were looking on calmly and were displaying no fear. When Peredonov had finished and was silent, Tvorozhkov gave his sons an attentive look. They stood even more erect and looked straight at their father.

"Go," Tvorozhkov said.

The boys bowed to Peredonov and left. Tvorozhkov turned to Peredonov:

"It's a great honor for us, my gracious sir, that you have deigned to trouble yourself in regard to my sons. Only we are informed that you have been going to many others and also demanding that the parents whip their boys. Can it be that suddenly in the gymnasium the fellows have gotten into so much mischief that there is no coping with them? Everything was fine, and now all of a sudden, one thrashing after the other."

"Well, if they are getting into mischief," Peredonov muttered distractedly.

"They do get into mischief," Tvorozhkov agreed. "Everyone knows how it is. They get into mischief and we punish them. The only thing that surprises me—you must forgive me, gracious sir, if I don't say it quite right—the thing that surprises me a great deal is that of all the teachers you alone trouble yourself with, forgive me for saying so, such an unsuitable pursuit. As everyone knows, when you whip your own son, then that's all there is to it if he deserves it, but peeking beneath the undershirts of other people's boys would seem to be somewhat of a superfluous business for you."

"It's for their own good," Peredonov said angrily.

"We are quite familiar with these procedures." Tvorozhkov objected immediately, without allowing him to continue. "If a student does something wrong, then he will be punished in the gymnasium, according to the rules. If he's bent on doing it, then the parents are informed or they are summoned to the gymnasium and the class prefect or the inspector will say what his guilt consists of. And the parents certainly know how to deal with him at home, depending on the boy and what his guilt is. But for a teacher to go around the homes on his own and demand that the boys be thrashed, there are no procedures governing that. Today it's you who come, tomorrow someone else comes, the day after a third person, and each time I'm to give my sons a licking? No, I'm sorry, your most humble servant, that is not acceptable, and you, gracious sir, ought to be ashamed of pursuing such a foolish business. Shameful, sir!"

Tvorozhkov stood up and said:

"I suggest that there is nothing more for us to talk about."

"Is that all you have to say?" Peredonov said sullenly, getting up distractedly from his chair.

"Yes, that is it," Tvorozhkov replied. "You will now excuse me."

"You want to raise nihilists," Peredonov said spitefully, backing awkwardly towards the door. "You ought to be denounced."

"We are capable of making a denunciation ourselves," Tvorozhkov replied calmly.

This response plunged Peredonov into terror. What was Tovorozhkov prepared to make a denunciation about? "Perhaps during the conversation," Peredonov thought, "I let something slip, blabbed, and he picked it up. Perhaps he has the kind of apparatus under his divan that records all the dangerous words." Peredonov threw a terrified glance under the divan—and there, it seemed to him, something shifted, something small, grayish, pulsating, trembling, jeering. He started to shake. "Just don't give yourself away," the quick thought flitted through his head.

"You won't catch me, not on your life!" he cried to Tvorozhkov and hastily left the room.

13. Of course, Peredonov hadn't noticed this. He was entirely absorbed in his own happiness.

Marta returned to the summer house after Peredonov had already left. She entered it with a certain fear: Vershina would say something.

Vershina was annoyed. Up until then she still hadn't lost hope of fixing Marta up with Peredonov and then marrying Murin herself. And now it was all ruined. She quickly and quietly heaped words of reproach, rapidly emitting puffs of tobacco smoke and glancing angrily at Marta.

Vershina loved to grumble. Her languid caprices, her fading, languid lust supported this feeling of dull displeasure, and it was expressed most comfortably in grumbling. If she expressed it aloud, it would come out as obvious nonsense, but if she were to grumble, all the absurdity would slip past her tongue—and neither she nor others would notice the incoherence, the contradictions, the uselessness of all these words.

It was perhaps only now that Marta understood how repulsive she found Peredonov after all that had happened with him and because of him. Marta gave little thought to love. She dreamt about how she would get married and would keep a good household. Of course, in order to do so she needed someone to fall in love with her and it was pleasant for her to think about that at the time but it wasn't the main thing.

When Marta was dreaming about her household, she would imagine that she would have precisely the kind of home, garden and orchard that Vershina had. At times she had sweet dreams that Vershina would make a present of it all to her and Vershina herself would stay on there to live with her, smoke her cigarettes and rebuke her for her indolence.

"You didn't know how to make him interested," Vershina said angrily and quickly. "You were always sitting there like a bump on a log. What more could you need! A fine young man, the picture of health. Here I am taking pains with you, trying, you might have at least appreciated and understood that. It was for you, you know, so you might have at least tried for your part to attract him somehow."

"I couldn't just foist myself on him," Marta said quietly. "I'm not one of those Rutilov girls."

"A lot of honor, this threadbare Polish gentry!" Vershina grumbled.

"I'm afraid of him, better I marry Murin," Marta said.

"Murin! Do tell, please! You have some grand ideas about yourself! Murin! As though he'd take you. The fact that he sometimes said some affectionate words to you, that doesn't mean perhaps that they were actually intended for you. You're still not worth a husband like that—a solid, serious man. You like to eat, but it makes your head hurt to think."

Marta turned a brilliant red. She did love to eat and could eat frequently and a lot. Raised in the country air, amid simple and rough work, Marta considered abundant and nourishing food one of the main conditions for human well-being.

Vershina suddenly rushed up to Marta, struck her on the cheek with her small dry hand and cried:

"On your knees, you good-for-nothing!"

Marta, sobbing quietly, got down on her knees and said:

"Forgive me, N [atalya] A [fanasyevna]."

"I'll make you stay the whole day on your knees," Vershina cried. "Don't fray the dress, if you please, it costs money, stand on your bare knees, raise your dress up and take your shoes off. You're no grand lady. Just you wait, I'm still going to thrash you with the rod."

Marta, obediently sitting down on the very edge of the bench, quickly took her shoes off, uncovered her knees and got down on the bare boards. It was as though she liked to subjugate herself and to know that her part in this oppressive matter was coming to an end. She would be punished, kept on her knees, perhaps even whipped. It would be painful, but afterwards everything would be forgiven. All this would happen soon, that very day.

Vershina walked back and forth past the kneeling Marta, felt pity for her and yet was hurt over the fact that she wanted to marry Murin. It would have been nicer for her to marry Marta off to Peredonov or someone else, and to take Murin for herself. Murin appealed to her in so many ways: he was big, fat, and such a good and attractive person. Vershina thought that she would be more suitable for Murin than Marta. The fact that Murin had become so engrossed in Marta and so enticed by her—well, that might have passed. But now, now Vershina understood that Murin would insist on Marta marrying him and Vershina didn't want to interfere. It was as though she were overcome with some kind of maternal pity and tenderness towards this girl, and she thought that she would sacrifice herself and give up Murin to Marta. This pity towards Marta forced her to feel kind and to be proud of the fact, while at the same time the defunct hope of marrying Murin inflamed her heart with the desire to make Marta feel the full force of her wrath and her kindness, as well as Marta's complete guilt.

Vershina particularly liked Marta and Vladya for the reason that she could give them orders, grumble at them and sometimes punish them. Vershina loved power and she was very flattered when Marta, after committing some fault, would unquestioningly get down on her knees at Vershina's order.

"I do everything for you," she said. "I'm not an old lady yet myself, I too might have still enjoyed my life and married a kind and solid person. Why should I look for husbands for you? But I'm more concerned with you than with myself. You've let one prospective husband slip away and now, just like for a little child, I'm supposed to lure another one, but then you'll snort again and scare this one off."

"Someone will marry me," Marta said shamefully. "I'm not a monster and I don't need other people's prospective husbands."

"Silence!" Vershina raised her voice. "Not a monster! So what am I, a monster! She's being punished and still talks. Obviously, the punishment isn't bad enough. Well, of course, you have to be properly punished, my little ones, so that you'll obey and do what you're told and not act smart. You can't expect any sense from someone who acts smart out of stupidity. You, sister, must first learn how to live yourself, but for the time being while you're still going around in other people's clothing you'll have to be a little more modest and obey, otherwise Vladya won't be the only one getting a licking."

Marta was trembling, and pitifully raising her tear-stained and flushed face, looked with timid and silent entreaty into Vershina's eyes. There was a feeling of submissiveness in her heart and a readiness to do everything she was ordered to do, to tolerate everything that they wanted to do with her—just as long as she knew, or could guess what was wanted of her. And Vershina felt her power over this girl and that made her head spin, and a kind of tenderly cruel feeling in her suggested that she had to treat Marta with parental severity, for her own good.

"She's become accustomed to beatings," she thought. "A lesson wouldn't be a lesson for them without that, they don't understand mere words. They only respect those who oppress them."

"Let's go home, my beauty," she said to Marta, smiling. "I'm going to treat you to some excellent whipping rods."

Marta started to weep anew, but she felt happy that the matter was coming to a conclusion. She bowed down at Vershina's feet and said:

"You are like my very own mother to me, I am bound to you for so much."

"Well, come on," Vershina said, poking her in the shoulder.

Marta got up obediently and followed barefoot after Vershina. Vershina stopped under a birch and looked at Marta with a grin.

"Should I break them off?" Marta asked.

"Break them off," Vershina said. "And nice ones."

Marta started to tear off branches, selecting the ones that were longer and firmer, and she stripped the leaves from them while Vershina watched her with a grin.

"Enough," she said at last and set out for the house.

Marta followed her and carried an enormous bundle of rods. Vladya met them and looked fearfully at Vershina.

"I'm going to give your sister a whipping right now," Vershina said to him. "You'll hold her for me while I punish her."

But when she arrived at the house, Vershina changed her mind. She sat down on a chair in the kitchen. She made Marta kneel down in front of her, bent her over her knees, raised her clothing from behind, held her hands and ordered Vladya to whip her. Vladya, who was used to whipping rods, having seen more than once at home the way his father whipped Marta, thought that if someone was being punished then it had to be done conscientiously, even if he did feel pity for his sister at the moment. And therefore he whipped Marta with all his strength, carefully tallying up the blows. It was extremely painful for her and she cried out in a voice that was partially muffled by her clothing and Vershina's dress. She tried to lie quietly, but despite herself her naked legs kept moving on the floor more and more forcefully, and finally she started to thrash about with them in desperation. Her body was already covered with wealts and spatterings of blood. It became difficult for Vershina to hold her.

"Wait," she said to Vladya. "Tie her legs up more firmly."

Vladya brought rope from somewhere. Marta was tied up firmly, laid out on a bench and bound to it with a rope. Vershina and Vladya took a rod each and for a long while thrashed her from two sides. Vladya made an effort to tally up the blows as before, under his breath, but calling the tens out loud. Marta's cries were sonorous and shrill, gradually subsiding until her shrill whining grew hoarse and intermittent. Finally, when Vladya had counted to a hundred, Vershina said:

"Well, that's enough for her. Now she'll remember."

They untied Marta and helped her into her bed. She was whining weakly and moaning.

She couldn't get out of her bed for two days. On the third day she got up, bowed down with difficulty at Vershina's feet, and then getting up, started to moan and weep.

"For your own good," Vershina said.

"Alas, I understand that," Marta replied and again she bowed down at her feet. "From now on don't leave me, take the place of my mother, and forgive me now, don't be angry any more."

"Well, God help you, I forgive you," Vershina said, holding her hand out to Marta.

Marta kissed it.

Introduction to the
"Sergei Turgenev and Sharik"
Fragments from *The Petty Demon*

T HE FOLLOWING FRAGMENTS from *The Petty Demon* were copied from
Sologub's notebooks to the novel (dated 1902), currently housed in the
Leningrad Public Library (Gosudarstvennaya publichnaya biblioteka
imeni Saltykova-Shchedrina; Lichnyi arkhivnyi fond F.K. Soluguba, No. 724,
Nos. 2 & 3). Most of this material was published in the newspaper *Rech'*
(April 15, 22, and 29, 1912), under the title "Sergei Turgenev and Sharik."
Some additional unpublished fragments on the same theme have been interpo-
lated into the basic material by the translator.

Insofar as this fragmentary episode has been generally unavailable to
Western readers this material constitutes a new page in the textual history of
one of the greatest twentieth-century Russian novels. Together with the variants offered in the 1933 edition of the novel (reprinted by Bradda Books in
1966), these materials provide us with the most complete text of *The Petty
Demon* which we are likely to have for the forseeable future.

"Sergei Turgenev and Sharik" recounts the episode of how two writers
pass through the town in order, as Sharik informs the participants at the masquerade ball, "to study your manners." They initially befriend the gymnasium
student Vitkevich, who then acquaints them with Peredonov, although not
before providing the inquisitive visitors with stories about the strange schoolteacher. Convinced that they themselves are among Russia's "newest men," the
authors see Peredonov as one of the same breed and develop an immediate fascination for him. The two perceive something "powerfully evil" in Peredonov,
respecting his "demonic" desire to whip children in order to prevent them from
laughing. Indeed, viewing Peredonov as the most curious example of Russian
"manners," each quickly decides to make the mad schoolteacher the hero of his
next novel. What follows is a series of humorous adventures which the two
writers experience while visiting with Peredonov and his fellow townspeople.
It is clear that the Turgenev-Sharik sequence is thematically tied to the main
plot of *The Petty Demon* by the *peredonovshchina* which corrupts, to one
degree or another, most of the characters and which forms a kind of connec-
tive tissue between virtually all of the novel's episodes and events. The two
writers are linked to the book's negative figures by virtue of their pettiness,
insincerity, ambition, and blindness to their own banality. Furthermore, insofar as language and theme are profoundly interconnected in *The Petty Demon*,

the verbal texture of the deleted portion demonstrates considerable linguistic affinities with the larger body of the text. Yet the overall lightness of the Turgenev-Sharik episode—its entire tonality of banter and almost slapstick humor—runs counter to the high seriousness with which Sologub approaches the major ideas of the novel: the nature of beauty and the role of creative fantasy in life. And there is good reason why this is so.

In point of fact, the Turgenev-Sharik episode, and specifically the character of Sharik, was conceived as a vicious parody of Maxim Gorky, which Sologub allowed himself to release only in 1912—ten years after its original composition. Relations between the two writers had never been particularly warm, and with the exception of *The Petty Demon* and the verse collection *Circle of Fire* (*Plamennyi krug*, 1908), Gorky had reacted in print quite unfavorably to Sologub's "decadent" works. Given their strong literary and political differences, it is not surprising that Sologub should have composed such a parody. But why he removed this episode from the novel shortly before its publication will remain a matter of speculation until his voluminous archives are made available to public scrutiny. There is no question, however, as to why Sologub published this material in April 1912; indeed, that year marked the culmination of the bitterness that each writer had long felt for one another. Their feud flared up in early March, when Gorky published an article about suicide (a popular theme in Sologub's early works and in the writing of many decadent/symbolist authors), entitled "On the Present Time ("O sovremennosti," *Russkoe slovo*, March 2 & 3, 1912). Ever-sensitive to the slightest negative allusion (real or imagined) to him and his works, Sologub could not have failed to notice this piece. Six weeks later "Sergei Turgenev and Sharik" appeared in *Rech'* (April 15, 22, and 29)—Sologub undoubtedly having found the time especially opportune for issuing his long-suppressed parody of Gorky. Nor did the matter end here. On December 16 of the same year, *Russkoe slovo* again carried a piece by Gorky—his third "Fairy Tale"—which was even more detrimental to Sologub and which included some slighting remarks about the writer's wife, the critic Anastasya Chebotarevskaya. In his response of December 23 to an angry letter from Sologub, Gorky categorically denied any intention of personally attacking him, although when mentioning Sologub in his letters, Gorky never failed to employ the most abusive terms.

In the deleted episode from *The Petty Demon*, Sologub attains at least partial revenge for Gorky's attacks on him. It is Sharik for whom Gorky serves as the model: the crude and self-righteous author whose Nietzschean heroes are bathed in cheap sentimentalism and distasteful amoralism, all of which reflects not "objective reality" but actually the writer-preacher himself. There is little doubt that Sharik's bathetic exclamation, "To hell with the truth! Truth is a horrible petite bourgeoise, a rumor-monger and a fool," echoes and lampoons Satan's famous line in Gorky's play *The Lower Depths* (written during the same year as Sologub's notebooks): "Man—now that's what truth is! . . . Truth is the god of a free man." However one approaches these fragments from *The Petty Demon*, they shed a new and interesting light on Sologub's timeless masterpiece.

Stanley Rabinowitz

(a) Peredonov met Vitkevich on the street in the company of Stepanov and Skvortsov, two writers who had arrived a few days before from the big city and whose acquaintance he had made the preceding day.

Stepanov (who now published under the name of Sergei Turgenev) wrote verse in the decadent spirit for fame and Marxist verse for publication. He also wrote stories that were of a dual content as well. Some were intended for fame— but no one would print them and they lay in the writer's desk, preserved for posterity. The others were printed willingly enough in journals and newspapers, but from time to time it did happen that the writer was criticized because they bore too close a resemblance to long-forgotten works by deceased writers who were unknown to the world. At that point Stepanov changed his pseudonym. The literary name of Sergei Turgenev was still not widely known. No one had yet succeeded in discovering the sources for his fresh inspirations, although sensing fresh booty, many diligent bibliophiles in godforsaken spots had been conducting zealous searches in their own literary hodgepodge as well as that of others.

The story-writer Skvortsov (who used the signature of Sharik) thought of himself as being the most up-to-date person in Russia and was very curious to know what would come after Symbolism, Decadence and various other new tendencies at the time. Moreover, he considered himself to be a Nietzschean. Incidentally, he still hadn't read Nietzsche in the original—because of his lack of knowledge of German—and he had heard that the translations were bad and for that reason he didn't read them either. But he wrote stories in the mixed style of Reshetnikov* and Romanticism of the 1830's, and, moreover, the heroes of these stories always possessed an unmistakable resemblance to Sharik himself. They were all strong people.

There was something akin in their external appearance despite the fact that at first glance they did not appear similar. Sharik was a lanky young fellow, scrawny, with shaggy red hair. He usually just called himself a "fellow." Turgenev was short, with a ruddy complexion, clean-shaven, somewhat balding. He wore a pince-nez in frames made of Warsaw gold and was always squinting. He was fussy and diffident in his movements. He would say of himself: "I am a poet." And at the same time he would squint blissfully. Sharik didn't wear glasses. His manners were exaggeratedly uncouth. They weren't badly dressed, just slovenly. Sharik was in a light-colored loose peasant shirt and Turgenev in a gray summer suit. Turgenev had a walking stick in his hands whereas Sharik carried a staff that was five feet long. Turgenev spoke in a languid fashion whereas Sharik hacked and hewed.

Sharik and Turgenev were jealous of each other, because they both considered themselves candidates to become Russian celebrities. But they pretended to be great friends while being guided by one and the same perfidious calculation: each of them was attempting to make a drunkard of the other and thereby ruin the other's talent.

Not long ago Sharik had even embroiled Turgenev in a duel with an apothecary. Before and during the duel everyone got properly drunk, both the duellers and their seconds. At the signal they fired at each other, but after they had turned their backs to each other with the calculation that the bullets would fly around the globe and strike where they were intended.

Carousing and seeking ever fresh means for facilitating the realization of their perfidious intrigues, they arrived in our town. Once they were here each

*Reshetnikov, Fyodor Mikhaylovich (1841–1871). A novelist of the 1860's with strong democratic views and a follower of Belinsky, Chernyshevksy and Dobrolyubov. His best-known novel was *The People of Podlipno* (1864) which dealt with the depressed and exploited lives of the peasantry and *Lumpenproletariat*.

of them considered himself close to his goal. For that reason they felt compla-
cent, gave themselves a small respite and even though they got drunk every day,
it wasn't carried to excess. It was Vitkevich who brought the writers together
with Peredonov. As a progressive student at the gymnasium he naturally considered it his responsibility to become acquainted with the writers and he even
wrote an essay for them: "The Influence of Slowacki on Byron."*

Even before the writers made the acquaintance of Peredonov they had been
suddenly consumed with a great curiosity about him. From the stories of Vitkevich
and others he seemed to be one of the new people. They sensed something powerfully evil in him and each of them immediately intended to use him as the hero
for their next brilliant novel. Yet, at the same time, by some strange whim of their
willful minds, they saw in him a common type as well, the "bright spirit" (the
authorities, i.e., the headmaster, Peredonov had said, were persecuting him).

"This here lad sure does praise you," Sharik said to Peredonov.

"He is overcome with pathos because of you," Turgenev said diffidently.

"He understands," Peredonov said sullenly, "that they're all blockheads
here. But he's not a bad fellow himself."

"We were just out for a walk," Sharik said.

"This is no time for a walk," Peredonov replied sullenly. "Come over to
my place and drink vodka and we can have lunch at the same time." The writers readily agreed. They all went to Peredonov's.

"These gentlemen of letters and myself were talking about an interesting
topic," Vitkevich said. "About down-and-outers."

"Yes, people say you shouldn't hit a man who's down—what nonsense!"
Sharik exclaimed. "Who should you thrash if not a person who's down!
Someone who's on his two feet isn't going to take it, but a man who's down is
a completely different matter. You can give it to him in the teeth and the mug,
the scoundrel!"

He gave Turgenev an affectionate glance, looking directly into a face that
was dissipated from protracted drunkenness.

"Give it to him hot, the villain!" Turgenev agreed as well, bestowing a
fond look on his friend and stroking him on his thin and fragile back. It seemed
to Turgenev that Sharik was already in bad shape and had contracted syphilis
of the spine from all manner of excesses.

"Do you agree? A submissive person should be pushed around?" Sharik
asked Peredonov with an affectionate tone in his uncertain voice.

"Yes," Peredonov replied. "And the boys and girls should be whipped and
as often as possible, and as painfully as possible so that they'll squeal like little
piggies."

"Why?" Turgenev asked with a painful grimace.

"So they won't laugh, otherwise they'll be laughing in their sleep,"
Peredonov replied sullenly.

"You hear!" Sharik exclaimed ecstatically. "So they won't laugh! There's
something demonic in that! To banish that vulgar, animal laughter out of that
vulgar childhood!"

---

*Slowacki, Juliusz (1809–1849). A Polish poet and dramatist whose early works
depicted the romantic image of the solitary and disenchanted hero. Much of his work was
written and published abroad (Paris). Together with A. Mickiewicz he belonged to the
foremost representatives of Polish revolutionary romanticism. Obviously he could have
had no influence on Byron (1788–1824), whose works preceded those of Slowacki's.

"Yes, that is repulsively beautiful," Turgenev said, out of diffidence to both Peredonov and himself.

"Yes," Sharik rejoined, "or exquisitely vile. But Turgenev hit it right on the head: repulsively beautiful! My friend Turgenev—there's none wittier than he in Russia."

"And just remark on his marvellous aphorism: exquisitely vile," Turgenev said. "Marvellously said! O, my friend Sharik knows how to find amazing words. Russia will be hearing about him."

Excerpts from the speech which he had prepared long ago to deliver at Sharik's graveside were activated in his mind.

They went on several paces in silence, smiling joyfully, each delighted with his intelligence and brilliance. Vitkevich walked alongside them with mincing steps and kept peering exultantly into their blissful faces.

"It's turned out just famously that we came to this backwash," Sharik said. His thoughts were on that remarkable person, Peredonov.

"There's nothing good here," Peredonov said sullenly.

"But there's you!" Turgenev exclaimed and gazed fondly into Peredonov's dull eyes.

"I'm all there is!" Peredonov said mournfully. "And I'll be leaving soon. I'm going to be an inspector, make the rounds of the schools and whip the boys and girls."

"What melancholy in these benighted lands!" Turgenev exclaimed.

"And what power!" Sharik rejoined. "This is greater than Foma Gordeyev."*

"A million times greater," Turgenev agreed.

These writers loved to compare and they always rejoiced if it were possible to exaggerate their praise of one person while simultaneously knocking someone else.

"There's no Foma Gordeyev here," Peredonov said. "But there is a Nikolai Gordeyev. He's good at chewing up bread and sticking spitballs on the ceiling."

"He's mad, isn't he, Turgenev?"

"Yes," agreed Turgenev. "But it's a profound madness."

"And Pylnikov is a scoundrel, but she didn't want to give him a whipping, his landlady," Peredonov said.

"Who are these people?" Sharik inquired.

"There's this gymnasium student here, a lodger at this landlady's. Kokovkina is a widow. He's a little sweetheart. People say he's a girl in disguise, looking to catch a husband. I went to his place and questioned him but Sasha wouldn't admit it. He ought to have been given a good thrashing. But she, the old lady, didn't want to. Now there's one you ought to castigate in print, the old bitch."

"Yes," Sharik agreed. "Bourgeois-liberal vulgarity has to be overthrown by all possible means. The vulgar bourgeois has to be shocked so that his eyes bulge out. With a fist right to his belly."

*Foma Gordeyev (1899) was the title of Gorky's first important novel. The hero of the novel, Foma Gordeyev, is the young son of a rich Volga merchant. He is disenchanted by the lack of spiritual values in both his father and the entire merchant class. When he tries to resist the traditional autocratic and undemocratic ways of his class, he is eventually destroyed. The novel was praised for the starkness and brutality of its portrayal of the merchant world.

He suddenly thrust forward his right foot and poked Turgenev in the side with his fist. Turgenev exclaimed:

"Easy! You'll kill me like that. Don't forget that I'm Turgenev."

"Sergei, but not Ivan," Sharik declared meaningfully and grinned sarcastically.*

Turgenev frowned and said:

"Well, that's beside the point, but the only thing I want to say to you, Mr. Peredonov, is that it's impossible to print the fact that this lady protested. It all has to be depicted symbolically, that is, the other way around. We'll print that she performed the punishment on her own initiative, on the basis of her unbridled, Asiatic despotism. Reproducing the incident in this fashion will correspond to the humane principles of our press."

Peredonov gave a loud yawn and said:

"The street is getting its back up."

The street rose to a small hill and then descended once more on the other side. A bend in the street between two miserable hovels was etched against a blue, sorrowful sky that was turning to evening. This quiet region of impoverished life was shut up in itself and languished in deep mourning. Even the writers grew mournful, the way it sometimes happens suddenly with children who are weak and tired out of boredom.

"Yes, a real pit," Sharik said and whistled.

Sergei Turgenev was silent, his head bowed listlessly. He was thinking that his sorrow was the sorrow of a great spirit that was languishing in the miserable bonds of false existence, and he was proud of his sorrow.

(b)   "To begin with," Turgenev replied, "be so good as to introduce us to your spouse."

Since Peredonov stood there motionlessly, goggling at the writers with his dull eyes, Turgenev thereupon stepped forward to Varvara with a gallant motion, scraped his foot, seized himself by the tie and gave his name:

"Allow me to introduce myself: Sergei Turgenev, man of letters. I beg your magnanimous forgiveness for intruding on your familial hearth at a time that is perhaps unfitting."

Varvara produced a smirk, offered the man of letters a sweaty hand that was dirty from fussing with the cat and said: "Pleased to meet you. Only forgive me that I'm in this work dress. I was just busy with all the housework here."

Sharik stepped forward as well, cleared his throat and said in a loud voice: "The writer Skvortsov. Sharik. All Russia knows Sharik."

Varvara smirked at him as well and shook his hand too. But all the while she was thinking about the cat and couldn't comprehend what Sharik the guest was talking about.

(c)   "We'll get him out, Auntie, don't you worry," Vitkevich said, winked at Varvara and as he stepped past her, gave her a nudge with his elbow as though by chance.

The writers exchanged glances. Sharik produced a soft whistle. Vitkevich's words and behavior gave them to understand immediately how they were supposed to act with Varvara.

(d)   The writers laughed. They saw the cat as being symbolic. It was precisely the way a Peredonov cat should be.

*A reference to Ivan Sergeyevich Turgenev (1818–83), one of the great triumvirate of 19th-century Russian novelists that included Tolstoi and Dostoevsky.

(e)   Dreamily, Turgenev raised his gray eyes to the ceiling that was pasted over with paper and said:

"Green-eyed cats that love to miaow on roofs over the human abode—now that is the prototype of the superman."

Sharik grinned scornfully.

"Well, what's your opinion then?" Turgenev asked.

"Sharik grew thoughtful, made a circular motion with his right hand, brushed a lock of hair back from his forehead and said:

"See here, I'm not denying the beauty of your definition. Generally, you're a master of spouting out that kind of poetic verbiage where there's more poetry than truth—and, basically I say to hell with the truth! Truth is a horrible petit bourgeoise, a rumor-monger and a fool. But this time I am defintiely not in agreement with you. It seems to me that there's another hitch here."

Sergei Turgenev, turning red from the praise and from the fact that he disagreed with what Sharik was saying, asked:

"And just what is the hitch?"

"You see, pessimism . . ." Sharik was about to begin. But Sergei Turgenev sharply and scornfully interrupted him:

"Well, sir, you're wrong, forgive me, pessimism is a dog, a bitch."

Sharik was struck.

"Well, you're right, of course," he said. "But what I wanted to say was: are cats wise or not?"

Sergei Turgenev replied determinedly:

"They are."

"Then note," Sharik continued, "I am speaking only about cats and not felines. But what I mean to say is that when cats make love they produce agonizing cries. Why? Suffering lurks at the very source of life. And bitter suffering miaows on all the streets and courtyards of the soul, on all the roofs of life. The more mournful and the more terrible the miaowing, the more fiery the striving for the ideal. The winged song of the poet slinks timidly among the cats wandering over the roofs."

Sergei Turgenev exclaimed ecstatically:

"Marvellously put! It miaows! What a symbolic word!"

Peredonov suddenly yawned and in the process his face was momentarily illuminated with an expression of pleasure—how sweet he found that yawn!

"What a demonic yawn he has!" Sergei Turgenev said pensively. "How profoundly symbolic is this yawning reaction against the banal tedium of vulgar life!"

Varvara suddenly exploded in reverberating laughter and said:

"Well, enough of your tomfoolery. Here, you'd better eat the cherries."

"Who cares about cherries!" Volodin objected. "Varvara Dmitrievna, don't go interfering with our conversation. We don't go into your kitchen when you're getting something ready for us to eat, so don't you interfere with us hearing about learned subjects."

Sharik and Sergei Turgenev started to talk to Varvara and in the process they clowned about, being immediately infected with the lack of respect shown her. It was the first time they had seen her, but she reminded them of something familiar and cheap.

Sharik indicated Varvara with a wink to Turgenev and asked him:

"She resembles Emma there at the 'Vixens',* doesn't she?"

Without the least embarrassment Turgenev gave Varvara the once-over and said:

"Yes, but she's even more like Zhenya in 'Old Japan'."*

*These are probably names of brothels in St. Petersburg.

"Well, I was never there," Sharik replied condescendingly.

Varvara smirked.

"What Emmas and Zhenyas are you talking about?" she asked. "Are they friends or something?"

"Yes, sort of like friends," Sharik said, smirking with particular significance.

"Girls," Turgenev said dreamily and then added tenderly: "Poor girls!"

"Why do you have such poor friends?" Varvara asked with a smirk.

"You see, Auntie, we ourselves don't have two kopecks to rub together," Sharik said with undue familiarity.

"What do you mean calling me Auntie!" Varvara said in an offended voice. "Do you really take me for an old woman?"

"Quite the contrary, my respected matron," Turgenev replied chivalrously. "It was only out of respect."

"Bust my gut, Mummy, if it wasn't out of respect," Sharik added as well.

"A lot I need your respect, just imagine, what next!" Varvara replied with a roar of laughter.

Vitkevich jumped into the conversation as well.

"Anyone finds respect flattering, Granny," he said impertinently.

But Varvara immediately cut him off:

"You're just trying the same, you little milksop."

Sergei Turgenev, smiling and rolling his glazed little eyes upwards, broke into a pleasant tenor:

> Emilia so marvellous,
> The friend I held in high esteem,
> A love that was miraculous,
> You were my lifelong, perfect dream.

His cunning gray eyes expressed something between pleasure and scornfulness.

Sharik listened with a condescending smile and finally broke into an unnatural laughter that was exaggeratedly loud:

"No, really, I find it even touching," Turgenev said. "There's something here that's so naive, so primitive—in short, almost Pre-Raphaelite."

Sharik grew pensive.

"Yes, quite likely," he agreed. "but still, pretty dumb."

"Of course!" Turgenev exclaimed. "Essentially, it's idiotically silly, but even that's what's good about it. We copied it down here in the cemetery," he explained to Peredonov. "And generally you've got a lot of amusing signs in the town. I wrote a few of them down. Here, I'll read them to you."

He pulled a soiled and tattered notebook out of a side pocket and started to read some extracts:

"Cookhouse For Twenty-Four Horses."

"School For Boys And Girls Of Both Sexes."

"Floor-Polisher And Electrician For Cheap Enlightenment."

"Male Trousers For Men."

"Musical Grand Pianos."

"Fine Wines and Biers."

Sergei Turgenev suddenly turned serious and said to Sharik:

"You know what? I'm going to insert this epitaph into my poem."

"Yes, it'll fit, go right ahead," Sharik agreed. "You know, ladies and gentlemen, Turgenev has decided to rattle off a poem. It's going to be something terrific!"

"Yes, if I manage to express what I want to," Sergei Turgenev said modestly. Sharik said hastily:

"Of course you'll manage! Just imagine, it'll be a really great mystical thing, and there won't be any Demon or Satan there. Who gives a damn about the devil! Rubbish, nonsense, a lot of big-sounding nothing! No, instead, that mighty spirit that is alien to everything ideal and which Turgenev has called 'The Banal.' Ah, what a name!"

Sergei Turgenev smiled modestly, the way a genius would smile who is confident of the greatness of his conception.

"Yes," he said bashfully, "it's a creation that is interesting and profound in its conception. I have already dedicated it to eternity and posterity. It will be a genuine chef d'oeuvre."

Peredonov suddenly burst into laughter. Sergei Turgenev shuddered and gave Peredonov a hateful look.

(f)   Now she imagined that she could entice one of the writers who were getting intoxicated in their wanderings hither and yon and get married to him. She invited them to a party together with her customary table companions: Peredonov and Varvara, Falastov, Volodin, Rutilov, the Prepolovenskys and a few other young officials.

The guests arrived early. Only the writers were missing for the time being.

(g)   However strange it might have seemed, Rutilov still hadn't lost hope of marrying off one of his sisters to Peredonov. For that reason he didn't care for any talk about Peredonov marrying Varvara and in order to change the conversation to something different, he started to talk about the writers' adventure the evening before. After a real drinking bout at Murin's, the the drunken writers had wandered about the streets and caused an uproar. The police had escorted them to the police-station. Since the chief of police was away on a trip that day and the assistant chief of police was passing the time at the home of the cathedral archpriest's, there was no one to handle the case of the writers and they had to spend the night in the "flea-bin" (the local name for the room at the police station where arrestees were detained by the police). They let them out the next morning and even apologized to them.

It turned out that everyone knew about the adventure. Nevertheless, they started to talk about it enthusiastically, laughing all the while, and they traded details that were obviously improbable with one another.

It was precisely at that time that the writers arrived. Turgenev was wearing a light-colored jacket and a string tie—he was trying to appear sophisticated and sensitive. Sharik was wearing a loose peasant shirt and affected exaggeratedly peasant manners.

They were showered with questions. Was it true that they had spent the night in the lockup? Was it true that the police had flogged them? Was it true that they had put their stamp on the wall? The writers gave an ecstatic and embittered account of their adventure.

Turgenev said with a bitter smile:

"It's only one out of a mass of similar deplorable facts from Russian reality. Regardless of where you look you find nothing but Russian stupidity, Russian insipidness and Russian dumbfoundedness!" he said with bitter scorn as he pronounced the word "Russian."

"Old Russia is the celebration of drink," Murin said with a laugh of approval.

The writers gave him an angry look and Sharik replied with rudeness:

"What you're spouting has absolutely nothing to do with it."

Turgenev added his support:

"Completely sober intellectuals are ending up in the flea-bin quite apart from the drunks. But there are masses of precedent for that in our judicial history. Our 'Rooshian' police—well, now, who doesn't know about them!"

"Yes, there's more than a few sincere fellows that are feeding the lice around our jails," Sharik said.

Turgenev started to preach:

"Russia doesn't have any of the essential characteristics of European statehood: the freedom of conscience, the freedom of the press, the sanctity of the individual, the freedom of movement without a passport."

At this moment Peredonov produced a totally unexpected and very loud yawn.

The writers didn't care for this in the least. They exchanged an irate look.

"Only Russians can yawn and sleep under a cloud," Turgenev said.

"Some snore, some roar," Sharik remarked sternly.

"But, nevertheless, our incident was exceptionally distressing," Turgenev said fervently. "Recently arrived men of letters, the cream of the intelligentsia, with the famous Sharik at their head, are doing honor to the town by paying it a visit. They ought to be regarded as respected guests, whereas the gendarmes go dragging them off to the lockup! Even Siberia is too good for people who do that. It is totally unacceptable that any policeman be ignorant of literature."

"That kind of villainy couldn't happen in the European countries," Sharik said with certainty.

Turgenev sighed, flashed his little eyes like a serpent and hissed:

"This incident will pass over into eternity! Some future day in the history of Russia my memoirs will appear. All of this will be told then."

"Well I'm not going to wait for posterity," Sharik declared. "I'll write a letter to a German or a Swedish newspaper."

"Won't you get in trouble for that?" Rutilov inquired timidly.

"No, it's possible to do it abroad, they don't pay attention to that sort of thing."

"It's pretty important business to be locked up at the police station," Murin said.

"And have you ever been locked up there?" Sharik asked with a quick burst of temper.

"Well, really, why would I have been there!" Murin replied, offended.

"Then you can't judge what it means to spend a night in prison," Turgenev began with feeling. "The damp gloom, the bare walls, the poisonous, stifling stench. On the other side of the wall the clanking of shackles, the fierce cries of sullen guards and someone's heartrending moans. Exhausted by this whole terror, you lie down on your cruel pallet—and suddenly the bedbugs, the lice, the fleas, the cockroaches and the tarantulas attack you and sting and sting you unbearably. You leap up, you want to get out, you bash against the doors in righteous indignation. But the ferocious roar of the drunken cutthroat, armed with our own native and universally renowned whip, brings you instantly back to submission. You collapse on the damp, filthy floor, you become oblivious for half a minute and you start dreaming—oh, those horrible, delirious prison dreams! Horrible, horrible, thrice horrible! Ignominy, ignominy, a hundred times over, ignominy! Despicable Russia."

"Incidentally, speaking of dreams," Peredonov said, "last night I had a dream too. It was terrible! Supposedly I had robbed Marta, bumped her off and then dragged her off to the rubbish heap."

Varvara started to giggle and said:

"And she deserves it, the bitch."

Turgenev looked on with perplexity and annoyance. No one had been struck by the force of his words. It was just as though a gnat had buzzed. Turning to Sharik he grumbled:

"A benighted simplemindedness."

"Mind-boggling!" Sharik muttered in response.

(h) They were inhibited by the presence of the new guests, the writers. For their part, the writers were smiling condescendingly and mockingly. Seeing that the ladies were looking at them at Grushina's party, Sharik said:

"What vulgar dreams there are gadding about in this town! Turgenev, tell them your dream about the avenue of omniscient birds. The atmosphere in it will take your breath away."

Turgenev smiled dreamily, raised his eyes to the ceiling and started to talk in a languid voice:

"It was a long avenue, an endless avenue. All the trees had their branches chopped off. A mystical fire blossomed between each pair of trees. And on each tree sat an omniscient bird, an owl*, blinking its eyes. A splendid atmosphere! But no, my friend, Sharik," he said, growing faint from languor, "they won't understand. They cannot understand it!"

"Amen, amen, be gone evil spirit!" Peredonov whispered.

Sharik envied Turgenev his dream. He was trying to think up a dream of his own that would eclipse all the other ones that had been described earlier— it was a dream that was obviously unlikely, with a multitude of details. It included a mighty-winged eagle (Sharik himself), a serpent, a crow and bloody-mouthed tulips. But Rutilov interrupted his story.

"I never have any dreams," Rutilov said. "And even if I do, then I forget them immediately. It's worth remembering them, truly!"

Rutilov wanted to uphold his dignity as an educated person in the eyes of the writers.

"What for?" Turgenev asked, shrugging his shoulders.

"I don't believe in dreams," Rutilov said. "We might be living in the provinces, but that doesn't mean we've become savages."

Sergei Turgenev gave him a condescending reply:

"Naturally, it's not every being who has the opportunity to come into contact with the eternal problems of reality."

Feeling wounded by the words of the writer, Rutilov said:

"Only the peasantry believe in dreams. It's not becoming to educated people."

Sharik smiled sarcastically.

"Such sophistication!" He said spitefully.

Pleased with the fact that he had related his dream, Turgenev was smug. He passed a hand through his hair and said:

"No, I'm not laughing at folk superstitions. I have a lot of sympathy for folk

---

*In Russian the bird is a "sirin," which is both a small owl-like bird and a mythological bird from ancient Russian folklore that has the face and breast of a young girl.

traditions. I'm the grandson of the common folk, I'm the nephew of prophesying woe. My cradle was fanned by prophetic dreams. My heart believes in all these tales—oh, I am a madman! Last night I also dreamed, there in the prison, that I was the Tsarevitch, handsome and youthful. My eyes were radiant like stars, my curls were spilling over my shoulders in a golden cascade, roses blossomed on my lips and exquisite maidens were kissing my white hand with lips as gentle as a dream."

Peredonov once again produced a sudden and loud yawn, and furtively made the sign of the cross over his mouth so that no one would see.

(i)   There was the smell of food. Grushina summoned the guests to the dining room. Everyone set out, jostling one another and affecting politeness. They sat down haphazardly.

"Help yourself. What do you desire?" Grushina regaled the writers who had sat down side by side.

Turgenev produced a melancholy smile, assumed an inspired look and said:

"Desires? But my desires are insatiable. I would desire to take wing and fly and fly . . ."

"And I would desire," Sharik declared sullenly, "to give some scoundrel a punch in the mug."

Turgenev objected:

"No, I want to have a woman who is as mad as I am! With reddish hair, with eyes that are green and wild, a woman who is long and supple like a serpent, and just as slender and wicked."

(j) The very same fancy simultaneously entered the minds of both writers. They exchanged winks, stood up from supper, went off to the side and started a heated conversation. They were trying to convince each other to marry Grushina.

"There's something bacchic in her," Turgenev said.

"Really, I wouldn't be at all opposed," replied Sharik, "but she suits you more."

And each of them tried to outdo the other in singing her praises: each was thinking of ruining his friend with this marriage.

(k) It was Murin, Sharik in a loose peasant shirt, Turgenev in a light-colored, light-weight suit with a pink tie, and their friends.

"Ah, the supermen!" Rutilov said with a giggle as he caught sight of the writers.

The writers took this salutation at face value and laughed.

(l)   "Really, mam'selle, don't you find it drafty down below?" Turgenev asked, as he sat Varvara in the carriage.

"I'm no mam'selle now, I'm a madame and I'll give you one right in the kisser."

"Aha, how stern!" Turgenev burst into laughter.

Sofiya was secretly rejoicing at the fact that the wedding was being marred. Her keen eyes were screwed up and glistening with pleasure and her thin lips were compressed in malice. But her movements were just as flowing and restrained as usual and her speech was just as unctuous and patronizing.

(m) The writers, Sharik and Turgenev, were already visiting the Khripaches that day. They were studying the local manners and for that reason made an effort to go everywhere. They started to talk about the latest town news, about Peredonov's marriage and his eccentricities in general.

"By the way," Lyudmila said, "what a handsome boy you have in the gymnasium, a Sasha Pylnikov—a picture of good looks."

Varvara Nikolaevna was amazed. It seemed to her that it was not in the least being mentioned "by the way." But the switch from Peredonov to the cute boy was incomprehensible to her and for that reason appeared even somewhat unseemly. She said:

"Actually, I don't know them, any of them. There are so many of them and I don't have anything to do with them."

"He's a new student of yours," Lyudmila said.

"Really? But I don't even know the old ones, let alone the new," Varvara Nikolaevna protested.

"It's that same boy that Peredonov thinks is a girl," Lyudmila explained.

"Ah, so that's it! Yes, I did hear something," the headmaster's wife drawled unwillingly.

Turgenev smiled craftily.

"Your Peredonov," he said, "has expressed this fact somewhat crudely. The hypothesis that a girl in disguise has entered the gymnasium, naturally, wouldn't bear any scrutiny. But, nevertheless, you do know who he is."

The headmaster's wife smiled benevolently. She was expecting that the writer would say something witty and amusing.

"So, he's nothing more than a young lad," Darya said. "Only he's cute."

"It's not quite like that," Turgenev insisted.

"Well, who is he then?" Lyudmila inquired.

"A hermaphrodite!" Turgenev exclaimed and for some reason raised his eyes to the ceiling.

There was a general confusion—the ladies didn't know that sort of word. Sharik translated:

"A boy-girl."

"But what's that supposed to mean?" a curious Lyudmila asked.

"How can I tell you!" Turgenev said. "If you like, it's a higher being. In him we find a self-fulfillment, a harmonious combination of the active and passive elements in the human spirit and nature. And, actually, not simply a combination, but rather a synthesis of these two elements. Each of us represents a kind of disunited being. But the perfect person is not a man, not a woman, nor even a man and a woman together, and is neither man nor woman. These two elements are united in him chemically, so-to-speak, in a supernatural process, so that the usual physiological path is abolished as being superfluous and leading nowhere. We are all either fertile or procreative, whereas he already represents the self-wrought fruit."

He would have gone on speaking for a long while, but Lyudmila suddenly burst into laughter. The headmaster's wife gave a restrained smile: she couldn't make out whether the writer was joking or speaking in earnest, and for that reason she had a smile on her lips whereas her eyes expressed something akin to pensive consideration of this eccentricity. Khripach had listened attentively and then he said:

"This is rather clever and perhaps in the abstract it is feasible as some specific hope, although at present it is only vaguely expressed in other trends that have come to pass. But in regard to the given individual case it has been exaggerated. Moreover, the path which you have indicated, whether supernatural or superhuman, is essentially the path of the Antichrist and the originator of that path, that is, the Antichrist, cannot, in any event (here Khripach smiled ironically) be a pupil at a state educational institution."

Turgenev had been offended by Lyudmila's laughter, all the more so because at first she had apparently been listening sympathetically. "A crafty wench," he thought and said as he shrugged his shoulders:

"If no one here cares for my hypothesis, then you are simply being deprived of one clear and elevated point of view of the subject."

(n) The writers, Sharik and Sergei Turgenev, were at the masquerade as well. On their way back to the capital they had once again stopped off in our town. Dissipated and jaundiced from hard drinking, they nevertheless still appeared quite the young fellows. They had strong constitutions although they were always assuring their trusting friends that they suffered from the ailment of "the great Nadson."* As always, Sharik wore his loose peasant shirt.

"This is the international costume," he explained to Volodin. "All intellectuals should be wearing it."

On his face he preserved an exaggeratedly disdainful and sullen expression. He despised this merry crowd. Turgenev was more polite. He had a condescending expression.

"There's something intoxicating in the banal and stupid merrymaking of the crowd," he said to Sharik. "You have exactly the same kind of impression as though you were taking a mud bath."

"Proto-banal!" Sharik muttered angrily.,

"Yes, all this glitter bores me, like other people's joy," Turgenev said. "Listen, Sharik, how do you like this comparison: boring, like other people's joy? I am going to insert it in my new novella."

"Marvellous," Sharik offered his praise. "A perfect fit. Really, other people's joy is a spectacle that is fairly loathesome."

Turgenev and Sharik went off to the buffet to drink tea.

"I drafted a critical study today," Sharik explained. "You'll be interested in the content."

"Naturally," Turgenev said. "What you wrote can't be other than interesting."

"Yes, of course," Sharik agreed. "So here's my theme: Nekrasov and Minaev."**

"Pfui!" Turgenev said scornfully.

"Wait," Sharik stopped him. "I am maintaining that Nekrasov—and note that I am maintaining it with facts—that Nekrasov was envious of Minaev."

---

*Nadson, Semyon Yakovlevich (1862–1887). Perhaps the most famous and inspirational of the democratically-minded "civic" poets. He died prematurely of tuberculosis. However, to the romantically-inclined, his death came as much from spiritual causes (disenchantment, sorrow and painful sensitivity) as from physical.

**Nekrasov, Nikolai Alexeyevich (1821–1878). Perhaps the most famous poet of the mid-nineteenth century in Russia and the leading representative of the realist-democratic tendency in "civic" poetry. In 1846 he gained control of the journal The Contemporary, which, until its suppression in 1866, was the leading journal in Russia, publishing both Turgenev and Tolstoy, as well as the civic critics like Belinsky, Chernyshevsky and Dobrolyubov. In 1867 he took over another influential journal, Notes of the Fatherland, which he published until his death. Minayev, Dmitri Dmitrievich (1835–1889). A translator and minor Russian poet who belonged to the Nekrasov school. He worked in various democratic journals of his day, including those owned by Nekrasov. Famous for his parodies, epigrams and puns on topical subjects.

"Aha!" Turgenev exclaimed and laughed. "Improbable, but nice. Immortally nice."

"Yes, yes, he was envious," Sharik said with conviction. "And in fact it was impossible for him not to be envious: envy is an essential attribute of the genuinely literary temperament."

"Yes, perhaps you're right," Turgenev said thoughtfully.

"I can understand Salieri."*

Meanwhile a crowd had gathered at the entrance to the buffet. They were looking at the writers and exchanging remarks. Sharik was angered by this. He stood up, frowned, scratched the back of his head and said in a rude voice:

"Hey, listen you characters there, what d'you want? What do you see here so interesting?"

"Sh-sh-sh," echoed in the crowd. "He's speaking, he's saying something."

Suddenly it became very quiet and Sharik's voice echoed with ruthless clarity in the midst of this perfidious silence:

"I came here to study your manners, not to dangle in front of you like a scarecrow. I am a man of letters and not a deep-sea diver, or even some bare-bellied Venus. You're wasting your time staring at me. I have the very same kind of mug as every other scoundrel here and I drink tea with my mouth and not with my nose or any other aperture."

"Well done!" someone shouted in the crowd.

Someone clucked maliciously, someone started to laugh. Sharik went on, with increasing loudness and anger:

"Sergei Turgenev and I sat down to sip tea, so you scram, hop to it! Rather than goggling at us you'd better read our books more carefully, otherwise you'll be gathering moss before you know it. Other men of fiction are merely my precursors . . . The precursors for me and Sergei Turgenev. So then, you go ahead and read us, learn some sense for yourselves, we won't teach you anything bad."

He turned away from the crowd, sat down, poured some tea into his saucer, set the saucer on his scalded fingers and slurped with deliberate loudness. The motley crowd gave the orator a round of applause and dispersed with laughter.

"He got rid of us smartly!"

"Now that's some writer!"

"He doesn't have to hunt for words."

"Smart fellow!"

"We fools really deserved that!"

"After all, what's the point of stating. Some wonder!"

The official with the besom was shaking it, clowning about energetically and repeating:

"This is a real bathhouse. They really steam our brother here."

Turgenev had made no attempt to stop Sharik. He smiled sweetly and dreamt that this tactless escapade would find its way into the newspapers and discredit Sharik. When the spectators had left, Turgenev gave Sharik a sympathetic handshake and said:

"This speech will endure as a famous fact in our biography. Write it down before you forget it, otherwise people will distort it!"

"Yes, thank you, I'll slap it down," Sharik said. "I myself feel that I did a great job of it."

*Salieri, Antonio (1750–1825). An Italian composer who lived in Vienna after 1766. He was reputedly insanely jealous of Mozart and a legend circulated that he had poisoned the great composer. Pushkin utilized that legend in his "little tragedy" entitled "Mozart and Salieri."

"You know," Turgenev said, "when a person hears speeches like that, the soul sprouts wings, white and sharp ones, like those of demons."

"That's a clever one you've come up with," Sharik encouraged him. "You and I are in good form today!"

Turgenev's eyes grew dreamy and he said:

"Today, while you were writing, I strolled through the woods outside of town. I conversed with the flowers, the birds and the wind. I was happy."

"If you take some vodka or rum with you," Sharik said, "then it's really something."

"No, I wasn't drunk," Turgenev protested. "My soul is akin to the clouds, those mutable and beautiful clouds. Do you see the tears in my eyes? Those tears are from a surfeit of sensitivity."

THE PETTY DEMON AND THE CRITICS

MURL BARKER

The Petty Demon, written during the years 1892 to 1902 was serialized in the journal *Voprosy zhizni (Question of Life)* in 1905. It was not until 1907 that it was finally published in book form, and then it received widespread recognition and Sologub's literary fame was assured. But not all of the early reviews and criticism of the novel were favorable; on the contrary, Sologub's contemporaries were often sharply divided in their views. While it is a rather flippant exaggeration to write off this initial reaction to the novel as a "collection of cliches,"[1] for today's reader, most of this early criticism seems dated, repetitious and lacking in perspective. Part of the problem was the pronounced tendency toward rhetoric; there was a great deal of plot recapitulation; generalizations abounded. I do not feel that extensive translations of this material are necessary to accompany an English edition of the novel intended for the non-specialist. But a brief overview of the various interpretations by those early critics will serve as an introduction to the recent criticism included in this appendix.

Many of Sologub's contemporaries reacted extremely negatively to the work (and its author) in their reviews. Anastasia Chebotarevskaya, Sologub's wife, was irked by the attacks and was provoked into an angry diatribe aimed at these critics. In an article which is really a defense of her husband's work, she questions these reviewers' intelligence, their talent and experience in dealing with literature: in Russia, she claims, virtually anyone can pass himself off as a critic—beginning with the uneducated schoolboy.[2] What prompted her article were the epithets directed at Sologub which she had gathered from the various critical articles written about him by his contemporaries. Sologub was characterized as "possessed," "a maniac," "sadist," "a morbid, mutilated talent with a psychopathic inclination," "abnormal," "decandent."[3]

Chebotarevskaya's observations are not confined to The Petty Demon; rather, she comments in general about the author's philosophy as dramatized by all of his works. She points out that one distinct thread in his works is his rejection of the world in its present, untransformed condition. Denial of the real world was not difficult for Sologub since death is viewed in such a positive light: it comforts, does not deceive and no one fears death—not even the children, who alone are called alive in this repugnant world. But Dream, too, may be a liberating force and with it, the creative process in particular. This idea is expanded in Sologub's various solipsistic proclamations concerning the power of the individual's "I" to create and affirm worlds within itself. And, Chebotarevskaya concludes, there is a striving in Sologub for the intimate to become universal.[4]

Certainly the trilogy provoked the more vitriolic outbursts directed toward Sologub.[5] But *The Petty Demon*, too, proved to be fertile ground for accusations leveled at the author. While it was generally agreed that Peredonov was the epitome of banality, stupidity, and cruelty, the crudest interpretation of the protagonist came from those critics who saw him as a self-portrait of the writer.[6] Other critics disagreed and the author addresses this accusation in the preface to the second edition of the work. Most critics agreed that the existence of Peredonovs was widespread in the Russian provinces, and indeed, shortly after the appearance of the novel, the word "Peredonovism" was coined and came into general usage. The more general view however was that there is some part of Peredonov in each one of us, that the character becomes a symbol of a universal truth, transcending his time and milieu. One of Sologub's most perceptive critics, Ivanov-Razumnik,[7] insists that one misses the whole point of the work if it is read merely as an account of provincial life. Rather, it is life in its entirety: life without aim or meaning—the philistines' rampant banality and cruelty are everywhere. It is not Peredonov alone who represents this terrifying vision of life: the other characters in the novel are no less horrible in their spiritual make-up than Peredonov; each one is striving for his or her "inspectorship."

The repulsive image of Peredonov as victimizer, as a thoroughly contemptible distillation of man's vile impulses, is balanced by those who saw him as a victim. While admitting to his baseness, still Peredonov was described as suffering from a persecution mania resulting from the forces pursuing him: his cohorts, the *nedotykomka*, even nature. Peredonov was seen as a victim of the weakness of human cognition: he did not understand the Dionysian relationship to nature and he was blind to beauty.[8] Peredonov elicited a sympathetic response because of his lonely battle with the *nedotykomka*: he was characterized as a new and tragic Don Quixote.[9] His tragedy was also seen as that of a lonely individual who can find no place for himself either on earth or in any higher realm.[10] He was seen to be vulnerable because he appeared to have no kind of armor; he was completely naked and unable to save his "I".[11] And the reader is asked to feel compassion for Peredonov who emerges as a symbol of human suffering.[12]

Peredonov's elusive little beastie, the *nedotykomka*, inspired many different interpretations among Sologub's contemporaries. The little grey creature was described variously as the petty demon of the title,[13] as a symbol of all that is terrifying in life—"the lie which he (Peredonov) accepted as the truth; it was more indubitable and more real than the whole of reality surrounding him."[14] One critic saw it as a symbol larger than the work in which it appears: "For Sologub, ghosts and devils, the secret, hostile forces inhabiting all of nature and quietly startling the weak, frightened individual were concentrated into the one sinister figure of the *Nedotykomka*."[15] In the criticism of Sologub's contemporaries there are frequent comparisons made between Chekhov's Belikov ("The Man In A Case") and Peredonov. This prompted one critic to see in the *nedotykomka* "a symbol of all that the 'man in a case' is guarding himself against."[16]

Standing in opposition to the gloomy and terrifying world of Peredonov and his *nedotykomka* are Sasha and Lyudmila. No other aspect of the novel seemed to call forth as many contradictory views as this "legend in the process of being created." On the negative side we read that the episode has no valid function in the novel but was only added for its "piquant aroma."[17] Another critic agrees that the story is in no way connected with Peredonov's history and that while Sasha and Lyudmila may remain innocent, "this boundless perversion is all the more depraved."[18] He asserts that Lyudmila fits very nicely into the banality surrounding her and that Sasha is nothing more than a little Peredonov.[19]

Alexander Blok, a great admirer of Sologub's, was most lavish in his praise for the Sasha-Lyudmila episode. He read it as ". . . a bright spot, a subtle thread, a fragrant aura," and he praises Sologub for his originality in discovering "a wellspring of unfathomable purity and *charm* . . ."[20] Blok wrote about the poetic nature of the story and was joined by another critic who praised Sologub's "tender and pure tones" in writing about this "impetuous passion of youth." He adds that the episode could "exist independently as a beautiful poem of young earthly love."[21]

Ivanov-Razumnik[22] states the obvious: that the relationship is an escape from Peredonovism. Beauty, and in particular the beauty of the human body can overcome the Peredonovism in life. The philistines know but two extremes in their relationship to the human body: either unconcealed debauchery or hypocritical modesty. But Sologub wants to transform the gloomy, grey meaningless life into a cult of the body, a pure esthetic delight, and he does this with the Sasha-Lyudmila story. He constantly suggests that the reader compare the relationship of those two with Peredonov and his associates who defile beauty and in particular, the beauty of the body (as exemplified by Peredonov with Varvara, Grushina at the masquerade and the authorial interjections regarding their actions). The attempt to avoid Peredonovism through a cult of beauty of the body turned out to be full of impossibilities and contradictions, notes the critic. So Sologub's concept of beauty broadened to include nature, the spirit and fantasy. And through the creative force of his "I," Sologub takes a piece of life and transforms it into worlds of fantasy from his imagination.

Scattered throughout this early criticism are comparisons between Sologub and his nineteenth-century predecessors. The most frequently mentioned names are Gogol, Dostoevsky and Chekhov. *The Petty Demon* is often viewed as a continuation of the Gogolian preoccupation with the banality, backwardness and madness of provincial life and of course, *Dead Souls* was the obvious novel of Gogol's to compare with *The Petty Demon*. More technical parallels were noted between the two authors' works: their use of repetitions, the preponderance of negatives and the predominantly "gloomy" vocabulary which pervades their works.[23] V. Botsyanovsky suggests that both Gogol and Sologub have an apparatus to enlarge each living thing into caricature. He does not mean to accuse them of exaggeration, but rather, he explains that it is as if each writer had a microscope in his brain. They put under it an imperceptible piece of human vileness and then it becomes visible to everyone.[24]

Again, the stifling atmosphere of the provinces, the banality, a mood of pessimism, the trivialities in which people are involved were the grounds for comparing Chekhov and Sologub. More specifically, Belikov, "The Man In A Case," was compared to Peredonov, with conclusions regarding their similarities and their differences.

With Dostoevsky, the comparisons swing from confusing (suggesting that Sasha and Lyudmila are as necessary in *The Petty Demon* as Kolia Krassotkin and Iliusha are to *The Brothers Karamazov*!)[25] to the vague (the gloom to doom atmosphere; the "Karamazov questions" about the meaning of life and innocent suffering). Character parallels were mentioned: the Underground Man and Smerdyakov with Peredonov for example.[26] Other critics emphasized the presence of the diabolical in both writers' works: this observation has the potential for a specific and rewarding comparison.[27] But as is often the case in this early criticism, a provocative idea such as this one is presented, but it is seldom developed satisfactorily.

After 1923, when Sologub was attacked as "anti-revolutionary" and "outmoded," he was unable to publish. Two reprints of *The Petty Demon* were issued in the Soviet Union in limited editions.[28] Orest Tsekhnovitser, in his Introduction to the 1933 edition, rails that Sologub, who came from such a modest background and suffered in the provinces, should have been ripe for revolution. Instead, Sologub is accused of having no social perspective, no belief in tomorrow. And his lack of well-defined political positions cheapens the novel. The work is praised though for its realistic portrayal of life in pre-Revolutionary Russia.

Soviet criticism continued to emphasize the realism of the novel. In 1969 an article[29] was published with documentation to prove that characters and events were drawn from real life experiences of Sologub when he taught in the provincial town of Velikie Luki. Included was a letter from an individual who had taught with Sologub as well as an unpublished interview with Sologub, who admits that he used as his model for Peredonov, a certain Strakhov, a teacher even more insane than Peredonov.[30]

A refreshingly sympathetic, sensitive and more sophisticated assessment of Sologub by a Soviet is found in the introduction to a collection of Sologub's poetry published in 1975.[31] In it, I. Dikman praises *The Petty Demon* as the author's greatest achievement in prose as well as being one of the most successful Russian novels at the beginning of the century. While pointing out that Sologub testified to the veracity of character and milieu, the author is applauded for his portrayal of the philistine psychology and for his creation of the *nedotykomka*, which is interpreted as a symbol of the banality and vileness of that philistinism.

In this introduction, the universal aspect of the novel is alluded to by the observation that readers and critics saw the work as a confirmation of the absurdity, the senselessness and incomprehensibility of life as well as the baseness and vileness of man in general. Dikman dismisses the Sasha-Lyudmila story as having no place in the novel, no realistically portrayed perspective.

There has been one book-length study of *The Petty Demon*, published in this country by Galina Selegen.[32] In her monograph, which is written in Russian, Selegen introduces the reader to the history of the symbolist novel in France and Russia, she discusses Sologub's philosophy and esthetics, then she turns to the novel itself, focusing on structure, methods of characterization and various aspects of the author's language. She writes about Peredonov as the embodiment of banality as well as its victim, the *nedotykomka* as that banality having taken form in his imagination. She points out that unlike other social novels, we do not have a biography of Peredonov, no explanation of social forces forming his character. She notes that there is no plot in the traditional sense, but rather that the novel is a series of the hero's spiritual experiences which reveal his character. She agrees with those who feel that the Sasha-Lyudmila plot stands outside of the artistic plan of the work.

The body of critical material about *The Petty Demon* in English was quite limited until fairly recently. John Cournos, an early translator of Sologub, published one of the first studies of the writer in English.[33] It has a certain antiquated charm; his comments on *The Petty Demon* are sensible if not always original. He sides with the critics who see Peredonovism as a universal human condition; he gives Peredonov credit for recognizing that the *nedotykomka* is an evil spirit and for fighting against it. He finds the Sasha-Lyudmila episode to be a relief from the novel's tragedy: "But the infatuation of a young woman for a young boy may in itself seem strange to the English reader." (!)[34] As for the "Karamazovian question" (Ivan's questioning the meaning of life), Cournos believes that Chekhov consoled himself with the hope of progress; Sologub finally realized that beauty and imagination might offer an escape for the individual, but not for all of humanity—so Sologub's great hero became Death.

Brief mention of *The Petty Demon* is found in various histories of Russian literature, the best probably that by D.S. Mirsky who called the novel "the most perfect Russian novel since the death of Dostoevsky."[35] Renato Poggioli[36] devotes some attention to the work with perceptive, if concise observations, and Robert Jackson's study[37] is also to be recommended. The articles reprinted here, and the suggested readings following them, represent the best criticism on *The Petty Demon* to appear in recent years in English. While ultimately the work must speak for itself, these thought-provoking analyses by contemporary scholars should enrich the reading of *The Petty Demon*.

NOTES

1. An observation by Andrew Field in the Introduction to his Master's Thesis, "Sologub's Prose: A Critical Analysis Of Its Symbolism And Structure", Columbia University, 1961 (unpublished). Field was the translator of the novel published by Random House in 1962.

2. A.N. Chebotarevskaia, "'Tvorimoe' Tvorchestvo," in A.N. Chebotarevskaia (ed.), *O Fedore Sologube. Kritika. Stat'i i zametki.* (Petersburg, 1911). This piece eppears in the collection of critical essays about Sologub, compiled by Chebotarevskaia. It is a selection of articles covering the writer's work in poetry, drama and prose. While a rather well-balanced assessment for the time (the articles were written between 1905–1911), it is not surprising that the general attitude is most positive. Ardis (1983) has reprinted the Russian original (ISBN 0-88233-849-8).

3. *Ibid.*, p. 79.

4. This is particularly true in Sologub's trilogy, *The Created Legend*, written between 1907 and 1913. Translated by Samuel D. Cioran and published by Ardis (Ann Arbor, 1979): Volume I, *Drops of Blood*; Volume II *Queen Ortruda*; Volume III *Smoke and Ashes*. The protagonist, Trirodov, is actively pursuing a Utopian ideal, a private idea being put into practice in order to transform other individuals and thereby transform reality.

5. See the "Introduction" by Samuel Cioran in *Drops of Blood* pp. 11–21 for a summary of the reaction to the legend. Of particular interest is his discussion of Gorky's estimation of Sologub.

6. Among others, A. Gornfel'd, "Nedotykomka" in *O Fedore Sologube*, p. 256; IU. M. Steklov, "O tvorchestve Fedora Sologuba," *Literaturnyi raspad. Kniga vtoraia* (Petersburg, 1909), p. 190.

7. Ivanov-Razumnik, "Fedor Sologub" in *O Fedore Sologube*, pp. 7–35.

8. A. E. Redko, "Fedor Sologub v bytovykh proizvedeniiakh i v 'tvorimykh legendakh'," *Russkoe bogatstvo*, No. 3 (March 1909), p. 77.

9. *Ibid.*, p. 75.

10. P.S. Vladimirov, "Fedor Sologub i ego roman 'Melkii bes'," in *O Fedore Sologube*, p. 315.

11. E. Anichkov, "Melkii bes," in *O Fedore Sologube*, p. 220.

12. Z. Gippius, "Slezinka Peredonova," in *O Fedore Sologube*, pp. 72–79.

13. Peredonov is often referred to as the petty demon too, which emphasizes the multiplicity of interpretations of the title.

14. R. Ivanov-Razumnik, *O smysle zhizni. Fedor Sologub. Leonid Andreev. Lev Shestov* (St. Petersburg, 1908), p. 45.

15. IU. Steklov, "O tvorchestve Fedora Sologuba," *Literaturnyi raspad*, II (St. Petersburg, 1909), p. 176.

16. E. Anichkov, *loc. cit.* Anichkov argues that Peredonov is not at all like Chekhov's schoolteacher.

17. Steklov, *op. cit.*, p. 200.

18. Gornfel'd, *op. cit.*, p. 259.

19. A. Gornfel'd, "Fedor Sologub," *Russkaia literatura xx veka 1890–1910*, ed. S. Vengerov, II, kn. 4–5 (Moscow, 1915), p. 47.

20. Aleksandr Blok, *Sobranie sochinenii* (Moscow, 1962), V, 126.

21. A. Izmailov, "Ismel'chavshii russkii Mefistofel' i peredonovshchina. 'Melkii bes'—roman F. Sologuba" in *O Fedore Sologube*, p. 293.

22. Ivanov-Razumnik, in *O Fedore Sologube*, pp. 7–35.

23. A. Belyi, *Masterstvo Gogolia* (Moscow, 1934), reprinted by Ardis, Ann Arbor, 1983.

24. V. Botsianovskii, "O Sologube, Nedotykomka, Gogole, Groznom i pr. (Kritiko-psikhologicheskii etiud)" in *O Fedore Sologube*, p. 146.

25. E. Anichkov, *op. cit.*, p. 217.

26. P. S. Vladimirov, *op. cit.*, p. 307.

27. V. Botsianovskii, *op. cit.*, p. 171.

28. Moscow-Leningrad, 1933; Kemerovo, 1958.

29. B. IU. Ulanovskaia, "O prototipakh romana F. Sologuba 'Melkii bes'," *Russkaia literatura*, XII, no. 3, (Leningrad, 1969), pp. 181–184.

30. For a more detailed discussion, see G.J. Thurston, "Sologub's *Meikiy bes*," *Slavonic and East European Review*, LV, 1 (January, 1977), pp. 31–33.

31. Fedor Sologub, *Stikhotvoreniia*, ed. M.I. Dikman, 2nd ed., Bol'shaia seriia, (Leningrad, 1975).

32. Galina Selegen', *Prekhitraia viaz' (Simvolizm v russkoi prose: 'Melkii bes' Fedora Sologuba* (Washington, 1968).

33. John Cournos, "Fedor Sologub," *The Fortnightly Review*, XCVIII (July-December, 1915), pp. 480–490.

34. Cournos, *op. cit.*, p. 486.

35. D.S. Mirsky, *A History of Russian Literature* (New York, 1926), p. 444.

36. Renato Poggioli, *The Poets of Russia 1890–1930* (Cambridge, 1960).

37. Robert Jackson, *Dostoevsky's Underground Man in Russian Literature* ('s Gravenhage, 1958).

Additional Articles of Interest:

Julian W. Connolly, "The Medium and the Message: Oral Utterances in *Melkij Bes*," *Russian Literature*, IX (1981), pp. 357–368.

F.D. Reeve, "Art as Solution: Sologub's Devil," *Modern Fiction Studies*, V, No. 2, (1957), pp. 110–118.

G. Roman Shchurowsky and Pierre R. Hart, "A Somber Madness: Dionysian Excess in *The Petty Demon and Professor Unrat*", *Germano-Slavica*, Vol. III, No. 1 (Spring, 1979), pp. 33–44.

G.J. Thurston, "Sologub's *Melkiy bes*", *Slavonic And East European Review*, Vol. LV, No. 1 (January, 1977), pp. 30–44.

A Chronology of Important Dates

Murl Barker

1863	February 17. Fyodor Kuzmich Teternikov born in St. Petersburg
1867	Father, a freed serf, later a tailor, dies. Mother becomes a domestic in the Agapov household
1882	Graduates from a teachers' institute; begins teaching in the provinces
1884	Publishes first poem, "The Fox and the Hedgehog" (*Lisitsa i ezh*) in *Vesna (Springtime)*
1892	Moves to St. Petersburg to teach, later becomes a district inspector. Associated with the journal *The Northern Herald (Severnyi vestnik)* in which he publishes poetry, short stories and his first novel, *Bad Dreams (Tiazhelye sny*, 1895). Adopts the name of Sologub.
1892–1902	Writes *The Petty Demon (Melkii bes)*, serialized in *Questions of Life (Voprosy zhizni)* in 1905, in book form, 1907
1894–1912	Writes novel *Sweeter Than Poison (Slashche iada)*, serialized in *The New Life (Novaia zhizn'*, 1912)
1896–1908	Publishes eight volumes of poetry
1896–1921	Publishes nine collections of short stories
1907	Publishes first play, "Liturgy to Myself" (*Liturgiia mne*) in *The Scales (Vesy)*. Sologub wrote twelve original plays, 1907–1922. Retires from education. Beloved sister and companion Olga dies.
1907–1913	Publishes trilogy. Original title is *Phantom Spells (Nav'i chary)*; as a later, revised version: *The Created Legend (Tvorimaia legenda*, 1914)
1908	Marries Anastasia Chebotarevskaya. *The Flaming Circle (Plamennyi krug)* published: His most popular collection of verses written from 1900 to 1907
1909–1914	Publishing firms Shipovnik-Sirin issue collected works in twenty volumes: one book of articles and tales, one of drama, five of poetry, six of short stories and seven of novels
1915–1921	Continues to publish collections of poetry, short stories and the novel *The Snake Charmer (Zaklinatel'nitsa zmei*, 1921)
1921	Denied permission to travel abroad; wife commits suicide
1923	Branded "out-moded" and "counter-revolutionary" and unable to publish. Works at translating and editing
1927	December 5, dies after a long illness

THE GROTESQUE IN FEDOR SOLOGUB'S NOVEL *THE PETTY DEMON**

LINDA J. IVANITS

THE PRESENT STUDY is an exploration of the relationship between *byt* and the fantastic in *The Petty Demon*. The very title of the novel hints at a possibility: that the pettiness and vulgarity of everyday life—*poshlost'*—are a mask of the demonic. The cosmos of the novel, appearing initially to be a typical provincial society, slips almost imperceptibly into an inferno. The artistic method through which *poshlost'* is integrated with the demonic is the grotesque.

A few words should be said about the concept of the grotesque underlying this study. Recently the grotesque has been described both as the trivial perceived as demonic and as the demonic made trivial.[1] This seems accurate with the qualification that in literature as well as in painting and sculpture the combination of the trivial and demonic takes a highly visual form. The grotesque is a particular distortion of the usual representation of man, and as such it implies a play with the concept of what it is to be human. This distortion is frequently achieved through a joining of elements from the animal, plant, spirit, and mechanical worlds with human elements. Often bodily confines are violated and extended to ludicrous or obscene proportions. In the case of nonhuman creatures the form is humanized, yet remains lacking in genuine humanity. In the grotesque object the trivial and the obscene yield to the uncanny and vice versa so that an uncomfortably estranging effect, perhaps best described as simultanenously ridiculous and sinister, results.[2]

The above understanding seems to apply to such figures as Gothic gargoyles, the strange creatures of Hieronymous Bosch's hell, Pieter Bruegel's illustrated proverbs, Jacques Callot's sketches for the Commedia dell'Arte, and many of the paintings and sketches of Francisco Goya—all of which are generally accepted as grotesque.[3] Other aspects of the grotesque include a particular type of motion which is gestic and apparently unmotivated and which tends to turn back on itself. The dance of death, consisting of jerky hops and strange contortions, has been called the archetypal grotesque motion.[4] Senseless, impromptu acts of spite, obscenity, and scandalmongering are common activities, and they imply abrupt, directionless motion. Insanity is a frequent motif accompanying the presentation of grotesque characters because it provides a cover for irrational behavior.

A particular type of scenery which conveys the feeling of a defined space and is at the same time cluttered and colorful is characteristic of the grotesque. Parties and masquerades are frequent settings because they provide an element of artificiality and estrangement. If the grotesque object is placed outdoors, then nature tends to come alive and acquire a hostile mien. Language is a significant factor in the presentation of grotesque characters. Words tend to lose their value as a means of exchanging ideas, and they often acquire a magical significance. A character's language, like his motion, tends to be abrupt and illogical.[5]

The Petty Demon contains an entire roster of grotesque figures. Three primary means of rendering characters grotesque are used: (1) the exaggeration and repetition of one or two salient physical features, (2) metaphor, and (3) literary allusion. The effect in most cases is that the chracters are not rendered so overwhelmingly unhuman as to be totaly fantastic. They remain a part of provincial *byt*, yet at the same time their essential humanity is called into question, and they are given identities within a demonology.

THE CHARACTERS

The major character and focal point of *The Petty Demon* is Peredonov, a paranoid schoolmaster who is obsessed by a desire to be promoted to the position of inspector of public schools. He was modeled on a teacher whom Sologub knew personally when he taught in the Russian provinces, and this prototype, like the character generated from him, was to Sologub the very incarnation of *poshlost'*.[6] Peredonov's is the most elaborate portrait in *The Petty Demon*, and it is possible to visualize him rather precisely. Basically he is drawn from the outside in, through externals which serve both to create a pictorial representation and to reflect the status of his soul. His face is ruddy, sleepy, and generally indifferent. He has small, puffy eyes framed in gold-rimmed glasses; his eyes are expressionless and as his insanity increases they become vacant "like the eyes of a dead man."[7] He has chestnut brown hair which is thinning, and he is gaining weight around the middle—suggestions that he is approaching middle age. To avoid catching cold, Peredonov wears an overcoat, even in warm weather. His tendency to encase himself in an overcoat indicates a fear of his surroundings, and thus points to his paranoia. The indifference and lack of emotion in his face and eyes suggest that he is somehow lifeless.

Comparisons of Peredonov to a corpse, a pig, a puppet, and a devil are especially important in rendering him grotesque. The metaphor of the walking corpse (*khodiachii trup*) is the logical culmination of a visual representation stressing lack of emotion and lifelessness. The comparison of Peredonov to a puppet serves to mechanize him; the suggestion is that someone other than he is in control of his movements. Significantly, this comparison is used when he is engaged in a hysterical, awkward dance, which may be considered a dance of death (257). Peredonov's mistress Varvara is the first person in the novel to call him a pig; it is her response to his spitting in her face. Possibly the most striking comparison of Peredonov to a pig is in the form of a pun on the word "piatachek," which means both "five-kopeck piece" and "pig snout" in Russian. Peredonov's friend Rutilov asks him if he has a five-kopeck piece (*piatachek*) and then reasons that if Peredonov has a pig snout (*piatachek*), he must be a pig (60–61). Terrified, Peredonov grabs his nose to make sure it is human, but when he asserts that he has a "human mug" (*chelovech 'ia kharia*), he uses a term which may also apply to a pig (*kharia*). The implication is that he may be a pig after all.

In folklore and the literary tradition the pig is a common embodiment of the devil, and no doubt in *The Petty Demon* too these images are intercon-nected.[8] While the metaphor of the pig points directly to Peredonov's vulgarity, that of the devil suggests the demonic side of his personality. Rutilov calls Peredonov a devil several times, and on one occasion calls him a devil in eye-glasses, thus adding a human and comic touch to the traditional image of the devil. Another significant instance in which Peredonov is called a devil occurs at the very end of the novel just before his murder of Volodin. Varvara, now his wife, repeats the common saying, "Husband and wife make one devil" (*Muzh da zhena—odna Satana*, 382). The suggestion may be that Peredonov's demon stature grows during the course of the novel; he is no longer an ordi-nary devil (*chert, bes*), but the "prince of darkness" (*Satana*).[9]

The metaphors used in Peredonov's depiction dehumanize him by empha-sizing his lifelessness and by suggesting that he has another, non-human essence—that of a pig/demon. The presence of bodily hungers—appetite—in the place of emotion and feeling tends to further dehumanize Peredonov. Vodka is perhaps the most obvious sign of appetite in *The Petty Demon*. A staple of Peredonov and his friends, it runs through the novel as a leitmotif accompany-ing Peredonov on visits, present at his parties, and present too at his slaying of Volodin. As Peredonov's paranoia grows, his intake of vodka increases until, towards the end of the novel, he begins to appear at the school drunk. Varvara excuses Peredonov's strange (insane) behavior as drunkenness, and this causes her no worry. Vodka and cards are the only means Peredonov has of enter-taining his friends, an indication of the meagerness of his imagination. Here too the folk tradition provides a framework for interpretation: it was believed that a drunk was one of the devil's favorite hosts and that card-playing was a com-mon entertainment among devils and witches.[10]

As is freqent in the creation of the grotesque object, the motif of the buf-foon is combined with that of the demon in Peredonov's characterization. This is most evident in the ridiculous yet sinister antics in which he engages. For example, on his wedding day Peredonov reddens his cheeks with Varvara's rouge, paints "P's" on his chest, attempts to wear one of Varvara's corsets, and, finally, tries to have his hair cut in an imaginary "Spanish style"—all to distin-guish himself from Volodin. The comic element in Peredonov's buffoonery is diminished by the error in conceptual thinking which underlies it. His paranoia is by now so acute that he believes Volodin will "crawl under his skin" and assume his identity, his wife, and the inspectorship. This series of antics is uncanny partly because it illustrates the power which words have acquired over Peredonov. A statement which originally was a general formulation of the fear that Volodin wanted to marry Varvara and become the inspector—"Perhaps he's even thinking of marrying Varvara and crawling under my skin, (71)"—has become for Peredonov a literal possibility.

In general Peredonov's language displays the same abruptness and lack of transition as his motion. His speech usually consists of short units, often of only one or two words. Although his language is vulgar, it tends to be gram-matically correct (in contrast to that of Varvara and Volodin). As a rule Peredonov does not initiate conversation, but rather reacts to someone else's words; and there is a notable absence of formal greetings and the usual polite-ness of social convention in his speech. He uses substandard words in place of the standard lexicon: for "face" (*litso*) he substitutes "mug" and "snout" (*kharia, rozha, rylo, morda*), and he refers to his friends by debasing diminutive forms of their names ("Varka" rather than "Varvara," "Pavlushka" rather than "Pavel").[11] For Peredonov language is a means of fulfilling bodily needs, of abusing, of spreading gossip, of charming, and of countercharming; words have lost their value as a means of exchanging ideas and opinions. Yet, at the same time, they have acquired magic powers: this is clear from the terror which the pun on "piatachek" inspires in Peredonov and from his fear that Volodin will literally "crawl under his skin."

The settings in which Peredonov is placed tend to take on his sullenness and become extentions of his personality. Hints are given that his apartment is dirty and smelly; it is certainly stuffy, since to avoid drafts Peredonov refuses to open the window. Nature particularly mirrors Peredonov's inner state. He is often pictured alone outdoors going to and from places. Streets, trees, grass, physical surroundings, and especially the weather take on his moods and reflect his boredom, anguish, and fear. As Peredonov's paranoia increases and he becomes deader, nature comes alive and seems hostile to him: "The heavens frowned. The wind blew straight at him. . . . The trees did not want to give shade. . . . But dust rose up in the form of a long, half-transparent gray serpent. Why is the sun hiding behind a cloud—could it be spying?" (285).

Peredonov's pictorial delineation, achieved through a combination of human, animal, mechanical, and demonic traits, is the first of many such creations in *The Petty Demon*. The two persons closest to Peredonov, Varvara and Volodin, are also genuinely grotesque. Varvara's physical representation is acheived through a juxtaposition of contradictions. She has a wrinkled face on which there is a lewd and spiteful expression, but her body is beautiful, like that "of a gentle nymph with the head of a withered harlot attached to it by the power of some despicable spell" (72). The motifs of mechanization and the mask are used in Varvara's characterization. The high heels she wears cause her walk to be jerky, and she is so heavily powdered and rouged that her blushing cannot be seen. In Varvara's creation there is a certain identity of mask and face: the vulgarity which her heavy make-up suggests is painted on top of the lewdness which accompanies her decaying beauty. For the social visits which she makes after her marriage, Varvara dons a new hat adorned with flowers in all colors. Thus another element, this time from the plant world, is added to the motley amalgamation which makes up her visual image.

Hints are given that Varvara has a witch nature. Peredonov senses that she has the power to charm him. He is alarmed because she cooks from a black book, a suggestion of sorcery; and he fears that she has the ability to cast a spell on him with cards. Indeed, Varvara, like the rest of the novel's society, believes in black magic. She is able to recognize her crony Grushina's abilities at sorcery, and she immediately suspects sorcery when a hat which Peredonov left in his former apartment is returned (46, 251).

The only person in the novel who sincerely likes Peredonov is Volodin, yet Volodin, is the person from whom Peredonov suspects the brunt of the attack against him. Volodin's physical creation is based on the motif of metamorphosis: he is, as his name implies, amazingly ram-like. He bleats his way into the novel, and, after Peredonov cuts his throat, he bleats, squeals, and chokes his way out (25,383). Even in a society characterized by a lack of intellectual interests, Volodin's bestial stupidity stands out. This is particularly evident in his language, which is totaly insipid and devoid of meaning. An especially incongruous touch is added to Volodin's depiction by Peredonov's attempt to marry him to Nadezhda Adamenko, an attractive, intelligent girl who spends her time reading books and has no part in the day to day affairs of the novel's town. As a couple they are a complete mismatch, both visually and intellectually. The costume Volodin grafts on his ram-like frame while courting Nadezhda renders him additionally ludicrous: he wears a tight fitting frock coat, a freshly starched shirt, a gaudy necktie, and his wooly hair is pasted down with pomade and scented.

The two widows Vershina and Grushina play a significant role in Peredonov's fate. Vershina wants to marry Peredonov to her ward, an awkward Polish girl named Marta, and she therefore beckons him into her house whenever he passes. Grushina is Varvara's confidante in her attempts to marry Peredonov, and it is she who forges letters promising Peredonov the inspectorship. But Vershina is also involved in the ruse of the letters. She instills suspicion into Peredonov about the authenticity of the first one, thus causing Varvara to have Grushina forge a second; moreover, at the end of the novel she tells Peredonov outright that the second letter was a forgery and thus directly precipitates the murder of Volodin.

Vershina is an obvious witch. She is a small, thin, prematurely wizened woman with black eyes and brows, a dark complexion, and dark yellow teeth, and she always dresses in black. Her gestures are smooth, almost imperceptible, her smile is crooked, and her tone of voice monotonous. Vershina is a chain smoker, and she should be visualized with puffs of smoke rising in front of her. Vershina's garden is an important part of her characterization; it is lush and vibrant with color, and it is chaotic. This garden and the gray house within it form the only setting for the many meetings between Peredonov and her, for, unlike most of Peredonov's other friends, she never visits him at his home. During these meetings he is in her territory, an enchanted realm, and the implication is that he is also under her spell.

While Vershina is depicted in black, gray is used for Grushina, and dust rather than smoke is her characterizing motif. She gives the impression that she never washes and that "if she were struck several times with a carpet beater, a column of dust would rise to the very heavens" (42). This emphasis on dirtiness is bolstered by Grushina's corresponding vulgarity, the immodesty of her conversation, and the general depravity of her life. Her house is slovenly, and her walls are decorated with poorly-drawn pictures of naked women. This house, like Vershina's house and garden, is an important locus of action in the novel. It is here that the forgery takes place and that Peredonov, during a party, makes his final decision to marry Varvara.

Certain parallels in the depictions of Vershina and Grushina are evident. Their names are phonetically similar, and each is drawn through the use of color (black-gray) and a corresponding motif (smoke-dust).[12] It seems, however, that Vershina's witch nature is more striking. Significantly, except for the business of finding Marta a husband, she scarcely seems to be a part of the provincial *byt* of the novel; she belongs almost wholly to the supernatural. It is likely that Grushina is also a witch; she is a known fortune-teller. Nevertheless, this witch nature is hidden under layers of dirt, and her involvement in the petty affairs of the town serves to ingrain her in *byt*. In a sense Vershina and Grushina may be considered the two aspects of a total grotesque personality: the demonic predominates in Vershina, but *poshlost'* is more obvious in Grushina.

The most unusual and most seemingly mismatched of the potential fiancées for the dull-witted, gloomy Peredonov are the three lively, attractive, intelligent Rutilov sisters. Even so, the possibility of a match between Peredonov and the Rutilov girls is to be taken seriously within the world of *The Petty Demon*. While it is repeated many times that the girls are attractive, gay, and lively, they are not drawn through emphasis on significant physical features. The sisters are characterized rather by secondary effects, such as the foods they eat and the atmosphere they create about them and, especially, by literary and folk allusions. The Rutilov home is an example of impeccable neatness and care; it is dust-free, pleasant-smelling, colorful—the very opposite of the Peredonov and Grushina households. The sisters' home conveys the appearance that those who live there belong to the best circles of local society and are in every way proper. But the foods they eat—fruit, nuts, halvah, and imported liqueurs—suggest something unusual.

The Rutilov girls are introduced into the novel through a curious scene. Their brother, so he thinks, has persuaded Peredonov to marry one of them. But Peredonov has a condition: he demands that each sister state how she would please him. The oldest Daria says she would bake pancakes; the second Lyudmila that she would collect gossip; and the youngest Valeriya tells Peredonov that he must guess for himself how she would please him. These answers provide a comic touch because, with their reference to appetite (pancakes), scandal, and eroticism (Valeriya's vague hint), they play directly to the *poshlost'* and coarseness in Peredonov. More importantly, this scene is a clear echo of the opening lines of Pushkin's fairy tale "Tsar Saltan" ("Skazka o Tsare Saltane" . . .") in which three fair maidens relate how they would please the tsar if he would marry them: the first would arrange a banquet, the second weave linen, and the third would give birth to a hero.[13] This allusion to "Tsar Saltan" casts the Rutilov girls into the roles of "fair maidens" of the Russian fairy tale, thus suggesting that they are best visualized as the perfect but nondescript beauties of Russian folk art. Peredonov by implication becomes a remolding of the tsar—and in a weirdly perverted way, his ability to choose from almost any of the young girls in town makes him a local autocrat. Of course, in Peredonov the color and splendor of the fairy-tale world have degenerated to *poshlost'*—appetite, scandal, and vulgar eroticism. Moreover, if the comparison between the scenes in *The Petty Demon* and "Tsar Saltan" can be sustained, there is the additional hint that at least the two older sisters may have evil powers. In the fairy tale the tsar marries the youngest, and the others, who become the palace cook and the palace weaver, work toward her destruction.

The suggestion that the fairy-tale beauty of the Rutilov sisters may conceal a sinister nature is borne out by comparisons of the sisters to witches. Peredonov calls them witches immediately after refusing to marry them. Moreover, in their frenzied drinking, singing, and dancing they are likened to witches celebrating their Sabbath on Bald Mountain (181). Perhaps it is in view of their identity within the novel's demonology, and not of their attractiveness and seeming propriety, that the sisters should be viewed as serious candidates for marriage with Peredonov.

Lyudmila attains an identity apart from her sisters in her relationship with Sasha Pylnikov, the fourteen-year-old schoolboy with whom she falls in love. The exotically sensuous games of the young couple run counterpoint to the coarse relationship between Peredonov and Varvara. Yet, aside from clear aesthetic differences, there are suggestions that Lyudmila may in fact be very much like Peredonov.

In addition to the metaphor of the witch, certain other comparisons play a vital role in Lyudmila's presentation: she is also called a *rusalka* and a devil. In Russian folk belief the *rusalka* was an unclean spirit, often descended from an unbaptized child, who appeared naked, with loose, flowing hair, and who often drowned or tickled her victim to death.[14] Lyudmila is first called a *rusalka* by Sasha after she wins a mock wrestling match. Later she compares herself to a *rusalka* and, at the same time, acknowledges her pagan love of bodily beauty and the joy she finds in pain (323). Some of her actions reveal that she, like Peredonov, is sadistic. She pinches Sasha's cheeks until red spots appear; she pulls his ear; and she makes him kiss her knees, during which she has an expression of "triumphant cruelty on her face" (216, 213, 318). Furthermore, she has an erotic-sadistic dream in which she takes pleasure in watching Sasha be whipped (182). Still another link connecting Lyudmila to Peredonov is the metaphor of the devil. Daria, referring to Lyudmila's relationship with Sasha, repeats the common saying "The devil has bound himself to an infant" ("Chort s mladentsem sviazalsia," 218) and then specifically identifies Lyudmila as this devil.

Sasha is introduced into *The Petty Demon* through a rumor which Grushina tells Varvara of a boy posing as a girl in order to snare Peredonov and find a husband. Thus, although a connection is not explicitly made, it appears that Sasha too is introduced as a possible bride for Peredonov. He is one of the few genuinely likeable characters in the novel, yet even he has a dual nature. The motif of metamorphosis is basic to his presentation; his physical delineation turns on his attractiveness and his resemblance to a girl. He is slender and dark, with mysteriously sad eyes and long blue-black lashes. His name too suggest a duality: he is almost always called "Sasha," a diminutive form of both "Alexander" and "Alexandra." The smoothness of his skin, his rosy cheeks and blushing, and his high chest cause him to be taken for a girl, and at the same time it is these traits which are the source of sensuous appeal for Lyudmila. The erotic games in which Sasha and Lyudmila engage play on the questionable status of his sex. Lyudmila delights in dressing Sasha in her own clothing, and she collaborates with her sisters in sending Sasha to the town masquerade dressed as a girl—a geisha.

The ambiguous nature of Sasha's sex seems to be connected with the metaphor of the werewolf. Varvara calls Sasha a werewolf almost as soon as she hears about him, and within a few pages the same term is applied to Peredonov's cat (142,146).[15] In a subsequent dream, Peredonov imagines that Sasha and his cat are enticing him somewhere in werewolf-like fashion: "Pylnikov led him along dark and dirty streets, and the cat ran alongside, and its green eyes glimmered . . . (230)." After Sasha's landlady surprises the couple and finds Sasha dressed as a girl, she forbids him to visit Lyudmila. Thus, for the fittings for the geisha costume and for the masquerade itself, Sasha must escape through the window of his room at night. These nocturnal ventures which he makes for the purpose of "appearing to be a girl" suggest metamorphosis and hint at his werewolf nature. Lyudmila also alludes to this when, during their erotic games, she puns on the expressions "who wants" (*kto zhelaet*) and "who bays" (*kto zhe laet*, 208).[16]

Even Sasha, the most appealing creature in the novel, has an identity within the demonology of *The Petty Demon*. The werewolf, however, has a particular significance in Sologub's art; it often stands as a symbol of a wistful, nostalgic longing for a primeval existence and an escape from everyday reality (especially *poshlost'*).[17] It is meaningful that Sasha's nostalgia should reveal itself particularly after a visit from Peredonov, the novel's prime embodiment of *poshlost'* (155).

In addition to the above characters, who play fairly major roles in Peredonov's life, the novel contains a vast number of minor characters, most of whom are also grotesque. Peredonov's disheveled and habitually drunk landlady is a striking example of a witch. It is she who has a spell cast on Peredonov's old hat, and she returns Peredonov's cat with rattles on its tail. As the town ruffians the Avdeev boys are responsible for the execution of much foul play: they tar Marta's gates, break Peredonov's windows, and throw litter into Peredonov's carriage after his wedding. They seem to "spring from the earth" and be "swallowed up by the earth," a suggestion that they are best understood as unclean spirits which, in folk superstition, appear and disappear in this fashion (251).[18] Even the town functionaries whom Peredonov visits to ward off possible slander are grotesque. They are drawn through the exaggeration of certain features and through the complementary presentations of their houses.

As we have seen in several instances, literary and folklore allusions shape the visual images of characters and aid in interpreting their activities. One of the more fantastic personages in *The Petty Demon* whose creation depends largely on literary allusion is the alleged author of the letters promising Peredonov the inspectorship, Princess Volchanskaya. The Princess never actually appears in the novel, yet, Peredonov suspects that she is nearby spying on him, and in his imagination she assumes the form of a two-hundred-year-old "yellow, wrinkled, hunchbacked, fang-toothed, evil" woman (336). He suspects that she may be hiding in a pack of cards as either the queeen of hearts or the queen of spades, and though he attempts to burn the whole pack, the princess rises up out of the flames, hissing and spitting on the fire (314).

The comparison of Princess Volchanskaya to the queen of spades is highly significant because it provides a clear reference to Pushkins's tale "The Queen of Spades." It is possible to observe a number of parallels in the plots of the two works. In Pushkin's tale the protagonist Germann relies on an old Countess to reveal a mysterious secret whereby he may win a fortune at cards. This thought becomes an obsession with him, and his entire fate is placed in the hands of the old woman. The vehicle through which he hopes to obtain an audience with the Countess is her poor-relative ward Lizaveta, and he courts her to this purpose. In *The Petty Demon* Peredonov is obsessed with his inspectorship just as Germann is with the secret of the cards; and he relies on the Princess, who is supposedly Varvara's patron, to obtain it for him.

The image of the old Countess of "The Queen of Spades" offers a visual referent for the grotesque image of Princess Volchanskaya. In Pushkin's tale the Countess appears as (1) a young, beautiful, but frivolous woman of the 1770's, (2) an ancient, hideous woman of the 1830's who is trying to preserve her long faded beauty, (3) a corpse, (4) an apparition, and (5) the queen of spades.[19] A particularly grotesque image of the Countess is achieved through the incongruity of her puffy, decrepit flesh and the various adornments she grafts on it to make herself younger: a powdered wig, rouge, elegant dresses which are sixty years out of fashion, and, an item from the floral world, roses.

There is a suggestion that the Countess, like Princess Volchanskaya, may have a witch nature, the last thing Germann calls her before drawing his pistol to force the secret from her is "old witch."[20] But the Countess does not reveal the secret while she is alive, and this leads to another similarity between the Countess and the Princess. Even though Princess Volchanskaya never appears corporally in *The Petty Demon*, she exercises an overwhelmingly destructive infuence on Peredonov's fate. His belief that she has turned against him leads him into a deeper terror and suspicion of others which culminates in the murder of Volodin and his collapse into total senselessness. Similarly, it is not as a living woman, but as a corpse, an apparition, and as the queen of spades that the Countess has her most powerful influence on Germann's fate. She squints at him from her casket and then appears to him as an apparition to reveal the secret by which he can win his fortune. And, on the final day of gambling, when Germann draws the queen of spades instead of an ace, he perceives in the card figure the old woman mocking him.[21] Germann, like Peredonov, collapses into total insanity. The similarities in plot structure between "The Queen of Spades" and *The Petty Demon*, the image of a decaying witch-like woman, and, above all, the shared metaphor of the queen of spades suggest that Princess Volchanskaya is best understood as a literary reincarnation of Pushkin's old Countess.

The Petty Demon also contains a number of grotesque characters whose creations proceed not from the usual image of man, but rather from the non-human world. In these characters the grotesque is achieved largely through humanization. These bizarre creatures include card figures, Peredonov's cat, and the *nedotykomka*. In his delirium Peredonov sees playing cards strutting before him and assuming the forms of familiar people. The eights become "werewolf-students," and he recognizes in the postman, who brings the second forged letter, a knave who caused him to lose at cards (255, 310, 256). His cat too becomes an object of terror. Unlike the usual black famulus of witches and sorcerers, it is white and fat; but Peredonov fears that it has the power to bewitch him, and he suspects that it has denounced him to the authorities (242). In his imagination the cat assumes fantastic proportions, now becoming the fairy-tale "puss in boots," now a young man with a red moustache who cannot stop sniffing (337, 287).

The most important of the non-human creatures in *The Petty Demon* is the *nedotykomka*, a gray spirit which appears in the midst of the incense during the blessing of Peredonov's new apartment and torments him from this point to the murder of Volodin. The name "nedotykomka" means "not-quite-pokeable-female-creature," and it points to the spirit's elusiveness. In contrast to all the other characters, the *nedotykomka*'s pictorial delineation is not the product of the distortion of a familiar form. It is "faceless," a creature of "undefined outlines" (156). Therefore, it is difficult to visualize the spirit, although not entirely impossible. An abundance of perceptual criteria is used in the spirit's delineation: it is smelly; noisy, and extremely active. These traits perhaps indicate that the *nedotykomka* is primarily a presence to be felt, and only secondarily a creature to be visualized.

The spirit is gray, and the repetition of this color suggests that it is to be understood as a characterizing epithet. As a color gray conveys a feeling of drabness—colorlessness—rather than of pigmentation and thus is of limited value in attempting to picture the *nedotykomka*. Other attributives point to the sense in which the spirit's grayness is to be understood: it is also "dirty" and "dusty" (286, 308). Probably the main function of the color "gray" is to link the *nedotykomka* and Peredonov to each other; gray is indicative of the boredom, squalor, and *poshlost'* of his existence. One of the most highly sensual traits used in the depiction of the *nedotykomka* is smell. The spirit is called "stinking" (*voniuchaia*, 308). Although smell provides an obvious feeling of the spirit's presence, the use of this particular word, which is vulgar and characteristic of Peredonov, suggests that it may be a way he perceives it, rather than an actual attribute of the creature. This trait too joins the *nedotykomka* to Peredonov's soul and to his apartment, which is foul smelling and which is, in its way, a mirror of his soul.

Sound and motion are other essential ingredients in the creation of the *nedotykomka*. The spirit continually laughs and jeers at Peredonov, and it is this mockery which more than anything else instills horror into him and drives him to such acts as chopping the table under which the spirit is sitting (310). The *nedotykomka* is continually quivering, fidgeting, rolling about on the floor, and jumping. Both the spirit's tremendous noise and its quivering, whirling motion connect it with Peredonov's psychic state. They provide an index of the restlessness and agitation in his soul. These traits also suggest a possibility for visualizing the *nedotykomka*.

Although the *nedotykomka* does not smile (image), but laughs (sound), one may construe the visual representation of this laughter as a taunting smile, a smirk, or a leer. The spirit can perhaps best be pictured as a leer implanted on a small, amorphous grayish mass, which is continually whirling about Peredonov, yet which is impossible to touch or approach. If this is correct, then the leer adds a human element to the delineation of the *nedotykomka* and renders it grotesque.[22] Moreover, the spirit's motion may be understood as an uninterrupted dance of death.

Peredonov is the only character in the novel who sees the *nedotykomka*, and he, of course, is insane. Yet, while there can be no doubt that the spirit reflects his soul and is symptomatic of his insanity, there is reason to believe that the *nedotykomka* has a broader meaning than would be possible if it were merely the projection of a madman's fantasy. Rather, this gray spirit is integral to the total vision of the world in *The Petty Demon* and, possibly, in Sologub's work in general. This is suggested partly by the spirit's presence outside the novel; the *nedotykomka* is the subject of an earlier lyric.[23] However, the most convincing evidence that the spirit is a reality existing beyond the confines of Peredonov's consciousness is the particular way in which it is presented in the novel itself. Although Peredonov is the only character who sees the *nedotykomka*, nevertheless, it is never presented totally through his vision. Unlike the other fantasy creatures, the spirit never occurs in a dream; and, it is never presented through interior monologue, which would bring the reader directly into Peredonov's consciousness without the obvious presence of the narrator's voice. Rather, the *nedotykomka* is always presented as a statement of fact within the narration, and this signifies that the narrator shares in the vision of the spirit.

Here one must consider the particular nature of the narrator. In *The Petty Demon* there is minimal distance between the implied author and the narrator who retains almost absolute control over the telling of the story. We can term this narrator "reliable": his testimony is to be considered true and his judgment is valid.[24] When the *nedotykomka* is introduced, the narrator's voice is totally dominant. The language is highly poetic and thus uncharacteristic of the dull-witted, vulgar Peredonov; rather, it is close to that of the earlier lyric: "An amazing creature of indefinite features ran out from somewhere—a small, gray,

, nimble *nedotykomka*. It chuckled, and quivered, and whirled around
lonov. . . . It quivered and teased—gray, faceless, nimble (156)."[25] In later
ages the device of narrated perception is often in evidence.[26] Here, though
the spirit's presence is narrated, Peredonov's experiencing consciousness is
brought in through the use of modal words characteristic of him and of the
present tense: "The *nedotykomka* ran about . . . and squealed. It was dirty,
smelly, repulsive, and terrifying. . . . If only someone would deliver him with
some word or sweep it away. But there are no friends here . . . (308–9)."

The *nedotykomka* must be considered a feature of the cosmos of *The Petty
Demon* and not just the hallucination of a madman. It is perhaps best understood as a symbolization of evil. The creature's eerie laughter hints at a diabolical nature, and the attributive "faceless" may link it to the devil who is also
faceless. Some of the forms which the spirit assumes, such as that of a dog and
column of dust, are linked to beliefs about the devil in folk superstition.[27]
Particularly meaningful is the guise of the serpent which it assumes at the masquerade. As the form of the devil in the Biblical story of the Fall, this guise con-
nects the spirit with primordial evil. Yet, while the *nedotykomka* is no doubt a
manifestation of the evil which pervades the cosmos of *The Petty Demon*, it
should not be understood as a gradiose symbol of denial. Rather, the spirit
embodies petty evil—*poshlost'* and spite raised to cosmic dimensions. The
grayness, dirtiness, and dustiness of the spirit point clearly to this.

A recent critic has suggested that the real import of the *nedotykomka* is
that it signals Peredonov's contact with another reality.[28] His vision of the spirit can in fact be understood as a sort of self-transcendence. He is initiated into
a truth beyond himself and beyond the limits of visual reality—for the other
characters do not see it. Of all the characters in the novel, Peredonov seems the
most total in his devotion to petty evil. If, as an emodiment of this evil, the
nedotykomka can be considered his "god," then, in religious terms, Peredonov
is a fully integrated man. He has reached a stage of "transfiguration," albeit in
a negative sense, and his vision of this dirty, gray spirit can possibly be construed as the converse of the vision of light of Orthodox mysticism.[29]

THE COSMOS

Implicit in the delineations of most of the strange creatures of *The Petty
Demon* is the motif of the mask; in most cases a human identity veils a perhaps
truer identity within a demonology. The idea of the mask was, in fact, basic to
Sologub's conception of art. He believed that the purpose of art is to remove
appearances or masks (*lichiny*) and to reveal the true Countenance of things
(*Lik*).[30] In *The Petty Demon* the tension between appearance and reality is basic
not only to the depictions of individual characters, but to the presentation of
the cosmos as a whole.

The aggregate of dual-natured creatures in the novel presents a picture of
an utterly bizarre society, and the physical environment in which these strange
characters are placed intensifies this impression. Among the more important
places of action are Peredonov's dirty, stifling apartment and Grushina's dusty
house; the unpaved dusty and muddy streets of a provincial town; Vershina's
lush, enchanted garden; a billiard hall filled with smoke; the pleasant home of
the Rutilov girls; and a splendidly colorful seventeenth-century Russian church.

These settings are too lush and too disparate to be typical of a normal, drab Russian provincial town. Rather, this is typical scenery for the grotesque. The visual world of people and places which emerges is an amalgamation of the ugly and the beautiful, the everyday and the exotic, the vulgar and the supernatural.

The activities of the town as a whole are significant in suggesting the true nature of the cosmos. Scandalmongering is a basic preoccupationn of this society, and it is also a sign of *poshlost'* and spitefulness. Rumor has it that the Marshall of the Nobility Veriga wears a corset; Grushina and Rutilov taunt Peredonov with stories that his students drink, smoke, and chase girls; Peredonov's visits to the town functionaries are prompted by fear of scandal, and the content of the conversations during these visits is largely gossip. Probably the most significant rumors are those concerned with Sasha. He is introduced through a story tha the is a girl. This rumor prompts Peredonov to visit Sasha and then to report the scandal to the headmaster and to spread the story throughout the school. Lyudmila, who is loved in the town for her charming, lively way of relating gossip, hears this rumor and, curious, goes to visit Sasha. Preposterous as it may seem; this rumor contains a glimmer of truth, for Sasha's characterization turns on the suggestion that he has the ability to change into a girl. Later in the novel Peredonov spreads a story that Lyudmila has perverted Sasha. Grushina and Varvara write letters about this to the headmaster, and he resolves to investigate. Lyudmila, however, enchants him into believing an outright lie—that her relationship with Sasha is perfectly innocent. Although Peredonov is telling the truth, he is vulgar, coarse, and obviously insane; Lyudmila is believed because she is attractive, sweet-smelling, and well-dressed. Rumor thus serves as a means of confusing appearance and reality. Moreover, in the strange world of the novel, the most believable tales seem to contain a hint of truth.

Although a sense of stagnation and inertia pervades the atmosphere of *The Petty Demon*, the pace of the action is frenzied. Much of the hustle and bustle is centered around getting people married. Most obvious are the attempts to catch Peredonov, but, in addition, Peredonov hopes to find a wife for Volodin, and Grushina and Vershina are looking for husbands. The desire to marry is prompted not by feelings of mutual attraction, but by an apparently rootless conviction that one simply should be married. Many petty abuses are connected with the business of marriage: Volodin is persuaded to have Marta's gates tarred because he was rejected as her fiance; Vershina tells Peredonov of the forgery largely because her plan to marry him to Marta failed; Grushina arranges for litter to be thrown into the carriage of the newly-wed Peredonovs. Marriage is, of course, a legitimate human concern, and, moreover, the wedding ceremony serves as an excellent reflection of a society's customs—an embodiment of *byt*. Yet, within folk superstition, weddings are among the most basic activities of witches and demons.[31] It is probable that in the world of the novel *byt* is a sham and the rage to marry is in reality deviltry.

The question of motivation is important. The sense of motion out-of-control conveyed by rumor and the instinctiveness of the desire to marry are indications that reflective, rational behavior is somehow absent from the cosmos of the novel. Yet, at least an appearance of cause-and-effect motivation can be found. At the outset, the basic intrigue unfolds as a conflict between Peredonov's quest for a promotion and the attempts of various townspeople to marry him. Peredonov's visits to the town officials, his attempts to find Volodin a wife, his frequent attendance at church, as well as Varvara's arranging for the forgery of the letters and Vershina's maneuvers to get Peredonov into her garden all fit into the development of this intrigue and are thus provided with a seemingly clear motivation. It is true that these events are at times accompanied by other, seemingly unmotivated acts, such as Peredonov's molesting his cat, soiling his walls, teasing his students, and, especially, by malicious town gossip—all of which seem to originate in pure spite. But, at least for the first part of the novel, this secondary strain is subordinate to and integrated within the mainline development of Peredonov's quest and the attempts to marry him. It is possible to say that the image of the cosmos which emerges in this part of the novel is one in which there exists a certain logic to human behavior.

However, about the time of the appearance of the *nedotykomka*, the uninterrupted, sequential development of this intrigue is broken, and many small episodes, having very little to do with Peredonov's quest for promotion or attempts to marry him, are introduced. Just prior to the spirit's appearance an incident in which Peredonov steals a pound of raisins and blames his servent is related; Sasha is introduced and Peredonov visits his lodgings. Just after the *nedotykomka*'s appearance the narration shifts to the story of the tarring of Marta's gates and then to Peredonov's meeting with the headmaster of the school. Now too the erotic affair between Sasha and Lyudmila gets underway. In a word, the narration becomes fragmented, and events are neither a development of the main intrigue nor are they provided with a clear motivation. The rational ordering of the world of *The Petty Demon* is revealed as an illusion; chaos, within which the *nedotykomka* has its existence, replaces cosmos.

The motif of insanity, which often accompanies the presentation of the grotesque, plays a significant role in *The Petty Demon*. Peredonov suffers from paranoid schizophrenia, and this affliction is portrayed with clinical accuracy. He lives in suspicion and fear of both people and objects, and his most specific fear is that he will be poisoned. In taking measures to defend himself, Peredonov displays an amazing degree of activity. Serious aberrations in conceptual thinking are evident in Peredonov's portrayal, and these are perhaps best reflected in his language: words take on a literalness and acquire magic properties. Medically speaking, the central event in Peredonov's insanity is the appearance of the *nedotykomka*; this signals the point at which he enters into a fantasy world and begins to have hallucinations.[32] The accuracy of Sologub's depiction of paranoia caused one of his contemporaries to cite the novel as an example of new, psychological, rather than sociological, realism.[33] However, it seems that like *byt* and motivation, psychological verisimilitude is another mask in the novel. It provides a protective veil and an acceptable explanation for outrageous behavior and fantastic creatures. This is most strongly suggested by the objectivity of the *nedotykomka*: the spirit is a fact of the world of the novel and not solely of Peredonov's fantasy. The indication is that Peredonov's insanity grants him a vision of the truth that the world is chaotic, hostile, destructive, and evil.

The true face of the cosmos of *The Petty Demon* is revealed at the masquerade. Most of the weird creatures whom the reader has met one by one in the course of the novel are now gathered together under one roof. The masquerade includes the motif of insanity in two ways: it suggests that the entire town is insane, more like a madhouse than provincial Russia, and it removes the protective veil of "insanity" from what Peredonov perceives and reveals that his vision of the cosmos is accurate. A conflict of appearance and reality is evident in the very announcement of the masquerade. Rumors circulate that the prizes will be a cow for the best female costume and a bicycle for the best male costume. But, as soon as the townspeople have become enthusiastic about the prizes, it is discovered that in reality only a fan and an album will be given. Even so, almost the entire town turns out for the event. The possible gaiety and festivity of the occasion is dampened from the beginning by the knowledge that the hall seems a little dirty and the crowd is already slightly drunk: *poshlost'* has invaded the realm of the exotic.

The costumes are significant. Varvara does not labor over hers; she wears a mask with a stupid face, rouges her elbows, puts on an apron, and goes as a "cook straight from the stove (347)." This slovenly outfit is similar to her usual dress; thus she goes as herself though slightly costumed. Grushina chooses to dress as the goddess Diana. Her costume is immodest, but it has many folds in which she can hide the sweets she steals for her children. The scantiness of this costume reveals that she has flea bites on her body. She is her vulgar, indecent self and, significantly, her costume is interpreted not as the goddess Diana, but the dog Dianka. The Rutilov girls do not fuss over their costumes: Daria goes as a Turkish woman, Lyudmila as a gypsy, and Valeriya as a Spanish dancer. They dress exotically, but not outlandishly, and in this sense they too are themselves. Sasha, of course, goes as a geisha, and the import of this costume is that it plays on the ambiguous status of his sex. Neither Volodin nor Peredonov wears a costume. Volodin displays his ram-like, bestial nature by stomping wildly and by tearing ferociously at Sasha when the crowd attacks him. Peredonov has no need of a costume; he has achieved an inverted sort of integration in his devotion to petty, spiteful evil, and in him mask and face are one. It is at the masquerade that the *nedotykomka* too is finally attired in its true garb: the evil serpent.

In all individual instances the costumes worn (or not worn) tend to reveal the identity of the character rather than to hide it. This is also true of the crowd as a whole: it is drunk, vulgar, spiteful, and bestial. This bestiality, to the point of mania, is revealed especially in the savage attack it makes on Sasha after he receives the prize for the best female costume. After the actor Bengalsky has rescued Sasha and taken him from the hall, the final event in the revelation of the true nature of the town occurs. Peredonov, prompted by the *nedotykomka* in the form of a serpent, sets fire to the clubhouse. The townsfolk have gathered together, their bestial and demonic natures have been revealed, and, with Peredonov's arson, the suspicion that this is an inferno becomes a visual reality. The masquerade is now vested in its mask—fire, which is really its face.

The world of *The Petty Demon* is visually close to that of Bosch's hell and Bruegel's proverbs. It is a world in which petty, spiteful evil pervades the atmosphere and swallows up the characters. The *nedotykomka* is the ruler of this world, and Peredonov is the spirit's faithful servant. But, he is only the first of many lesser servants, for the entire cosmos of the novel is populated with petty, spiteful beasts, witches, and devils. The artistic means through which *poshlost'* and the demonic are integrated is the grotesque.

In *The Petty Demon* one can see a continuation of the tradition in Russian literature which perceives evil as petty; Peredonov may legitimately be considered a relative of both Gogol's Chichikov and Dostoevsky's Smerdyakov. It is also possible to see in this novel an inversion of attempts in Russian and world literature to depict the totally good man. In this sense a recent critic's understanding of Peredonov as a *fin de siècle* redoing of Don Quixote is justified.[34] But there is no reason why this comparison cannot be extended to include other saintly figures. Peredonov might also be understood as an inversion of Dostoevsky's Myshkin. Sologub seems to be attempting to depict the totally evil man in the totally evil society. In the final analysis it may be possible to understand the novel as a reversal of the Christian myth of redemption in which Peredonov is an inversion of Sologub's conception of Christ.

NOTES

*This study is a revised version of a much longer study which appeared under the same title in R. Freeborn, R.R. Milner-Gulland, and C.A. Ward, ed., *Russian and Slavic Literature* (Cambridge, Mass: Slavica Publishers, 1976), pp. 137–74.

1. Respectively, Victor Erlich, *Gogol* (New Haven: Yale Univ. Press, 1962), p. 5, and Lee Byron Jennings, *The Ludicrous Demon: Aspects of the Grotesque in German Post-Romantic Prose* (Berkeley and Los Angeles: Univ. of California Press, 1963), p. 17. In general, Jennings closely approximates what this study understands as the definition of the grotesque.

2. Jennings (*The Ludicrous Demon* . . . p. 10) says that the grotesque object is perceived as simultaneously ludicrous and fearsome.

3. Wolfgang Kayser, *The Grotesque in Art and Literture* (New York: McGraw Hill, 1963), pp. 32–33, 181, suggests that the grotesque effect in Bosch may be weakened because his paintings seem to contain a symbology which is decipherable within the usual Christian framework. Kayser postulates a vision of cosmic absurdity as a condition for the grotesque.

4. Jennings, *The Ludicrous Demon*, p. 20.

5. Often in a literary work the creation of the grotesque is accompanied by an uneven narrative style which draws attention to the vocal texture by employing such devices as verbal nonsense and cacophony. Ludmila Foster defines the literary grotesque totally in terms of a style which "employs the devices of distortion and shift to create an effect of absurdity of estrangement," "The Grotesque: A Method Of Analysis," *Zagadnienia rodzajów literackich*, Vol. IX, No. 1 (Lódz, 1966), p. 81. She also suggests that in *The Petty Demon* the grotesque effect is weakened by the absence of this style. "A Configuration of the Non-Absolute: The Structure and Nature of the Grotesque," *Zagadnienia rodzajów literackich*, Vol. IX, No. 2 (Lódz, 1967), p. 39.

6. A.A. Izmailov, "F. Sologub o svoikh proizvedeniiakh, *Birzhevye vedomosti* (Oct. 16, 1906), p. 3. B. Yu. Ulanovskaya maintains that the model for Peredonov was a certain Ivan Ivanovich Strakhov who taught with Sologub in the Velikie Luki district in the late 1880's. Ulanovskaya also appears to have located prototypes for Varvara and Volodin, "O prototipakh romana F. Sologuba *Melkii bes*," *Russkaia literatura*, Vol. XII, No. 3 (1969), pp. 181–84.

7. F.K. Sologub, *Melkii bes*, in *Sobranie sochinenii*, Vol. VI, S. Peterburg: Shipovnik, 1909–14. All subsequent quotations from *The Petty Demon* will be from this edition and will be indicated by page number in the text.

8. Gogol is perhaps the best-known Russian author to use the pig in this sense. For a discussion of folk beliefs about common forms of the devil see S.V. Maksimov, *Nechistaia sila. Nevedomaia sila*, in *Sobranie sochieneii*, Vol. XVIII (S. Peterburg: Prosveshchenie, 1908–13), p. 11.

9. *Ibid.*, p. 12

10. *Ibid.*, p. 8.

11. Galina Selegen', *Prekhitraia viaz'* (Washington: Victor Kamkin, 1968), pp. 147–76, discusses the language of *The Petty Demon* at length.

12. The names "Vershina" and "Grushina" are interesting. The word "vershina" denotes a "summit" and the phonetically similar verb "vershit," is commonly used in the sense of "to sway destiny" (*vershit' sud'bami*). Her name thus suggests that she may be the major witch of the novel, and it points to the influence which she has on Peredonov's destiny. Grushina's name is from the Russian word for "pear," and it adds a comic touch to her delineation.

13. A.S. Pushkin, *Polnoe sobranie sochinenii v desiati tomakh*, Vol. IV, (Moskva: AN SSSR, 1963), p. 429.

14. Vladimir Dal', *Toklovyi slovar' zhivogo veliko-russkogo iazyka*, vol. III (S. Peterburg, Moskva, 1914), p. 1744.

15. The word "oboroten' " is not an exact equivalence of the English "werewolf." It has a broader meaning and signifies a creature which is able to change from a human to an animal or plant nature at will. See Maksimov, *Nechistaia sila*, p. 118.

16. Maksimov reports similar punning on the part of *rusalki*. See *Nechistaia sila*, p. 118.

17. See, for example, Sologub, "Belaia sobaka," *Sob. soch.*, Vol. VII, pp. 11–18.

18. Maksimov, *Nechistaia sila*, p. 260.

19. Pushkin, *Polnoe sobranie* . . ., Vol. VI, pp. 319–56.

20. *Ibid.*, p. 341.

21. *Ibid.*, p. 355.

22. Mikhail Bakhtin maintains that the mouth is most significant in creating a grotesque image of the body, *Rabelais and His World* (Cambridge: M.I.T. Press, 1968), p. 316.

23. Sologub, "Nedotykomka seraia," *Sob. soch.*, Vol. V, p. 14.

24. See Wayne C. Booth, *The Rhetoric of Fiction* (Chicago: University of Chicago Press, 1968), pp. 169–209, for an extended discussion of reliability.

25. See Sologub, "Nedotykomka seraia," *Sob. soch.*, Vol. V, p. 14.

26. For a discussion of narrated perception see Ronald J. Lethoce, "Narrated Speech and Consciousness," Doctoral Dissertation, University of Wisconsin, 1969.

27. Maksimov, *Nechistaia sila*, p. 8.

28. F.D. Reeve, *The Russian Novel* (New York, 1966), p. 315.

29. Anon., *Orthodox Spirituality* (London: S.P.C.K., 1968), pp. 96–97.

30. Sologub, "Edinyi put' L'va Tolstogo," *Sob. soch.*, Vol. X, p. 196.

31. Maksimov, *Nechistaia sila*, p. 8.

32. Sologub's depiction of paranoia is in accord with the following: Sigmund Freud, "On the Mechanism of Paranoia," *General Psychological Theory* (New York, 1963), pp. 29–49; Carl G. Jung, *The Psychogenesis of Mental Disease in The Collected Works of C.G. Jung*, Vol. III (New York, 1960); and Jacob Kasanin, ed., *Language and Thought in Schizophrenia* (New York, 1944).

33. Kogan, *Ocherki* . . ., p. 106.

34. Andrew Field, "Translator's Preface," in F. Sologub, *The Petty Demon* (Bloomington: Indiana University Press, 1970).

Symbolic Patterning in Sologub's *The Petty Demon*[1]

Charlotte Rosenthal and Helene Foley

THE PARALLELS AND contrasts between the main plot of *The Petty Demon* and the subplot involving Lyudmila and Sasha are repeated and striking, but difficult to evaluate. To give but a few examples: in one scene, Peredonov and Ershova dance, and Peredonov's movements are described as mechanical and lifeless.[2] In another scene, Lyudmila and her sisters dance, and their movements are described as ecstatic and lively.[3] While Peredonov declares that he fears incense and hates all aspects of the Orthodox Church ritual, Lyudmila confesses to Sasha that she loves precisely the ritual accoutrements of the church (137 and 299; 357). How are we to understand the relation between the two plots, and how does the world of Lyudmila and Sasha illuminate or undercut the larger world of the novel? How are we to understand the curious mixture of pleasure and pain which dominates, in different ways, the behavior and emotions of all the characters? Why do both plots end in a violent act of ritualized destruction, a sacrifice or a near sacrifice? In this paper we argue that the task of interpretation must begin with an understanding of the system of allusions in the novel to classical and particularly Greek antiquity.[4] Sologub makes the world of Sasha and Lyudmila represent the beauties and dangers of the pagan. By contrast, Peredonov and his world are insensitive to or eager to pervert the natural world and the possibilities it offers. As the narrator emphasizes, Peredonov did not experience the vital, elemental, Dionysian ecstasies of the natural world because he was blinded by delusions of a separate, individual existence (310–11). A fuller understanding of the "Dionysian ecstasies" which Peredonov finds repellent and hostile, and to which Lyudmila and Sasha are allied, is central to an interpretation of the novel.

The world of Sasha and Lyudmila is defined through a network of allusions to nature and classical mythology. Natural images, especially the sun, flowers, and perfumes[5] dominate their world. Lyudmila would like to melt away under the sun like a cloud (356). She calls Sasha by the affectionate terms "my little sunshine" (245) and "my little sun" (245). Sasha's surname, Pylnikov, is derived from *pyl'nik*, "anther," the pollen bearing part (male) of a plant, usually a double sac.[6] Lyudmila's room always smells of flowers, branches, or the perfume which she loves (228, 365). All the Rutilov sisters, but especially Lyudmila (206) are associated with flowers. Their house has "carefully arranged plants by the windows" (403). Valeriya's kiss to Sasha is like an apple blossom (237). The scenes between Sasha and Lyudmila revolve around flowers and perfume, as Lyudmila responds to the boy like a desiring flower to the sun overhead (244–45).[7] In a poem quoted by Ivanov-Razumnik,[8] Sologub describes beauty as "fragrant"; the beauty of the world of Sasha and Lyudmila is imminent in its natural perfumes.

In Chapter 26 Lyudmila wears Japanese perfume to visit Sasha. The sisters take as the model for Sasha's geisha costume at the masquerade the label on a chorilopsis perfume bottle (379); the robe is patterned with large fantastic flowers by now emblematic of the relation between Sasha and Lyudmila. In an article entitled "The Enmity and Friendship of the Elements,"[9] Sologub finds that the Japanese—like the pagan Greeks to be discussed shortly—celebrate nature, while the Russians are hostile to the elements. Japanese paintings are radiant with the sun's light; their flag displays the rising sun, a red disk on a white field, while the royal standard of the imperial family showed a golden chrysanthemum on a red field. These color groups—red and rose, gold and yellow—pervade Sasha's and Lyudmila's world. Sasha's geisha costume is made from yellow silk and red satin; his parasol and stockings are rose colored silk. Lyudmila's perfume atomizer is dark red glass patterned with gold. Even her cyclamen perfume is described as red and gold: its scent is compared to the reddish-gold glow of the setting sun (243). Lyudmila's room is yellow and gold (237). Her hat is rosy yellow (349), her arms are covered with a yellowish rose material (240), and she loves brightly-colored clothes. Her surname, derived from the Latin "rutilus," meaning red, suggests the brillilant red gems cut from the mineral rutile. In short, while the world of Peredonov is filled with grey and black, the world of Sasha and Lyudmila is brilliant with the passionate colors of flowers, sun, blood, and wine.[10]

Like many of his contemporaries, Sologub admired and idealized classical antiquity. In an article, "Canvas and the Body," for example, Sologub berates modern man for not enjoying the harmony of the naked human body and the natural elements as did classical antiquity.[11] Sologub shared the general "Dionysian" mood of the modernists. Nikolai Berdiaev records Sologub's participation in an imitation Dionysian mystic rite.[12] As Sologub was reticient about influences on his literary development, we do not know the precise sources of Sologub's views on classical antiquity. He was certainly acquainted with the work of I.F. Annensky, the classical Greek scholar, educator, and poet who translated Euripides' *Bacchae* in 1894, accompanied by an introduction and three extensive essays.[13] The influence of this play on *The Petty Demon*, as we shall argue shortly, seems unmistakable. The classicizing poet Dmitry Merezhkovsky used imagery in his early poems which may have inspired Sologub. These poems, written before Sologub finished *The Petty Demon*, include: "Leda," the "mother of beauty," and "The Song of the Bacchae," which praises the sacred howls and Dionysian laughter of its gay maenads, and their abandonment of middle-class morality.[14] Sologub's sources also may have included the French Symbolists, whom he knew well, Volynsky's and Minsky's articles on Nietzsche published between 1895 and 1900, the writing of Lev Shestov on Nietzsche (*The Good in the Teaching of Count Tolstoy and F. Nietzsche*, 1900), and the writings of Nietzsche himself.[15]

For Nietzsche, the classical Greeks lived the purely aesthetic life celebrating creativity, a life which Lyudmila tries to instill in Sasha. Lyudmila, the life-affirming pagan, contrasts with the church-going marionettes of "peredonovshchina." Like Nietzsche, Lyudmila rejects philistinism, stifling conformity, and prudery as a betrayal of nature. Both celebrate the amoral search for a pleasure that encompasses both joy and pain. Sologub's wife, Anastasia Chebotarevskaya, connected Sologub and his fictional heroiness explicitly with the Nietzsche of *Thus Spoke Zarathustra*.[16]

Through the Lyudmila-Sasha relationship, Sologub offers an alternative to "peredonovshchina," a world modeled on an idealized pagan Greece, in harmony with nature, through which the participants can immerse themselves in creativity, joyfulness, self-oblivion, and a pantheistic communion with the natural flux of the universe that Nietzsche calls Dionysian. Through Dionysus man achieved a creative unity with nature and a universal spiritual power. The Dionysian artistic energy bursts forth "from nature herself, *without the mediation of the human artist*," and offers "an intoxicated reality which likewise does not heed the single unit, but even seeks to destroy the individual and redeem him by a mystic feeling of oneness."[17]

Specific allusions to pagan antiquity permeate the world of Sasha and Lyudmila. Her patronymic, Platonovna, Plato's daughter, makes her a spiritual descendent of the pagan philosopher. Lyudmila becomes a goddess or priestess of a Dionysian and pagan cult, while Sasha emerges as the young god himself. Lyudmila's tender kisses remind Sasha of the wave that gave birth to Aphrodite, the Greek goddess of love (235). He calls Lyudmila a *rusalka* (247), as she does herself (356). In Russian folk belief this female figure was a nature spirit, associated with water or the fields, and sometimes a dangerous temptess who brought death to he victims. Lyudmila, too, like the Greek goddess Aphrodite and the *rusalka*, is a nature spirit, a temptress, and a destructive force.

Lyudmila espouses a pagan, and often specifically Dionysian philosophy. She loves the Christian church only for its ritual, incense, singing, and weeping—pagan features that stress ritual, not doctrine, beauty, not repression. Her cyclamen perfume exudes the pagan power of ambrosia and sun (244). She advocates a philosophy of beauty, centered on the human body (356). To Sasha Lyudmila argues that she is a pagan, and should have been born in Athens. She urges on the boy the view that happiness and wisdom are achieved only through madness, self-oblivion, and intuition (361). This same celebration of madness, of the achievement of happiness through self-oblivion, dominates classical literature on Dionysus, and especially the choral odes of Euripides' *Bacchae*.[18]

Sasha, like Lyudmila is explicitly associated with the ancient world through his study of Latin and Greek. Lyudmila calls him a "classicist" and complains that Kokovkina keeps him home to study the Greeks; Sasha asks Lyudmila to cuddle him for good luck so that he can get an "A" in Greek (247). One of Lyudmila's favorite costumes for Sasha is that of a barefoot Athenian boy (360). Peredonov puns that Sasha lives in a "pension without classical languages" (195). While he thus associates Sasha with prostitution and his own fearful, vulgar fantasies, he instinctively, if negatively, associates him with classical culture.

Sasha is Dionysian first and foremost through his sexual ambivalence.[19] His name is either male or female. Throughout the novel his sexual identity causes confusion and he readily passes for a girl at the masquerade. Dionysus in human form was frequently represented as a beautiful young man of ambiguous sexuality, with an enigmatic smile, and dark eyes like the "mysteriously sad" dark eyes of Sasha (212).[20] Zeus entrusted his motherless son Dionysus to be brought up by nymphs, while Sasha is temporarily raised by the nymph-like Rutilov sisters.[21] Both god and boy, through the geisha costume, are associated with the East. Each changes shape and identity through costume. Each, when he enters a new environment, causes widespread and insidious social disruption through his ambivalence and beauty, and threatens to convert his followers to a new cult.[22] Lyudmila visualizes Sasha as a god of beauty, an idol (356), and a boy equal to a god (356); the narrator makes the same point (357). Sasha's immature sexuality stimulates female fantasy rather than lust for direct sexual consummation, as does Dionysus as the leader of women's cults in the *Bacchae*. Dionysus liberates the female in the male, the male in the female, thus undermining traditional gender identity.[23] He turns Pentheus into a woman, and his female followers into men. Peredonov, like Dionysus' royal opponent in the *Bacchae*, is attracted to the Sasha/Dionysus figure, but resists and debases his attraction.

Dionysus, often incarnate as a beast, makes us see the beast in man, not the socially restricted human being. In Lyudmila's pun on the words "who is that barking" (*kto zhe laet*) and "who wishes" (*kto zhelaet*), Sasha becomes a dog; for Sologub the dog can demonstrate its receptivity to nature through its sense of smell.[24] In Lyudmila's first dream a snake wears Sasha's head. Dionysus, himself often manifest in the imagination of his followers as a snake, makes his female followers wreathe their heads and bodies with snakes.[25] The effect of one of Lyudmila's perfumes is like the touch of "joyous, nimble, scaly snakes" (252). Sasha, disguised as a geisha, is described as "nimble" (395), and the *nedotykomka*, which after Sasha's arrival causes madness in Peredonov, is also "nimble" (185,186), and a "nimble little snake" (401).[26] Sasha, through his divine and bestial associations, comes to represent pagan divinity and an ecstatic identification with nature, while Peredonov, like Dionysus' enemy Pentheus in the *Bacchae*, is finally punished and haunted by the very nature he rejects and fears. Pentheus fails to recognize Dionysus' divinity, unlike the other Thebans (and Lyudmila in the novel), in his sexually ambivalent human guise. Hence he is punished with a madness in which he sees the god in bestial form. The mad Peredonov comes to see Sasha as a cat, an evil member of the family of unclean spirits in Russian folk belief.[27]

In his article on the theater, Sologub insists on the inseparability of good and evil, pleasure and pain.[28] The Dionysian cult, like the relation between Lyudmila and Sasha, dissolves the boundaries between madness and sanity, pleasure and pain, tears and laughter. Lyudmila recommends to Sasha suffering and the sweetness of suffering which can be achieved through a full experience of the physical self (356). Passion combines sweetness and youth with pain and tears (361). Lyudmila asks Sasha, "Do you understand, my little sun, when something feels sweet and joyous and painful and you'd like to cry?" (245). Her response to the crucifixion is consistent with this attitude: "You know, sometimes in my dreams,—he's on the cross, and there are droplets of blood on his body" (358). Sasha, in response, wants to sacrifice his body and blood to her desire and his own shame (362).

The Dionysiac is beautiful and dangerous, festive and violent. This ambiguous yet liberating dissolution of cultural oppositions marks Lyudmila's and Sasha's relation from its inception. Her puns to Sasha often mix beauty and cruelty: "Do you want me to scent/suffocate you?" (230) Her pun on *rozochki* (diminuitive of "rose" and of "switch," 245) makes a Dionysiac reconciliation between beauty and violence. In the *Bacchae* Dionysus is "beyond good and evil"; for us, as Tiresias says, "he is what we make of him."[29] The boy-god Sasha has an equally disturbing effect. His blushing cheeks, which he shares with Dionysus, hint at innocence and guilt, or something beyond either. Stories of student orgies and drunkenness are mysteriously associated with his presence, and lead to Peredonov's random and unjust punishments and whippings.

Lyudmila's laughter with Sasha is liberating; for Peredonov the laughter of the Rutilov sisters feeds his paranoia and fear of mockery. In the *Bacchae* the smiling god brings joy to his followers and humiliating mockery to Pentheus, who, like Peredonov, fears such laughter above all things.

Lyudmila's sequence of "torrid African dreams" about Sasha become increasingly destructive, and foreshadow the violence of the masquerade scene. In the first dream, her desire for Sasha is expressed in imagery simultaneously borrowed from Dionysiac cult and biblical Eden—the tree of knowledge (Dionysus was also a tree god).[30] In the second, Lyudmila lies at the shore of a lake, regal in a golden crown. Sasha as a swan suggests the Greek myth of Leda, impregnated by Zeus in the shape of a swan.[31] In Russian folk belief the swan, a former woman, was the most sacred of birds,[32] and a metaphor for a bride in folk songs. The mixture of traditions suits Sasha's ambivalent sexuality. The setting of the second dream introduces a note of decay that undercuts its passion: "It smelled of warm, stagnant water and slime and grass languishing from the sultry heat." (212) In the third dream Lyudmila observes Sasha publicly beaten by naked youths. As he laughs and cries, Lyudmila experiences the ecstasy of self-oblivion and death. Like the "affair" between Lyudmila and Sasha, the dream sequence moves from the innocent, mythic realm to mortality and sexuality, from private to public.

Lyudmila's passion remains unfulfilled and her pleasure in violence is always tinged with beauty and sensuality. Peredonov's similar impulses are gross, literal, and unecstatic. He revels in the ugly violence of tearing off wallpaper (57), whipping school boys, performing a mock funeral for his landlady (71), ripping Varvara's dress (186), and subduing her beautiful body with its harlot's head to his gross lust (102). The Rutilov sisters, when drunk, sing, dance, and become ecstatic and frenzied like Greek maenads (211); the drunken Peredonov dances like a puppet or mechanical doll (69).[33] The Rutilov sisters drink cherry liqueur; Lyudmila asks Sasha on their first meeting if he likes grapes (207). Their drunkenness is by implication Dionysiac, while the vodka-drinking Peredonov never reaches the ecstasy of a union with nature. He fears the country, and feels safe only in closed and stuffy interior spaces.

The climactic masquerade[34] and Peredonov's "sacrificial" killing of Volodin reveal the destruction that ensues from the denial of the Dionysiac. Euripedes' *Bacchae*, the ultimate literary prototype for the festival turned destructive, offers remarkable parallels to Sologub's text. In the *Bacchae*, Dionysus revenges himself on Pentheus for rejecting his cult. He dresses the king as a woman and sends him off to be torn apart by his mother, two aunts, and the women of Thebes, who have been maddened by the god. The festive ecstasy of the women explodes into mob violence. In Greek myth, women (usually three women) often tore apart their children under the influence of Dionysus; in Orphic myths the young god himself is torn and dismembered by Titans.

In Sologub's masquerade, the three fantasy-loving Rutilov sisters, dressed exotically as a gypsy, a Turkish woman, and a Spanish woman, take revenge on the town which has threatened to destroy Lyudmila's affair with Sasha by dressing the young "god" as a geisha and sending him off to a festival in which he barely escapes being torn apart. The townspeople are overpowered by the greed, jealousy and impulse to revenge that has characterized them throughout the novel. In the *Bacchae*, a silence which offers a terrible parody of the preliminary stages of sacrificial ritual proceeds the lynching of Pentheus.[35] A comparable moment of silence intervenes before the judging and the explosion of the crowd at the masquerade (393). Gudaevskaya, significantly costumed as a fertility figure—an ear of corn—leads the lynch mob.[36] But at the last moment the actor Bengalsky, dressed as a beautiful foreigner, wards off the logical tragic consequences of the action as a kind of *deus ex machina*.

Masquerades and festivals allow the participants to break the standard rules of behavior in a temporary fashion that releases social tension and restores a sense of community. But the possibility of explosion remains imminent. The action at the masquerade can be suggestively read in relation to René Girard's theory concerning the origins and role of sacrificial ritual and festival in human society.[37] For Girard, early society enforced the social order through religion. The origin of the religious system and of sacrifice can be found in the unanimous lynching of a scapegoat. Through this generative act, the violence of the community, which results from an uncontrolled proliferation of "mimetic competition," is transferred to a deity.[38] Through religious ritual the community continues to re-act this relation to the god(s), whose beneficial violence ensures peace and order. During times of social crisis, a human sacrifice can serve to re-unite the community and to restore or re-create the religious system. Such "sacrificial crises" emerge when a society is trapped in the kind of religious atrophy and uncontrolled "mimetic competition" and vengefulness that we see in Sologub's novel. Like the Thebes of Pentheus, the townspeople reject Lyudmila and Sasha's Dionysiac cult in its benign form. Yet Peredonov's world fails to enact the mythical scenario of the *Bacchae* in which the sacrificial death of Pentheus establishes the Dionysian cult by violent means. Sasha escapes, and the masquerade aborts and is forgotten. Bengalsky, the *deus ex machina* who interrupts the expected scenario, seems, like Sasha, to have associations with Dionysus. Dionysus was god of and actor in Greek tragedy, and Annensky (XCIV) notes that every two years the god returned from a campaign in India. Like Dionysus in the *Bacchae*, those who consciously adopt the Dionysiac transformation of self through costume and enter into his festival voluntarily remain in control.[39] Dionysus, the seer Tiresias, and Cadmus know how to act. Similarly, for Bengalsky, Sasha's disguise is a mere prank, the masquerade no more than a play. And indeed, this theatrical intervention in a scenario that almost completes the plot of Euripedes' play, does turn the masquerade of the novel into a mere play; for the world of Peredonov is, apparently, not yet ready for a real tragic conversion to the Dionysiac. Instead, Peredonov's perverted sacrifice of Volodin removes the memory of the scandal from the minds of the townspeople, while the scandal itself is obscured by lies.

Peredonov, the embodiment of anti-festivity, comes to the masquerade simply as himself, and ends it by sending the hall up in smoke. Throughout the novel Peredonov, the Pentheus figure, has opposed and perverted the Dionysiac. The main plot of the novel precisely inverts the world of the subplot between Sasha and Lyudmila. Peredonov's sexual and sensual life is gross and devoid of liberating visions of beauty. His pleasure in violence unjustly destroys the lives and property of those around him. He accentuates the worst characteristics of his world and mobilizes it against Sasha. He tries to convert the town, which is only too susceptible, to his own special "religion" of anti-fesitivty and sadistic violence. Like Pentheus, Peredonov cannot understand his own sexuality. He rejects healthy brides for the false Varvara. Pentheus falls prey to the Dionysiac in himself and is lured by Dionysus to dress as a woman. Peredonov at one point tries to differentiate himself from Volodin by wearing a woman's corset (313).

Pentheus fences with Dionysus' false image in a palace which goes up in a blazing demonstration of divinity about him; Peredonov tries to destroy his private demon, the *nedotykomka*, by setting fire to the hall in which the masquerade takes place. In both cases obsessive resistance to Dionysus leads to a distorted view of reality and finally to madness. Yet in the *Bacchae* the mass sacrifice of Pentheus leads to the establishment of the Dionysiac cult in Thebes. In *The Petty Demon* Peredonov helps to destroy the masquerade with his fire. He then substitutes a purely private ritual, performed in isolation from the community, for the cult-establishing public lynching. Peredonov's pervasive fear of nature and its Dionysiac mysteries are finally embodied for him in his double, Volodin the ram, whom he kills by slitting his throat; just as Dionysus in the *Bacchae* sacrificed Pentheus dressed in his ritual garb, Peredonov, in a paranoid rage at the failure of the town to accept his views of the world, sacrifices his ritual double in an explicitly pagan fashion.[40] Both the choice of victim and the mode of death are borrowed from ancient sacrificial practice. But while Peredonov pre-empts the Dionysiac sacrificial scenario for his own perverted ends, the effect of Volodin's death is to distract the town from either the sublimation or recognition of its own greed, vengefulness, jealousy, and repressed sensuality displayed at the masquerade.[41] The parallels with the *Bacchae* serve to underline the almost total repression of the Dionysiac in Sologub's fictional Russia.

The ambiguities of Lyudmila's and Sasha's relationship are precisely those expressed by Euripides in his presentation of Dionysiac cult in the *Bacchae*.[42] Dionysus promises the city of Thebes happiness and ecstasy through his cult, a liberating mixture of pleasure and violence (the tearing apart of wild animals). The women of Thebes, safely isolated from society in the wilds, participate in the cult without becoming directly involved in sexuality. But as the city rejects and intervenes in the cult, the new religion becomes increasingly dangerous. Finally, when the city fails to incorporate the Dionysiac into its social structure by peaceful means, the god forces them to accept it through violence. Similarly, the affair between Sasha and Lyudmila begins quite innocently; Sasha's youth makes consummation impossible from the start. Lyudmila at first obscures the impossibility of the romance from herself, denying Sasha's schoolboy reality in a haze of perfume. In the privacy of her house she can play a modern day Aphrodite or *rusalka*, liberating mind and body through fantasy, maenadic dance and folk song, the medium which for Nietzsche contained "Dionysiac elements" at its core.[43] In isolation her pursuit of pleasure and pain remains innocent. Yet the increasing pressures of the outer world make the amorality of Lyudmila's romance immorality, and turn her to violence and revenge. Daria's song introduces morality into the affair; the naked shepherd leads the naked shepherdess to the water's edge, where "fear chases shame, shame chases fear," and the shepherdess orders the shepherd to forget what he has seen (209). Sasha and Lyudmila are forced to lie, and to resist shame.

Only a life lived apart from the town remains untainted by shame, gossip, and jealousy. Nadezhda ("Hope") Adamenko alone escapes town involvement and gossip in a world of books and gracious hospitality. She generously ignores Volodin's impertinence in proposing to her. The Rutilov sisters act vengefully in a Dionysiac style; they tolerate Peredonov's refusal to marry them, and content themselves with mockery until the town threatens their private life. Nevertheless, they participate in some of the town's activities and are partially susceptible to its mentality. Hence they are increasingly trapped between two worlds.

We conclude, then, that through a system of allusions to the pagan (Greek, Japanese, and Russian), Sologub creates in the Lyudmila-Sasha relationship a world of Dionysiac amoral beauty, violence, and creativity which is opposed and finally destroyed by the unnatural, mechanical, and perverted vengefulness and pettiness of the world of Peredonov. Like Dionysus' cult in the *Bacchae*, the former at first appears to be beyond morality and culture. The hostility of non-initiates direct the volatile, innocent mixture of pleasure and pain toward an explosion of violence. Sasha and Lyudmila resort to lies and deception; her increasingly violent fantasies lead to the near sacrifice of Sasha by the masquerade crowd. The masquerade fails to affirm the unity of contradictions in life, or to unify the town in a collective Dionysiac experience which could transform their way of life. The festival is aborted and forgotten in the wake of Peredonov's mad crime. Like Euripides, Sologub refuses to judge Lyudmila's myth of liberation and beauty; we only know that the world of Peredonov has remained impervious to it.

NOTES

1. This is a slightly revised version of "Symbolic Patterning in Sologub's *Melkii bes*," which appeared in *The Slavic and East European Journal*, Vol. 26, No. 1 (Spring 1982), 43–55.

2. Fedor Sologub, *Melkii bes* (reprint ed.; Letchworth, Eng.: Bradda Books, 1966), 69. All subsequent references to the novel, placed in the article in parentheses, are to this edition.

3. *Ibid.*, 211. Some of the vocabulary that Sologub uses to describe this dance echoes that used by Innokenty Annensky in his essay "Dionis vlegende i kul'te" describing elements of the Dionysiac cult intended to induce ecstasy: ". . . agonizing dances, whirling (a ritual act), running, wild howling, the heady noise of flutes . . . intoxicating drinks." Annensky uses the word *khorovod*, a folk dance form, to refer to the Maenads' dance. See *Vakkhanki, tragediia Evripida*, tr. Innokentii Annenskii (St. Petersburg: Tipografiia Imperatorskoi Akademii nauk, 1894), LXX–LXXI, LXXVII. Subsequent references to this book are placed in parentheses.

4. G.J. Thurston, in his article "Sologub's *Melkiy bes*," *Slavonic and East European Review*, 1 (Jan. 1977) sees the connection between Dionysus and *The Petty Demon*, but he does not work out the implications of this allusion for an interpretation of the novel. The authors of this paper formulated their interpretation without knowing of Thurston's work. We are delighted, however, that he confirms the general direction of our argument.

5. Irene Masing-Delic sees these perfumes as "symbols of the flesh 'transsubstantiated' into ethereal beauty." See "'Peredonov's Little Tear'—Why Is It Shed?," below. Annensky emphasizes the intimate connection between Dionysus and nature. The aim of Dionysiac ritual, he writes, was to fuse man with nature and Dionysus was associated with the forces of nature (LXXI, LXXVII).

6. Stanley Rabinowitz has stressed this derivation in his article "Fedor Sologub's Literary Children," note 22 (see below.) *Pyl'nik* also means "dust coat" or "duster," perhaps indicating simultaneously Peredonov's obsessive perception of Sasha—a symbol of beauty and innocence—as the omnipresent, hateful dust. Masing-Delic suggests that Sasha's surname hints at his ultimate surrender to the "realm of *dust*" (114). Dionysus was the god of the vine, the bringer of fruit.

7. Rabinowitz sees these "ever-present flowers and sweet perfumes" as creating "a climate of sensuality which can only accelerate Sasha's physical desires." Though the discussion of cyclamen perfume reflects Lyudmila's own feelings, it can also be interpreted as an "allegory" about "the course of Sasha's own sexual growth." See below.

8. Ivanov-Razumnik, *O smysle zhizni: F. Sologub, L. Andreev, L. Shestov*, 2d ed. (St. Petersburg: n.p., 1910; reprint ed., Letchworth, Eng.: Bradda Books, 1971), 47. It is also curious that Dionysus was associated with fragrance—Annensky mentions this twice in his essay on Dionysus (LXXX and LXXIII).

9. *Sobranie sochinenii* in 12 vols. (St. Petersburg: Shipovnik, 1909–1912), X, 217.

10. The narrator tells us that Peredonov specifically did not like the colors of the sunset, fire red and gold (320).

11. *Sobranie sochinenii*, X, 210. This is only one of many points in common with Nietzsche. In *The Birth of Tragedy*, Nietzsche praises the Greek "man of culture" for his unalienated, celebratory view of life which differs so radically from that of modern man. See *The Birth of Tragedy*, tr. Walter Kaufmann (New York: Vintage Books, 1967), 59–61.

12. Nicholas Berdyaev, *Dream and Reality: An Essay in Autobiography*, tr. Katharine Lampert (New York: The Macmillan Co., 1951), 162. Thurston also remarks on this incident, 38–39, n. 41.

13. See Nt. 3. Thurston posits this play as "the most important source available to Sologub," 39. He is particularly strong on noting parallels between the *Bacchae* and the novel, especially the identification between Dionysus and Sasha, and Pentheus and Peredonov.

14. Nietzschean themes appear in Merezhkovksy's poetry as early as 1892. One of Lyudmila's dreams recalls the myth of Leda and the swan. Some elements of the landscape in the dream may have been suggested to Sologub by Merezhkovsky's poem. The latter can be found in: D.S. Merezhkovksy, *Sobranie stikhov, 1883–1920g.* (reprint ed., Letchworth, Eng.: Bradda Books, 1969), 77–79. The "Song of the Bacchae" was first published in 1894 in *Severnyi vestnik*, No. 12, 42. On Nietzsche's influence on the Silver Age, see Ann Marie Lane, "Nietzsche in Russian Thought, 1890–1917" (Ph.D. dissertation, University of Wisconsin at Madison, 1976), Chapter One; Bernice G. Rosenthal, "Nietzsche in Russia: The Case of Merezhkovksy," *The Slavic Review*, Sept. 1974, 429–52.

15. For a complete list of writings about Nietzsche in Russia during this period, see Richard D. Davies, "Nietzsche in Russia, 1892–1917: A Preliminary Bibliography, Part 1," *Germano-Slavica*, Vol. II, No. 2 (Fall 1976), 107–46. Davies points out that much of the Russian intelligentsia undoubtedly read Nietzsche in the original German or even in French translations (108).

16. Anastasiia Chebotarevskaia, "Aisedora Dunkan v prozren'iakh Fridrikha Nichshe," *Zolotoe runo*, 4 (1908), 83.

17. *The Birth*, 38. In the preface to the English translation of *The Petty Demon* of 1916, Sologub emphasizes that Peredonov represents the lonely, isolated individual, incapable of directing himself into "the general path of universal life." This notion is similar to Nietzsche's "gospel of universal harmony" and "the mysterious primordial unity," 37 in *The Birth*.

18. See especially *Vakkhanki*, lines 72–82, 378–86, 416–31, 902–11.

19. Thurston refers to several passages in the *Bacchae* in which Dionysus betrays a sexual ambivalence, and, like Sasha, is described as pretty, with a fair, delicate skin, flushed cheeks, and the aroma of perfume. Also like Sasha, he spends all his time in the company of females. See 39–40 for these details and others that we have noted.

20. See *Vakkhanki*, lines 453–59, the *Homeric Hymn to Dionysus*, or Vases Like the Pronomos Vase (*ARV2* 1336). See also the description of Dionysus on p. 5 of Annensky's translation. Annensky points out that Dionysus was a mixture of masculine and feminine features (XCVIII), and that Praxiteles' statue of Dionysus shows him as a beardless, beautiful youth (XCIX).

21. Thurston notes that in their frenzied drinking, dancing, and singing, they were behaving like maenads under the impact on them of the "Dionysian" Sasha (37). Annensky recounts a number of legends connected with Dionysus involving three sisters on LXXXIV, LXXXVII.

22. Myths about Dionysus tend to feature the god in a sexually ambivalent disguise entering new cities and causing great social disruption until his cult is accepted.

23. For a discussion of cross-sex dressing in Dionysiac cult and the broader effects of Dionysus' undermining of traditional gender restriction, see Clara Galllini, "Il travestimo rituale di Penteo," *SMSR*, 34 (1968), 211–28 and C.P. Segal, "The Menace of Dionysus: Sex Roles and Reversals in Euripides' *Bacchae*," *Arethusa*, 11 (1978), 185–202. In the *Bacchae* the king Pentheus believes that Dionysus sexually corrupts his female followers, but he is proved wrong. Instead, he succumbs to the suppressed female element in himself,

dresses as a woman, and is destroyed by the mad and masculinized women of his city.

24. See Vsevolod Setchkarev, *Studies in the Life and Work of Innokentii Annensky*(The Hague: Mouton, 1963), 223. Merezhkovsky compares the bacchae to dogs in his poem "The Song of the Bacchae." See p. 4 of our text.

25. Annensky, *Vakkhanki*, LXXI, LXXVII.

26. Thurston makes the connection between Peredonov's visit to Sasha and the subsequent appearance of the *nedotykomka* (36). Rabinowitz has noted this verbal connection. Sasha and the *nedotykomka* are further connected through the verb "to squeal."

27. Pentheus, unlike the chorus in the *Bacchae*, cannot see the bestial side of the god until he goes mad. Peredonov typically sees the Dionysiac in a threatening guise. Another whole series of animal images plays a major role in the novel in the characterization of Peredonov and the town. But these images are used differently by Sologub to dehumanize his grotesque characters in the Gogolian tradition. See Masing-Delic, 111.

28. This article is found in the collection *Teatr, kniga o novom teatre* (St. Petersburg: Shipovnik, 1908). See p. 191.

29. E.R. Dodds, *Euripides' "Bacchae"* (2d ed., Oxford: The Clarendon Press, 1960), xiv.

30. Thurston has pointed out that the snake was one of Dionysus' symbols, 39.

31. See the discussion above of Merezhkovsky's poem "Leda."

32. S.A. Tokarev, *Religioznye verovaniia vostochno-slavianskikh narodov XIX—nachala XX v.* (Leningrad: AN SSSR, 1957), 51.

33. See Masing-Delic on the novel's puppet and dance motifs, 110. Thurston also notices Peredonov's inability to experience ecstasy, 30, 40.

34. Thurston interprets the masquerade as "a comic version of a Dionysian Festival" (40). He also elaborates on the many parallels between the *Bacchae* and the masquerade scene, 41–43. In his article "The Theater of One Will," Sologub views the masquerade as a means of engaging the spectator in play-acting, a hybrid form between play and spectacle. It could serve as a stepping-stone toward the higher attainment of "mystery" (*tainstvo*) in the theater. See 183.

35. *Vakkhanki*, lines 1084–85.

36. Kay Louise Robbins notes the satirical import of this costume: "The disguise, as a projection of the individual's interior, evokes satire as Yulia Gudaevskaya, the notary's wife, a thin dry woman who engages in promiscuous affairs, comes dressed as an ear of fertile courn. . . ." See "The Artistic Vision of Fedor Sologub: A Study of Five Major Novels" (Ph.D. dissertation, University of Washington, 1975), 73. Annensky mentions that an ear of grain (*kolos*) played a role in Dionysiac mystery (XCIV).

37. René Girard, *Violence and the Sacred* (Baltimore: John's Hopkins Press, 1977). See especially his interpretation of the *Bacchae* using this approach, 119–42.

38. A full explanation of Girard's terms or his theory is impossible here. In "mimetic competition" each member of a community desires what his neighbor has, and is drawn by this desire into a proliferating process of imitation of the other that culminates in violence.

39. In *The Birth of Tragedy* Nietzsche sees this ability at the heart of the Dionysian experience (see 64).

40. Thurston views Volodin as Peredonov's scapegoat rather than his double, 42. On the god's victim as his ritual double in Dionysiac myth, see H.P. Foley, "The Masque of Dionysus," *TAPA* 110 (1980), 130, n. 2. The parallels between Sologub's novel and the *Bacchae* become very complex here, since Peredonov does not become the god's victim like Pentheus, but instead adopts Dionysus' own role as sacrificer. Similarly, in the masquerade the role of Dionysus is split between Sasha and Bengalsky.

41. In terms of a Girardian analysis, Peredonov's success in taking the violence of the community on himself, and obscuring its culpability through this action, might imply that he has temporarily succeeded through his sacrifice in establishing his own anti-Dionysiac "religion" in the community.

42. For the most complete discussion of the essential amorality of Dionysiac religion and its ambiguities, see R.P. Winnington-Ingram, *Euripides and Dionysus: An Interpretation of the "Bacchae"* (Cambridge, Eng.: The University Press, 1948).

43. *The Birth*, 53.

"PEREDONOV'S LITTLE TEAR" —WHY IS IT SHED?[1]

(THE SUFFERINGS OF A TORMENTOR)*

IRENE MASING DELIC

THE PROTAGONIST OF Sologub's novel *The Petty Demon*,[2] the sadistic schoolteacher Peredonov, has evoked diametrically opposed reactions— love and hatred—in two Russian writers: Zinaida Gippius and Evgeny Zamyatin. The latter, in his essay "Fyodor Sologub,"[3] sees the Russina *Professor Unrath*[4] as the epitome of the seemingly indestructible philistine, that "mold" (221) which grows everywhere without being cultivated.[5] He notes that the author punishes Peredonov with immortality. To die is the fate of the tragic and romantic hero, Zamyatin argues, to live that of the vulgar man. Peredonov is not worthy of being "killed," only of being whipped—with the lashes of satire. To Zamyatin the novel is a romantic writer's satire on the "philistine snout," Peredonov not qualifying for the name *homo erectus* as he is a mere wheedling, tail-wagging and cowardly beast. The "Scythian" Zamyatin rejects Chichikov's famous statement that there is no merit in loving the virtuous and that it is considerably more difficult, thence laudable, to love the wicked. Zamyatin demands hatred for the ugly, common and "immortal" philistine snout which distorts the ideal image of man; he does so in the name of love for the future man who will have overcome the Peredonov within himself.

Zinaida Gippius in her essay (cf. footnote 1) likewise evaluates Peredonov as a poor specimen of a human being; nevertheless she proposes a different treatment of him than the one Zamyatin was to suggest later. The "vulgar fool" (41) Peredonov deserves sympathy, even love in her view. As a poet of metaphysical anxiety and unceasing unrest, Gippius cannot be accused of taking up a "Chichikovian" position in regard to human deficiencies, in spite of her "love" for the pettily wicked Peredonov.[6] But having described his own soul as a dull satiated snake (*She*, 1905), the poet would feel some sympathy for the spiritual dullard Peredonov.[7] This does not mean that Gippius's self-critical poet should be seen as "another Peredonov," their spiritual development obviously being on different levels.[8] Still, the problem of spiritual insufficiency, whatever its degree, was one which occupied Gippius. As a religious poet and thinker, she is interested in an aspect of Peredonov's existence, which Zamyatin—more concerned with man than God—does not heed: the "injustice" of having been born a petty, shabby, limited creature. Repulsive Peredonov's morality is of less concern to her than the motivation of Him Who created the "living Peredonovs." Gippius takes up the stance of a God-fighter to fling out the question: "*How did He dare* to create this creature? And how will He *answer for him*?" (43)

327 THE PETTY DEMON

In her critique of the Creator Gippius extends the Ivan Karamazov arguments against the given world order: "It is incumbent upon us to justify 'the little tear of the tormented child' because we must know: for what crime? why? for what purpose? But similarly it is incumbent . . . upon me to justify each of Peredonov's elephant tears . . ." (43).

Gippius claims as her own the discovery that Peredonov's situation is to be equated with that of the "tormented child" within the context of the theodicy problem. She even denies the author himself, i.e., Sologub, any knowledge of Peredonov's sufferings, subtitling her essay "What Sologub Doesn't Know." But K. Chukovsky rightly pointed out that Sologub "does know"; he sees Peredonov's "little tear," and even "positively drowns the novel in the tears of this morose sufferer," as the critic put it.[9] To judge from Chukovsky's facetious tone he does not take Peredonov's sufferings much to heart; nevertheless he gives a penetrating explanation of them. Peredonov's misfortune, the critic declares, is that he lacks the gift of creatively transforming reality and therefore cannot conjure up the wondrous land *Ojle* where tortured minds may find rest.[10] Here is indeed the key to Peredonov's situation.

Gippius correctly depicts Peredonov as a being deeply wronged by his creator. But whereas she offers God an opportunity to "explain Himself," Sologub's deity is the Demiurge of the Gnostics whose evil intentions are only too clear. The "Satanist" and "Lucifer worshipper" Sologub created a poetic world which would seem to find its best explanation in Gnostic-Manichaean terms. The critique of the Demiurge's faulty creation—our imperfect world and those clay puppets called human beings—forms the all-dominating thematics of Sologub's works in any genre. The novel *The Petty Demon* is no exception, demonstrating in full detail the situation of one of the Demiurge's victims: the clumsy, gross and particularly unsuccessful creation which was labelled Peredonov.

The task of this study is to discuss the specific causes and attributes of Peredonov's sufferings and to link these into a picture of this existential situation in the Demiurge's evil world. Its aim is to show how Peredonov's situation may be compared to that of the "tormented child" (in spite of the fact that Peredonov himself is a tormentor of children); it should demonstrate that Peredonov's life forms a critique of "divine powers," identified here with the Demiurge. In order to achieve this aim Peredonov's problematics may be divided into two interlinked categories. His fundamental problem is that his soul is captured in the prisonhouse of his body, so that he cannot attain true knowledge (*gnosis*) of reality. He attempts to rectify his situation by engaging in a quest for an identity (self-knowledge) during which he becomes a "suffering usurper."[11]

Peredonov's soul is imprisoned in his body—as is that of most men. In their compact grossness, human bodies cannot but trap the spirit. The Demiurge's creative work was "presumptuous and blundering" in its entirety but this characterization applies particularly to the creatures called human beings.[12] To make them, the Demiurge chose coarse clay as raw material which he shaped into crude and graceless forms. He then "deposited" in these "clay receptacles" a "spark of life." He himself was not the source of this "life energy" but stole it from the transcendent Spirit, the "living God" of the novel (300). The Living God is the true God Whose image the Demiurge has usurped in his pursuit of power. But in vain does the usurper compete with the Spirit—his creative failures give him away. His creatures ought not to be called men as they are but barely animated clay puppets, "golems," "homunculi," "Frankenstein monsters."

A glance at the outer form of the inhabitants of Peredonov's symbolic town proves that the Demiurge's creative talents are indeed limited. Many an "accident" takes place in his "laboratory." Often the wrong "parts" have been put together, as may be seen from crooked smiles, disproportionate eyes and heads which do not fit their bodies. In some cases the puppets have been daubed with too much "paint," in others with too little. The result: ruddy and greenish faces.

The "spark of life," without which these clay figures would "crumble to dust," is too feeble to move their heavy frame. They are therefore provided with a "mechanism" which propels them forward. Consequently their movements are jerky. The puppets are run on "electric batteries" and pulled by "strings." Their imitation of life is often successful, but at times a battery runs out, or a string snaps. Then it is evident that the Demiurge's creatures are "automatons." Prepolovensky, e.g., is a "faulty phonograph" who repeats the same story over and over again, until somebody takes off the "cracked record," i.e., interrupts him.[13] To sum up: the puppets are programmed—not for that complex form of being called "life," but for the existential mode of "dancing."

A dance is a series of formalized steps, which are repeated over and over again. Thus it is a movement which puppets may master, whereas the unpredictable movements of life lie beyond their capacity. The frequently recurring dance motif of the novel serves to emphasize the mechanical quality of marionette life. The motif reaches its apogee in the tumultuous scenes of the masked ball, when the puppets run amok, demonstrating yet another creative failure in the Demiurge's handicraft. When the puppets are overwound, control over their movement is lost.

Aesthetic and mechanical defects are not the only ones in the Demiurge's clay creatures. They are also fragile and perishable in spite of their apparent sturdiness. They are easily "broken," they "crumble" and disintegrate, and, in addition, engage in mutual destruction.

When the inebriated Ershova threatens to tear Varvara apart by her legs, this seems a real possibility in regard to a puppet (65). In a variant text, describing the Gudaevsky household, the parents think that tugging their child in opposite directions, they have torn him apart! (435) It is not surprising that Peredonov who agrees that his mistress Varvara should be "pulverized," fears ending up between the grindstones of a mill (286). This is in any case the "way of all flesh," as the Demiurge's "clay" is also termed. It is bound to disintegrate into dust. Dust envelops the cemetery city of "dead souls" in which Peredonov lives.[14]

As may be expected from such primitive creatures, the range of their activities is limited. As mechanisms they are only capable of feeding, coupling and reproducing themselves. In the grossness of these activities they are "animals." Thus, in addition to being a "show-booth" where coarse comedies are played, Peredonov's town is also a "zoological garden," where (domestic) animals inhabit stuffy, smelly cages—in the manner of the "captured beasts" of Sologub's poetry (We Are Caged Animals, 1905). In town we find: sheep (Volodin), ducks (Varvara), "scalded puppies" (Grushina's children), dogs (the Gudaevskys) and "beasts" of various other kinds, as the favourite address in town, skotina, indicates. People do not "agree" but have "sniff contact"; snjuchat'sja is a term Peredonov "borrowed" from Gogol's Poprishch. Grushina makes no distinction whatsoever between a human being and a dog, on the grounds that neither has a "soul" (338), and she often proves the truth of her words by behaving like a "bitch." Indeed the difference between humans and animals is minimal in Peredonov's town—in the Gogolian tradition.

Superficially Peredonov is no exception in his town. He too is barely illuminated by a "greedy but dull fire" (290), shining through his eyes,—that divine spark which flickers helplessly in the bodily prison. He too is a "wound-up puppet" (289, 290), a marionette pulled by the "strings" of his muscles (72). He too "dances," as in the scene with Ershova. She is a puppet equipped with a sound mechanism wherefore she emits squeaky noises at regular intervals (*povizgivala, pokrikivala*, 69)—the morose puppet Peredonov lacks a corresponding sound box. However both are equally subject to the inertia of mechanical laws; they cannot even "unlock" their embraces when they sit down at mechanically regular intervals to be "recharged." It is made plain in the novel that Peredonov's actions are never motivated by "will," but merely by mechanical motor impulses (72).

Peredonov adds to the zoological variety in the novel by being a "pig." Varvara calls him "swine" (55), emphasizing that this classification is based on close observation. Indeed it is stressed that Peredonov is not any other animal, e.g., a "bull," but a "downright swine" (*formennaia svin'ia*, 91), presumably of the Gogolian "demonic" type. Peredonov himself believes that he is one, laying claim to a "human snout."

Thus Peredonov's situation is that of all the people in town: a feeble spirit is trapped in a heavy, clumsy and inert body. The uneven struggle between spirit and matter inevitably leads to the defeat of the spirit. But there is a difference, nevertheless, between Peredonov and the other townspeople. They are satisfied with their condition, Peredonov is not. He feels uncomfortable in his "cage"; he is terrified of being a "pig," whereas e.g., Volodin is eminently happy as a "sheep."[15]

The Demiurge is not only a "blunderer"—he is also jealous. Forced to endow these creatures with a "spark of life," as "batteries" alone cannot maintain their life functions, he ensured that the separate sparks would not fuse into a spiritual fire. The existence of such a force would threaten his security on the usurped throne. Therefore he placed the "sparks" in bodies which were designed to make communication between them, as well as contact with outer reality, difficult.

The bodies which the Demiurge gave his creatures are prisonhouses. Their compactness is comparable to that of prisonwalls. The "windows" of the bodily prison, i.e., the five senses, transmit a minimal amount of information which, in addition, is distorted. They are "dirty windows" which allow the prisoner a view of a small and ugly corner of the prisonyard, i.e., the world of *realia*, whereas the vision of the sky, i.e. the realm of *realiora*, is blocked.[16] The imprisoned "sparks" are thus effectively isolated from reality outside as well as from an exchange of information. Unable to communicate with each other, barred from correct information, they cannot attain *gnosis*. This is the general human condition, which Peredonov shares (311).

But, primitive as Peredonov is, he nevertheless, is an exception in his town, yearns for the truth (both *pravda* and *istina*, 345/6). In this regard he is a human amongst "animals." He even seeks the truth in the right place, i.e., "beyond the world of matter" (366). But there is "noise" in his information channels and his senses delude him, instead of enlightening him. Thus Peredonov is doomed to constant fear, the inevitable result of confusion and ignorance. Fear leads to aggression. In the final analysis, it is ignorance which is the source of Peredonov's sadistic and criminal acts.

Peredonov is constantly deceived by his defective senses. His sleepy small eyes which almost drown in his bloated face are "muddy ponds" or "dirty mirrors" (325) which grotesquely distort reality. His nose cannot register aromatic smells, wherefore they seem unpleasant to him. His taste in food is of the grossest kind, and cannot afford him genuine pleasure. Consequently he is doomed to live in a hell of unrelieved ugliness, as one eternally damned.

To the constant flow of distorted information Peredonov reacts as a frightened animal would: by withdrawing into a dark corner. He attempts to stop the flow of impressions altogether. He puts cotton wool in his ears, in the classical "man in a shell" fashion, and never airs his room, keeping all "windows" locked. In the language of the gnostics this means that he blocks all his senses. The teacher of literature, Peredonov, refuses to read, thus barring himself from a valuable source of knowledge. All these attempts at withdrawal naturally result in even more distorted notions of reality and Peredonov is trapped in a vicious circle of delusion and fear. Insanity must ensue. But Peredonov's insanity testifies to the fact that—unlike many others in town—he is still able to react, even if only negatively.

Grace alone can save the damned. Peredonov could have been saved by a gracious vision of beauty, but, as Chukovsky pointed out, the ability to perceive or create beauty has been denied to Peredonov. Thus he is cut off from the source of life and *gnosis*. This becomes clear from Peredonov's reaction to the mystery of transubstantiation.

When Peredonov visits church—for practical, not spiritual reasons—he is frightened of the beautiful liturgy, the fine priestly vestments and the aromatic incense (as devils are wont, 137). This is so because "the mystery of the eternal transubstantiation of inert matter into a power breaking the fetters of death was forever veiled from him" (299/300). The "walking corpse" (300) Peredonov, i.e., the Demiurge's lifeless clay puppet, cannot understand or believe in the "living God and His Christ," i.e., the true divinity of the transcendental realm where life eternal resides in ideal forms of imperishable beauty.[17] Beauty transubstantiates the mortal flesh.

Beauty could heal Peredonov, but under the given circumstances, it becomes an additional source of horror. Peredonov feels that "beauty is not for him" and that ugliness "suits" him better. Driven by bitterness he recoils from beauty or destroys it. But his overreaction to it, as well as his strange interest in the beautiful androgynous Sasha Pylnikov testify to his dim awareness of this alternative beyond his grasp.

In nightmares Peredonov sees how Pylnikov, smiling seductively, beckons him to another realm, but to deluded Peredonov it assumes a sinister aspect (261).[18] The windows of his room are transformed into Pylnikov's eyes, staring at him (363). This symbolic delusion expresses Peredonov's simultaneous fear of and yearning for a beautiful world beyond his prison. Peredonov cannot transport himself to this realm of beauty and life everlasting. This failure is Peredonov's misfortune, but not crime.

Others are more fortunate than Peredonov. Lyudmila *Platonovna's* refined senses are capable of perceiving the realm of *Platonic* ideas; so are those of her "god-like youth" (*otrokbog*, 357). As long as these reincarnated Aphrodite and Eros do not give in to the realm of *dust*—as *Pylnikov* presumably sometime will—they may partake of the transubstantiation mysteries. They attempt to realize these mysteries in their dressing up games which have the purpose of emulating the androgynous being. Donning the garb of the opposite sex, they symbolically unite both sexes in one perfect being.[19]

The idea of the androgynous being is beyond Peredonov. Also in this respect he is the sly Demiurge's victim. This usurper-deity firmly implanted lustful desires in his clay creatures (*nizkii soblazn*, 102) as well as other forms of greed. The crudely animalistic and purely utilitarian reproduction system serves the Demiurge's power schemes, as it scatters the divine spirit ever more sparsely amongst an increasing number of clay creatures.[20] The atomization of the spirit is counteracted by the Dionysiac ecstasies of spiritually androgynous beings who in their perfection demand nothing from one another but beautiful impressions. Such ecstasies fuse the scattered sparks of the spirit. But the majority of people continue to "wallow in lust," thus fettering themselves to the realm of dust. Lust and dust are directly linked in the novel.

Peredonov thus has no access to Lyudmila's aromatic world of refined love; her perfumes—symbols of the flesh "transubstantiated" into ethereal beauty—frighten Peredonov, used as he is to his stuffy cage.[21] But although used to his cage, Peredonov is not happy in it. His *realia* world, while made up of gross, solid and heavy building material, such as mud, clay and flesh, lacks stability. It is a temporal world where change rules and where disintegration triumphs in the end, as there is no force in it which could oppose "decrepit chaos" (345). The symbol of this world of gross but fluidly vague *realia* is the formless and faceless (*bezlikaia*, 186) *nedotykomka*.[22] She and the reality she represents elude Peredonov's grasp (185).

The elusive *nedotykomka* is described in negative terms, as she is the product of the inexpressible horrors of the *realia* world. Her gliding movement from form to form (*zybkaia pliaska*, 341), her incessant metamorphoses, demonstrate the shapelessness of the material world of phenomena. These are open to any interpretation, as the eternal ideas are but weakly reflected in them and furthermore are perceived by defective senses. All phenomena therefore dissolve into that amorphus dust where the *nedotykomka* likes to hide. Beauty is the only adhesive capable of binding disintegrating mattter into a lasting form. The Demiurge is however incapable of creating beauty. He is a skillful "mechanic" but only the "living God" creates a "thing of beauty."

The Demiurge has tamed the forces of chaos, residing in matter, and is also capable of keeping them in a state of uneasy equilibrium, as the existence of the material world proves. The clay puppets "exist," but as their compact bodies are impenetrable to light, these unillumined beings hide dark chaos within themselves. This ancient heritage they frequently express in acts of senseless destruction.

Peredonov is a destructive creature. But his criminal acts demonstrate more than the chaotic quality inherent in all "clay": they are acts of rebellion. Peredonov realizes yet another "ancient heritage": that of Cain's rebellion against his own creator.

The Demiurge is often identified with the Old Testament God.[23] In the Sologubian version of the Old Testament fratricide, the role of the shepherd Abel together with that of sacrifical lamb is played by sheepish Volodin.[24] Volodin is so like a sheep because he in fact has renounced his human countenance by extinguishing the "spark" within himself. He therefore feels happy in the Demiurge's world, in which he lives obedient to the "Law" (319). Peredonov attempts to be obedient, but it costs him effort and anxiety. For his attempts to please he is not rewarded, or, in terms of the Old Testament, his "sacrifical offerings" are not accepted. Like Cain's, his heart becomes "embittered" (345), as he watches how his "brother," the happy hypocrite Volodin, lives in harmony with his creator. Dark chaos stirs in Peredonov's subconscious (345), which perhaps still carries the racial memory of Cain's deed. Growing awareness of existential injustice fills Peredonov with bitterness and fury; these same feelings overwhelmed the Demiurge's first creatures upon their discovery that they were "clay" and thus mortals. This bitterness was forgotten by the

"Abel-line" of mankind, but preserved and transmitted through the line of Cain.

Peredonov's purely negative rebellion against the Demiurge does not qualify as "Promethean." This (true) path is taken by Lyudmila. She has understood that a "separate existence" (311) furthers the atomization of the divine spirit and her attempts to kindle the fire of exquisite ecstasies qualify as "stealing fire from the gods," here the Demiurge and his "archons." Her fires differ positively from Peredonov's insane acts of pyromania. These too have the purpose of burning the prison of existence, guarded by the "wicked sorceress" of delusion (cf. the epigraph to the novel), but arson offers no solution.[25] Not the burning of houses, but the melting down of the "cages of individuation" offers true liberation. By increasing chaos Peredonov remains his creator's puppet, a devil's miniature copy: a petty devil.

As a petty devil Peredonov is a frightened one. He fears punishment in all forms—mostly as death. His pyromania may be partly explained as a death fear. He would like to burn down houses where people have died, apparently hoping to erase death itself in this way. What Peredonov does not understand, however, is that his rebellious crimes destroy only the outer manifestations of terror while the roots of human misfortune remain untouched. It is true that Peredonov has a "counterplan" to the Demiurge's faulty creation, but it is a poor one. A "beast" and "puppet," Peredonov can think only of a mechanistic utopia in which machines work, while men satisfy their animality (368, 369). Those moments when Peredonov satisfies some basic need are the only ones when he feels that he truly exists. Therefore he would like to prolong them (364) into a constant activity which would, furthermore, last for centuries. In Peredonov's utopia (parody of the land *Ojle*) men will reach extreme longevity.

But the fleeting moments of reality when Peredonov, stuffing his belly, may forget his fears, are too short to maintain his sense of being. Barred from *gnosis*, Peredonov ever more finds himself in a phantom world where he himself is a shadow amongst shadows. Peredonov ceases to feel his own reality and in the end he becomes alienated from the very interests and goals which he so fervently pursues (293).

Whereas ignorance caused Peredonov to misinterpret the signs of reality until it eluded his grasp, his own irreality is brought home to him by his fear of observation. In spite of his apparent smugness, Peredonov senses that he is but a "ridiculous insect," unworthy even of taking up "space" in the world. He feels that he is an "absurd" creature and therefore also an "unreal" creature, as the absurd, by defintion, contradicts the "real." Peredonov is afraid of being exposed as unreal. The words "observation," "ridicule" and "annihilation" are synonyms in his vocabulary. Observation to Peredonov implies the judgement of unworthiness and the punishment of annihilation. These elements are evident in is persecution mania, which is founded on his lack of ontological certainty.

Peredonov feels himself subjected to constant observation. The "eyes" (*sogliadatai*) which pursue him assume various forms, the most"Boschian" being the *glaz-ptitsa* which "consists" of one eye and two wings (317–318). At times even the sun itself, symbol of the Demiurge's power, takes part in the "observation game" (317).[26] But whatever form the spies assume, they all have one purpose: to observe Peredonov, find fault with him (*pridrat'sia*, 294), pronounce him to be insignificant, ridiculous and unworthy of existence and finally to push him into the void of nonbeing. Peredonov's situation is that of the rider in the poem *The Devil's Swing* (1907). Precariously placed, his clumsy ride and inevitable fall are the source of great mirth to both superterrestrial demonic spectators as well as earthly devils. Thus Peredonov's paranoiac visions express a complex protest against divine (in)justice. Had he possessed poetic gifts, he could have formulated his dark fears and muddled sensations in terms such as these: "*Ihr*[the divine powers] *führt ins Leben uns hinein, / Ihr lasst den Armen schuldig werden, / Dann überlässt ihr ihn der Pein, / Denn alle Schuld rächt sich auf Erden.*"[27] Peredonov was born "poor" in the sense of spiritually deficient; he was "made" ridiculous and is punished for being so. In this regard he is an innocent sufferer, pursued by "laughing furies" (318) for crimes he could not but commit, i.e., for being what he is and did not choose to be.

Peredonov's yearning for an inspector's post is thus primarily a desire to avoid an inspection which would literally reduce him to nothing. Having a post (*mesto*) to Peredonov means the certainty that he takes up space (*mesto*), i.e., that he exists; it means having found a place (*mesto*), safe from inspection, as no one inspects inspectors. The acquisition of a post is indeed a matter of life and death to Peredonov, as he repeatedly states (346, 390). He can no longer suffer the "withering" glances of ridicule, which mercilessly "murder" him. There is of course ambition in Peredonov's pursuit of a career, but is is the absurd ambition of an "insect" and "zero," clinging to the futile hope of becoming the opposite of what he is.

Thus Peredonov is yet another "injured and insulted" petty clerk of Russian literature, one of those who "stung" by vanity, attempt to redress both social and metaphysical wrongs by aspiring to a higher post and who in these acts of "usurpation" are led to their ruin. Their limited imagination sees in the table of ranks the "ladder of being" where they discover "symbols of real value," "a way of defining a person."[28] Peredonov, like his predecessors, believes that he will acquire a personality by becoming an "important person- age." The higher ranks to him offer the right of unquestioned being.

Peredonov's combined career pursuit and identity quest show fatal mis- conceptions, as might be expected. Thus he confuses the concepts "self-knowl- edge" and "renown." Seeking an identity, Peredonov does not choose the Socratic path of "knowing himself" but hopes that renown will show him who he is. He dreams of inducing reactions of awe and terror by flinging out threats, which would make other people into mirrors of his self, reflecting his grandeur and thus proving his existence. Peredonov twists the proverb "knowledge gives power" into "renown gives power over being." The *znatnye*, he believes, have control over reality (335) and the *nedotykomka* does not plague them (343). Following the inertia inherent in all untransformed matter, Peredonov chooses "being known" instead of "knowing." Had he broken "automatism" and cho- sen the active alternative, he might have reached the goal of his quest: to attain a sense of reality. Renown, the substitute of knowledge, escapes him.

To be known implies uniqueness. The identity of a "distinguished" person cannot be mistaken, and such a person's "place" in life is safe from usurpation. An anonymous "nobody" is constantly threatened by the danger of being "replaced" by someone equally undistinguished and undistinguishable. Peredonov, the faceless nonentity, is haunted by fears of being "replaced," i.e., having his "place" or "post" taken from him.

As a "Darwinian" Peredonov knows that "not everyone can be an inspec- tor" (210). In the "struggle for existence" (210) there are only two alternatives: to usurp another's place or to have one's own usurped, to replace or be replaced. Peredonov chooses the first alternative but does not enjoy his usurpation activities. His aggression is a "flight forward," and he sees his denunciations and murder as "defense measures" (340, 415). As a "man in a shell" Peredonov dislikes "expansion" and favors "shrinking." Had there been a nook dark enough to hide him from "inspection," he would have chosen to hide.

Peredonov's persecution phobias are of course based on misconceptions, but they are not entirely unreasonable. Observing life in his town, Peredonov sees that "replacement" is eminently easy amongst "puppets" and "animals," which have no unique and irreplaceable identity. Substitution constantly takes place.

Observing the marriage market and himself taking part in the "exchange of goods" (218), i.e., partners, Peredonov sees how easily the "merchandise" changes hands. There is no such thing as a non-eligible partner or an irreplaceable one. Anyone may be coupled with anyone else in that dance (macabre) where a change of partner merely leads to a new "tour."

Peredonov takes an active part in the "replacement games" in town, amateurishly playing his role of usurper. For example, by punishing children who are not his own, he usurps paternal rights. Here, perhaps, he again unwittingly imitates the Demiurge, who punishes his "children" frequently under the same pretext which also Peredonov uses, i.e., that it is "for their own good."

Peredonov also usurps marital rights, replacing Mr. Gudaevsky in Madame Gudaevskaya's bed. But whereas the Demiurge, in his usupration acts, goes free from punishment, being on the top of the hierarchy of oppression, Peredonov is pursued by nemesis (260). Perhaps it tells him that just as easily as he replaces others, is he himself replaced. Replacement is possible anywhere—in Varvara's bed and at school, where the director "whets his teeth" (79), obviously planning Peredonov's "pulverization." But "pulverization" also threatens from the "director of the universe," from him who instituted the whole "replacement principle" by denying men a unique and irreplaceable identity.

Pursued by nemesis, Peredonov develops into a Golyadkin senior, yet another petty clerk "bitten by the bug of desire to be somebody."[29] He acquires his rival and double in Volodin who is as amorphous as the *nedotykomka* and, therefore, like her capable of metamorphosis. Volodin is so devoid of inner content (his chest rings hollow when he beats his fist against it) that he can absorb foreign content into himself, which, in fact, he does in regard to Peredonov, whose speech and gestures he imitates (the scene of the proposal to the Adamenko girl). Even Peredonov has his "ape."

Whilst waiting for the usurped identity, Peredonov guards his own. Worthless as it is, there are even more worthless ones (Volodin's). For the purpose of identification he paints the letter P all over his body, an idea which is not entirely absurd.

Peredonov lives in a world where all personal value may be read from similar signs as the letter P. Uniform buttons, cockades, pins, epaulettes and collars determine who you are and what you are "worth." The dead souls of Peredonov's town prop up their hollowness by insignia of rank and thus indicate who they are. Peredonov accepts the conventional meaning of these signs which to him are as incomprehensible as any others. All of reality is to him a system of signs which he cannot decipher. He merely imitates established patterns and models, e.g., the example of the town official Veriga.

Before his wedding Peredonov rouges himself, because he believes that ruddy Veriga does; he plans to put on a corset—an item which props up a disintegrating form—for the same reason. He chooses Veriga as the idol of his fetishistic cult because he recognizes him to be what he himself would like to

335 THE PETTY DEMON

be: a successful usurper. Veriga will presumably reach his goal, a governor's post (132, 157), whereas Peredonov does not reach his, the inspector's post (178). This difference between Peredonov and Veriga applies generally. Peredonov is a singularly unfortunate "devil" in a world where many a "man" realizes his dreams.

Amongst the genuine philistines, the Verigas and Volodins, these "darlings of the gods," Peredonov is not an innocent child, but a weeping devil thrown into a world where he is as lost as the purest child. Like any innocent child, Peredonov interprets reality (and language) literally and is therefore lost in a world of conventional form and hypocritical lies. Peredonov is victimized by the Demiurge's true accomplices: the race of human adults, the liars and hypocrites, the descendents of Abel. These are so evil that even "devils" of Cain's lineage compare favorably. "There's so much evil among men that often old Satan suddenly will cry like an offended child."[30] Peredonov is no worse than a "wicked child."

To sum up: Peredonov's concept of identity as well as his "model of the world" are reflected in the hierarchy of cards in those games he likes to play but always loses. Some cards have a "face"; knaves, queens and kings are the "big-eyed inspectors" (281). The majority of cards lack a face and are marked only by conventional signs and numbers. These are the "inspected" ones which lose all value when confronted by a "face card." People are to Peredonov "cards" (342).[31] Schoolboys, e.g., are neglible quantities, recognizable only by their coat buttons. Peredonov aspires to becoming a "face card." Above these there is only the ace, so important that his face cannot even be imagined, as is the case also with the Demiurge. But the Ace needs no face. As a "walking belly" it represents to Peredonov the pinnacle of being—existence as constant feeding (141). This ability remains, after all, the only criterion for reality and identity which Peredonov can wholeheartedly embrace. But is he to be blamed for his pitiful conclusions, or his Saturnine creator who devours his own children? Is he, to repeat the public prosecutor's, Avinovitsky's, question—"a criminal or a victim? (143).

Naturally a sympathetic or antipathetic view of Peredonov must remain a matter of personal attitudes. Within the context of the novel it would appear however that the reader is not asked to castigate Peredonov but rather to feel pity for him, as well as all mankind, humiliated by the "human condition." The reader is perhaps also encouraged to experience fear—not at the grandeur of Peredonov's misfortunes, but at their humiliating pettiness, which increases their horror. In other words: the reader is offered the opportunity to experience the catharsis which is denied Peredonov himself. Pity and fear would save the reader from sharing in "peredonovism" rather than "laughter" which, presupposing the distance of superiority, precludes identification.

Peredonov's existential situation appears too complex to be (only) laughed at, in the spirit of enlightenment—however bitterly. The light which could illumine Peredonov is not the light of reason; reason could dispel Peredonov's misconceptions of reality but not change his attitude towards it. Peredonov needs thinking less than feeling and perceiving—i.e., he needs the illumination of the Spirit, the source of knowledge beyond reason. "Animals" cannot be taught anything but to "sit," but they can be enchanted by "music." The Dionysiac frenzies and their purifying fires could perhaps transform the dancing doll Peredonov into at least a dancing satyr.

The novel is in my reading a religious-philosophical allegory, showing the path to salvation through both negative and positive instruction. Its satirical elements are centered around the "Volodins" of the novel who are the true "philistines"—not Peredonov. The novel is filled with the "burning problems" of its day: the "revaluation of good and evil," the "salvation through beauty" and the "restoration of human dignity" in a Nietzschean spirit. Rebellious but humiliated Peredonov represents the whole misery of mankind, dimly becoming aware of its condition.

Peredonov, as a representative of human misery cannot be surrounded by the sombre majesty of "great Satan."[32] Comparing the petty demon Peredonov to Pushkin's Germann ("The Queen of Spades") as, through many allusions, is often done in the novel, it is Peredonov's lack of romantic aura which emphasizes the compelling need for a new human dignity in the face of "higher powers." The role of romantic rebel may reconcile man with his situation. The relentless depiction of Peredonov's existential struggle precludes a reconciliation with the "human condition."

Peredonov's "romance with Fate" is pure imagination—he does not even set eyes on his queen of spades, the elusive princess Volchanskaya. His bragging lies about having been her lover is the wishful thinking of a man who never was "the darling of Fate," old cocotte as she is. All this is essentially true of Germann also, but this bitter truth is hidden under the veil of romantic events and the hero's tragic aura. Grotesque Peredonov serves the symbolist "non-acceptance of the world" better than the romantic Germann.

In his role of "victim without immediate appeal" Peredonov does not stand alone in contemporary literature. In Bryusov's poem "The Madman" (1895) Peredonov's situation is given "in a nutshell."[33] Gippius, in her stories about "subhuman creatures" posed the question "how did He dare" more than once. In Merezhkovsky's *Leonardo da Vinci*, the artist—himself not a model of virtue in the accepted sense—does not condemn a wicked little boy, as he knows him to be one of "those innocent in their wrongdoing, because by nature formed for evil."[34]

Crudely simplifying a literary debate it could be said that the function of protagonists "by nature formed for evil" is the following: to demonstrate the need for a sympathy without bounds, a love without limits. These spiritual forces—it was hoped—would overcome even the crudest evil, the source of which resided in matter. The best manner in which to "vex" the Demiurge was to "infiltrate" matter with spirituality. Thus "black coal" could be transformed into "brilliant diamonds (Vl. Solovyov), or "mud receptacles" into "alabaster amphoras."[35] Spiritualization would transform "animals" into (super)human beings who would master their own fate. During the reign of the Spirit it would finally be acknowledged that the world of *realia* is unreal and this insight would break its evil spell. The power of the Living God would be reinstated and the Demiurge dethroned. A new world of imperishable beauty would then be bound to arise and in it there would not be a single tear—neither that of the innocent child, nor the frightened devil.

NOTES

*From *Scando-Slavica*, 24 (1978), pages 107–124. Reprinted by permission of the editorial board.

1. The quote refers to Z. Gippius's essay "Peredonov's Little Tear." This and subsequent quotes from the essay are from Sharon Leiter's translation in *The Silver Age of Russian Culture*, eds. C. and E. Proffer (Ann Arbor: Ardis, 1975).

2. The edition consulted for this study is: *Melkii bes, (Shabby Demon)*, Letchworth, Hert.: Bradda, 1966. Page references (in parentheses) in the text are to this edition.

3. The article is quoted from *A Soviet Heretic*, Essays by Yevgeny Zamyatin, ed. and transl. by Mirra Ginsburg (Chicago & London, 1970).

4. For this parallel, see Edmund Kostka, "A Literary Quandary: Fyodor Sologub and Heinrich Mann," *Glimpses of Germanic-Slavic Relations from Pushkin to Heinrich Mann* (Lewisburg, 1975).

5. Cf. Ivanov-Razumnik's view that the novel was not a satire on provincial life but a horror vision of the "philistinism of life generally." See his *O smysle zhizni (On the Meaning of Life)*, Letchworth: Bradda, 1971, p. 40.

6. The tensions in Gippius's paradoxial religiosity are well defined in Olga Matich's *The Religious Poetry of Zinaida Gippius*, München 1972.

7. The *persona* of *She* is masculine.

8. The question as to whether Peredonov is a "portrait" of the author may be answered in similar terms. Peredonov may well be Sologub "without the latter's intellect, talent and passionate self-criticism" (Gornfeld) but in this difference lies their incommensurability.

9. K. Chukovskii, "Putevoditel' po Sologubu," *Sobranie sochinenii v shesti tomakh* 6 (M. 1969), p. 342.

10. Omry Ronen has interestingly deciphered the names *Ojle, Ligoj* and *Mair* in his "Toponyms of Fedor Sologub's *Tvorimaja Legenda*," *Die Welt der Slaven* 13, 1968, pp. 307–316.

11. The expression is taken from Richard F. Gustafson's "The Suffering Usurper: Gogol's *Diary of a Madman*," *The Slavic and East European Journal* 9, 1965, pp. 268–280. Peredonov's situation is remarkably similar to Poprishchin's as defined in this fine study. The allusions to Poprishchin are manifold in the novel; cf. the *Spanish* hairstyle Peredonov wants to acquire before his wedding, Varvara's desire *"po-frantsuzski nasobachit'sia,"* etc.

12. For a characterization of the Demiurge, see *The Encyclopedia of Philosophy* 3, New York & London 1967, title "Gnosticism."

13. The puppet motif was not only frequently used by the Symbolists but also discovered by them in other writers, e.g., Chekhov, whose characters in *The Cherry Orchard*, according to Bely, are "automatons." See his "Vishnevyi sad," *Vesy* 2, 1904, p. 48.

14. Cf. A. Belyi, "Liudi poshli ot pyli: vot kosmogoniia Sologuba"; "Dalai-Lama iz Sapozhka," *Vesy* 3, 1908, p. 66.

15. He and many others in town are "hylic," i.e., "fleshly beyond redemption." See *Baker's Dictionary of Theology*, Grand Rapids, Mich., 1960, p. 163.

16. For a discussion in stylistic terms of the *realia-realiora* tension in Sologub's world, see Carola Hansson, *Fedor Sologub as a Short-Story Writer*, Stockholm 1975 (Stockholm Studies in Russian Literature 3).

17. Christ belongs to the "eternal messengers" which the true God at times sends to earth with a revelation of the truth. Others are Buddha and Zoroaster.

18. In this pose Pylnikov appears as a variant of the paintings of Bacchus and St. John, as presented in D. Merezhkovsky's "historical romance" *Leonardo da Vinci* (1902). Both these "divine figures" are androgynous, "fair as a woman" and point, smiling mysteriously, to something beyond themselves. See pp. 458–462 in the New York 1976 ed.

19. For a discussion of the androgynous being as the model of the future "super-man" and similar ideas of the times, see, N.Å. Nilsson, "Strindberg, Gorky and Blok," *Scando-Slavica* 4, 1958, pp. 23–42.

20. Cf. Hans Jonas, *The Gnostic Religion*, Boston 1963, p. 59: "The very creation of Eve and the scheme of reproduction initiated by it subserve the infinite further dispersion of light . . ."

21. A. Blok stressed that the function of the Lyudmila episode was the demonstration of the "spiritualized flesh." See his "O realistakh," *Sobranie sochinenii*, 8 vls., Moskva & Leningrad 1962, vol. 5.—Lyudmila's perfumed world is comparable to Trirodov's alchemistic wonderland (*The Created Legend*).—Her name has the "flavor" of a heathen goddess's name.

22. Galina Selegen suggests that the creation of the *nedotykomka* may have been inspired by J.K. Huysman's novel *En route*, where a similar creature appears. See her *Prekhitraia viaz'*, Simvolizm v russkoi proze: "Melkii bes" Fedora Sologuba (Washington 1968), p. 87.

23. The Demiurge is "clearly a polemical caricature of the Old Testament God," the *Encyclopedia of Philosophy (op. cit.)* states. For a discussion of "revengeful Adonai" versus "allgood Lucifer," see J. Holthusen, *Fedor Sologubs Roman-Trilogie*, The Hague 1960.

24. In the view of the gnostics Cain and Esau are positive figures, whereas Abel becomes their "whipping-boy." Interestingly enough Abel has retained his "gnostic status" in J. Olesha's *The Cherry Stone*, where the well-adapted Soviet communal leader of a "flock" of obedient citizens (*pastva*) is called *Avel'*.

25. Cf. Peredonov's horror vision of a fortress built by angry men in red shirts (p. 317).—In Sologub's works there often appear "wicked sorceresses" whose function it is to veil the vision of true reality from eyes yearning to see it. Such an "evil witch" is Lepistinya ("The Earthly to the Earth") or the Old Woman ("The Poisoned Garden") who wants to hinder the Youth from looking into the enchanted garden by pulling the "curtains" of his "windows."

26. Paranoiac motifs are very common in symbolist literature. The agents of Bely's novels are not only connected with the Third Section. Blok's poem *Est' igra* . . . (1913) deals with metaphysical secret agents.

27. J.W. von Goethe: *Wer nie sein Brot mit Tränen ass.*

28. Gustafson, p. 272.

29. Gustafson, p. 279.

30. Quoted from O. Tsekhnovitser's "*Predislovie*," included in the Bradda edition, p. 20.

31. Cf. Peredonov's vision of people as "cards" with Chekhov's early story "Whist."

32. Tsekhnovitser drew a line of development from Lermontov's "great Satan" to Sologub's *The Petty Demon*. "Predislovie," p. 14.

33. For a discussion of this poem, see my paper, "Limitation and Pain in Bryusov's and Blok's Poetry," *The Slavic and East European Journal* 19, 1975, pp. 388–402.

34. Op. cit., p. 77. Another example of a blatant "revaluation" of the times is L. Andreev's "Judas Iscariot" (1907).

35. The alabaster amphora made transparent by an inner light of fire is the symbol Merezhkovsky chose for the ideal relationship between spirit and matter, content and form, the inner and the outer. See his programmatic article "On the Reasons for the Decline and on the New Tendencies in Contemporary Russian Literature." (*Polnoe sobranie sochinenii* 5, Moskva 1914, [reprint] Hildesheim & New York 1973, p. 217.).

Fyodor Sologub's Literary Children: The Special Case of *The Petty Demon*

Stanley J. Rabinowitz

MONG THE MANY thematic components of the prose fiction of Sologub, one in particular is repeated with remarkable constancy: the theme of the child. A detailed investigation of this theme leads to the complex metaphysical issues which pervade Sologub's work; it also provides a key to understanding his highly idiosyncratic vision of reality.[1] Vyacheslav Ivanov's famous contention that "the child is the central point of [Dostoevsky's] doctrine concerning the world and concerning man,"[2] is equally true of Sologub; indeed, it might serve, if one were interested in the problem, to initiate an extremely fruitful comparison of the two writers.[3] Children appear in well over half of Sologub's sixty-odd short stories in his Decadent-Symbolist period of 1894–1914,[4] where they are, by and large, the author's major focus of attention. Furthermore, in each novel of this period (*Bad Dreams*, 1895; *The Petty Demon*, 1905; the trilogy *The Created Legend*, 1907–14; *Sweeter than Poison*, 1912), children play a crucial, if not a central role. Sologub's use of these characters is especially interesting from a structural point of view, for while the child is almost invariably the hero in his stories, this same character in his larger works serves an ancillary function: he is always closely and vitally associated with the adult-hero who is now at the center.[5] Any attempt to understand the behaviour of Sologub's protagonists, as well as the ideas and issues they embody, must take into account the special position which the child assumes.

With few exceptions, Sologub's stories read like elaborations of Ivan Karamazov's litany of child abuse before his rebellion of the *The Legend of the Grand Inquisitor*. Imprisoned by his earthly existence, the child is tormented by a wide range of forces which Sologub is careful to define as inevitable and unvanquishable. In this sense they are, like Ivan's children, a movingly effective device for uncovering life's irrational and terrible evil. Arguing Sologub's inheritance of an important component of Dostoevsky's philosophy by noting his similar use of the child to express and justify his metaphysical rebellion against the insensitive laws of the universe, R.V. Ivanov-Razumnik claims that Sologub

intentionally limits the field of his artistic creation by this circle of [children's suffering] just as Ivan Karamazov with the same circle outlined his ethical questions. And the reason is the same. The absurdity, meaninglessness of life, its evil, its horror can be seen more clearly in children who still, speaking in Ivan's words, have not eaten the apple and are still not guilty of anything.[6]

Children, however, are more than mere vehicles for expressing moral outrage in Sologub's fiction; they exist not only to pose ethical questions. The earliest stories betray the author's profound concern with the purely personal dimensions of childhood. Works such as "Shadows" (1894), "The Worm" (1896), "In Captivity" (1896), and "To the Stars (1904) are essentially dramatizations of the emotional trials, of the late-juvenile or early-adolescent state which Sologub views as the most complex and crucial period in the development of human consciousness.[7] Whatever else they may accomplish, the best examples of the writer's short prose make abundantly clear the inseparability of Sologub's interest in the psychic world of children from his broader philosophical concerns. The terrible anguish of a youngster on the border of two conflicting states—sexual innocence and sexual maturity—inevitably indicates a more general sense of ontological malaise which results from life's "fatal contradictions."

Despite the undeniable mixture of abstract and intimate elements in Sologub's child-centred stories, it would be inaccurate to argue the predominance of an emotional perspective in them.[8] Nor, for that matter, do these sketches of childhood provide a thoroughly satisfactory literary portrayal of this perspective. The Soviet critic M. Dikman views Sologub as the creator of a fictional world where "that which was earlier a state, a psychological situation, becomes a philosophical position, a myth."[9] Only A. Gornfeld's observation of Sologub's somewhat depersonalized embodiment of the child in his short fiction suggests the imbalance which exists between these psychological and philosophical positions. "It is impossible," he writes, "to say that in [Sologub's children] there exist many different images: all of them in essence are fused into one image."[10] And his further contention that "the child" is not so much a person as he is an object of fate—a necessary conclusion of [Sologub's] conception of life,"[11] rightly emphasizes the writer's intent to invoke the child in a manner which resembles Ivan Karamazov's strategic presentation of children.

Only when Sologub turns to the novel—namely to The Petty Demon—do we find a considerably more personal and specifically psychological treatment of the child. Nowhere in Sologub is the child's inner chaos better understood and more subtly depicted, nor indeed the psychological and metaphysical levels more effectively integrated, than in this, his most highly regarded fictional work.[12] This may partially be explained by the difference in genre, but Sologub's failure to delve as elaborately into the peculiar realm of the young psyche in his other novels suggests that he is guided here by more than formal considerations alone. Indeed, The Petty Demon occupies a singular position in Sologub's oeuvre. No other of his works discusses so candidly and convincingly the philosophical basis of what is to Sologub, life's tragic sense. That this same work should contain the writer's frankest investigation of complex youthful emotions is more than coincidental. Sologub's honesty about the psychological world of children reflects, and goes hand in hand with, his openness in revealing a skeptical and disquieting vision of reality.

Seen against the background of his predecessors in the stories, the central child figure of The Petty Demon, Sasha Pylnikov, alerts us to a critical stage in Sologub's thought and helps us to appreciate the unique quality which characterizes this novel. Most of the stories which contain children were written before 1905, the year that Sologub published The Petty Demon in the periodical Questions of Life. Up until this time, Sologub's work reflects the writer's growing pessimism, which in many respects The Petty Demon, and Sasha in particular, epitomize. But after 1905 (and certainly by 1907, when The Petty

Demon appeared in a separate edition) Sologub's writing assumes a more upbeat mood, the seeds of which can be found already in Sasha's role in the novel. There is, admittedly, something contradictory and ambiguous about the child's combination of fear and faith on Sologub's part, but it is just this unsettling mixture which constitutes the novel's special quality. *The Petty Demon*— if we cast our glance most fixedly on its central child character—stands on the brink of two fairly distinct psycho-philosophical states of mind in Sologub.

Of all Sologub's children, Sasha Pylnikov, the gymnasium student who becomes the object of Lyudmila's amorous advances, is the most genuinely three-dimensional. His characterization exemplifies the writer's most artistically original and psychologically sophisticated portrayal of the confusion, ambivalence and emotional turmoil which typify the transition from boyhood to manhood. Lyudmila's observation that "the best age for a boy is fourteen-fifteen, he can still do nothing and doesn't really understand, yet he senses everything, absolutely everything,"[13] undoubtedly echoes Sologub's own sentiments. His use of pre-pubescent children betrays an enjoyment of those tense climactic moments before change is finally affected and transition ultimately achieved. The frequent appearance of the child-adolescent in Sologub's fiction demonstrates the author's delectation in the perfect mixture of, and balance between, the two starkly diametrical opposites which this unique state represents, however brief it may be. Sologub's penchant for capturing the heightened moment, when the Dostoevskian combination of psychological and metaphysical antipodes is at its peak, seems best gratified in the incipient struggle between child-like and adult forces within the newly awakened youth.[14] Sologub was not a writer who specialized in scenes charged with dramatic tension and excitement, yet where such moments do exist, they are most likely to involve children. Sasha Pylnikov represents the fullest realization of this element of drama in Sologub's prose.

The significant interrelation of levels in *The Petty Demon* can be appreciated when one realizes that Sasha's movement from a condition of passive innocence to a state of heightened sexual awareness occurs against the background of Peredonov's and Lyudmila's peculiar worlds. The specifically personal struggle within a child between conflicting temptations toward adult sin and boyhood purity is indivisibly linked to a more general opposition between life's vulgarity and cruelty and some transcendent ideal which must be found to counteract it. Peredonov symbolizes the former, Lyudmila and her "legend in creation" the latter. The Sasha episode of *The Petty Demon* best exemplifies Dikman's observance of co-existing psychological and metaphysical planes in Sologub. "Philosophical reflections about the world and about man," she writes, "are inseparable from the spiritual world of Sologub's lyrical hero . . . and they become a personal, intimate theme."[15] Indeed, in terms of the writer's use of the child, *The Petty Demon* most fully realizes an objective which Sologub would later state in his preface to the collection of verse, *The Fiery Circle* (1908): "I want the intimate to become the universal." The psycholgical polarities in the individual child reflect and repeat the metaphysical dualities of the world. Sasha's internal drama, his conflict, to use the poet Blake's terms, between innocence and experience, is externalized in the collision between Lyudmila's spiritual realm of dream, poetry and the lyrical mood and Peredonov's material world of *byt* and banality.[16] On a deeper level, Sologub conceives the child's emotional disjuncture as no less than the contrast between the ideal and the real, the ability of beauty to maintain its integrity, or to exist at all, in the face of earthly powers.

The distinction between "moment" and "movement" defines the fundamental difference in Sologub's portrayal of the major child-figure in *The Petty
Demon*. In his short stories, Sologub chooses to click the shutter, as it were, on
the precise instant of the young self's recognition of psychological transition,
preferring to concentrate on the atmosphere of fright which it induces. The ultimate strength of many a child-centered story in Sologub lies less in its success
as a psychological character-study than in its effect as a mood piece. In *The
Petty Demon*, however, Sologub departs from this somewhat detached and
abstract approach, exemplifying rather than symbolizing the process of "spring's
awakening."[17] The writer concentrates on the *development* of a character as he
experiences the awareness of his own sexual maturity and as he undergoes the
conflicting emotions resulting from this self-discovery. In switching his narrative focus onto Sasha Pylnikov, Sologub not only presents a more personalized
portrait of childhood by delving into the inner workings of the blossoming adolescent's mind; he also acknowledges the complexity of the child's emotional
world as well as the integrity of his personality. Among the major Russian writers,
only Dostoevsky before him had so extensively depicted the special psychological tensions of youth.[18] As V. Ilin has noted,

> Sologub was impressed most of all by [Dostoevsky's] astonishing and uncanny
> details devoted to children's nightmares, tragedies and defects. In this sense,
> Sologub must be considered as the successor of Dostoevsky, who was the first
> both to reveal this new existential child's world and to make it the subject of
> great literature.[19]

The existential world of the child, which Ilin conjures up, is epitomized in *The
Petty Demon*. Sasha represents Sologub's attempt to have the child function on
more than an abstract, symbolic level by assuming more complex human characteristics as he experiences the concrete pain of inevitable personal growth.

In the characterization of Sasha, Sologub is concerned with a young boy's
gradual maturation, marked by the latter's growing consciousness of his own sensuality and physical attractiveness. Sologub traverses a broad range of sexual development in this "raw youth" from the time that Sasha "still had never been curious to
find out whether he appeared attractive or ugly to people" (p. 247) until his wildly
flirtatious behaviour as a geisha who, quite dexterous in sensual matters, "curtsied,
lifted her small fingers, giggled in a choked voice, waved her fan, tapped now one
man and now another on the shoulder with it" (p. 388). Beginning with his bashful kissing of Lyudmila's elbow and proceeding to his considerably bolder contact
with other parts of her body, Sasha becomes more deeply involved with a young
woman who rouses within him the first feelings of passion and desire. The immediate uniqueness of this episode lies in its focusing upon the shameless dynamics of
young love. This is a subject which Sologub had never treated before, and one
which, as we will observe, he handles with unquestionable originality. Sologub subtly relates Sasha's discomforting manipulation by Lyudmila and his awkward
engagement in sensuous games, his bitter-sweet reactions to his blossoming sexuality, and his troubled thoughts over "impossible dreams" and "contradictory feelings." Such scenes demonstrate a sophisticated understanding of the young adult's
psyche, years before Freudian theory had penetrated widely into literature. The
steady transformation of what initially are unclear stirrings and confused impulses
in Sasha into more precisely and better perceived sensual desires creates a convincing glimpse into the world of experience.

Sasha's responses are either conveyed via internal monologue (as is his early sense that Lyudmila "came and went . . . and left only . . . a vague excitement in my soul, which is creating a sweet dream," p. 235) or reported by the omniscient narrator (as is his later query: "What is this mysteriousness of the flesh? How could he sweetly sacrifice his blood and his body to Lyudmila's desires . . .?" p. 362). Yet in each case they reveal undeniable insights into his own psychological growth and emotional condition which had not been admitted, or not so clearly expressed, in the case of Sologub's other children. To be sure, Sasha's experience with Lyudmila reveals more than Sologub's awareness of the child's capacity for deep, complicated emotion; L.N. Tolstoi, for one, had already treated this phenomenon in his *Childhood* (1852). Rather, the incident demonstrates an acknowledgement of this character's *own* awareness of his ability to arouse passionate interest while he himself experiences erotic desire. In this sense, Sologub expands considerably the dimensions and possibilities of literary portraiture of the child. He handles the theme of the child as a sexual subject in a new way by viewing the problem largely through the child's eye. No longer is the latter's characterization limited to a conflict free sexuality as observed from a removed or dispassionate third-person perspective.

Such a perspective is conspicuously present, for example, in Tolstoi's description of Nikolenka Irtenev's inner development in *Adolescence* (1854). "But none of these changes which had taken place in my outlook on things struck me more than the one in which I had ceased to see a housemaid of ours merely as a servant of the feminine gender, and began instead to view her as a *woman*,"[20] the narrator reflects. The grown-up Nikolenka's recollection of the time when he first noticed Masha's enticing voluptuousness and strove to imitate his brother's sexual advances to her is characterized by sobriety and distance. Yet precisely such qualities preclude the kind of convincing evocation of those complicated feelings and tense emotions, so prevalent in Sologub's depiction of a similar psychological passage. Dostoevsky's literary account of such a moment, "A Little Hero" (1857), also eliminates, or at least diminishes, the sense of tortured anxiousness and fearful confusion which accompany the youngster's awareness of his amorous feelings toward an older woman and his realization that his childhood had ended. For all three writers the incident is virtually identical; however, Sologub's narrative technique and his emphasis on the sexual aspects of the maturation process signal his originality.

William Rowe notes that images such as the sun, drops of water and sweet fragrances highlight both Dostoevsky's and Sologub's accounts of the child's emotional growth.[21] But Sologub's imagery creates a provocatively sensual and suggestively erotic atmosphere which more effectively captures the child's innermost thoughts and desires at this stage. The frequent references to heat which accompany the Sasha-Lyudmila relationship reinforce the boy's awakening passion as he increasingly burns with excitement in the presence of his young temptress. Lyudmila's "torrid African dreams" about Sasha, her bright, sunny room with its colourful wallpaper, all create an exotic, tropical and seductive background, more conducive to Sasha's ripening sexuality. Her ever-present flowers and sweet perfumes also provide a climate of heightened sensuality which can only accelerate Sasha's physical desires. Her spraying him with fragrant scents, like the moistness of her chamber, contributes to the sticky, vapourish atmosphere, so suited to their erotic carnal games. This spraying also recalls an act of baptism—in this case into Lyudmila's avowed religion of the flesh.

But the imagery works on yet another level. The negative connotation of heat and fire in the novel—Peredonov's incendiary act at the masquerade ball and the book's epigraph, "I wished to burn her, the wicked witch," are but a few examples—suggests the decidedly destructive aspect of Sasha's ardent love. Lyudmila loves to sprinkle Sasha with drops of perfume, yet she also perversely delights in the drops of Christ's blood as He hangs from the Cross. And the same seductive charms which lure the boy into Lyudmila's world of pleasure, also hypnotize him, much as Peredonov is mesmerized by Vershina as she entices him into her luxuriant garden. Sasha is very much the victim in his erotic escapades, rendered submissive and helpless by the very things which have stimulated and attracted him. Thus the imagery which Sologub employs to describe the inception of first love implies the bitter-sweet, contradictory nature of Sasha's private adventure while also integrating it into the broader thematics of the novel. The unmistakably decadent view of sex as a sweet and pleasurable experience which is nonetheless connected to decay, perversion and ultimately death, penetrates the very core of Sologub's nightmare of a once-beautiful world condemned to corruption and *poshlost'*.

On the narrative level, Sologub achieves a unique effect in portraying Sasha Pylnikov, an effect which his predecessors fail to realize with their overly articulate and emotionally steady characters. Sasha's conflict is related not necessarily through clearly articulated utterances, but rather through the recounting of his vague and ambivalent feelings, his timid, hesitant movements and his often faltering speech—all of which more persuasively conveys the confusion and sense of incomprehension which the child experiences at this crucial stage in his life. By eliminating the emotional control and rather even tone which predominate in Tolstoi's and Dostoevsky's renditions, Sologub presents more dramatically the sense of growing catastrophe as the distressing process of adolescent maturation continues.

The wide variety of feelings which Sasha endures—pain, joy, shame, exhilaration—are all the more significant because they contrast so poignantly with the deadened senses of those characters who people the protagonist's lifeless realm. Sasha's personal experience seems particularly refreshing in a loveless, feelingless world of mechanized puppets: the merchant Tishkov thoughtlessly spurts his mechanical rhymes; Vershina's ward Marta dreams about her virtues dressed as dolls; and Peredonov himself moves slowly and apathetically like a "wound-up doll" (p. 289). Tortuous as it is, the child's ordeal asserts the existence of natural human feelings, genuine emotional tenderness and the presence of concerns and drives which are neither perverted nor destructive. Sasha's realization of the full implications of his and Lyudmila's amorous adventures, coming on the heels of his questions, "And what does she want?," provokes a reaction of excited animation and free, spontaneous movement, unlike anything else in the book.

> And suddenly he blushed purple and his heart pounded ever so painfully. A wild ecstasy overcame him. He did several somersaults, threw himself on the floor and jumped on the furniture. Thousands of absurd movements hurled him from one corner to another, and his joyful, clear laughter resounded throughout the house. (p. 358)

Yet despite such happy moments, the broader dimensions which Sasha's personality attains neither continually evoke simple joy nor do they totally possess positive qualities. With the onset of desire and sexual appetite arises the problem of how this newly acquired strength will be applied—constructively or destructively. Lyudmila characteristically ignores the question when she insists that her and Sasha's stimulations "were far from coarse, loathsome attainments" (p. 246). Yet in a thoroughly Dostoevskian manner, Sologub acknowledges that beneath desire can lie a drive toward dominance and that hatred as well as love can express affection. That these contradictory tendencies extend to children, too, is seen by Sasha's perplexed state of mind after he has been kissed by Lyudmila.

> [Her] tender kisses aroused languid, dreamlike thoughts. He wanted to do something to her, pleasant or painful, tender or shameful—but what? To kiss her legs? Or beat her, long and hard, with supple, long twigs? So that she laugh from joy or cry from pain? Perhaps she desired both. . . . How could he sweetly sacrifice his blood and his body to her desires and to his shame? (p. 362)

Sasha's momentary vacillation between the urge to fondle or torture recalls another literary child who exhibits a corresponding capacity for opposing impulses toward love and hate: Liza Khokhlokova in *The Brothers Karamazov*. Admitting her approval of parricide and her delight in child-suffering, the lame fifteen year-old is more articulate and extreme about her own propensity toward evil. But Sasha at least shares a similar potential for such feeling. Whether it is an expression of *Weltschmerz* or sadism, the tendency of each toward cruelty is undeniable. In Liza's case this cruelty comes to light in the chapter significantly entitled "A Little Demon" ("Besonok"), when she personally substantiates Alesha's observation that "there are moments when people love crime." With Sasha the revelation occurs when, for example, we learn that "contradictory feelings mingled in his soul—dark and nebulous: perverse because they were premature and sweet because they were perverse" (p. 349). The little demon which is seen harbouring in Liza's soul is not without its counterpart in Sasha. The predominance of conscious irony as well as the continual use of double entendres in Sologub's novel make Kokovkina's reaction to her boarder's exhilaration particularly meaningful. "Are you possessed or something?" ("chto eto ty besnueshsia!" p. 358), she exclaims. In the root of the verb is found the same "bes" which characterizes Peredonov and which constitutes the book's very title. The implication here is that Sasha contains within him at least the seeds of evil, and as such he mirrors—as does Liza—the adults, who are more central to the novel's action and plot.

By suggesting Sasha's corrupt tendencies, Sologub's analysis of the child's psyche becomes disturbingly double-edged. The novel is built on a series of paradoxes which gradually unfold to jolt and perplex the reader. A fundamental one is connected with Sasha Pylnikov. The very honesty which allows Sologub to reveal the uniqueness of this personality by investigating its complex emotions during "spring's awakening" also serves to debunk its special status. The Romantic fallacy of the child's unquestionable innocence is now destroyed. With his inclination toward desire and enjoyment of drives heretofore dissociated from his character, a likeness to an ordinary adult is intimated. Duality pervades everything. Upon further investigation, even the seemingly inviolable purity of childhood must be questioned. Yet it is precisely this discovery of duplicity in Sasha's emotional world which signals his full importance in the novel. The psychological crisis of conflicting good and evil which Sologub depicts in the individual child mirrors the metaphysical calamity which underlies his larger vision of the world. Sologub's newly found doubts about Sasha on the behavioural level find their counterpart in his suspicions about life in general on the philosophical plane, and both work hand-in-hand in contributing to the book's pervasive sense of nervousness and insecurity. It is here that *The Petty Demon* supports Dikman's claim of the inseparability of psychological states from metaphysical issues in Sologub's art. The intimacy which Sologub achieves in his personalized portrait of Sasha adds credence to the more general dimensions of his ideological argument.

Sasha's assumption of negative worldly qualities—aggressiveness, deceptiveness, vanity—inevitably results from his continuing integration into adult life. However, beyond its significance as an important factor in the child's personal history, this metamorphosis contains crucial and far-reaching metaphysical implications. The novel's pervasive sense of tragic gloom is eventually extended to the world of children in a passage whose tone of inevitable doom resonates with growing intensity throughout the remainder of the work.

> Only the children, tireless and eternal vessels of God's happiness on earth, were lively and ran and played. But sluggishness descended even upon them, and some sort of faceless, invisible monster, nestling behind their shoulders, looked out now and then with its menacing eyes on their suddenly dulled faces. (p. 141)

Here Sologub strikes a major theme which Sasha's characterization vividly realizes. Because of the omnipresence of a demonic energy in life, all beauty is ultimately rendered invalid and all things, even the purest, face gradual and inevitable extinction. This destructive force reaches its most devastating impact when it strikes Sasha, but is is already forecast in Lyudmila's tale about the cyclamen, "which gives pleasure and induces desires, both sweet and shameful, and stirs up the blood" (p. 245). This tale is an allegory which refers specifically to "spring's awakening" in the child. Lyudmila's attribution of three colours to the flower and the corresponding sensations which they provoke— all in order of the increasing intensity of their sensuality—actually charts the course of Sasha's own sexual growth. That the flower's own transformation from joy, to desire, to passionate love represents the extermination of childlike beauty is verified during the remainder of the novel. Once again the imagery works on two levels: Lyudmila's flowers are as much "fleurs du mal" as they are fragrant blossoms of beauty and enchantment.

References to Sasha's increasingly destructive strength or to his unattractively "heavy, awkward hands" (p. 359) indicate the child's continuing degeneration. But nothing signals this process as blatantly as the symbolic scene in which Lyudmila leads Sasha into a ravine in order to continue their amorous games. The languid atmosphere and the specific vocabulary which Sologub uses to convey the setting are highly suggestive. The description of the "warm, heavy air . . . [which] recalled that which was irrevocable, [where] the sun, as if sick, was shining dully . . . in the pale, tired sky, [where] dry leaves lay peacefully on the warm earth, dead" (p. 350) signals the final realization in Sasha of the corruption to which Sologub had earlier doomed all things, in the scene of similar colouring and tonality cited above. "Irrevocable" suggests Sasha's permanently lost innocence; the lifeless leaves imply the extinction of a once-blossoming plant, of Sasha-the-flower-himself.[22] Images of heat and warmth, which the writer formerly used in a positive manner, are now exclusively negative. Significantly, it is here, against the background of exhaustion and death, that the child's transformation reaches its apex. Its accomplishment confirms the ultimate sense of disaster which continually hangs like a pall over the novel. If *peredonovshchina*—the constant slippage of all phenomena into an intensified state of corruption and decay—represents the major component of Sologub's philosophical vision in *The Petty Demon*, then it is Sasha's psychological metamorphosis which demonstrates the potency of this vision.

To be sure, a story-like reading of Sasha's emotional maturation as a metaphysical allegory about the movement of all things in life toward *poshlost'* is possible. But unique to *The Petty Demon* is the notion that ideal childhood, the integrity of whose borders Sologub had always reverentially distinguished, itself resembles—even if only partially—the grown-up world. Sasha's less complicated counterparts in the author's shorter fiction are unanimously terrified as their precious spring-like existence approaches its termination. Adulthood is base and sinful and these characters invariably resist it. In Sasha's case, however, the soothingly clear distinctions between good and evil, which the child symbolizes in the stories, are far from firm. The portrayal of Sasha precisely in this gray area helps make *The Petty Demon* Sologub's most disquieting work. It is here, through Sasha, that Sologub first seriously contemplates the existence of original sin; a possibility which leads to the highly disturbing idea that everything in life is inherently evil. Otherwise stated, through a psychological portrayal of a child who is unable to distinguish firmly between an exclusive like or dislike of his sexuality, Sologub helps raise the disturbing metaphysical question of whether the beautiful ideal can be possible at all in a world where the absolute is lacking.

Not the least important characteristic of Sasha's behaviour is the ambivalence he exhibits toward his own sexual awakening. His actions often reveal a response to maturity which is based not entirely on fear and remorse. Like Lyudmila, although initially cautiously and confusedly, he enjoys being "immersed in passionate and cruel dreams" (pp. 356–57). Rather than avoiding or rejecting the pangs of desire, Sasha frequently accepts them, while displaying a willing participation in acts during which they are satisfied. In another example of his awareness of his emotional metamorphosis, Sasha intuits the effect of Lyudmila's perfume—"sweet but strange, enveloping, radiantly misty, like a golden, early, though sinful sunrise behind a white haze" (p. 243). The imagery here is obvious and, as in the allegory of the cyclamen, refers to Sasha's sexual transformation. The seeming harmlessness of the perfume's white mist (like Sasha's own purity) conceals a dangerously sensual world of desire, yet the child shows no resistance to being transported by the potion's scent to Lyudmila's realm of erotic pleasure, where the new age of passion commences. We later learn that a "shameful and passionate feeling was aroused in him" (p. 356). However, instead of opposing this form of initiation into the adult world, as one might expect in a Sologub story, Sasha almost encourages it, by dreaming: "If I could fall down at her feet as if by accident and snatch off her shoe and kiss her lovely foot." The loss of shame and the "fall from grace," which previously carried such categorically harmful connotations, here contain an element of sweetness. Consequently the child's complicity in, as well as enjoyment of, "spring's awakening" tend to put its former implications into a new light. Indeed, whatever the extent of Lyudmila's role in Sasha's "adulteration"—and it should not be under-estimated—Sasha's own culpability would appear to place at least some of the burden of guilt on his shoulders.

The various ambivalences, which the penetration of the child's psyche reveals, necessarily mark a change in regard to the Sologubian ideal which this character had previously symbolized. To the extent that Sasha demonstrates a potential for it, if not a predisposition toward it, genuine evil may be a part of this beauty. Certainly this hidden, unknown force may explain both Peredonov's and Lyudmila's intense curiosity toward this "mysterious person" (p. 236). The former's interest is a result of a paranoic fear that beneath the seeming guise of a harmless student could lie a threatening deceiver. The latter's concern is based on an erotic urge to lead the boy to the exciting brink of sin without his ever actually reaching it, although "herself not noticing, Lyudmila awakened in Sasha the first, albeit still vague manifestations of yearning and desire" (p. 240). Whether she understands it or not, Lyudmila's growing need to clothe the boy in different costumes implies an unnaturalness or inadequacy in Sasha which heretofore did not exist. The ability of Sasha, by the end of the book, to camouflage skillfully a less-than-ideal appearance behind a mask of unspoiled innocence and perfection suggests the alarming possibility that beneath what may seem to be the beautiful absolute could easily lie its polar opposite.

In this sense, Sasha would appear to differ from the children of Sologub's stories at least insofar as through them the writer indicates the presence of a higher, flawless reality. Beneath Sasha's exterior he evidently uncovers a somewhat less-than-perfect state. Robert Maguire, noting a somewhat related reversal of roles in the novel's protagonist, observes that "it is likely that Peredonov is an unconscious parody of [Vyacheslav] Ivanov's idea of the artist."[23] What Maguire means, of course, is that Sologub's character, far from performing the traditional Symbolist role of penetrating the higher spheres of reality to find beauty, instead descends into the lowest realms of life, where he envisages ugliness and *poshlost'*. To the extent that Sasha's depiction is as contrary to that of the customary Sologubian child as Peredonov's is to the normal Symbolist-hero, an affinity between the two may be plausible. With its increased signs of taintedness which can be only cosmetically disguised, Sasha's beauty is open to question. The very vocabulary Sologub uses to convey the child's aggressive behaviour while adorned as the geisha seems to confirm such doubt. Two words in the sentence "geisha, iurkaia i sil'naia, vizzhala pronzitel'no, tsarapalas' i kusalas'" (p. 395)—"iurkaia" and "vizzhala"—have been used previously to describe the quintessence of *peredonovshchina*, the nasty and foul *nedotykomka*. Indeed, one might argue that Sasha's gradual but inevitable sexual maturity serves as a thematic counterpart to Peredonov's increasing acts of vileness and destruction. The process of each runs as two parallel lines and these lines finally intersect during the masquerade ball. Here the triumph of Sasha's sexuality is complete when he convincingly acts the role of the geisha, much as Peredonov's destructiveness reaches its peak when he sets fire to the club and prepares to murder Volodin.

Sasha's aunt does not necessarily admit to any change in her nephew's beauty even though she remarks ironically that "he is exactly the same child as he was, or is he so spoiled that he is deceiving [me] even by his face?" (p. 400). However, her doubt meaningfully re-enforces the schoolmaster Khripach's wise observation that "appearances are sometimes deceptive" (p. 200), a remark that plants an inescapable note of suspicion in the reader's mind concerning any final determination about the characters. Whether recognized or not by Sasha's aunt, the mere suggestion of the possible illusiveness of the absolute, the implication that the seeds of evil may be contained within, and nurtured by, beauty itself, seriously challenge the existence of any redemptive ideal or absolute harmoniousness.

As the major figure to intimate the deceptiveness of a previously assured incarnation of innocence, Sasha best indicates the lack of fixity and uncertainty which pervade Sologub's world view. He is the character who most unambiguously establishes the importance of the theme of reality and illusion which is first sounded in the novel's opening paragraph and then reverberates throughout: "it seemed as though people were living peacefully and harmoniously in this town. Even happily. But it only seemed that way" (p. 37). Sasha's characterization strikes at the very core of the neurotic dualism and instability which permeate the narrative tone and overriding philosophy of *The Petty Demon*. This instability extends to the stylistic level of the book, whose dual-leveled imagery, double entendres and numerous puns signal a breakdown in the integrity of language itself: words no longer communicate clear and unqualified meaning. The depiction of Sasha reflects the nervous interplay and deep-seated ambiguity which exist between the demonic and "Dionysian" forces continually at work in the novel. In this sense the Sasha episode may be considered to represent the structural and philosophical center of *The Petty Demon*. Both Peredonov and Lyudmila need Sasha, both vie for control of him, in order to prove the predominance of their respective world views. Through him Peredonov attempts to demonstrate that all must be dragged down into the mire, while Lyudmila tries to establish that in order to have beauty man need only create it.

Sasha's transformation surely gives some credence to Peredonov's suspicions, if not to his extreme reactions: evil does threaten everything, even the absolute of beauty. In its own way, the child's metamorphosis questions just how "mad" Peredonov actually is, as does Lyudmila's observation that "only in madness is there happiness and wisdom" (p. 361). But more importantly, Sasha's characterization challenges the absolute validity of beauty itself. Indeed, through this figure the writer finds that truth and beauty are not necessarily the same. The child serves as a persuasive example of the applicability of a Peredonov-oriented ideology, which insists that a world ruled by necessity is artificial, false and ultimately corrupting. However, in questioning the absolute integrity of the ideal, Sologub, through the character of Sasha, in no way argues that man can exist without it. As the central focus of Lyudmila's dream, the child shows that her illusory vision of beauty is still purer than Peredonov's mundane and vulgar reality. Her corruption is less harmful than his deliberate destruction of the boy. Sologub manipulates Sasha in *The Petty Demon* to prove that although beauty must inevitably be soiled by the evil inherent in man, paradoxically—and tragically—man needs the very thing which he himself destroys. It is true that when Lyudmila corrupts her ideal she complies with the world as it necessarily is and thereby substantiates its power. But her stubborn insistence on believing nevertheless in the inviolabilty of Sasha's beauty, demonstrates a faith and an individual will which are even stronger and more compelling than the "truth." So important is Lyudmila's need to love a beautiful image of Sasha that she believes in the child despite the change which she helps to effect in him.

Sasha's unique structural position in *The Petty Demon*, as the person whose fate the two major characters vie to control, shows Sologub's condemnation of certain contemporary social and ideological outlooks. As the quintessential representative of a society where respect is gained soley by rise in position and power and where interest in higher spiritual values is all but gone, the emblematic Peredonov exhibits his greatest evil when he abuses children and denies the child in others. To the person who considers the ultimate achievement in life to be his treasured inspectorship, any absence of the all-pervasive *poshlost'* of this world or any trace of the intangibly non-earthly is deemed threatening and unnecessary. Peredonov's malicious teasing of the peasant Misha Kudriavtsev, his bullying of the harmless Kramarenko, the innocent Antosha Gudaevsky, and the defenseless brother of Marta, Vladia, and, finally, his unceasing torment of Sasha Pylnikov himself are, in fact, but individual examples of society's more widespread and even fiercer hostility toward any form of beauty whatsoever. This is demonstrated at the masquerade ball where the crowd's perpetration of collective evil against the geisha, as it symbolically destroys the unique beauty which she represents, validates one of the narrator's saddest admissions and most bitter social commentaries: "truly in our age it is beauty's lot to be tainted and violated" (p. 102). Sasha's function in this scene, as well as in the novel at large, is to suggest (recalling the argument, if not the apocalyptic overtones of Dostoevsky's *Idiot* and *The Devils*) that in a society where the concept of beauty is absent or defiled, man is reduced to a beast and is doomed to inevitable disaster. Beauty's place is preserved—and by extension, spiritual transformation is assured—only in a world which is oblivious to the petty concerns of everyday life and which reserves a place for the adoration of the non-material. Lyudmila's appreciation—indeed, idolatry—of an ideal perfection, ephemeral and decadent though it may be, signifies a joyous diversion and ecstatic escape from vulgar and demeaning *byt*. By ignoring (as Peredonov cannot) the phenomenal realm of foul nature and ugly matter, which she does for example during her walk with Sasha to the ravine, Lyudmila seems to negate, or at least to undermine, its ultimate importance.

Lyudmila's incarnation of the ideal in the person of the child mirrors nothing less than Sologub's similar practice in his fiction. Through her, the writer restates a Dostoevskian belief that "beauty will save the world,"[24] not so much because it is truthful, but rather because it is the touchstone of a faith without which man's vision would be hopelessly bleak and his individual will totally powerless. "If the entire world lies in the bonds of necessity, then what of my freedom which I also feel as a necessary law of existence?," Sologub would later ask in his article "Art in Our Day." "The Symbolists' individualism was not a rebellion against social mindedness, but a revolt against mechanical necessity, against an excessively materialistic world view."[25] The writer might have easily been talking about Lyudmila as well. On its most vital philosophical level, *The Petty Demon* rehearses the struggle for faith in light of a nightmarish vision of reality which does everything to disprove it. Insofar as the object of this faith is itself ambiguous in *The Petty Demon*, we might infer that Sologub believed it could be gained, to use Dostoevsky's words, "only through the crucible of doubts."[26] If this is the case, then Sasha fulfills his function perfectly.

Sasha Pylnikov ultimately suggests a need for faithfulness to an ideal of beauty, the loyalty to which transcends the truthfulness of this beauty. As such, the boy's characterization reflects Sologub's agreement with Dostoevsky's feelings about his ideal, namely that "even if it were proved to me that Christ was outside the truth, I would still prefer to remain with Christ than with the truth."[27] Yet having said this, we must acknowledge that the portrayal of Sasha represents a fictively demonstrated "proof" which Sologub would never again allow himself to repeat. In his next novel, the trilogy *The Created Legend*, he returned to his "abstract musings" by rendering his most symbolic child-portraits: that of the hero's mysterious son, Kirsha, and of the eerie, supernatural "quiet children."

NOTES

*From *Canadian Slavonic Papers*, 21 (1979), 514, n.22, pages 503–519. Reprinted by permission of the editorial board and the author.

1 Sologub's literary children rarely received the serious attention of his contemporaries. The critic Iu. Steklov cited them to prove that Sologub's "works evoke interest mainly for psychiatrists" (Iu. Steklov, "O tvorchestve Fedora Sologuba," *Literaturnyiraspad.* 2 vols. [St. Petersburg, 1908]. II, 166); V. Kranikhfel'd charged Sologub with being unable "to refrain from his piquant mystical experiences" when portraying children (V. Kranikhfel'd, "Fedor Sologub," in *V mire idei i obrazov* [St. Petersburg, 1912], p. 45); and L. Voitlovskii claimed that these characters "were cheap imitations of Dostoevskii" (L. Voitlovskii, "Sumerki iskusstva," *Literaturnyi raspad*, II, 50).

2. V. Ivanov, *Freedom and the Tragic Life* (New York, 1960), p. 95.

3. In addition to the works cited in this article which deal with Dostoevsky's influence on Sologub, two others should be noted: A. Dolinin, "Otreshennyi: K psikhologii tvorchestva Fedora Sologuba," *Zavety*, 1913, no. 7, pp. 55–85, and A. Zakrzhevskii, *Podpol'e Psikhologicheskie paralleli* (St. Petersburg, 1911), pp. 29–54.

4. Although rigid periodization of Sologub's work is difficlut, World War I may be seen to constitute his second period, while his third phase is represented by the post-revolutionary span of 1919–27. The child is rarely encountered during the latter phase.

5. The sole exception, where it is the child who is the hero, is *Sweeter than Poison*. Significantly, this novel was an extension of an earlier story, "Shania i Zhenia," which Sologub published in 1897.

6. R. Ivanov-Razumnik, *O smysle zhizni* (St. Petersburg, 1908), p. 36.

7. For a brief discussion of children in some of Sologub's stories, see Murl Barker's "Introduction" to *The Kiss of the Unborn and Other Stories by Fedor Sologub* (Knoxville, 1977), pp. xiii–xxxvi.

8. Early critics insisted on the predominance of lifeless elements in Sologub's portraits of children, and one in particular berated him for his "wandering among abstract musings." See A. Volynskii, "Novye techeniia v sovremennoi russkoi literature—Fedor Sologub," *Severnyi vestnik*, 1896, no. 12, p. 238.

9. M. Dikman (ed.) *Fedor Sologub—Stikhotvoreniia* (Leningrad, 1975), p. 27.

10. A. Gornfel'd, "Fedor Sologub," in S.A. Vengerov (ed.), *Russkaia literatura XX veka, 1890–1910*, 3 vols. (Moscow, 1914–16), II, 56.

11. *Ibid.*

12. *The Petty Demon* is the only work of Sologub's prose which has been reprinted in Russia since the revolution. The latest edition appeared in 1958 and was published in the small city of Kemerovo. Only in the West has the novel received sustained critical attention, although even this has been insufficient. The most recent study of the novel, which treats its mythical elements is G.J. Thurston, "Sologub's *Melkiy bes*," *Slavonic and East European Review* LV, no. 1 (January 1977), 30–44.

13. F. Sologub, *Melkii bes* (Letchworth, Hertfordshire, 1966), p. 250. All subsequent citations are from this reprint of the 1933 Moscow edition and are noted in parentheses in the text.

14. For several interesting ideas on some similarities between Dostoevsky's and Sologub's "collisions," see Dikman, p. 25.

15. *Ibid.*

16. The question of which world ultimately predominates in *Melkii bes*—Peredonov's or Lyudmila's—has engaged critics since the book's publication. See particularly A. Gornfel'd, "Nedotykomka," in *Knigi i liudi* (St. Petersburg, 1908), pp. 32–40, and A. Blok, "*Melkii bes*," in *Sobranie sochinenii v vos'mi tomakh* (Moscow, 1960–63), V, 124–29.

17. The phrase "spring's awakening" is particularly appropriate since it is the title of a play (1891) by the German dramatist, Frank Wedekind, the Russian translation of which (1907) Sologub edited and supervised and which his wife, the critic A. Chebotarevskaya reviewed. There is no question that, in Chebotarevskaya's words, Wedekin's "picture of that upheaval, of that psycho-sexual tragedy which occurs in children at the dawn of their lives," had considerable influence on Sologub. See *Russkaia mysl'*, 1907, no. 10, pp. 196–99.

18. Anton Chekhov was also interested in child psychology, although the overall role of children in his fiction is not as extensive as it is in Dostoevsky's or Sologub's. For an informative survey of this topic, see Iu. Aikheval'd, "Deti u Chekhova," in *Siluety russkikh pisatelei*, 2 vols. (Moscow, 1914–17), II, 211–26.

19. V. Il'in, "Fedor Sologub—Nedobryi i zagadochnyi," *Vozrozhdenie*, no. 158 (1965), p. 61. This suggestive observation has failed to attract the critical scrutiny it deserves.

20. L.N. Tolstoi, *Sobranie sochinenii v 20 tomakh* (Moscow, 1960–65), I, p. 143 (emphasis in the original).

21. See W. Rowe, *Dostoevsky: Child and Man in His Works* (New York, 1965), p. 71.

22. The name "Pylnikov" is derived from the Russian word for anther, "pyl'nik." Names in *The Petty Demon* generally carry symbolic import much as they do in Gogol's earlier vision of a vulgar world of *poshlost'*, *Dead Souls*.

23. R. Maguire, "Macrocosm or Microcosm? The Symbolists on Russia," in *Russia: The Spirit of Nationalism* (New York, 1972), p. 133.

24. This comment is attributed to Prince Myshkin in the *Idiot*. Not surprisingly, the clearest incarnations of the beautiful ideal in both writers exhibit child-like qualities. Regarding Myshkin, we recall his Swiss doctor's claim about the young man: "A child, absolutely a child!"

25. F. Sologub, "Iskusstvo nashikh dnei," *Russkaia mysl'*, 1915, no. 12, p. 44.

26. Quoted in K. Mochul'skii, *Dostoevskii: Zhizn' i tvorchestvo* (Paris, 1947), p. 535. Dostoevsky noted this comment in his notebooks to *The Brothers Karamazov*.

27. F.M. Dostoevsky to N.D. Fonvizin, March 1954. Quoted in *Letters of Fyodor Michailovitch Dostoevsky to His Family and Friends*, trans. by E.C. Mayne (New York, 1961), p. 71.